The Birth of Intimacy

The Birth of Intimacy

*Privacy and Domestic Life
in Early Modern Paris*

Annik Pardailhé-Galabrun

Translated by Jocelyn Phelps

upp

University of Pennsylvania Press
Philadelphia

First published in French as *La Naissance de l'intime*,
© Presses Universitaires de France 1988

First published in English 1991 by Polity Press in
association with Basil Blackwell

First published in the United States 1991 by the University
of Pennsylvania Press

U.S. Library of Congress Catalog number LC 91–050607
ISBN 0–8122–3124–4

Printed in Great Britain

Contents

Acknowledgements

Without the contributions of so many people and institutions, this book could never have been completed. We are grateful for the warm, friendly atmosphere of the Sorbonne's Centre de Recherches sur la Civilisation de l'Europe Moderne and for the resources it provided, and we would especially like to thank François Crouzet, the Centre's director. We also thank Michèle Merceron, Geneviève Oger, and Marie-Yvonne Alquier for their efficient help and their discreet, smiling presence. Then there were the enriching meetings of the Seminar, where it was always a pleasure to see Madeleine Foisil, Jean-Paul Poisson, Marie-Christine Varachaud and others. The Centre National pour la Recherche Scientifique provided us with material support, the University of Paris-Sorbonne and its president, Jacques Bompaire, welcomed us, and Marie-Paule Ricque and Mme Desgardins gave us access to the technical expertise of the cartographers at the Centre de Recherches d'Histoire Quantitative at the University of Caen. We are also grateful for the devotion and the personal skill of the personnel of the French national archives, especially at the Minutier Central, and last but not least, for the patience and friendship of Marie-Josée Serizier. To all those who offered us help and encouragement, we offer our heartiest thanks.

A. P.-G.
P.C.

Scholars whose Research and Writings Contributed to the Preparation of this Book

Authors of pre-doctoral monographs (*mémoires*): Colette Abadagan-Azokpota, Véronique Aronio de Romblay, Yves Aubry, Marie-Ange Bianchi-Boulanger, Pierre-Denis Boudriot, Marie-Dominique Bost, Anne-Charlotte Capitaine, Claire Catta, Roger Charneau, François Colodiet, Claudine Corneloup, Marie-Caroline Coutand, Geneviève Crombez de Montmort, Marie-Jeanne Curis-Binet, Nicole Denquin, Myriam Descamps, Françoise Dommanget, Christine Droniou, Marie-Pierre Dumoulin, Dominique Durier, Laurence Duschenes, Véronique Estève, Laurence Gaveau, Louis Gresset, Bernard Guiblain, Dominique Henrard, Sophie Lacoste, Martine Landrier, Isabelle Landrivon, Patrick Le Chanu, Marie-Pascale Lefèvre, Christine Legrand, Thérèse Leridon-Segui, Catherine Marais, Maravillas Mataix, Atiyanee Mathayomchan, Claire Ménez, Françoise Merel, Gérard Neveu, Afsaneh Pakravan, Véronique Paquet, Véronique Paupert, Isabelle Petitclerc, Gaëlle Piot, Christine Rideau, Geneviève Rodier, Florence Roussel, M. Vandertaelen, Dominique Villate, Marie-Pierre Zuber.

Doctoral thesis: Pierre-Denis Boudriot.

Preface

The warmth that radiates in these pages from these Parisian hearths of the seventeenth and eighteenth centuries – what Michelet liked to call 'The great century, I mean the eighteenth' – results from the particular shape that has been given to a study conducted under the auspices of the Centre de Recherches sur la Civilisation de l'Europe Moderne at the Université de Paris-Sorbonne. This synthesis is based on fifty preliminary monographs and one doctoral thesis directed jointly by Annik Pardailhé-Galabrun and myself. She worked directly with the students, and their work was introduced and discussed during our weekly Tuesday seminar from 5 to 7 p.m. Since several heads are generally better than one, this Tuesday evening brain-storming session enriched us all. No one can say who had a given idea: it simply sprung there out of the encounter, our discussion and our friendships.

Several of the most active members of this seminar were particularly helpful, and Annik Pardailhé-Galabrun is most grateful to them. Madeleine Foisil knows so well how to dig beneath a deceptively simple surface appearance and unveil its hidden significance. Together with Jean-Paul Poisson, our expert in notarial evaluations, she deserves a special mention. Madeleine Foisil, Annik Pardailhé-Galabrun, and I formed such a solid team that there was no compartmentalization among us on this research project. The study was a collective effort, and a list of the fifty-one students involved, many of whom are already recognized scholars in their own right, is printed in the Acknowledgements. But this book is an individual accomplishment. Annik Pardailhé-Galabrun held the rudder from the time I put it into her hands in 1978, and she brought the ship into port. She held the pen as well. She guided the process of organizing the information, and she led and completed the proposed project. In short, she was both the master builder and the architect.

Many people love Paris. A bibliography of this city would fill several volumes. The general idea that we developed in *La Mort à Paris* holds here as well: a city of 400,000 inhabitants in 1640 and slightly more than 600,000 on the eve of the French Revolution, Paris between 1640 and 1790 knew slow but steady growth. The city underwent more accelerated growth before and after that era. London overtook Paris in the middle of the eighteenth century. But for one and a half centuries, in terms of population, wealth, resources, levels of personal consumption and trade, though Paris possessed only 2.5 per cent of the population of France, it was the biggest city in the world. Literature, the arts and accounts left by contemporary travellers all bear witness to the fact. Paris consumed four times as much meat per capita as all the rest of France, drank a share of its coffee, chocolate and tea, and published at least as much if not more than the rest of France.

The higher we look on the scale of complex consumer goods, the greater is the relative share going to Paris. Broadly speaking, Paris was the aristocrat of French and European cities during the Enlightenment. Furthermore, thanks to its notaries, the city also enjoys a wealth of documentation on its history. Paris in this period offered a juxtaposition of individuals seeking to build a new world and, drawn along in their wake, broad strata of society that were much slower to evolve, and more closely bound to the past than open to the future. Anyone who wanted to do a study of how life was actually lived in a great city enlivened by the spirit of the emerging modern world would obviously choose Paris as its focus.

What you will read here is not based on the testimony of single witnesses, even such oft-cited sources as Louis-Sébastien Mercier or Restif de La Bretonne. The material underlying our assertions has been taken down by the notary and tallied according to age-old tradition, using handwritten card files. This may seem rather old-fashioned, but either our computers have somewhat short memories, or we have not yet discovered how to use them effectively in order to take in at a single glance the hodge-podge of 3000 Parisian households gone over with a fine-tooth comb in the inventories compiled after deaths. As with our earlier study on death, we built up our sample by trial and error. The rock on which this information is based is 2783 inventories done after deaths, with a larger share from the eighteenth century than the seventeenth, and more from the right bank of the Seine than the left bank and the Cité, where the records of 110 notarial offices (out of 122) were examined.

A broad range of supplementary documents are also examined in the light of these inventories. I would mention in passing the marriage contracts used in Roland Mousnier's study and the 10,000 wills used for *La Mort à Paris*. As units of study, we used the street, the neighbourhood, and the socio-professional group, as well as the apartment building, an aspect which has been carefully studied by Pierre-Denis Boudriot. We are grateful for the condition in which we found the marvellous Z1J series in France's National Archives.

The average ordinary house changed more between the first and last quarters of the eighteenth century than it had during the two preceding centuries or during the century that followed. By the end of the reign of Louis XV, it took 29 tons of materials, 41 tons including earthworks, to house one Parisian in accordance with the new standards and expectations for average to high-quality housing. That meant a fireplace in every room; with the same amount of wood, these fireplaces would reflect four times as much heat into the room as those broad, straight, gaping fireplaces that predated the progress made by heating technology. This was one of the modest steps made in the eighteenth century, the century of privacy, toward the earliest form of well-being, or *confort*, to use a word taken almost intact from English: a more intelligent use was made of effort, and there was a greater economy of movement. I doubt that a single room in the physical setting of this life has escaped the attention of Annik Pardailhé-Galabrun and the students whose work she guided so well.

What criticisms can be made of our sample? So that you can judge its reliability, we present it here in detail, placing our (note) cards on the table. Inventories were made following 10 to 15 per cent of all deaths. The work of Parisian notaries and the Coutume de Paris greatly facilitated our task. Our geographical distribution coincides fairly closely with the distribution of people and lodgings. We entered one house in ten, over a period of 150 years, from 1640 to 1790, during which time 2,500,000 persons died in 600,000 households. Paris was a city of some 100,000 homes in 1640 and some 150,000 on the eve of the Revolution. In 150 years, Le Sage's famous 'diable boiteux' or limping devil lifted the roofs and let us peep into one household out of 200. Our national opinion polls today make do with less in order to have election results ready for the evening news.

Of course, I can imagine your reply: our sample is not a perfectly straight-forward photograph of the Paris population. It is biased by the use of the inventory after death, slightly more than was our sample of testators in *La Mort à Paris*. Louis-Sébastien Mercier, ever the demagogue, proclaimed that notarial documents were outrageously expensive. The reason for this dearness has since been explained by the Colins Clark-Fourastié law. In a society in which services were held in the same esteem as sophisticated household appliances today, the scribblings of the notarial clerk cost a day labourer who carried water on his shoulders a fair share of the sweat from his brow. Yes, the inventory is a selective device. But though it narrows the base of the pyramid and slightly alters the proportions, it does not distort the basic form. Individuals from every level of society, every profession, every degree of fortune are present, but the thin chorus of voices they raise may not reproduce the exact proportions of each group in the hypothetical general population. If we were to attempt one day to estimate the total number of objects contained in the 25,000 Parisian houses on the eve of the Revolution, half of which date from the eighteenth century and half from the previous 250 years of the seventeenth, sixteenth and late fifteenth centuries, we should have to assign weighted values, or in other words, deflate our figures.

At this degree of precision, our sole aspiration is to let you imagine what you would have seen and touched if you could have entered some of these dwellings, whether 'a town house of thirty-one rooms occupied by its owner, the widow of the marquis so-and-so', or the furnished room in which a day labourer lived with his wife, where they had sought to use modest screens to sketch an outline of privacy in their poor man's palace. In examining this authentic slice of life standing several stories high, we must simply bear in mind that our social pyramid places proportionately more people on top than there actually were, and fewer at the bottom than there must have been. What we have eliminated are the wanderers, the unsettled, the migrants of misery, the unassimilated, the vagabonds. After all, from Arlette Farge to Christian Romon, not to mention the excellent study by Daniel Roche, who selected the least privileged third, this fringe has received so much attention that we run the risk of forgetting the rest of the population. In between the Court society at Versailles and the pensioners of the Hôpital Général, we believe that those whom the Constituent Assembly shamelessly called *citoyens actifs* (gainfully employed citizens) also have a claim to a place in history. More than half of these were Parisians born and bred.

Under such conditions, is it any surprise that our true Parisians seem like villagers, who love their street, their neighbourhood, the church of their parish, who are curious about the daily lives of their neighbours and who pursue the professions of their fathers? Paris in the eighteenth century was not the dangerous city of a Jack the Ripper. The Paris contained within the gates of the Farmers General, but without omnibuses or the Métro, could appear to travellers to be a sprawling ensemble unequalled anywhere else in the world, but it was also a juxtaposition of small neighbourhoods, each a warm focus of existence in which neighbours actually still knew one another.

For this we have great quantities of evidence. I shall cite a single example. Paris at the beginning of the eighteenth century already contained almost a thousand streets, but it was not until 1728 that they acquired official names and that the owners of houses on street corners were required to install tin plaques bearing these names, which were then progressively replaced by engraved stone tablets. As for the street numbers which private initiative had placed here and there, these were not standardized until the imperial *décret* of 4 February 1805. Of course there were shop signs. If Delamare's count was accurate, there was an average of one for every seven or eight houses at the end of the seventeenth century. Parisian space was a space that had not yet been marked, delimited and numbered. It was a space of names, like any country hamlet in Hurepoix or Brie, but it was also a space mapped in memory, and therefore a space that could be recounted.

In order to find one's way in Paris, it was not enough to have eyes, it was also useful to possess the language. To make sure we were on the right track in interpreting the clerks' indications, we often had recourse to the testimony of good or bad neighbours. In short, people found their way in Paris then as they do today in Tokyo, by asking for directions. 'Et il n'y a de bon bec que de Paris', wrote Villon: 'No one can gab like the Parisians.' This sort of space remains, out of vital necessity, a space of close conviviality. How could it be otherwise? The bachelor has his meals brought in, and with the exception of wine, salt and a few sticks of firewood, no one keeps any provisions. As a result, everyone hops down to the merchant ten times a day for a handful of this or a glass of that. Water is carried up on the bearer's shoulder, and both rich and poor live in the midst of a tangle of little debts. The memory of a Parisian of the Enlightenment is also a largely unwritten book filled with a multitude of small accounts.

Annik Pardailhé-Galabrun and her clerks, those of yesterday and those of today, will show you around the entire social scale. You will therefore receive confirmation of what you may already have suspected: this city was at the heart of the state, and therefore of justice and finance; it was based on services of all types. Our notaries do not say much about the linen maids who looked after the comfort of lonely inn guests. Our sources examine the daylight world and see little of the grey realm that appeared after nightfall. We can indeed speak of the 'tertiary' sector, and you will realize to what extent this was a city that lived by word of mouth, on frills and flounces in the well-being that foreshadowed comfort, and on reading and prayer as well.

It was not easy to live well there. We realize how costly life was. And it was ruinous for those not lucky enough to be servants. Jacqueline Sabattier has already said almost all there is to say on the lackeys thrown out of their extended families, who swelled the ranks of aggressive flunkeys on the eve of the 'great troubles' that marked the end of the century.

Indeed, everything was horribly expensive in Paris, where everyone was the creditor of everyone else. Rarely has anyone measured with such exactitude this network of debts and assets. Letters were for the rich – everyone else made do with notes and their word. A person's word established the borderline between who was honourable and who could not be trusted.

Misery, even more than debauchery, is closely and strangely bound up with death (besides, the realm of misery in Paris is a serious one, and by far the most populous, so we leave questions of debauchery to other scholars). It therefore follows that the test of conjugal love is the obsessive fear of leaving behind a widow without means of support. Romon saw the widow of a counsellor to a provincial Parlement die of cold on the doorstep of a church. But much more simply, it was *horribly expensive to die.* The modest ambition to leave at least enough for a decent funeral was an idea that I too had as a young man.

There is something else you will discover with Annik Pardailhé-Galabrun: a stroll through Paris in the eighteenth century is almost as much a stroll through time as it is through space. Every now and then you find yourself practically in the twentieth century, as part of the impressive mass of men and women who ensure our complete continuity and contiguity with the France and Europe of the eighteenth century, 99 per cent of whom lived in the fully inhabited, 'filled in' world of traditional Latin Christianity.

With us, you will be surprised by the fantastic revolution the house has undergone. Only one discovery rivals in importance the transition from *vertical* to *horizontal* housing, in my opinion, and that is Annik Pardailhé-Galabrun's discovery – one which nobody can dispute with her – of the progressive shift in Paris during the eighteenth century from cooking in a crouching position to cooking standing up.

In both cases, the result is a great avoidance of bodily pain, a more rational organization and a better economy of physical effort. Add to that what we knew already: the change from piling things in chests to arranging, classifying and placing them flat in closets.

It is important to note, however that these revolutions did not happen everywhere at the same pace. Look at residential buildings. In Paris, people did not live in their own houses. They rented them out, or rented as tenants. Most of the 14 per cent who were owners of their homes did not belong to the top of the social ladder. Does that mean that it was not done to live in one's own house?

What I do know is that by the middle of the eighteenth century, horizontal living was beginning to carry the day. Narrow houses with their rooms on top of each other cost less. They were also harder to heat. They were run down. The taste for old buildings is a rich person's luxury and a recent passion. Old buildings in the eighteenth century were merely run down.

Between the beginning of the seventeenth and the end of the eighteenth century, the gradual progress made was immense; indeed, it finally amounted to a world of difference. There were many more objects, much more space. As I noted in *La Mort à Paris*, it is the nineteenth century, not the eighteenth, that becomes encumbered with accumulated possessions.

There are four or five times as many objects, and yet possessions remain rare, precious and fragile (the Industrial Revolution did not produce junk, but rather more solid articles). In the eighteenth century people did not yet throw things away. They accumulated them. Perhaps they did so because of the bonds of affection between a humble object and the humble landmarks of the setting to which our shreds of memories are attached.

The disappearance of red in favour of green was not to be expected. Nor was the role of the bed, that cathedral that represented 15, 20 or 25 per cent of the value of the furniture, that temple of life, the site of conception, where the soul was captured, and of death, when it was released. I remember the bed of a duchess that was worth the price of a small farmhouse in the Beauce region. But the bed was not a privilege of the rich. Nor were the screens that offered an inkling of privacy in the corners of a single-room home, or in the kitchen where the maidservant slept. And the kitchen itself reveals the subtle art of the palate.

Books provided nourishment for the spirit. Paradoxically they also argue, along with the images on the walls, for a sense of continuity. Books and images lend strength to Philippe Ariès's, and nuance to Michel Vovelle's, lessons on death. In fact, it was the notary who strove to expurgate the use of pious formulae in his documents. At the moment when the Commune of 1793 was preparing to force the legislature down the path of lightning de-Christianization, Paris refused to part passively with the warmth of affectionate piety, or with the daily meditation practised by the majority on dolorist Christian themes: these focused on the dolorous mysteries of the Passion of Christ and yet were simplified, practical and straight to the point.

Paris may have been the aristocrat of Enlightenment France, but Paris was also rooted in France, and the warmth of its homes could not foreshadow the coming revolutionary fury. But that is another story. We hope simply that the contagious glow of these 3000 Parisian hearths will warm you with a little of the happiness we had in bringing them back to life.

Pierre Chaunu
Institut de France

Introduction

The numerous travellers from France's provinces and from abroad who visited
Paris from the reign of Louis XIV on could not heap sufficient praise on the city:
it was 'one of the most beautiful and magnificent in Europe, and in which a
traveller might find novelties enough for six months of daily entertainment, at
least in and about this noble city', wrote the English scientist Dr Martin Lister
in 1698.[1] The second largest city in Europe after Rome attracted the curiosity
of tourists during the seventeenth and eighteenth centuries, and Paris was the
subject of a wealth of descriptions in guides and travel accounts of the times, two
literary forms whose success grew continually from the 1650s.

Many of these visitors recorded their personal impressions on the appearance
of urban housing in their diaries. Though subjective, often repetitive from
one writer to another, and sometimes biased and inaccurate, these observations
are nonetheless interesting because of their spontaneity, and they reveal the
environment in which the capital's inhabitants lived as seen with the fresh eyes of
travellers. Taken together, the various comments set down by these authors
sketch out a bird's-eye view of Paris: in the centre of the city, the streets are
dark and narrow, lined with houses of different heights, giving a general impression of great height and verticality. Each house shelters some twenty persons.
In the close suburbs or *faubourgs*, the houses are lower, more run down, and
semi-rural. This was a city of contrasts: between buildings constructed as rental
properties with ordinary, cramped façades, and the town houses or *hôtels* of the
nobility, with carriage entrances, standing between their courtyard and garden on
spacious lots. These contrasts between the appearance of the centre and that of
the new neighbourhoods to the west were accentuated during the eighteenth
century by the frenzied building that took place in the latter area.

These characteristics of Paris on which travellers focused were corroborated by
Louis-Sébastien Mercier's descriptions from the eve of the French Revolution.
'Hauteur des maisons' (On the height of the buildings) is even the title of a
chapter in his *Tableau de Paris*,[2] and in *Parallèle de Paris et de Londres* the same
author insists again on this elevation and adds that 'this passion for stacking up
people this way, from the cellar up to the rooftops, concentrates bad air in filthy
streets, so that it is extraordinary that the plague does not break out there'.[3] His

Tableau de Paris also echoes the progress in urban planning from which the city had benefited in the last years of the *ancien régime*: 'Immense structures grow from the earth as if by magic, and new neighbourhoods consist solely of the most magnificent *hôtels*. The fury to build ... is marking the city with an air of greatness and majesty.'[4] The writer was thrilled at the numerous changes taking place in the capital and noted that 'the city has indeed changed its appearance in the last twenty-five years'.[5]

Though the many descriptions of Paris from this period give us a tiny idea of the various types of housing in the urban fabric and of the customs and habits of the population overall, they tell us almost nothing about the housing conditions of the city's inhabitants, nor about how they lived within their households. The travellers who have left behind diaries for posterity belonged to wealthy and educated milieux, and they stayed in the finest hotels or furnished rooms of the capital. A small number of them, especially the English and those travelling during the second half of the eighteenth century, described in great detail their apartments in the most fashionable hotels of the period, located in the faubourg Saint-Germain or, after the 1770s, near the Palais Royal. The only private homes in which these outsiders were received were those of the social and intellectual elite. This is not a representative sample of the Parisian population. To cite an example, one of the well-known regulars at Mme du Deffand's salon was Horace Walpole. Despite the interest such writings by travellers hold for the historian, they generally do not make a great contribution to our understanding of daily life in the privacy of the city's households.

Just what kind of lodgings were hidden inside these buildings of which most travellers saw only the façades? What sorts of objects, enclosed behind these walls, created the setting for the daily existence of their inhabitants? Driven by the desire to know more about the life-styles of these pre-revolutionary Parisians, we looked for a way to slip inside these dwellings and visit them from top to bottom, from the attic to the cellar. What better guides could we find than notaries to explore these homes of old Paris? In fact, it was in the notarial archives that we found the ideal document, the key that would let us enter these households and unveil the secrets of their inhabitants: the inventory compiled after death. This stroll through time and space which we shall present throughout these pages is founded on the detailed and systematic analysis of some 3000 inventories dating from the period between 1600 and 1790. Only 17 per cent of these date from the seventeenth century, and 83 per cent from the eighteenth. Though the shortest of these documents are just two pages long, the most extensive cover 100 pages or more, and the average length is approximately eight to ten pages. Examining such a wealth of information, which totals some 50,000 pages, represents a considerable amount of work that would exceed the capacities of a single scholar.

As a result, this book is the fruit of a vast collective study directed by Pierre Chaunu, member of the Institut de France and professor at the Université de Paris-Sorbonne. Some fifty students preparing their *maîtrises* and *troisième cycle* degrees participated in this research project, each one making his or her contribution to the reconstitution of the Parisian home from the century of Louis XIV and from the age of the Enlightenment, which we have tried to grasp in both its totality and its diversity.[6] In addition to their written work, the comments and suggestions of various scholars who took part regularly in Pierre Chaunu's seminar also contributed to the elaboration of this work.

The 2783 inventories providing the basis for this study were drawn from approximately 100 of the 122 notarial firms listed in the Minutier Central[7] for the eighteenth century. We have complemented this basic documentation with other sources such as notarial acts involving either the deceased and his or her family, e.g. marriage contracts, wills, *partages* (divisions of property among co-heirs) or the dwelling, e.g. leases, deeds of sale, works estimates or reports by sworn building experts, all found in series Z1J in the French National Archives, as well as illustrative documents from the print department of the Bibliothèque Nationale. The inventory remains, however, the primary focus of this study. Indeed, the great interest this document holds for French and foreign historians is well known, ranging geographically across western Europe, the Ottoman empire and Nouvelle France (the French possessions in Canada), and temporally from the fourteenth to the twentieth centuries. Used systematically along with the marriage contract in the 1960s and 1970s in the field of socio-economic history,[8] it has earned its place more recently, in conjunction with the will, in the field of cultural history and the history of *mentalités* or attitudes.[9] Numerous specific studies have been made using inventories and wills, and their advantages and failings have been emphasized by various scholars.[10]

The inventory is certainly an indispensable source for reconstructing daily life through the relationships between individuals and the spaces and objects in their households. However, it cannot be considered as providing a photograph of Parisians at home, and because of its gaps and its imperfections, it must be used with some prudence.

To what extent is this document representative of the Parisian households we have attempted to understand? It would seem that on this point, three major flaws must be attributed to the inventory:

1 By its very nature, it is produced when the family is breaking up, and it presents a household torn by the drama of death: a widow or widower is left alone, a father or mother of a family must bring up small children, minor orphans are placed in the care of guardians, and so forth. This means the inventory can never reproduce the portrait of a happy, normal household.

2 Generally speaking, the inventory involves individuals having reached an advanced stage of life: in three-quarters of all cases, the act was drawn up after ten years of married life, at an estimated age of forty to fifty (specific indications of age are rare). Consequently, this document does not always provide enough evidence to identify typical families, since some or all of the children have left the parental home.

3 The inventory was a legal document used as a means of defence by heirs, minors and creditors, and was not intended for general use. It reflects a specific situation. Inventories were compiled when:

(a) minor heirs were to be placed in guardianships;
(b) The heirs requested it and would not accept the inheritance without an inventory having been made;

(c) one of the spouses requested that the property in the estate be divided (this was often done when remarriage was planned).

It has been calculated that just 10 per cent of all deaths were followed by an inventory at the start of the eighteenth century, and the figure was 14–15 per cent on the eve of the French Revolution.[11] Although the place of the inventory in notarial work was greater than that of the will, it was nevertheless small, as polls carried out for the years 1698 and 1749 indicate. Out of 2458 legal documents drawn up in three notarial offices chosen at random, just twenty-four inventories were completed in 1698, which accounts for less than 1 per cent of the total.[12] The percentage of inventories seems to have increased in the first half of the eighteenth century: in a sampling of 2416 deeds drawn up in 1749 in four different offices, 100 inventories were noted, representing 4.1 per cent of the total.[13]

It is also important to emphasize that the inventory was selective from a social point of view. This was a document for the rich, or at least the well-off, because of its relatively high cost for common folk, e.g. 15–20 livres (hereafter abbreviated L) around 1700 and 30–40 L around 1780, or more than twenty days of work.[14] On the eve of the Revolution, Louis-Sébastien Mercier denounced, in his somewhat demagogical way, the 'awful dearness' of notarial deeds 'because one does not have the right to negotiate and set their price in advance'.[15]

The goal of this study, however, is not specially to enter the households of the poor, so that this failing in the inventory is not seriously damaging for our purposes. Furthermore, we have attempted to counterbalance this situation by including specific studies of the most humble levels of the Paris population, such as servants, day-labourers, and *frotteurs* or floor polishers, as well as the inhabitants of the Saint-Marcel and Saint-Antoine faubourgs, both recognized as being essentially working-class neighbourhoods. Those people of the second half of the eighteenth century who had no true home, and who lived in the misery of unhealthy and impersonal furnished rooms located in the narrow, dirty streets and cul-de-sacs of the central city, leave no trace through inventories, since often all they possessed was a bundle of rags. They have been examined in numerous studies based on police archives,[16] but they cannot hold our attention here, since we are seeking to capture the actions of daily life as portrayed through the elements of material culture. Though they fail to be representative in this aspect, the inventories have given us the means of assembling a fairly broad social and professional sample, excluding this drifting population of the abject poor who were often from the provinces and had come to Paris at the end of the eighteenth century to find work.

Among other difficulties, the inventory contains gaps or inaccuracies touching on three aspects of our study: the deceased person and his family, the dwelling and household objects.

1 Although the inventory almost always specifies the deceased person's name and surname, title, profession and marital status, it almost never mentions his age. Though it generally indicates the date of the will, if any, and of the individual's death, it rarely offers information on the last illness or circumstances

surrounding death. Occasionally expenses for doctors, surgeons, apothecaries or nurses may be noted, as well as funeral expenses, under the heading of the deceased person's debts, at the end of the document.

In the area of marital status, we made one salient observation: whereas no mention of male bachelorhood is ever made in the preamble to the inventory, unmarried women are always referred to as *filles majeures* (spinsters). It could therefore only be assumed hypothetically that a man might have been unmarried. If the deceased person was married, the duration of the marriage or the existence of a prior marriage can be determined only if one or more marriage contracts are mentioned in the list of documents or papers.

Nor is the inventory a very sure source regarding the individuals composing the household. Children of the deceased are always named as heirs, with the exception of those having taken religious orders, as they would not be beneficiaries of the estate. The ages of minor children are usually indicated, but it is not always easy to know how many of them actually lived in their parents' home. This is because the document never specifies whether a given child was put out to nurse, being apprenticed, or boarding at school. For married or grown-up children, it is equally difficult to determine whether they were living under the same roof, unless the document specifically indicates a different address. Since houses were not numbered, there must be some doubt if the offspring's domicile is merely given as in the same street without further information. Finally, children from a previous marriage, who had no rights to the estate, were not named in the preamble to the document, even if they lived in the same household as their dead stepfather or stepmother. Servants or boarders having no blood relationship with the deceased appear in the inventory only if they served as witnesses to the document or if a room in the house was associated with their name, thereby preserving their memory. The presence of servants in a household may be revealed by statements of wages due to them.

The inventory is clearly not a reliable source of demographic information. It must therefore be used with extreme caution when dealing with the question of population density in Parisian housing.

2   The inventory does not give a good indication of the external appearance of houses, nor of their internal layout. Many details – the number of stories or of windows per story, building materials, dimensions, and the age and state of repair of the buildings – cannot be known from this type of document alone. The presence of a carriage doorway, a pedestrian entrance, of one or more buildings, a courtyard, a garden or a well is never mentioned directly. Nor can the inventory be used to reconstruct the picture of a tenement house, as it is impossible to find all the descriptions of the various apartments it contained.

The inventory's limitations also become apparent when we try to re-establish the layout of a dwelling. As we follow the valuers' footsteps from one room to another, it is difficult to imagine the appearance of these interiors. It is often hard to distinguish the transitions within these living areas, as the notary fails to mention passageways such as stairs or corridors, void as they would be of any possessions to be inventoried. Servants' quarters containing their personal belongings could even go unnoticed.

Nor are the functions of various rooms evident from the terms used by the notary, with the exception of the kitchen, bedrooms, dining room or shop. This failing may, however, be attributed to the fact that, more often than not, rooms at that time did not have specific functions, as we shall see later. Any idea of the dimensions of a room or the number of openings or fireplaces can be obtained only indirectly, from the dimensions of tapestries covering the walls, window curtains or door curtains, or the presence of fire irons.

Last of all, the impression gained of the arrangement of furniture in each room from the bare listing of all the items in the household is often hazy and may sometimes even be inexact in certain details. The last illness or the death may have tended to modify the way space was organized, and the notary's arrival could add to these changes if it was necessary, for instance, to provide him with a table in a room which normally did not contain one, or to collect similar objects together in order to facilitate their evaluation. However, since rooms did not have specialized functions, these slight modifications are of little importance.

3   Of more direct concern to our study are the gaps and inaccuracies relating to household objects. On this point, the flaws inherent in this type of document are due to three factors: the psychological and practical conditions in which the operation took place, the degree of cultural sophistication of the notaries and valuers, and the time elapsed between the date of death and that of the inventory.

The valuation of the estate took place under conditions that could vary considerably from one home to another, according to the social status and the wealth of the household being inventoried. In a well-to-do family accustomed to dealing with the notary,[17] the procedure took place in an atmosphere of trust and in conditions of comfort which contributed to the quality of the drafting of the document but reduced the attention paid to detail. With more modest folk, completely unfamiliar with legal matters and often living in a single, badly heated, poorly lighted room, the description and valuation of objects inventoried tended to be more summary and hastily done, as the objects had little value. Since trust was not as great, however, the listing of possessions is minutely detailed, and the contents of outbuildings and annexes were carefully verified.[18] Sometimes, in the case of low-income families, descriptions were simplified in order to reduce costs: the inventory of a master painter dated 9 January 1748 mentions 'a bundle of linen which was not described in more ample detail at the request of the parties, in order to avoid the cost'.

The detail and accuracy of descriptions and the sale value attributed to objects were also dependent on the cultural sophistication of the notary, his clerk or the valuers in charge of the inventory. The descriptive vocabulary used may therefore be misleading in certain cases by its very lack of precision. The notary often failed to recognize the subject matter of engravings or pictures and simply noted 'picture with figures' or 'devotional picture' without further indication. The same is true of books, which were frequently valued in a general manner, by packets of the same format, without any mention of authors or titles. Completely heterogeneous objects might be valued together: a commode with a prie-dieu, for instance, or a Christ in ivory, an umbrella and the lid of a pot. Some objects were not even described because the notaries or valuers decided, quite arbitrarily, that they were 'not worth describing'. Common kitchen utensils in stoneware, pottery or iron, were sometimes designated as 'items for various uses' or 'not worthy of more ample description'. As for objects in pewter, they were sometimes lumped together under the heading 'pots, platters, plates and other utensils in real pewter'. There exist numerous such examples demonstrating the vagueness of the notaries' vocabulary.

Devotional objects, and especially pious engravings, received no mention by the notary, unless the objects had a certain sale value, as was the case with a Christ in ivory, a gold cross or a rosary in coral. Some objects were described as old, broken, worn or torn, and were assessed at a pittance, according to a clearly subjective and random evaluation by the valuers.

Despite their inaccuracies, most of these descriptions contain a striking amount of detail: the notary's eye observes everything, even the number of curtain rods, the presence of a bundle of old linen or boards, some cracked cups and saucers, or a broken table leg.

The conspicuous absence of certain objects in these inventories may be attributed to the time that elapsed between the death and the drawing up of the document. Legally, the inventory could not be made less than three days after death, and a 1667 edict set the maximum time limit at three months. In practice, however, when there was a new marriage or a guardianship, this time limit was largely exceeded and could extend to one or even several years. In going over the inventories of *gagne-deniers* (market porters) and *frotteurs* (floor polishers), we observed extremes of one day and twenty years. But these cases seem exceptional, and the overall average limit is about one to one and a half months. The longer the time that elapsed between the death and the inventory, the greater the odds that the appearance of the household had changed. Because seals were rarely placed on the belongings of the deceased, the heirs could, even in a short period of time, remove or sell objects.

Every scholar who has studied inventories has noted omissions concerning three types of objects:

food supplies (which is understandable) as well as fuel supplies, even in winter;

clothing and articles for children;

everyday objects of little value, e.g. pocket knives, household objects such as brooms, pamphlets or religious images.

The inventory therefore cannot be considered as an exhaustive source detailing all the objects in a household. It is even less reliable as a means of evaluating wealth. This is because most objects were in fact valued below their real worth by the valuers in order to benefit the heirs. The prices indicated can therefore give only a general idea. As a result, we have not attempted to use these notarial data to study the financial status of these Parisians.

Despite its flaws, the inventory nevertheless remains the richest and most concrete source we have in our archives. It allows us to follow the example given by Lesage in *Le Diable Boiteux* (1707) and to look under the roofs of buildings in an attempt to rediscover, through the notary's eyes, the texture and the warmth of life in the Parisians' domestic world.

1

Geographic Location of Households in Paris and its Suburbs

Within the space of the city and its suburbs, where were these 2783 households inventoried by the notaries located? There were 2664 (96 per cent) in Paris itself and 82 (3 per cent) in the surrounding villages. Unknown or imprecise addresses account for 37 (1 per cent of the total).

One introductory note: with the exception of those located in the *banlieue* or outlying suburbs, which constitute a very small part of our sample, the residences which we are trying to position spatially were apparently rarely entire buildings. Most often they were rental lodgings containing one or more rooms within a tenement house. In the absence of a distinguishing number, sign or other indication on the outside of the building, it is possible that households living in the same street occupied different stories of a single house, though such assumptions cannot be based on the documents.

It is therefore impossible to state with certainty that the notaries visited 2664 houses in the capital. As a result, because the addresses are so vague, it is not easy to determine how representative our sample is in relation to the total number of houses in the city: according to an account preserved in the Delamare collection,[1] there were 20,207 houses in 1668. Saugrain estimates that there were 22,000 in 1726,[2] and Expilly calculates that 23,565 houses were subject to the capitation tax in 1755.[3] As the capital began to grow rapidly in the 1760s, this number was probably greater than 25,000 on the eve of the French Revolution.[4]

Addresses in Paris

The data in the preamble of the inventories give us information about the parish and the street in which the deceased had lived and, indirectly, through street names, about their neighbourhoods.

The parish

This unit provided the framework for both religious and daily secular life in the seventeenth and eighteenth centuries and remained very important until the Revolution. Our 2664 Parisian households were spread over forty-five parishes within the city walls, over a surface area of some 3000 hectares, according to boundaries set in 1702 by the city's division into twenty neighbourhoods as they appear on the 1773 Jaillot map during the reign of Louis XVI.

Of forty-five parishes recorded in Paris, we counted nineteen on the right bank, in the city and its faubourgs, fourteen on the Ile de la Cité and the Ile Saint-Louis, and twelve on the left bank, around the university and its faubourgs.

We know that the number of parishes in Paris between the end of the sixteenth century and the Revolution varied around the forty mark. In addition to the thirty-eight parishes existing at the end of the sixteenth century, six others were created during the seventeenth and three more in the eighteenth century, but five of the fourteen parishes on the Ile de la Cité were eliminated during the eighteenth century. If we refer to Abbé Lebeuf, the first person to undertake a topographical description of Parisian parishes around 1754 in his *Histoire de Paris*, there were twenty parishes at that time on the right bank, twelve on the left bank, and nine on the Ile de la Cité, making a total of forty-one parishes. Taking into account the changes that were made in the second half of the eighteenth century – the construction of Notre Dame de Bonne Délivrance, a new parish, in the Gros Caillou neighbourhood in 1776 and the elimination in 1786 of the Saints-Innocents parish, merged with Saint-Jacques-de-la-Boucherie after its cemetery was closed – the figure of forty-one parishes remains valid until the Revolution.

Of the 2664 heads of families in Paris whose addresses we know, 1907 (71.5 per cent) lived in nineteen parishes on the right bank; 679 (25.5 per cent) in twelve parishes on the left bank, and seventy-eight (3 per cent) in fourteen parishes on the Ile de la Cité or the Ile Saint-Louis (see maps I and II, where the unit 1 *toise* = c. 6 feet).

If we look at the distribution of households by parish, it appears that more than 80 per cent of the households were located in the old parishes in the city centre. According to the population estimations done for each parish by Expilly in the middle of the eighteenth century, these were the most heavily populated parishes: Saint-Eustache and Saint-Sulpice both included 90,000 inhabitants, Saint-Nicolas-des-Champs 50,000, Saint-Germain-l'Auxerrois and Saint-Paul 40,000, Sainte-Marguerite, Saint-Laurent, and Saint-Etienne-du-Mont 30,000 each, Saint-Roch 24,000, and so on.[5] The parishes in the centre of Paris, where most of our households were located, were very ancient territorial structures that emerged as early as the eleventh century within an ecclesiastical domain. As it became a true administrative unit in the thirteenth century, the parish contributed to the decline of seigniorial institutions and to the development of city unity. Except for a few boundary changes and a small number of new creations, the boundaries of parishes as they appear on Junié's map of 1786 were inherited from the Middle Ages. The seigniorial origin of these districts explains the puzzle-like aspect of this map, as well as the disproportionately small parishes on the Ile de la Cité compared with the far-flung parishes of Saint-Sulpice, Saint-Etienne-du-Mont, Saint-Eustache or Saint-Nicolas-des-Champs.[6]

Because of the great variations in surface area, the value of comparisons between the numbers of inhabitants from one parish to another in our sample is only relative. On the other hand, we noticed a bias in favour of the right bank, with 71.5 per cent, versus 25.5 per cent (or slightly more than a quarter) on the

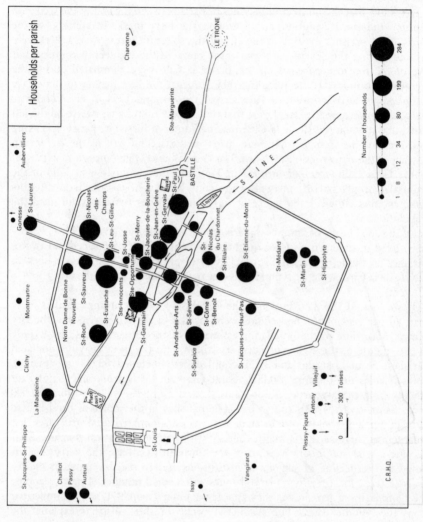

I Households per parish

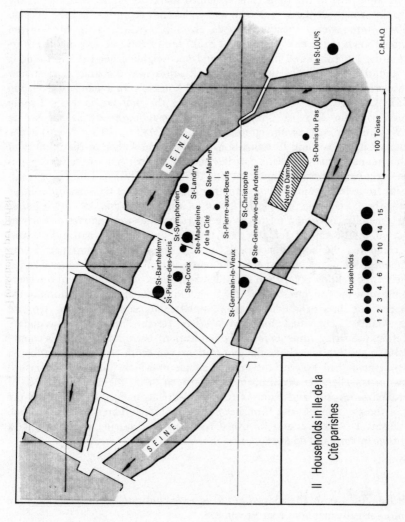

II Households in Ile de la Cité parishes

left bank. The tendency of our sample to favour the right bank is not the only explanation for this imbalance. In fact, the right bank's demographic predominance becomes clear as early as the Middle Ages, if we consider the list of parishes and of homes in 1328, attributing 80 per cent of the urban population to the thirteen religious districts within what were then city limits.[7]

The population of the right bank remained markedly higher than that of the left bank throughout the seventeenth and eighteenth centuries, and the division of Paris into twenty neighbourhoods in 1702 (which assigned fourteen neighbourhoods to the city (on the right bank) and its suburbs, five to the university (on the left bank) and its suburbs, and one neighbourhood to the Ile de la Cité and the Ile Saint-Louis) took this situation into account, as each new neighbourhood included an average of 17,000 houses, with a standard deviation of 255.[8] Of the 23,565 Parisian houses paying the poll tax in 1755, Expilly counted 6484 (or 27.5 per cent) in left bank neighbourhoods, as opposed to 14,608 (or 62 per cent) on the opposite bank, and 2489 (or 10.5 per cent) in the Ile de la Cité. According to estimations by the same author of the number of inhabitants per parish, left bank parishes housed 31.5 per cent of the Paris population, right bank parishes 65 per cent, and those in the Ile de la Cité 3.5 per cent.

Aside from demographic factors, another consideration of the same order helps explain the bias of our sample in favour of the right bank. Inventories after death generally concerned relatively aged persons who were natives of Paris or had lived in the capital for a certain time. It appears that native Parisians, who composed the bulk of notaries' clientele, lived for the most part in the neighbourhoods of the city, whereas the opposite bank was much better adapted to shelter the drifting population of students, soldiers on the move and travellers arriving from the provinces or abroad. It should be noted that in addition to the Sorbonne, the three neighbourhoods of Saint-Benoît, Saint-André-des-Arts and Place Maubert contained forty-two *collèges* (establishments for secondary education, preparing students for higher education), according to Jaillot's count.[9] We also know that as early as the end of the seventeenth century, the faubourg Saint-Germain had become the area of choice in which hotels and furnished rooms for travellers set up in business.[10] Between them, the neighbourhoods of Saint-André-des-Arts and Saint-Germain-des-Prés contained a total of 28 per cent of the city's hotels and furnished rooms in 1765.[11] The occupants of such establishments – *collèges* and furnished rooms – were usually spending only a short time in Paris and do not appear in inventories.

The street

Aside from the parish, the address of the deceased indicated in the heading of the inventory usually mentions a street name.

Out of 2664 Parisian addresses, we know the street in 2218 cases (83 per cent of the inventories). Using these documents, we have listed 545 public roads. Saugrain estimated the number of streets in 1720 at 960; Sauval believed there were over a thousand in 1724.[12] Jaillot seems to be the most reliable author, as he lists and maps all the streets by neighbourhood: in 1773, he counted 864, to which should be added eighty-two cul-de-sacs, seventeen *places*, fifteen *quais*, twelve bridges, and six intersections (*carrefours*). If we take into account the more than 100 roads whose construction was undertaken in the new neighbourhoods from the 1760s on, then Paris on the eve of the Revolution must have boasted between 1000 and 1100 streets.

Using the Jaillot map of 1773, we were able to identify almost all the 545 streets noted in the inventories. Though streets rarely changed their names during the seventeenth and eighteenth centuries, some of them had names that were hardly exclusive, such as rue Neuve, rue Basse or rue des Fossés, and the spelling was highly variable. Others, while located in different parishes, bore the same or very similar names. It should be noted that the new streets laid out toward the end of the eighteenth century, serving the west of the city in the sectors of Ville-l'Evêque, Roule, Chaussée d'Antin and Gros Caillou appear only rarely in our study.

Addresses are noted in this inexact and unclear manner because streets did not acquire a properly official identity until 1728: it was only in January of that year that the government decided to fix the names of city streets by placing tin name-plates bearing the names permanently in large black letters at the corner of each street. The following year a police order required the owners of houses on which these plates were placed to begin progressively replacing them with 'one-and-a-half-inch thick tablets of sandstone, sufficiently large to engrave thereon' the name of the street as well as the number of the neighbourhood.[13] House numbers as we know them today, however, came much later. They date from an imperial decree of 4 February 1805. Some Parisian houses received numbers as early as the sixteenth century: such was the case in 1512 with the sixty-eight houses on the Pont Notre Dame that belonged to the city. Until they were demolished in 1786, they kept their numbers. The houses on the Petit Pont, which were also property of the city until they were destroyed by fire in 1718, were identified by numbers as well, dating from the same period. The communal houses of the Marché Neuf on the Ile de la Cité were also numbered at the beginning of the eighteenth century. These numbers were simply a practical census-taking measure used by the city in specific areas. In application of instructions issued in 1723, 1726 and 1728, houses in the faubourgs were numbered for the same census-taking ends. In 1726 these numbers began to make a timid appearance in the *Almanach royal* to facilitate the identification of houses: in particular, some homes of counsellors in the Parlement or in the Chambre des Comptes are mentioned with their numbers.

These references became more frequent in the following decade. One Marin Kreenfelt de Storcks, chargé d'affaires for the Elector of Cologne, became editor of the *Almanach de Paris* in 1779 and was the first to have the idea of systematically numbering the houses in Paris, for the useful and modern purpose of assigning the inhabitants specific, practical addresses. The project met with a hostile reaction from Joly de Fleury, the *procureur général* of the police, as well as from the Parisians, who suspected its potential tax applications. As conceived by Kreenfelt, the project was carried out only in the neighbourhoods of Saint-Denis and Saint-Germain-des-Prés before being discontinued, as Louis-Sébastien Mercier regrets in his *Tableau de Paris*. Numbers were assigned in a continuous fashion, without separating odds and evens, and were assigned to each door rather than each house. During the Revolution, each section attempted to establish its own numbering system, without any plan or method.[14]

In the almost total absence of numbering – we found only three numbered houses in all of our study – the addresses given in the inventories sometimes employ other elements indicating location in addition to the name of the parish and the street, e.g. a shop sign or the name of the neighbouring street, a town house, a church, a convent or a well-known building nearby, or even the location with regard to a barrier marking the city limits, where taxes were paid on merchandise being brought into the city before the wall of the Farmers General was built in 1784. Expressions found in the notarial documents situate inhabitants in relation to these topographical landmarks: e.g. 'touching on' a building, 'at the entrance' or 'at the end' of a way, 'facing' or 'in front' of a given building, 'at the corner' or 'making the corner' of two streets.

We also noted the presence of signs in these inventories, above the doors of 177 houses, including sixty-nine in the seventeenth century. This number may appear very small; it may be insufficiently representative, either because some notaries failed to note their presence or because students failed to record the information. But houses and shops in the city did not all bear signs systematically, as we might imagine. A count dated 14 October 1670, taken from the Delamare collection, found 2982 signs.[15] This meant that signs were to be found on some 15 per cent of all residences in the city at that date. Even *cabaret* owners, wine and beer merchants, café owners, and innkeepers did not always announce their presence to passers-by with a sign.

These signs, in stone, clay, wood or metal, were usually attached by rings to iron brackets, and therefore posed a threat to passers-by during heavy winds. 'Because each merchant and each craftsman struggles to outdo his neighbour or his colleague by the height, size and weight of his sign', an ever increasing number of signs hanging out made the streets seem narrower and, in shopping streets, diminished 'considerably the view from the first story of houses and even the lamp light, creating shadows that threatened public safety'.[16] In consequence, a police *ordonnance* of 17 December 1761, which actually repeated earlier orders, declared that all signs were to be attached in the form of plaques to the walls of shops or houses, and were not to stand out or have a thickness protruding more than 10 cm from the bare wall.[17]

Given the rarity of signs and other geographical indications, it was most often necessary to refer to common knowledge and to relationships between neighbours on a given street or on neighbouring streets in order to find the address of a given city dweller – as is still the case today in Japan. In fact, through daily contacts among neighbours or at work, everybody seemed to know each other within a building, along a street and sometimes even within a parish.

For the 545 streets listed, we have calculated the distribution of households. A single home was found in 208 streets, (38 per cent of the total). In each of 234 streets (43 per cent), two to five of the deceased had been housed. Some six to ten families from our sample lived in each of sixty-three streets (11.5 per cent). There are only forty streets (7.5 per cent of all roads noted) in which we find more than ten addresses: these included a total of 824 households among the 2218 for which we know the address (i.e. 37 per cent of the whole). In twenty-six streets, eleven to twenty households were to be found; in seven streets, we located between twenty-one and thirty. Between thirty-one and forty addresses were indicated in each of the five following streets: rue Mouffetard, thirty-two addresses; rue Saint-Denis, thirty-six; rue Saint-Antoine, thirty-eight; rue du Faubourg Saint-Antoine, thirty-nine; rue Saint-Jacques, thirty-nine. Finally, the rue Saint-Martin and rue Saint-Honoré are named respectively in fifty-one and sixty-two of the inventories examined (see map III).

As any map shows, the most heavily populated streets in our sample were also the longest and most important roads in the city. There are sixty-two of our households located on the rue Saint-Honoré. Measuring some 853 toises (1680 metres) long, stretching across the three neighbourhoods of Sainte-Opportune, Louvre and Palais Royal, this road led from the rue de la Ferronnerie in the east to the Porte Saint-Honoré in the west; until its destruction in 1733, this gate separated the street from the rue du Faubourg Saint-Honoré. In the seventeenth and eighteenth centuries it was considered to be one of the longest, most beauti- ful and most shop-filled streets in the city and, according to Jaillot, was the street 'where you find the most churches, convents and remarkable buildings'.[18] In fact, the proximity of the royal palaces encouraged the nobility to build there and attracted a wealthy population connected with the Court, banking, trade and the literary world. Located on the route taken by royal and princely arrivals and other important processions, this was the main west–east artery leading to the centre of Paris.

Beyond the Porte Saint-Honoré, the faubourg of the same name was inhabited by nineteen of our Parisians. In this zone bordering on the city, bursts of urban growth and the capital's westward extension were marked throughout the centuries by the shifting location of the Porte Saint-Honoré. At the end of the twelfth century, this gate stood on what is today the Place du Palais Royal, an opening in Philippe Auguste's ramparts. When Charles V built his ramparts, a second gate was constructed in 1380, just beyond the Hospice des Quinze-Vingts. This gate was demolished in 1636, once the bastions ordered by Louis XIII were completed. It gave way to a third gate, located at what is now the intersection of the rue Royale and the rue Saint-Honoré. After this last gate was demolished in 1733, the city opened directly on to the suburb, but the notion of the gate survived the structure itself: an address dating from 1780 reads '11 rue and porte Saint-Honoré'.

In the eastern part of the city, the rue Saint-Antoine and the rue du Faubourg Saint-Antoine, which contained seventy-seven households altogether, were also major axes, studded with famous religious establishments such as the Jesuits' house of vocation, the Foundling Hospital and the Abbaye de Saint-Antoine. These roads led from the Place Baudoyer to the Place du Trône and also figured on the itinerary for royal parades and processions.

In the faubourg Saint-Antoine, a heavily working-class area that was growing rapidly in the eighteenth century, two other heavily populated streets appear in our study: the rue de Charenton and the rue de Charonne, both leading into the rue du Faubourg Saint-Antoine. The first, in which fifteen deceased persons had lived, was the oldest road in the Saint-Antoine suburb. Its existence predates Roman occupation, and it was part of the road running from ancient Lutetia

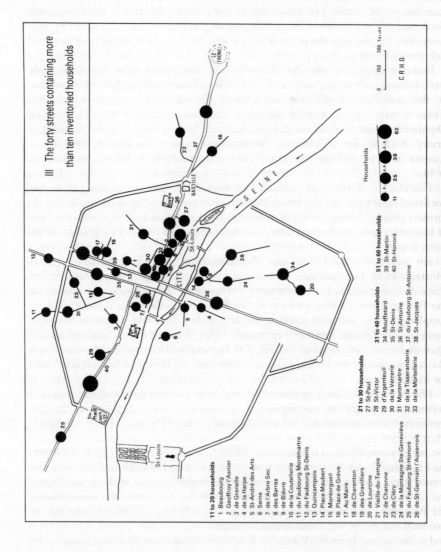

III The forty streets containing more than ten inventoried households

to Melun. This was where Robert de Cotte had the barracks for the Black Musketeers built at the end of the seventeenth century. This company was disbanded in 1775, and Cardinal Louis de Rohan, director of the Hospice des Quinze-Vingts, transferred the blind residents of his hospital in 1780, after receiving a very high price for the sale of the grounds on which the hospital, founded by St Louis, had stood between the Palais Royal and the Carroussel, bordering the rue Saint-Honoré. The rue de Charenton had also been the site, since 1660, of the convent of the Filles Anglaises de la Conception, a preserve of rich young foreign women.

Building along the rue de Charonne, on which sixteen of the households were located and which was formerly the way leading from Paris to the village of the same name, did not begin until early in the seventeenth century. Three monasteries stood along this street: the convent of the Filles de la Croix, a Dominican order established in 1641, and two communities of Benedictines, the priory of Madeleine de Traisnel, for which the cornerstone was laid by Anne of Austria in 1644, and the convent of Notre Dame de Bon Secours, founded in 1648.

The Place de Grève was located in the heart of Parisian municipal life. It was bordered on the east by the Hôtel du Boccador, built in 1606–8 on the site of the former 'pillared house' in which municipal governments had met since the time of Etienne Marcel in the fourteenth century, and on the north by the Hospice du Saint Esprit. This square lay in the centre of a densely populated neighbourhood which was home to 110 of our Parisians from the adjoining streets of la Mortellerie, la Tisseranderie, la Verrerie and la Coutellerie. The bustle on the Place de Grève and in the surrounding streets was connected with the presence of the Port de Grève, a centre of intense activity because of its fundamental role in supplying the capital with wood, grain and wine. These roads were used by the numerous teamsters transporting merchandise that had been unloaded on the Quai de Grève. Notorious as the site of public executions, the Place de Grève was also known for its fireworks, especially following *Te Deums* at Notre-Dame, and for its traffic jams.

The city's north–south axes are also frequently mentioned among the deceased persons' addresses. The rue Saint-Martin, some 586 toises (1151 metres) long, is mentioned fifty-one times. Taking its name from the famous priory of Saint-Martin-des-Champs, this street begins at the corner of the rue de la Verrerie and the rue des Lombards and ends at the Porte Saint-Martin, which opens on to rue du Faubourg Saint Martin. This was one of the major north–south axes cutting across Paris. In fact, it was prolonged in the neighbourhood of the university by the rue Saint-Jacques, and if we include the rue des Arcis, the Pont Notre Dame, the Petit Pont and the streets crossing the Ile de la Cité which join together the two banks of the Seine, these streets, aligned to one another, cross Paris from one end to the other, from the Porte Saint-Martin to the Porte Saint-Jacques, over a distance of 2000 *toises* or almost 4 km.

On this subject Sauval wrote, 'As for the rue Saint-Jacques and the rue Saint-Martin, which divide the city into two equal parts, or come close to it, together they form a street so long and so straight that travellers admit they have never seen another like it, or any that could be compared to it'.[19] Running parallel to the rue Saint-Martin, the rue Saint-Denis was the address of thirty-six of our homes. Measuring 645 *toises* (1278 metres), it was often called the Grande Rue Saint-Denis, and was included in both the neighbourhood of Saint-Jacques-de-la-Boucherie, from the Grand Châtelet to the rue aux Ours, and in that of Saint-Denis, where it led to the gate of the same name. It was extended by the rue du Faubourg-Saint-Denis, where twelve of the deceased persons had resided. The eighteenth century marked the beginning of the decline of the rue Saint-Denis, which came to be overshadowed by the rue Saint-Honoré and developed into an increasingly working-class street.

As the extension of the rue Saint-Martin on the other bank of the Seine, the rue Saint-Jacques contained the residences of thirty-nine of our Parisians. Another centre of population in the university sector was the Place Maubert, the site of various activities in the heart of a neighbourhood of religious communities, colleges, and merchants. The Place Maubert, together with the rue Saint-Victor and the rue de la Montagne-Sainte-Geneviève, housed fifty-five of our households.

Finally, we found one other concentration of habitation on the left bank, at the heart of the faubourg Saint-Marcel, in the rue Mouffetard and the rue de Lourcine. In these streets thirty-two and fifteen households respectively were located. The river Bièvre, whose source lies near Saint-Cyr to the west of Paris, was only completely covered over in Paris in 1910. Until then, it ran along the rue de Lourcine and crossed the rue Mouffetard beneath the Pont aux Trippes. This river was, of course, at the root of this neighbourhood's development as a craft centre. The presence of the river encouraged the establishment of slaughterhouses there, and with them, the arrival of several branches of the leather trade: tanners, curriers (*baudroyeurs*, also involved in hide preparation), shoemakers, cobblers and *mégissiers* or tawers (who prepared skins for fine leather goods). Certain tinctorial qualities in the water of the Bièvre made possible the development of a dyeing workshop, founded in 1447 by the 'scarlet dyer' Jean Gobelin, originally from Rheims, and established the reputation of the high-warp tapestry factory that became the famous Manufacture Royale des Gobelins under Colbert. By the end of the seventeenth century, the works were spread over four and a half hectares at the end of the rue Mouffetard, and employed 250 weavers.

Churches, convents, hospitals and gardens were also prevalent in this neighbourhood. The rue Mouffetard, the main artery in the Saint-Marcel suburb, was home to three parish churches: Saint-Hippolyte, the parish of the Manufacture des Gobelins, Saint-Martin and Saint-Médard, which earned a place in history because of the riot of 27 December 1561, during the struggle between Protestants and Catholics, and on account of the Convulsionaries who visited the tomb of Deacon Pâris between 1727 and 1732. The rue Mouffetard was also the site of the convent of the Dames Hospitalières, founded in 1656 by an order of Augustinians to take in and care for the sick. In the rue de Lourcine stood the Abbaye des Cordeliers, which dated from 1289.

We shall not look in such detail at all the densely populated roads in our survey, but before ending this examination of the distribution by streets, two observations may be made: first, among the forty streets mentioned on the left bank, a minority of just ten are cited as addresses in more than ten inventories each. This corroborates the hypothesis stated above on the distribution by parishes. Second, these streets, and even the names by which they were called, are all very old: the rue de Montorgueil, rue Montmartre, rue Saint-Martin, rue de la Mortellerie, rue de la Tisseranderie, rue de la Verrerie, rue de Lourcine, rue Mouffetard and rue Saint-Jacques had all borne the same names since the thirteenth century. Other streets, such as the rue Saint-Honoré, rue Saint-Denis, rue Saint-Antoine and rue de Seine already existed during this period, but under different names. It is therefore logical to assume that in the seventeenth and eighteenth centuries a number of houses dating from the end of the Middle Ages and the sixteenth century were still standing in these streets.

Addresses in the Area Surrounding Paris

These eighty-two addresses, which represent 3 per cent of all residences inventoried, are divided among thirteen parishes in the outlying Paris area. There were seventy-five deceased persons residing in the parishes of the ecclesiastical suburbs of Passy, Auteuil, Chaillot, Montmartre, Charonne, Clichy and Vaugirard; two in Aubervilliers and Gonesse, parishes of the archdiocese of Paris within the deanery of Montmorency; and five in parishes of the archdiocese of Josas (Antony, Issy and Le Plessis-Piquet, within the deanery of Châteaufort) and Villejuif within the deanery of Montlhéry. There were sixty-nine inventories for households in Passy and twenty-three involving residents of Auteuil.

The study of the eighty-two inventories from households in these surrounding villages takes us outside the city limits and broadens our horizons to include areas that, despite their proximity to the capital (the farthest outlying villages, Antony and Gonesse, lie respectively just 3 and 4 leagues (15 and 20 km) from Paris), had preserved an essentially rural character. Chaillot, though it lay just a half league outside the city, was described in 1779 as a gay village standing on a hill, with a few vineyards, gardens, and tilled fields.[20] According to Abbé Lebeuf, Passy, which stood on a delightful hill near the right bank of the Seine about a league outside Paris, owed its reputation not only to the Monastère des Minimes, whose inhabitants were also called the Bons Hommes (good fellows), but also to its many mineral water springs and its lovely country houses. In describing Auteuil, the same author noted that the plain in which the village lay was better adapted to tilled fields than to grape growing. Aubervilliers, situated at the end of the faubourg of Saint-Laurent, to the north-east of the capital, was known for its garden produce and vegetables, especially cabbages and lettuces. Antony, on the road leading from Paris to Chartres via Bourg-la-Reine, was surrounded by cultivated fields, meadows and vineyards. Le Plessis-Piquet stood two leagues from Paris in the midst of hedge-bordered fields. Villejuif, on the high road leading from Paris to Lyon, was an area of vineyards and cultivated fields.

The scanty population of these parishes emphasized their rural character. According to the *Dictionnaire Universel de la France* published in 1726, the villages of Le Plessis-Piquet, Aubervilliers and Auteuil (population: 480) had fewer than 500 inhabitants. Eight of the villages surrounding Paris – Issy,

Vaugirard, Chaillot (population: 538), Antony, Passy (population: 646), Clichy, Charonne and Villejuif, were home to between 500 and 1000 souls. Montmartre reached the thousand mark, and Gonesse, a borough known for its wheat market and the quality of its bread, had some 3000 inhabitants.

Despite their rural appearance, these suburban villages were connected to Paris by close bonds (the term 'suburb' or *banlieue* is used here in a broader sense than its definition in the *Encyclopédie*, which limited its use to areas within one league around the city). The population and the activities of these villages in the suburban ring developed in symbiosis with the city. Certainly villages like Versailles, Saint-Germain-en-Laye and Fontainebleau played a role in the monarchy and the government. But the villages encompassed by our study also maintained cultural and economic links with the capital. Well-off Parisians chose either to buy or to rent a house in the immediate environs of Paris, whether as their sole, main or second home.

Their choice fell especially often on Passy and Auteuil, where the shining lights of the literary and art worlds chose to live in the seventeenth and eight-eenth centuries. Boileau resided in Auteuil, Racine is supposed to have written *Les Plaideurs* there, and Molière and his friends frequented one of the town's fashionable cafés of the period. The painter Quentin La Tour had his studio in the rue d'Auteuil, in a house purchased in 1772 by Madame Helvétius. The salon she held there in the late years of the century was famous and received the high society of the age. The seigniorial Château de Boulainvilliers in Passy enjoyed a period of splendour under the Farmer General Le Riche de La Popelinière, a munificent patron and protector of the arts; through the château between 1746 and 1762 passed celebrities of the Court and the world, men and women of letters and illustrious artists. According to Mercier, on the eve of the Revolution Passy and Auteuil also attracted members of the 'petite bourgeoisie, all dressed up in their Sunday best, who rushed off to mass so that they could have the rest of the day to themselves. They arranged to dine in Passy, Auteuil, Vincennes or in the Bois de Boulogne.'[21]

The village of Vaugirard, one league outside Paris on the road to Issy, Meudon and Versailles, drew a more 'popular' crowd and was known for its *cabarets*: the *Dictionnaire Universel de la France* states that it was full 'almost exclusively of *cabarets*, and profited from an extraordinary arrival of people, especially on the feast day of Lambert, who is the patron saint of the said place'. Vaugirard, according to Mercier, was where the suburb of Saint-Marcel flocked on Sundays, and the people there 'danced barefoot, and spun about endlessly, men and women who raised so much dust within an hour that in the end they could no longer be seen'.[22] One wine merchant ran a shop under the sign of St John the Baptist in Vaugirard. Charonne, to the east of the faubourg Saint-Antoine, also attracted a popular clientele to its open-air cafés on holidays. One inventory from this parish helps us re-create a wine merchant's business, where clients were received in a shop and *cabaret* hall that opened in fair weather on to a garden provided with tables and benches.

We have also found the inventories of two other *cabaret* owners and a wine merchant who lived in Villejuif and in Montmartre, as well as four hotel owners who resided in Antony, Villejuif, Aubervilliers and Gonesse. These professions required vast structures with several outlying buildings in order to lodge clients and shelter horses, carriages and wagons. In these villages on the city's periphery, they found space that could be expanded more easily than within city walls. Daniel Roche has written a lovely description of the special role of the *cabaret* in popular culture and ways of life.[23] Settled outside the city barriers for tax reasons, these entertainment establishments emerge in our study through a few inventories, and they drew most of their clientele from the capital. In a way, they formed the link between the populations of the city and of rural villages.

The location of these businesses, situated on the city's periphery, is generally indicated with great precision. The addresses of inhabitants of Passy are distributed among ten named streets or are designated by place names or well-known buildings such as the enclosure in the Bois de Boulogne, the Courtyard of the Bons Hommes (in reference to the monastery of the Minimes de Nigeon) or the royal Château de La Muette. As for Auteuil, we noted the names of seven streets, in which sixteen households were located, as well as references to a place named Le Point-du-Jour, to two buildings – the presbytery and the church – and to a sign. In the other villages, the notary has often indicated street names: the rue de la Paroisse in Villejuif, the rue Rochechouart in Montmartre, the Grande-Rue in Aubervilliers, the Place du Marché in Gonesse, and so on.

Now that we have seen the lie of the land, let us turn to the men, women and children, those flesh-and-blood human beings of all ages who belonged to all social classes and professions. These are families stunned by the loss of a relative, ageing couples or solitary individuals, priests, widows, bachelors, and others.

2

A Sample of the Population of Paris

We can now turn to discovering the inhabitants of these households, in both their social and their family lives, using the indications revealed to us in the inventories. What social and professional categories did they belong to? What did they do to earn a living? How many people were living under the same roof? What were the bonds that brought them together?

Looking at Social and Professional Categories

Even though the inventory after death is a relatively selective document, we managed to collect a sample covering a wide social and professional range. In order to handle a great diversity of titles and professions that differ markedly from those we know in the twentieth century, we attempted to classify the deceased into categories. It should be noted that, with the exception of a few rare women who had a trade or who were listed as spinsters, the women in this sample are classified according to the title and profession of their husbands. Because of the complexity of the *ancien régime's* order-based society, any attempt to classify social groups must necessarily encounter great difficulties. In order to avoid taking sides in the debate, we do not claim to offer a new model for social stratification. The classification used here is purely empirical and was elaborated as a function of the categories we encountered in the documents; it is simply a research tool.

While attempting to group together people of comparable social rank, we also wanted to avoid creating too many headings in order to remain clear and simple. Therefore twelve categories (or thirteen including the 'unknowns') were finally adopted and are presented in the following pages (see table 1).

Group 1 is composed of 164 members of the clergy, representing 6 per cent of the total sample. This percentage seems relatively high, as the ratio of male ecclesiastics to the population was one per hundred inhabitants, at least in the seventeenth century,[1] according to periodic studies done of the households of Paris priests. Our sampling of members of society's first order includes abbés, who were generally of noble birth, as well as canons who belonged for the most

Table 1   Socio-professional groups

	Category	No.	%
1	Clergy	164	6
2	Nobles	67	2.5
3	Magistrates, office holders, king's counsellors	61	2
4	Accountants, financiers, officers of the domain, secretaries to the king	124	4.5
5	Members of legal professions	150	5.5
6	Doctors, surgeons	27	1
7	Merchants, bourgeois of Paris	622	22.5
8	Masters of urban trades	753	27
9	Artisans	435	15.5
10	Servants	189	7
11	Members of the military and related professions	47	1.5
12	Spinsters, miscellaneous	96	3.5
13	Unknown	48	1.5
	Total	2783	100.0

part to chapters of Paris churches, and curés and priests assigned to a parish in the city or elsewhere. We also found dignitaries and teachers at colleges and the university, as well as various priests, some of whom fulfilled clerical duties as chaplains, vicars, or priors of religious communities, and others who were without specific functions and apparently led the cultured lives of men of leisure (see table 2).

Group 2 is made up of sixty-seven members of the nobility (2.5 per cent of the total). Their status was determined either solely by their titles or by their titles and their military duties. These include gentlemen holding title to dignitary estates (*fiefs de dignité*), marquis or counts, as well as *écuyers* (squires) and high-ranking army officers.

Group 3 covers office holders from the judiciary world: magistrates at the king's courts, *Maîtres des Requêtes* (supervising magistrates), Counsellors of State, as well as certain office holders of comparable social rank in the households of the king and princes and other ordinary king's counsellors. These comprise sixty-one persons (2 per cent of the sample). Some thirty of these office holders, including a few members of certain illustrious families of judges, are members of the king's courts, the Parlement, the Chambre des Comptes, the Cour des Aides, and the Cour des Monnaies. *Maîtres des Requêtes* and counsellors of state also bore prestigious family names. Among the officers of the king's and the princes' households, it is interesting to note the presence of a few musicians, such as Antoine Boesset, director and superintendent of His Majesty's music, or François Francoeur, superintendent of the king' music; one Henri Beausire, architect, general master of His Majesty's buildings and of the city hall; and François-Augustin Paradis de Moncrif, a member of the Académie Française.

Table 2   Ecclesiastics

Abbés	14
Canons	23
Curés	20
Priests with parishes, vicars, sacristans, chaplains, *habitués* (clergy without parish duties)	38
Priests without defined duties	33
Various	36
Total	164

Group 4 includes 124 individuals who were accounting officers, members of the financial world, or officers of the city and the king's domain, as well as various secretaries to the king, representing 4.5 per cent of the whole. Financiers and accountants, the great majority of whom were office holders, make up more than half this group.

Group 5 is composed of representatives of the legal professions and ministerial office holders. Its 150 persons comprise 5.5 per cent of our total sample. There were ninety-two lawyers (*avocats*) at the Paris Parlement and in the king's council. The other members of this group are *procureurs* (attorneys or solicitors), notaries, *huissiers* (bailiffs), sergeants and *commissaires* (commissioners) at the Châtelet (the headquarters of the criminal jurisdiction) or court clerks.

Group 6 consists of doctors and surgeons and includes only twenty-seven individuals, barely 1 per cent of the total. This low figure is not surprising, as there were fewer than 150 doctors in Paris on the eve of the Revolution: more precisely, there were 113 in 1650, 105 in 1675, only seventy-seven in 1773, and 144 in 1789.[2] Surgeons, who belonged to the artisanal and trade communities of the city, were considered ordinary manual labourers until the publication in 1743 of a more favourable royal declaration that recognized them as members of a scientific body on a par with doctors: henceforth, they were required to possess the diploma of *maître ès arts* in order to be received as master surgeons, and they also won the right to be members of the university and enjoy all the privileges connected with that title.[3]

Group 7 contains the merchants, who number 477, as well as 140 members of the Paris bourgeoisie and five bourgeois from provincial cities whom we have included here. This category also encompassess those trade masters who are also designated by the title of merchant, as well as certain providers of food and lodging who did not hold the title of merchant, such as innkeepers, *cabaret* owners, and hotel keepers. This group covers a total of 622 persons or 22.5 per cent of the whole.

Group 8, the trade masters, is larger than any other group: with 753 persons, it represents 27 per cent or more than a quarter of our sample. To the grouping of trade masters we have attached a certain number of the deceased who did not possess the title of master but who practised intellectual or artistic activities that were not strictly mechanical professions: these include printers, painters,

Table 3 Servants

Coachmen, postilions, foot valets, grooms, saddlers	39
Chamber men, chamber valets	21
Chambermaids, governesses, companions	21
Maîtres d'hôtel, kitchen squires, kitchen officers, cooks (male and female)	31
Servants, domestic servitors, maidservants, individuals 'living in the service of ...,' individuals 'residing in the service of ...'	25
Doorkeepers, concierges, commissionaires, bailiffs, *Tourières* (nuns in charge of supplies), body guards	19
Various: gentlemen, *agents d'affaires*, intendants, officers, secretaries, gardeners	17
Others	16
Total	189

sculptors, musicians and manufacturers of musical instruments. Some of these craftsmen and artists held offices in the king's household.

Group 9 includes artisans generally: journeymen, craftsmen without qualification, day labourers, and other workers. In all, these 435 persons comprise 15.5 per cent of our survey.

Group 10 is made up of servants and contains 153 men and thirty-six women, or 7 per cent of the sample. This percentage probably under-represents the actual social reality, as servants were a numerically significant group in the city: Abbé Expilly estimated that they represented 8 per cent of the population, according to the poll tax rolls of 1764.[4] In this category we have included sixteen royal servants who held offices in the household of the king and the princes. Servants in the service of nobility, of titled persons or of members of the bourgeoisie were liveried or kitchen employees or belonged to the chamber personnel. Others were employed as guards or intendants. Finally, other servants had no specific duties and were designated simply in general terms as servants, household servants, or maids (see table 3).

Group 11 consists of members of the military and related professions, i.e. members of various bodies responsible for the police and for safety in the capital, but who were not noble. They number forty-seven, representing 1.5 per cent of the total.

Group 12 is made up of seventy-two *filles majeures* (spinsters) and twenty-four persons who could not be easily classified in any of the eleven previous categories, whom we have brought together here under the heading 'miscellaneous' for a total of ninety-six deceased persons (3.5 per cent of the sample). Spinsters are classified under this heading if they were designated as having no profession; female servants or women artisans, even if they are indicated as single, are of course listed in the corresponding professional category. Unmarried women were apparently quite numerous in Paris. Mercier is particularly ferocious towards them and sketches this portrait: 'The number of maids who have passed the marrying age is incalculable. Nothing so hard to come by as a marriage, not because the knot is eternal, but because a dowry must be deposited with a notary. There is an abundance of ugly girls of marriageable age. The pretty ones have a hard time making a place for themselves ... In any gathering, all you meet are old maids who have fled the duties of wives and mothers and who trot from house to house.'[5]

The deceased whose names are not accompanied by any mention of title or profession are classified with the unknown cases, who number forty-eight, or 1.5 per cent of the total.

As table 1 shows, the social composition of our sample is characterized by the clear predominance of groups 7, 8, and 9 – merchants, members of the Paris bourgeoisie, masters and artisans. These groups include a total of 1810 of the deceased, or 65 per cent of our sample. Even if we exclude from this set the 145 bourgeois from Paris and provincial cities, who were in fact often retired merchants or trade masters, this slice of the shop- and stallkeeping world still contains 1665 persons or 60 per cent of the total.

It should be noted that all other social groups form very small minorities here, and none represents more than 6 or 7 per cent of our sample. These are the percentages attributed respectively to ecclesiastics and servants. As we have already indicated, these figures seem rather high for the first group, in view of various studies that have been devoted to it. The proportion of representatives of the legal professions is probably also overestimated by our study. The percentage of members of society's second order, in contrast, is probably fairly close to the actual situation in Paris, since there were less than 30,000 members of the sword and robe nobility on the eve of the Revolution, or 4.5 per cent of a population estimated at 660,000 souls.[6]

This image of Paris in the seventeenth and eighteenth centuries, which our poll reflects as being dominated by the worlds of commerce and trades, seems accurate at least in some aspects. Jacques Savary estimated that trade masters alone, without including the members of their families, numbered some 40,000 in the middle of the eighteenth century. Of course our study, which produced ten reports dealing with trades, does tend to emphasize these categories. But commerce was omnipresent in every neighbourhood, as can be seen from the comments of provincial or foreign visitors to the capital during the seventeenth and eighteenth centuries.

Gianpaolo Marana, an Italian, wrote in 1692 that Paris was resplendent with 'an infinity of shops in which they sell only things of which you have absolutely no need. You can imagine the number of other shops in which you buy what is necessary.'[7]

Joachim Christopher Nemeitz, a German scholar, considered in 1718 that 'Paris is a place where you find an inestimable quantity of all kinds of merchandise. Wherever you look, you see shops in which there is something for sale.'[8] Guidebooks for travellers and books of useful addresses oveflowed with information on the numerous businesses in each neighborhood. Shopping in the luxury stores of the capital appears to have been one of the favourite pastimes of 'tourists' of the period, as their diaries attest. Mrs Cradock, a well-known English

Table 4 Fields of economic activity (for a total of 1665 deceased persons)

Food	243
Beverage sellers	161
Decoration, luxuries	141
Amenities	137
Textiles	131
Wood	121
Clothing	108
Labour	95
Construction, building	83
Haberdashery, commerce	73
Hospitality	58
Metals	55
Transportation	52
Leather, pelts	51
Land	44
Body care	36
Book and paper sellers	27
Containers	22
Glass	18
Various	9
Total	1665

traveller and wife of a rich patron of the arts,[9] and the Baroness d'Oberkirch, who belonged to an old family of the nobility of Alsace,[10] visited the finest stores in the city during their stays in Paris between 1782 and 1786.

It would seem, then, that our sample does not much exaggerate the number of Parisians working in the fields of commerce and trades. However, there is no doubt that this poll is too heavily weighted in favour of merchants and trade masters, at the expense of the common people such as journeymen, workers and unqualified craftsmen. In fact, the *Journal général de la France* estimated in 1789 that the lower classes included some 200,000 persons, or 30 per cent of the population.[11] The distortion here in favour of the more prosperous categories of the working class is due to the very use of notarial sources. As mentioned earlier, this tends to impose a certain social selection. Nonetheless, through these inventories, our study highlights the variety and the diversity of the trades practised, whether by rich merchants and trade masters or by modest journeymen and apprentices.

Based on information about the deceased person's profession found in the preamble of the inventory, we listed more than 180 different trades in which 1665 persons were employed. It seems reasonable to believe that the major trades practised in Paris at that time appear on our list (see table 4). The inventories mention mostly traditional and corporate trades. The almost total absence of factory workers is worthy of note: their very low social level and the instability of their wages closed the doors of notaries' offices to them.

At the highest level of activity, the commercial elite of the capital was made up of six corporations of merchants, representing clothiers, spice merchants, haberdashers, furriers, hosiers, and goldsmiths. They were delegated to represent the city's merchants at official ceremonies, royal and princely parades, receptions for important figures, performances of *Te Deums*, processions, celebrations of births and marriages, or funerals of princes. They were rich enough to cover the costs of appropriate clothing for such circumstances. Indeed, when summoned to these various occasions by the bureau of the Hôtel de Ville, they were expected to appear in ceremonial garb.

Since the edicts of 1581 and 1597, artisans in the city had been required to join one of the craft or trade communities. The number of such communities oscillated throughout the seventeenth and eighteenth centuries: from about sixty before 1673, it jumped to eighty-three at that date, then to 129 in 1691, before being reduced to 124, then to 120, as certain trades were merged during the first half of the eighteenth century.[12] This was the situation until Turgot abolished masterships, *jurandes* (corporations bound by the mutual oath sworn by their members) and all the merchants' and artisans' corporations and communities, by the edict of Versailles in February 1776.

Other trades which did not have the 'right to form corporations and communities' were said to be 'free' (i.e. were not bound by the system of masters and *jurandes*), but were considered by the social hierarchy that attributed a specific rank to each corporation at public ceremonies to be inferior to the trades bound by a sworn oath.[13] In certain neighbourhoods of Paris, artisans could set up shop as they saw fit and practise their trades without belonging to any corporation, even in good locations.

It is difficult today, in the computer age, to imagine how people worked in this traditional society. Names of trades from the period have little relation to our contemporary ideas about the same terms. Haberdashers or *merciers* provide a typical example: the small shopkeepers referred to by this name today bear very little resemblance to their seventeenth- and eighteenth-century counterparts, who occupied the third rank in the merchant aristocracy made up of the six corporations. They sold merchandise ranging from fabrics, muffs, bonnets, stockings and leather goods to tapestries, brass objects, hardware and mirrors – household goods as well as luxury items. Other trades from this period have completely disappeared in the twentieth century and are designated by terms that may seem ambiguous: for instance, the *ferrandinier* was not an ironsmith, as the name might suggest, but a manufacturing merchant who made or oversaw the production of *ferrandine*, 'a cloth whose warp is in silk and whose woof is in wool, *fleuret* [low-quality silk], or cotton', according to Savary.

Concerning the distribution of various fields of activity in the parishes of the city, we observed little clustering of trades in specific spaces, with such well-known exceptions as gardeners in the suburbs, printers and booksellers in the rue Saint-Jacques, or textile and clothing trades in the Saint-Eustache and Saint-Germain-l'Auxerrois quarters. Generally speaking, these trades seemed to be widely spread throughout the capital as a whole. If we calculate the number of trades mentioned per parish, it becomes possible to obtain an overall view of the neighbourhoods most receptive to the fields of commerce and craft production. If we stay within the city walls, excluding from our calculations the sixty-six deceased persons from the outlying suburbs, then 70.5 per cent of the 1401 members of trades for whom we have an exact address are found on the right bank, 26.5 per cent on the left bank, and 3 per cent on the Ile de la Cité. It should be noted that these percentages are very close to the figures for the population sample as a whole (i.e. 71.5, 25.5 and 3 per cent).

The area near Les Halles, around the parishes of Saint-Eustache and Saint-Germain-l'Auxerrois, was a major business centre in which 28 per cent of the trades found on the right bank were located. Predominant among them were foodstuff and beverage distribution and textile and clothing. The five parishes in the Marais, Saint-Nicolas-des-Champs, Saint-Jean-en-Grève, Saint-Gervais, Saint-Paul and Saint-Merry, together encompassed 35.5 per cent of the artisanal activity on the right bank. Trades dealing with textiles and decoration were most numerous, followed by beverage sellers and manual labourers. The clothing, textile and woodworking trades were also well represented. The faubourg Saint-Antoine alone, dominated by the parish of Sainte-Marguerite, was home to 12 per cent of these professions. Trades involving foodstuffs, fresh produce and furniture, including woodworking and decoration, were the most common there. Other parishes in the city, in the neighbourhood of the rue Saint-Denis and rue Saint-Martin, housed another 30 per cent of the deceased who had worked as merchants and artisans. Textile and woodworking captured first place here. Finally, the Saint-Honoré quarter, within the parishes of Saint-Roch and Sainte-Madeleine-de-la-Ville-l'Evêque, contained 6.5 per cent of the trades practised on the right bank.

Across the Seine, the parish of Saint-Etienne-du-Mont reveals the largest number of trades involving business and craft trades: we counted ninety-two, or a quarter of the total for the left bank. A great diversity of activities can be identified there. The three parishes of the Saint-Marcel faubourg – Saint-Médard, Saint-Hippolyte, and Saint-Martin – contain another 25 per cent of all trades, the main sectors of activity involving textiles, tapestry, building construction, and beverage sales. In the other eight parishes in the environs of the university, where a total of 185 members of trades, or 50 per cent of the left bank sample, were to be found, we observed that these activities were widespread.

Villages in the outlying suburbs, where we noted sixty-six trades, were prone to develop specific fields of activity, such as hotel- or *cabaret*-keeping, various types of farming, or laundering.

It appears that artisans' trades serving the daily needs of inhabitants tended to be spread throughout the central neighbourhoods of the city where the population was most dense, whereas the bulk of the more industrial trades, such as weaving, metal- or leatherworking and building preferred to locate in the suburbs, where they had access to greater space and could recruit from a working-class labour force that sometimes lacked any specific training. Examining addresses street by street confirms this broad distribution of trades across the city. At the same time, it reveals that all social classes dwelled together within a given street or even a given building. The wealthiest occupants lived on the lower stories, while the most modest inhabitants occupied the stories just beneath the roof.

Certain examples taken from the most populous streets of our sample are eloquent on this point. Of the forty-six inhabitants on the rue Saint-Honoré whose social and professional category we identified, there were four members of the clergy, four nobles, three officers of the king's domain, one lawyer at the Parlement, one interpreter to the king, one surgeon, four bourgeois from Paris, five merchants, fourteen trade masters, three artisans, including one day labourer, four servants and two spinsters. They practised their trades in such sectors as foodstuffs, beverage distribution, clothing, decoration, decorative arts, leatherworking and construction. To take the example of the rue de la Verrerie in the neighbourhood of the Place de Grève, a shorter and lesser-known street than the rue Saint-Honoré, its inhabitants nevertheless still cover the full range of social ranks: there are two priests, three nobles, a counsellor to the king, an accounting office holder, a secretary of the king's chamber, four members of the legal professions, two bourgeois from Paris, seven masters of various trades (e.g. foodstuffs, clothing, decoration, transportation) and one servant. On streets such as the rue Saint-Denis, rue Saint-Martin, or rue de la Tisseranderie all social ranks rub elbows, as on the above-mentioned roads. This seems to be the situation in the oldest neighbourhoods.

In contrast, the social mix on the rue du Faubourg Saint-Antoine is much more 'popular': there was not a single inhabitant belonging to either of the first two orders, nor any office holders. The inhabitants are for the most part unqualified tradesmen, of whom there are thirteen, in addition to ten trade masters, nine merchants, two servants, one Paris bourgeois and a municipal employee. The employments of these working class people were very diverse. In the same neighbourhood, the rue de Charonne and rue de Charenton were similarly populated by common folk, as were the rue Saint-Médard and rue de Lourcine in the faubourg Saint-Marcel. Yet in these streets inhabited by modest folk, as in other more 'bourgeois' streets, all sorts of trades worked side by side. The rue Saint-Jacques offers a final example: seven artisans from the book industry count among their neighbours a priest, an officer of the king's domain, three lawyers at Parlement, three Paris bourgeois, a master cloth and ribbon maker, a tailor, a master carpenter, a master shoemaker, a master painter and gilder, another painter, a musician and a spinster. This pot-pourri of trades and social classes in a same street would seem to characterize the old Paris of the seventeenth and eighteenth centuries. The social 'zoning' which reached its zenith in the second half of the nineteenth century was just making a tentative entry on the edges of the city in the 1770s, with the construction of new residential neighbourhoods towards the west, around Sainte-Madeleine-de-la Ville-l'Evêque and the Chaussée d'Antin.

Nonetheless, the social and professional portrait of old Paris as it appears through these inventories should be regarded with some reservations. There are sometimes actually several generations separating the various inhabitants mentioned in a given street. It seems logical that since the period we are studying was characterized by the stability of its households as well as its professions, a family could spend generations in the same house, or at least in the same street or quarter. Parisians, whatever their social rank, seemed to be attached to their streets, their parishes and their neighbourhoods, as is demonstrated by a study of their movements and changes of address. We discovered dynasties of clothiers occupying the same store from one generation to the next in the Saint-Eustache neighbourhood. Likewise, on the rue Saint-Jacques, printers and sellers of engravings also founded dynasties dating back to the beginning of the seventeenth century. It therefore seems probable that the social and professional portrait of the oldest neighbourhoods in Paris underwent few modifications between the middle of the seventeenth century and the second half of the eighteenth.

But our curiosity about these seventeenth- and eighteenth-century Parisians cannot be satisfied completely by knowing their social rank or what they did for a living. Using the inventories, we would like to enter into the privacy of the family circle and re-create the human warmth of the households visited by the notaries.

Families Composing the Households

Homes broken by a death, families torn apart by the loss of a father or a mother – these are the households into which the notary leads us. To understand how the harmony of family life has been upset and what emotional trauma resulted, we must read between the lines of the inventory and look behind the identities of the survivors: widows or widowers left alone, or very young children who have lost their father or mother or both. Though of inestimable value for capturing daily life through the objects it presents, the inventory, unlike the will, makes little allowance for the familial and emotional aspects of human relationships. The life-style rendered there through its material aspects alone resembles a still life without a soul. Yet beyond this appearance, do not these objects, described minutely and coldly by the valuers, call forth the memory of the household's inhabitants? The jewels or toiletry articles of the wife, the painting of a son or daughter, a child's chair or a servant's bed all bear witness to the presence of these people within their homes. Such notes in the inventory, as well as indications of heirs to the estate and witnesses to the document, help us to reconstruct the family circle gathered around the dying person, most often made up of close relatives, the spouse, children or perhaps servants, who probably watched over the deceased in his or her final moments and saw to the details of the funeral arrangements.

As we shall see, there were also numerous individuals living alone, but in their cases it seems reasonable to assume that in a world where people were much less isolated than they are today, and where the sense of community was stronger, married children, collaterals, more distant relatives, or even neighbours, members of the parish or professional colleagues came to help and comfort the dying person. When the place of death is indicated in the inventory, it is generally the home of the deceased: 'in his chamber', 'in her dwelling', 'at home', or 'in the house'. The vast majority of Parisians actually died in their beds, in the bosom of their families. The 'deceased's bedroom' or the 'room in which the deceased died' is usually well placed in the inventory, among the first rooms visited by the valuers. Death surprised some of these Parisians far from their homes, as was the case with two soldiers who fell in the king's service during the War of the Austrian Succession; a widow who died in her country house in Athis; or two other women who were staying with members of their families.

Some sick persons ended their days at the hospital, the Hôtel-Dieu or the Charité des Hommes. The widow of a day labourer from Auteuil declared that 'since her husband had died at Hôtel-Dieu in Paris, his old clothes and garments were to remain there, as was the custom'. A 33-year-old crockery merchant entered the same hospital on 6 December 1784 and died there four days later, after being helped 'both spiritually and bodily'. The causes of death were generally unknown, and the last illness is never indicated, with the exception of a pulmonary ailment that carried off a 21-year-old stringed instrument maker in 1774. Examining the wills written by ailing persons in the days before their deaths does not shed any further light on the subject.

While the inventory may reveal the financial distress of widows left to bring up their children alone, it almost never leaves a trace of the pain of separation suffered by the survivors. The grief of a widowed squire and infantry captain was recorded in the inventory after death in the following terms: 'momentarily leaves his house because of the sorrow into which he has been plunged'. The affliction of the widow of a master writer over the death of her husband was also captured under the pen of the notary's secretary: this woman had forgotten to have a very large sum of money recorded, but the inventory specifies that this 'omission was caused only by the grief and agitation which the loss of her husband has caused her'. Such indications are extremely rare, and therefore all the more precious. This age did not lend itself to emotional outpourings. Philosophical books and even private diaries written in France during the seventeenth and eighteenth centuries are very reticent about personal emotions, in contrast with English diaries of the same period.[14]

Working from the inventory data, we can attempt to reconstruct these households as they were before death struck, depriving them of one of their members. How many people lived under the same roof? What were the bonds that connected them? These documents provide us with sufficient material to study family structures, but not enough for a true demographic approach. Of course inventories make a significant contribution in the area of demography, especially where Paris is concerned,[15] compensating for the destruction of its huge wealth of birth and death registers during the Commune of 1871. However, we have not scrutinized our documents for information on age at marriage, number of children, intervals between births or age at death. Even when supplemented by the marriage contract, the inventory is not a highly reliable source of answers to such questions. The ages of the deceased are almost never indicated; the number of children per woman is necessarily approximate, since children in religious orders, children already deceased or those born of a prior marriage and therefore having no rights to the inheritance were not mentioned in the inventories. For these reasons, we have limited our scope to a study of the composition of these households.

One cautionary word before we begin: the *foyers* (or households from the orig-

Table 5 Family structures

Category	No.	%
Nuclear families	1233	44
Extended families	55	2
Couples without children	549	20
Widow(er)s with children	113	4
Widow(er)s without children	283	10
Unmarried	440	16
Unknown	110	4
Total	2783	100

inal meaning: 'hearths', or *feux*, to use a period expression) whose sizes we are trying to evaluate do not appear to be very representative of the Paris society of the times. Despite the gaps in our documents with regard to the ages of the deceased, it seems reasonable to assume that the households where death struck were often made up of elderly persons who had reached their twilight years; these are families in which some or all of the children are married and have left the parental home, or widows or widowers spending their old age in solitude. Of course death also carries off men and women in the prime of life, as is indicated by the presence of young children. Looking at households through the inventories would seem generally to underestimate their size, because of the excessive number of homes housing no children or occupied by widows or widowers.

Inventory data about the number of children or servants actually living in a household are also frequently inaccurate. In contrast, the notary's secretary always made careful note of the marital status of the deceased, with the exception of bachelors. It is therefore easier for us to determine family structures than the actual size of households.

Family structures

It should be borne in mind that the nuclear or conjugal family, i.e. the modern family composed of parents and their children, has been the dominant form in western Europe since the fourteenth century. Philippe Ariès has written elegantly of how the sense of family developed around the unit of the couple and gave rise to a wealth of imagery.[16] That the family clung together as a unit is reflected in our sample: with 44 per cent of the total, homes containing parents and children are easily the largest group (see table 5).

As the matrimonial nucleus was reinforced and notions of lineage began to fade, extended families in which the parents–children group was enlarged by the assimilation of other, ascending or collateral members became extremely uncommon. It had disappeared almost completely by the second half of the eighteenth century. An outdated structure, especially in the Enlightenment, only fifty-five such households were found, representing just 2 per cent of the total. Polynuclear families, consisting of several couples and their children, were exceptionally rare. Indeed, they seem as rare in Paris during the seventeenth and eighteenth centuries as in England, as represented in 100 communities studied by Peter Laslett and a group of demographic historians at Cambridge.[17] It was common practice for children, once married, to leave their parents and found a new household. However, in the face of old age, sickness or hardship, these Parisian households seem much more open than ours today, marked as we are by contemporary individualism. Elderly or ailing relatives came to live out their last days in the homes of their married children. The daughter of a barrel maker took refuge with her parents because she was 'separated from her husband, who beats her and mistreats her, though she is pregnant'. The wife of a master saddler took in her young brother Denis, an orphan aged sixteen, in addition to her three children, and the boy's uncle taught him the saddle-making trade.

Households of couples without children numbered 549, or 20 per cent of the whole. A certain number of these, probably half, had had the joy of bringing children into the world. When these children are mentioned in the inventory as heirs to the estate, those living at a different address from their parents have usually reached majority, aged 25 or more, or are married. If a child had died before its parents, the child's name rarely appears in the document. As for children who had taken religious vows or who were born of a previous marriage giving them no rights to the succession, we remain most often unaware of their existence. Finally, a certain number of couples had no children. Sterility was slightly higher at the time than it is today and affected some 10 per cent of all couples. Nor can we exclude the cases of young couples that were rent asunder by a death early on before they had time to procreate. The total absence of children is rarely specified explicitly in the inventory. Households of childless couples did not hesitate to expand by occasionally taking in in-laws such as a mother, a brother, a sister, a cousin, a granddaughter, or a nephew.

The mortality rate in this traditional society made itself felt in the composition of these households. Matrimonial units already ruptured by the death of a spouse and entering into a new period of mourning numbered 396, or 14 per cent of our sample set: 10 per cent of these widows and widowers were childless and 4 per cent had children to bring up. The statistics also reveal the extent of widowhood, 64 per cent, versus 36 per cent of survivors who were widowers. As everyone knows, women live longer on average than their partners, and this was true during that period as well, despite the relatively high number of deaths during childbirth. Furthermore, women usually did not remarry as readily as men, especially if they found themselves with children to look after. Some of these single adults took in a grandchild, a nephew or a niece as boarders. To escape their solitude, the oldest widows and widowers sometimes moved in with their children.

Whether these men and women were living with their spouses, surrounded by their children, or were widows or widowers, 80 per cent of the deceased had been married at least once. Because of the omnipresence of death, matrimony was a precarious state, and unions lasting longer than thirty or forty years were rare. Our information on the marital status of the deceased reveals how frequent broken families were. Couples could be parted by death at the birth of the first child. The duration of marriages varied considerably but on average rarely exceeded fifteen to twenty years.

Remarrying was in many cases a necessity for men left alone with young children, or for widows with very limited financial resources. In a world lacking in material comfort, solitude simply increased the hardships of daily life. Imagine the work involved, for instance, in preparing a simple meal in an age without running water, gas or electricity. We may overlook the constraints and burdens of everyday existence bound up in the slightest household tasks, accustomed as we are in the late twentieth century to flicking a switch to obtain light or heat or to cook our food. Without a servant or another family member, a single individual could not take care of both the demands of a trade and those of a household, in addition to caring for one or more children. Remarrying within a short period of time therefore often appeared to be the best solution.

In a sample set of 895 couples, we calculated that in 28 per cent one or both spouses had been married more than once. A slightly higher number of men than women seemed to tie the knot a second or even third time. Our study paints a portrait of some of these patchwork families, torn by death, in which children from different marriages were trundled from one couple to the next with each new union. These were unstable and complicated families, characteristic of this *ancien régime* society.

Our data set also includes 440 unmarried people, or 16 per cent of the total. Their number includes 164 ecclesiastics. The 276 others comprise 159 men and 117 women. We should note that when a woman was unmarried, her single status is always indicated, while this can only be assumed for a man, in the absence of any sign of a wife. Some of these men may be widowers whose marriage left no trace. When single women are indicated as having a trade, they frequently worked as servants or washerwomen. These were humble and precarious jobs that offered only a modest income. Mercier used the term *grisette* for 'the young girl who, being neither well-born nor propertied, is obliged to work for a living ... these girls leave their poor parents at the age of eighteen, take a room and live according to their fancy'.[18] Some of these single people, both men and women, lived with a brother, a sister or a nephew or niece.

It is worth emphasizing the extent of bachelor- and spinsterhood in Paris at this time, and it was actually on the increase during the eighteenth century. Mercier declared exaggeratedly that 'half the inhabitants of the city are therefore condemned to the single state, and most of them dread any offspring, for fear of not being able to feed them'.[19] If we add together the unmarried people and the widows without children, one-person households make up 26 per cent of the total, or 20 per cent if we exclude ecclesiastics. We should note that this number of households includes those single women, numbering fewer than a dozen, who were separated from their husbands or abandoned by them. The proportion of these Parisians who died alone is comparable to the estimated 25–30 per cent of testators who did so, as indicated by Pierre Chaunu's study on death in Paris.[20] Solitude in the city is not an aspect peculiar to the twentieth century. This characteristic of Paris, a sign of modern times, emerges through the inventories as well as through testaments.

Last of all, there are 110 deceased people (4 per cent) whose marital status we cannot establish with certainty. They are classified with the unknowns.

Children in the Home

While more than a quarter of the homes in our data set housed single persons, and were therefore reduced to the simplest form of household, 1450 households, or 52 per cent of the total, were enlivened by the presence of children. Their number varied from one to ten per family. It is not always easy, however, to determine how many children were actually living in the family home. Those named among the heirs, even when minors, were not necessarily living with their parents: young ones could have been put out to nurse, according to the custom of the times; older ones might be apprenticed out, or boarding at a college or convent; grown-up children listed as living in the same street could have lodgings independent of their parents' home, either in the same house or in a neighbouring one. The inventories are far from supplying us with the necessary details to answer these questions. Nonetheless some of them do allow us to fill in the blanks, where a debt to a nurse or the cost of board are set down.

As far as signs of the presence of children in the home are concerned, the inventories are notoriously reticent, and no one using these documents has failed to emphasize these gaps. The various objects intended specifically for children do not appear clearly in these interiors. A few pieces of furniture are recorded, such as children's beds, described as 'a small child's bunk in the form of a cradle, dressed with a straw pad and two small mattresses' or 'a dressed cradle', 'a wicker basket used by a child' or 'a child's bed in ticking, stuffed with feathers'; chairs, such as high chairs or little armchairs; and even a little commode for a child. We also find baby bottles, plates and casseroles for baby purée, and children's tableware or baby spoons, often in silver. And of course there were layette articles, bundles of nappies, children's clothes and a necklace, and even a whip.

Toys are rare: there are rattles, sometimes in silver, including one 'having crystal points with bells and a silver handle, evaluated at 12 L'; a small children's carriage and a cabriolet, and a child's wagon. This last toy was no doubt very popular at the time, as it figures on an engraving by Nicolas de Larmessin entitled *L'Enfance* (Childhood) from the first half of the eighteenth century. The scene pictures a little boy and a little girl pulling a small wagon with a cord. In the wagon is a young child being held by two small girls. To the right of the scene, two young girls are conversing, while a woman, book in hand, is teaching two others how to read. In fact, pictorial sources are much richer in information about children's play than the inventories: in a set of eleven eighteenth-century engravings of scenes from childhood, some eighteen different toys were identified.

The presence of children in a household may also be discerned indirectly, through the indication of a bedroom reserved for their use, or even through adults' clothing altered to fit them: the undergarments of one deceased person were adapted 'for the children's use'; 'the remaining garments were given to be adapted for her daughter's use'; or 'the extra shirts are used for the children'.

Just as the valuers may not mention any objects for children's use in a family with young progeny, by the same token the homes of couples living alone sometimes contain a layette or other articles previously used for the care of children who had since married or died. There is nothing astonishing in that; as we have already seen, this was a world in which nothing was thrown away, out of respect for the value of possessions.

Despite all the inexactitude of our documentation, we estimated that our 1450 households sheltered approximately 3120 children and that the average number of children residing in the family home was slightly greater than two. It should be emphasized that this does not imply an average birth rate per family, which was of course higher. We did a survey, using a sample set of 800 families, on the distribution of children: households with a single child were most common, at 36 per cent of the total. Next came the two-child families, at 29 per cent, then those with three, at 16 per cent. Families of five or six children or more, representing 10 per cent, were slightly more frequent than those with four children, accounting for 9 per cent. Large families seem to have been unusual, although it was quite common to see half-brothers and half-sisters living together under the same roof. But any estimate made on the sole basis of inventories must be considered to represent a minimum family size.

We also wondered about the age of children living with their parents. Once again, the inventories do not always provide as much detail as we might wish. Valuers frequently settled for the vague terms of 'minor' and 'major'. Nonetheless, we noted the ages of 773 minor children and sorted them into three age categories: four years and under, five to fourteen years, and fifteen to twenty-five years. The largest category were the five- to fourteen-year-olds, constituting 44.5 per cent of the group. Then came the young children, accounting for 31 per cent, and finally adolescents aged fifteen years or more, who made up 24.5 per cent of the whole. This means that three-quarters of the children who lost their father or mother and found themselves orphaned of one or both parents, were under fifteen years of age. If we take into account that the average age at marriage was twenty-five to thirty, then the age of children living in the city at the time of an inventory conducted following the death of one of their parents corroborates Daniel Roche's conclusion that three-quarters of the Paris population died at between forty and fifty years of age.[21]

Household Servants

We have already discussed the numerical importance of servants as a social and professional category in the Paris of the seventeenth and eighteenth centuries. As they were generally lodged in their employer's home, they became part of the family unit and made a place for themselves in a number of our households. Because they were tightly bound up in the lives of their masters, they were part of the family circle, constituting a sort of extension of the family. The inventories reveal their presence in several ways: they may be mentioned in the heading, either because they were the guardians of the seals placed on the deceased person's possessions or because they were present at the valuation 'to show and describe the possessions'. The latter case seems to have been more frequent. A servant might also figure among the parties to the estate as a creditor. During the valuers' visit, a room assigned to a given servant might be designated as 'the cook's room', a 'lackeys' room' containing three bunks, or 'the room called the coachmen's room, because it is above the stables', with two high-post beds. It was not uncommon to find the debts for wages due to one or more servants among the deceased person's papers.

In some cases, the clerk noted down a declaration made by a servant concerning the disappearance or removal of a piece of furniture, for example, or of an object belonging to the servant. On other occasions, a simple detail, such as 'a window curtain for the chamber maid' betrays the presence of a servant in the house. Finally, wills provide a complement to inventory data, in that they tell us about a master's generosity towards his servants.

Thus a certain degree of chance is involved in discerning the presence of servants in the households visited by the notary. Consequently, the inventory cannot be considered as a reliable source for discovering either how many families employed domestic personnel or how many such employees there were per household. We encountered servants in 27 per cent of our households. The inventories tell us that in 623 homes, of the 749 employing help, there were a total of 1046 servants. This would yield an average of 1.6 household employees per household. The vast majority of the Parisians in our study who lodged servants had only one such employee, designated under the title of maid, maidservant, manservant, or simply servant. In homes where there was just one servant, this position was predominantly filled by a woman, the sole servant and forerunner of the nineteenth-century French *bonne*, who was responsible for all the housekeeping tasks. Priests, on the other hand, often preferred to employ male workers.

When a household boasted two or even three servants, these were assigned specific functions, as suggested by the terms identifying them: chambermaid, *femme de charge* (who was responsible for managing household valuables such as linen or silver), chamber valet, governess, cook, kitchen girl, or butler. Households employing the services of three persons generally had a cook, a chambermaid and a servant. Liveried servants, lackeys, coachmen, postilions and so forth were encountered exclusively in the wealthy households of the nobility and of bourgeois office holders or financiers. In households employing more than four servants for specific jobs, the personnel became predominantly masculine.[22] This is due to the fact that women were hired only as chambermaids, cooks or, more rarely, as governesses. We should point out that in counting servants, we included boys, apprentices and journeymen, who were often lodged by the merchants and trade masters for whom they worked.

Which households were likely to have domestic help? Certain members of the nobility, office holders and financiers all had a wealth of servants. Having such a variety of domestic employees was indicative of a life-style that only members of society's upper echelons could afford. Clergymen, who most often lived in relatively modest circumstances, generally employed one or two servants. Lawyers and doctors rarely had more than two or three persons in their employ. Certain merchants, having become rich, indulged in the luxury of numerous domestic helpers. But in the shopkeeping and artisanal trades, the household personnel, boys, apprentices or journeymen lodged by their masters were employed in the store or the workshop. Keeping a servant in that age was a common practice, not to be considered as a sign of luxury or wealth. It was nonetheless rare to find servants in households where the value of the estate was less than 2000 or 3000 L.

For all the reasons we have explained, it is difficult to calculate precisely the number of servants, children, or other household members surrounding our 2783 Parisians on the eve of their deaths. Nevertheless we have attempted to make an approximation of the number of individuals living in these households. Because of the many uncertainties, we have been obliged to extrapolate, and we are aware of the hypothetical nature of the figure we propose. According to our estimates, the population encompassed by our study represents a minimum of 9000 Parisians – 9000 men, women and children of all ages and social classes, living alone, in couples, in families or larger households. These are 9000 persons whose everyday actions and behaviour we have attempted to understand through the indications furnished by the notaries. The households in our data set apparently contain an average of slightly more than three occupants. This average is low because of the great number of bachelors and widows, the almost total absence of extended families, and the small percentage of large families. Extensive households that were home to ten or fifteen persons do exist, but they are rare.

Are not the Parisian households we discover through these inventories actually quite modern? With an average of fewer than four occupants, they seem to be eighteenth-century forerunners of our contemporary households, which are characterized by their isolation and the small numbers of children in them.

3

The Parisian Home

From Vertical to Horizontal

The following glimpses taken from the mass of our data highlight how extremely diverse housing arrangements were in seventeenth- and eighteenth-century Paris: a town house with thirty-one rooms was occupied by its owner, the widow of a marquis, and her ten children and six servants; in a section of another house comprising eleven rooms lived a lawyer of the Parlement, his brother, and two servants; a hay trader living with his wife, two children and a maidservant rented a four-room apartment; a single room on the second story of a house had been sublet to a single woman; a cavalryman of the mounted constabulary of the Ile de France lived with another horseman in a room located in an outbuilding of the royal Château de La Muette; a five-room apartment at the *Collège* de Cambrai was home to the school's headmaster; and a bourgeois of Paris died in a furnished room.

The relationship between social status and lodging will be the first point addressed below. Following in the steps of the notaries, we shall then cross the threshold of these houses and have a look at the actual space in which the inhabitants lived out their lives. Using the information provided in the inventory, we shall follow the notary through these houses, from one room to the next, from one story to another, in an attempt to grasp the composition of these homes, the organization of their space, and the function of each room. Lastly we shall try to discern any traces left by the occupants on the space in which they lived, as well as their attachment to their homes.

Tenants or Owners?

Unlike modern-day France, where everyone, city and country dwellers alike, aspires to own his own home, Parisians in the seventeenth and eighteenth centuries were not averse to renting. Even wealthy families whose riches included houses in the capital or the outlying suburbs, were often mere tenants of their main residence. Of the 2113 inventories (i.e. 75 per cent of the documents in our sample) that indicate the status of the deceased occupants with regard to their homes, only 14 per cent were owners. The majority of those owning their residences were merchants, members of the Paris bourgeoisie or masters of one of the urban trades or crafts. Other well-represented social categories among these property owners were members of the liberal professions.

Renting lodgings was the most common situation, involving 77 per cent of the Parisians whose status we know. Tenants were drawn from all social and professional categories; even wealthy people possessing one or more houses that they had purchased or inherited might choose not to live in any of them themselves, preferring instead to keep them as rental properties. This was the case, for instance, with a fur merchant who owned a house with a carriage entrance and two outlying buildings. He rented it to a *Conseiller Contrôleur des Monnaies* (mint and treasury official) for the sum 700 L per year, while he himself lived in a much simpler house in exchange for an annual rent of 350 L. A certain number of tenants, usually belonging to the worlds of commerce or the artisanal crafts, are referred to as principal tenants because they leased an entire house and then in turn sublet lodgings to different sub-tenants. From the data in the inventories it is not always easy to determine which class of tenants is involved. If we are to believe Mercier, principal tenants had a bad reputation, but their position also brought certain disadvantages: 'A principal tenant is a merciless creditor, who seeks you out wherever you are, but he himself is hounded by the owner, who owes money to his builder, who in turn is unable to pay the collectors of the three *vingtième* taxes, who in turn make royal payment orders rain down, since they can have them reimbursed later at triple value.'[1] An elementary level of education and some accounting sense were indispensable to being a principal tenant. The inventories of several such people mention registers of rents received, covering a period of years. As for the sub-tenants, they were often humble people, simple artisans, spinsters or servants who occupied one or two rooms.

Aside from property owners and tenants, 4.5 per cent of our occupants were lodged by their employers, receiving room and board as part of their job. The greater part of these were servants living under their master's roof. They might be chambermaids, coachmen, doormen, kitchen workers or valets. To this group may be added the journeymen, apprentices and shop boys. Most of these household or shop employees lived in single rooms with very little space – cramped quarters in a single bedroom, a hovel or *bouge*, a booth or a closet, generally without a fireplace. The most unlucky did not even have a corner of their own, sleeping instead in the kitchen or the attic, or sharing a room above the stables, as was the case with coachmen. However, servants' living conditions were determined by their role in the household and by the social status of their masters. Royal servants, employed at the Château de La Muette or at the Tuileries palace, seemed to have been the most fortunate.

Among individuals housed by their employers we also counted some employees of the Gobelins tapestry factory and the lead-rolling mill on the rue Béthisy in the parish of Saint-Germain-l'Auxerrois, as well as certain occupants of the Louvre.

Another type of housing, communal lodging, representing only 2.5 per cent of our sample, applies almost exclusively to ecclesiastics, who were housed either in a presbytery or in a community of priests, in a congregation, or in a *collège*. While *curés* and their vicars often enjoyed fairly spacious housing in a presbytery, other priests attached to a parish sometimes lived in a communal house in which they generally were given one or two rooms. Ageing or infirm priests found refuge in the community of priests of St Francis of Sales, in the faubourg Saint-Marcel, established by letters of patent from Louis XIV in January 1700. Other communities that took in some of the priests in our data included the seminaries of Saint-Nicolas-du-Chardonnet and Saint-Magloire, the Maison des Révérends Pères de la Doctrine Chrétienne, and the Maison de l'Oratoire in the rue Saint-Honoré. The *collèges* of the Montagne Sainte-Geneviève also offered a wide range of lodgings not only to dignitaries, teachers and seminary students but also to ecclesiastics from the provinces.

One final type of housing which appeared in our documents concerned boarders in furnished rooms or with families. This was rare and applies to only 2 per cent of the Parisians in our sample. The capital was certainly well equipped with hotels and furnished rooms, and their number increased continuously from the reign of Louis XIV: from some 500 in the mid-seventeenth century, their number probably reached a thousand by the eve of the Revolution. However, this transient population, choosing to inhabit a furnished room for a short period, was hardly a typical source of clients for notaries. The handful of persons whom death overtook in this form of accommodation were almost always people living alone.

As for Parisians boarding with members for their family, their ranks thinned out progressively as the tradition of the extended family began to decline. These were elderly parents taken in by their children, or bachelors living with collaterals or other members of their family. In a small number of cases, the strength of family ties may be discerned through the type of housing.

Number and Types of Rooms

Inventories are a most precious source for our task of obtaining an idea of the number of rooms in Parisian homes of the period, and they provide specific information on the composition of more than 80 per cent of the dwellings in our data. Our calculations concern only the three main rooms in a house: the chamber, bedchamber or shop-chamber; the common room and its variants – dining room, sitting room or *salon*; and the kitchen, or chamber or room used as a kitchen. It should be noted, however, that among the two-room dwellings, we included dwellings consisting of a main room and either an adjoining room, be it a hovel, dressing room, office or alcove, or an outlying room, such as a shop, cellar, attic or garage. We classified these dwellings into single rooms, two- or three-room lodgings, four- to seven-room residences, and those of more than seven rooms.

By one-room lodgings, we refer to a single space enclosed within four walls, exclusive of any other room, however small it might be. Such rooms numbered 698 and sheltered 31 per cent of our households. Most of them were referred to by the valuers as 'chambers'. Our documents also make note of a few chamber-shops. In 1751, the dwelling in which a fruit seller and beer merchant lived in the faubourg Saint-Honoré, with his wife and daughter, did not include any of the three main room types, consisting solely of a 'shop and annexe areas'. A 'small alcove' installed at the back of the shop was the only refuge for the family's privacy.

Cramped though they were, these rooms fulfilled the functions of bedroom, kitchen, dining room and in certain cases, even those of a work space. The number of such lodgings remained essentially unchanged from the seventeenth century until the second half of the eighteenth; thereafter, they were on the increase, representing 33 per cent of a sample of 500 dwellings inventoried after 1750.

What do we know about the size of these single rooms? The valuers sometimes qualified them as small, medium-sized or large, but never indicated the surface area. The only potentially useful details the inventories make available to us on the subject come from the dimensions, given in *aunes* (about 1⅓ metres) of the tapestries 'going all around the room' or 'hung in the said chamber'. From these figures, we can draw only a very approximate idea of the size of such rooms, since no information is given about the width of doors, window or fireplaces. In the smallest rooms, the circumference covered by tapestries ranges from 4 to 8 *aunes*, or 5 to 9.50 metres. The largest perimeters noted by the valuers cover some 15 *aunes*, or almost 18 metres, varying on average between 10 and 15 metres.

These single rooms were generally located above the ground floor, though not necessarily in the uppermost stories. Based on a sampling of 300 inventories, we obtained the following distribution: 28 per cent of the lodgings were on the second storey, 23.5 per cent on the first, 21.5 per cent on the third, 15 per cent on the fourth, 8.5 per cent on the ground floor, and 3.5 per cent on the fifth storey. The relatively high proportion of single-room housing on the first storey, considered the most noble location, may seem surprising at first glance. However, there are two explanations: on the one hand, rooms on these floors were not exclusively occupied by members of the poorer classes, who were often housed under the eaves, and on the other hand, many servants were provided with rooms there so that they could be in close proximity to their masters on the first or second floor. Unless they worked as doorkeepers, gardeners or washerwomen, the occupants of these single rooms rarely lived on the ground floor, where tenants of shops preferred to make their home.

Who lived in these cramped quarters? The social range, generally fairly broad in the seventeenth century, apparently tended to narrow in on the working classes by the eve of the Revolution. In addition to the numerous small shopkeepers and artisans lodged in single rooms in the parish of Saint-Nicolas-des-Champs around 1640, there were also priests, musicians, a master surgeon and the widow of a purveyor to the household of the king.

In the 1750s these badly housed individuals still included small shop owners practising food trades among their ranks, pastry makers, bakers, butchers, fruit and orange sellers and roast meat vendors. But it had become rare to find wine merchants or beverage sellers who were not settled in more spacious abodes. In contrast, some members of the Paris bourgeoisie whose resources were limited also appeared among the ranks of occupants of single rooms. As for household servants, whether they were lodged under their master's roof or elsewhere, most of them were inhabitants of such housing. The same is true of journeymen, workers and unqualified tradesmen. Of sixty-two day labourers and floor polishers whose homes were inventoried between 1721 and 1761, 44, or 70 per cent, lived in single rooms.

Was living in a single room necessarily a sign of poverty, as we would naturally tend to think? To find out, we verified the values of inventories for 300 occupants of these humble abodes throughout the period studied. Of these poorly housed persons, 84.5 per cent had possessions worth less than 1000 L, and for 65.5 per cent the figure fell below 500 L; among the latter, we counted 18 per cent who were deeply impoverished, leaving an estate worth less than 100 L at the time of their death, be it in the reign of Louis XIII or after 1750. Only 15.5 per cent of the inhabitants of these one-room dwellings had fortunes greater than 1000 L. It is interesting to note that the wealthiest among these individuals, whether at the beginning of the seventeenth century or 150 years later, were people living alone – unmarried women, widows, or priests – and occasionally couples. It therefore appears that only a minority of Parisians could claim that living in a single room was not a patent synonym for misery. It seems safe to assume that the vast majority of these poorly lodged people, especially where entire families were involved, simply did not have means to rent a more spacious dwelling. Indeed, the difficulties they experienced in keeping a roof over their heads for a modest sum must have increased during the eighteenth century as rents rose constantly. Housing conditions, then, are generally closely related to wealth: the number of rooms increases proportionally with the value of the inventory.

As revealed by our investigation, crowding in these tight spaces does not appear to have been excessive. A solid proportion of the occupants figured among the many bachelors, widows or widowers and childless couples in our data. We are nonetheless aware of several examples of households with children living in cramped conditions within four walls. In 1662, a cook, his wife and their four daughters, aged seven and a half, six, five and three and a half, occupied a single room in a house located on the rue d'Angoumois in the Marais quarter. In 1680, the family of a master builder, including the parents and four young children, had no other home than their room in the rue des Poissonnières, furnished with a wall tapestry 14 or 15 metres long and 3 metres high. The dwelling of a master cabinetmaker, his wife and their two children, both under four years old, consisted in 1709 solely of a single room in a house on the rue du Crucifix in the parish of Saint-Jacques-de-la-Boucherie. Two households of six persons, one headed by a tobacco seller and the other by a coachman, were recorded in 1740 and 1742 as being lodged in similar circumstances, the former in the rue Saint-Nicaise in the parish of Saint-Germain-l'Auxerrois, and the latter on the rue Saint-Louis in the parish of that name. Last of all, there was the case of a construction worker in 1772 who lived with his wife and seven children in just one room located on the Quai des Ormes in the parish of Saint-Paul.

But was not that an isolated and exceptional case from among the notaries' clientele of that period? The other twenty-five one-room dwellings in the parish of Saint-Paul inventoried between 1770 and 1774 each housed a maximum of three people. Crowding in these modest homes visited by the notaries did not appear to be as dire in the second half of the eighteenth century as Mercier described when he wrote, 'An entire family occupies a single room.' The occupation rate in these dwellings hovered around an average of two to three persons per room until 1750 and even tended to decline toward the end of the eighteenth century, especially in the more prosperous neighbourhoods: the figure was 2.7 in Passy and Auteuil between 1740 and 1770, 2.3 in the parish of Saint-Etienne-du-Mont between

1761 and 1770, 2.18 in the faubourg Saint-Honoré during the second part of the eighteenth century, 1.9 in the parish of Saint-Paul between 1770 and 1774, and just 1.5 in the parish of Saint-Germain-l'Auxerrois between 1768 and 1790.

Of course these averages are certainly biased, and the actual figures must be higher: the most impoverished families and the innumerable poorly lodged persons living in dilapidated buildings in the centre of the city or in the humble houses of faubourgs like Saint-Antoine or Saint-Marcel are scarcely represented in our study. On the other hand, the size of our sample of inhabitants of single rooms is swelled by individuals of various social origins, who boarded with their family or in a furnished hotel or who were lodged by their employers. To these numbers must be added the priests housed within a community.

The vast majority of our housing sample is composed of two- or three-room dwellings. With these we included one-and-a-half-room homes, as single rooms extended by an annexe were designated: numbering 960 units, they make up 42 per cent of the lodgings in our data. The finest dwellings in this category include a chamber, a common room and a kitchen, which might be supplemented by one or two adjoining areas, e.g. a hovel, wardrobe, office or alcove, or by outlying spaces such as a shop, cellar, attic or loft. Such dwellings were a cut above housing limited to a single room. Nonetheless in lodgings with one and a half or two rooms, crowding could be fairly severe, as a few examples will show: in 1675, a master builder, his wife, and their five children, ranging in age from five and a half to twelve, lived in a 'room with adjoining hovel' on the first floor of a house on the rue d'Arras in the parish of Saint-Nicolas-du-Chardonnet. The household of one saddle merchant consisted of both parents and three young children, who made their home in two rooms and a shop in 1706. At about the same period, a master chasuble embroiderer with his wife and their eight children, ranging in age from seven months to twenty-one years, were jammed into two rooms and an attic on the fifth story of a house on the rue Saint-Denis. A master gardener from the faubourg Saint-Antoine who died in 1760 was settled with his wife and three children in two rooms. This was the case with a printer's family, also composed of five persons, living in the rue des Sept Voies in the parish of Saint-Etienne-du-Mont in 1768.

The occupation density of these two- or three-room dwellings varied considerably from one household to the next. While some modest families with five or more members lived in the most crowded conditions, couples and single persons belonging to the world of commerce, small office holders, or the *basoche*, as legal clerks were called, were much more at ease. Such was the case of a widower, a *procureur* at the Paris Parlement, who lived all alone in two rooms and an office in 1682, a wine merchant and his wife, who rented three rooms with a cellar in 1708, or a haberdashery merchant in the faubourg Saint-Antoine who, in 1760, enjoyed the use of three habitable rooms. There were also spinsters, with or without servants, in these two- or three-room habitations. The average number of occupants for such lodgings was 3.8 in Passy and Auteuil towards the mid-eighteenth century, 2.5 in the faubourg Saint-Honoré after 1750, 3.3 in the parish of Saint-Paul around the 1770s, and 2.7 in the parishes of Saint-Germain-l'Auxerrois and Saint-Etienne-du-Mont during the same period.

There were 446 residences consisting of four to seven main rooms, representing 20 per cent of the sample. These were small houses with one or two stories, or, more often, parts of houses or even apartments. It is interesting to note that as the number of rooms increases, there is a proliferation of annexes and outlying spaces of all sorts, which extend the habitable surface area considerably. These residences were a prerogative of the wealthy classes: office holders, accountants, lawyers, merchants, masters of the urban trades or crafts and their like, whose inventories were generally evaluated at several thousand livres. These homes might house large families as well as couples or individuals living alone. The valuers often mention the presence of one or two domestic servants. A master furniture maker in 1706 occupied a two-story house, with his wife and four minor children, on the rue Saint-Jean-de-Beauvais in the parish of Saint-Etienne-du-Mont that included four rooms, a kitchen, a *cabinet* or office, as well as a cellar and an attic. At about the same period, a *greffier* (court secretary) and *contrôleur du guet* (officer of the city guard) lived with his wife and their eight young children in a four-room apartment on the second floor of a house on the rue de Bourbon in the parish of Saint-Laurent. The lack of space is flagrant in this case, but families with so many children were hardly common, as we have seen, in seventeenth- and eighteenth-century Paris.

A sculptor for the king's buildings, his wife and their six children occupied seven rooms in 1750, plus a workshop and a shed, in a house on the rue Mouffetard. The household of a haberdashery merchant on the rue Saint-Antoine, which in 1772 was made up of nine persons, including two shop boys, made use of five main rooms, a small *cabinet*, two lofts, a shop and a cellar. But these spacious quarters were often more sparsely inhabited: the widow of a squire resided with her maidservant early in the eighteenth century in a four-room apartment on the second floor of a house on the rue Saint-Denis. One widower who was a sworn canvas measurer lived with his manservant in five rooms and a cellar on the rue Saint-Honoré. Six rooms on the rue des Fossés-Saint-Germain were the home in 1740 of a clerk to the *Greffe Civil* (court secretariat) of the Parlement, his wife, one child and a servant. The residence of the Maréchal de La Fare, who lived alone in the company of two servants, also included six rooms. In the parishes of Saint-Paul, Saint-Germain-l'Auxerrois, and La Madeleine-de-la-Ville-l'Evêque, the occupation rate of these dwellings in the second half of the eighteenth century is fairly low, varying between 3 and 3.5 persons.

Dwellings of more than seven rooms comprise a minuscule part of our sample and concern only 164 (7 per cent) of the deceased. These residences, which represent a part of a house, an entire main house or outlying building, or an *hôtel* or town house, were the preserve of privileged households belonging to the highest spheres of Paris society, such as old nobility, *robins* or magistrates, office holders, financiers, lawyers or wealthy merchants and traders. The values of their inventories, which sometimes included only a part of their possessions, often exceeded 5000 L and could in certain cases attain very considerable amounts. Among the wealthiest households, enjoying such a vast residence, either as its owner or as a mere tenant, was simply one facet of a generally high standard of living. Other signs revealed the extent of these fortunes: the presence of ranks of servants, the maintenance of a stable, the possession of works of art or decorative objects, or the pursuit of distractions or hobbies.

At the top of this wide range of housing were the *hôtels* or town houses reserved almost exclusively for the families of nobles, judges or financiers. This rarefied, aristocratic environment is well known through the extensive research devoted to it[2] and was not a primary focus of our work. The occasional town house inventories incorporated in our data were uncovered by chance during the examination of notarial minutes performed for a given notarial firm or parish. These seigniorial residences, especially those belonging to dukes or peers, were of course sprawling: to cite only a few examples, there were forty-nine rooms in the Hôtel de Créqui on the rue de la Cerisaie in the parish of Saint-Paul, which the Duc de Lesdiguières occupied in 1638; fifty-five rooms for the Duc de Vendôme on the rue Neuve-Saint-Honoré in 1665; and fifty-one rooms in the Hôtel de Guise on the rue de Chaulme in 1688.[3]

The town houses that began to appear in the faubourg Saint-Honoré in the 1720s and 1730s were every bit as impressive, both in size and in splendour. A surface area of some 4000 square metres was required for an *hôtel* built for the Maréchal de Contades, with its courtyard and garden, on the rue d'Anjou around 1723–4. Facing it from across the street was the town house completed in 1726 for Antoine Mazin, Knight of the Royal Order, *Militaire de Saint Louis*, engineer to the king and director of His Majesty's plans and places. This structure presented a monumental façade on the street, pierced by twenty-two windows, not including the six basement-level windows. On the ground floor were six casements, flanked at each end by two carriage doors; on the first floor were eight bay windows, and there were eight dormer windows on the floor under the eaves. The scale and splendour of the town houses built by the Farmers General during the eighteenth century in the new neighbourhoods to the west – the faubourg Saint-Honoré, the area around the boulevards or Montmartre – is equally well known.[4]

A sizeable household, including at least as many servants as masters, often inhabited these town houses. In the parish of Saint-Jean-en-Grève, there were thirteen inhabitants, of whom eight were servants, in the rue des Deux-Portes home of Jacques-Honoré Barentin, counsellor to the king in his council, *Maître des Requêtes Ordinaires* for the king's household, and president of the Grand Council, who died in 1665. This house counted fourteen rooms, excluding the five annexes and seven outlying structures. The town house of Jean du Tillet (died 1668), counsellor to the king in his council and in the Grand Chamber of his Parlement, in the rue Neuve-Saint-Catherine in the parish of Saint-Paul, contained fourteen chambers, three main rooms, a kitchen, three *cabinets* or studies, a dressing room, a furniture storage room, a table-service room, two dispensaries, a loft, four cellars and a stable. It seems to have housed at least twenty persons, including seven masters. The house in which Madeleine de Gontaut de Biron, widow of the Marquis de Bonnac, died in 1739, consisted of thirty-one rooms and was home to seventeen persons, including six servants. The *hôtel* of the Comte de Chastellux, lieutenant general of the king's armies and lieutenant general and commandant of the province of Roussillon, contained six-teen main rooms in 1742, to which must be added eleven storage rooms and five separate structures. Its eleven occupants were the count and his wife, five young children and four servants.

While these noble dwellings are not completely absent from our sample, they remain nonetheless exceptions. The majority of lodgings classified as having more than seven rooms rarely aspired to such dimensions. Many wealthy bourgeois families frequently chose to live in houses having eight to fifteen rooms. The furrier Pierre Goblet, who died in 1705, lived with his two children and two servants in one nine-room section of a house, not including alcoves and two cellars, in the parish of Saint-Germain-l'Auxerrois. At about the same period, a man employed in the affairs of His Majesty, his wife and two servants occupied ten rooms of a house with cellar on the rue Saint-Sauveur. It was in a nine-room house with woodshed and attic on the rue Saint-Denis that an office holder who was a provincial *contrôleur général*, bourgeois of Paris and former alderman chose to reside with his wife, one grown-up child and two servants.

These spacious quarters, unlike the noble town houses, were sometimes underpopulated: a lawyer of the Parlement, who was also a bachelor, shared his lodgings with two servants in an eight-room section of a house on the rue Neuve-Saint-Magloire in the parish of Saint-Leu–Saint-Gilles. He also had a cellar and an attic. In one sixteen-room house with cellar and attic on the rue Saint-Denis we found a bourgeois of Paris, his wife and two servants. Nor was there any crowding problem for Jacques Girard de La Soisson, lawyer at the Parlement, who lived in 1765 with his brother and two servants in eleven rooms on the ground and first stories of a house on the rue de Bièvre in the parish of Saint-Etienne-du-Mont. In another house on the same street, in 1766, the widow of a doctor also dwelled spaciously with one servant in nine rooms, similarly divided between the ground and first floors.

Many hotel- and innkeepers were just as spaciously housed, as were certain *cabaret* owners, wine merchants and beverage sellers whose profession led them to offer bed and board to passing clients. However, their cases must be examined separately. Because family space and work space tended to become closely intermingled in these households, it is very difficult to determine which rooms were reserved for private use and which were business areas. Two very distinct zones comprised the latter: on the one hand, the shop or *cabaret* rooms on the ground floor, above the cellars, and on the other hand, furnished rooms available to clients in the upper stories. Thérèse Morel's hotel on the rue Saint-Martin had eleven furnished rooms ready to receive guests in 1744. The innkeeper Claude Audinet had seventeen rooms in his lodgings on the rue du Pavé near the Place Maubert in 1765. The inventory of the wife of a beverage merchant on rue Saint-Honoré, compiled in 1765, listed nine handsomely decorated bedrooms. In the home of another beverage seller living on the rue Geoffroy l'Angevin in the parish of Saint-Merry in 1784, there were eighteen rooms, each described as containing a bed. In such households, it is hard to draw the line between the bedrooms intended for clients and those used by the family. Though the inventory is rich in other detail, it grants hardly any means of grasping exactly what was the habitable space of Parisians practising hospitality trades. These were times when professional and private life were closely intertwined, and both often were lived out in the same spaces.

These lodgings include not only the three main room types that we attempted to count and classify , but also a multitude of secondary rooms and outlying buildings. In these habitations where the tiniest available space and the smallest corner were put to use, these annexes extending the available surface area are significant. They might serve as makeshift rooms in a very tiny dwelling, or as storage areas in the absence of cupboards. Despite their secondary roles, the dimensions of these rooms could vary considerably, and they were not always cramped. The presence of a 'large *cabinet*' (in the sense of an office or study), for instance, is noted by several valuers. Installed under a stairway, in a corridor, 'beside' or 'at the back' of a main room, these annexes were designated by a surprising variety of terms: *cabinet*, antechamber, dressing room, boudoir, office, alcove, loft, *bouge* (hovel), furniture storage, entry, recess, garret or shopback, to name a few. In all, we noted more than twenty different names: this variety reveals the complex and disjointed structure of habitations in that period.

The number of annexes per dwelling is often closely related to the number of main rooms. A purchase agreement for a house on the rue Saint-Honoré, dating from 1669, exemplified how such annexes, in this case dressing rooms, were distributed like satellites around a room: the document mentions an outlying building at the back, consisting of 'three large chambers with fireplaces, one above the other, and three other chambers, smaller, serving as dressing rooms for said large chambers'. While two- or three-room lodgings rarely included more than one or two annexes, those with four to seven rooms, and of course the great houses, could contain many more. One bourgeois of Paris who sold fine foods and wine in the faubourg Saint-Marcel, and who died in 1732, had six *cabinets* in addition to the ten main rooms. In the home of another wine merchant from the same faubourg, residing on the rue Mouffetard in 1739, the eight main rooms were supplemented by six *cabinets* and one alcove.

There was as much variety among outlying areas as among annexes: here again we counted at least twenty types. The names most frequently used in describing them were: shop, cellar, attic, pantry, garage, hangar, stable, cowshed, grange, bakehouse, greenhouse, warehouse and workyard. More individualized than the annexes, these outlying areas almost all had specific functions, and a certain number corresponded to a specific socio-professional category or trade.

Shops were indicated in some 21 per cent of the dwellings inventoried; they were to be found exclusively in the homes of merchants and artisans. Other types of premises, also designated by specific terms, were typically associated with other activities, such as the furniture maker's workyard, the painter's studio, the baker's oven and bolting rooms, the butcher's slaughterhouse and boiler room, or the washerwoman's draining area. Some of these outlying areas were actually the work spaces of the deceased. It was common in those times to find them located near the home, either in the same building or in the courtyard. Some of these spaces may be identified with a given social category. Horse stables, for example, were to be found only in the wealthiest of households, those equipped with equestrian transportation, unless they could be considered as professional premises for renters of horses and carriages and carters. In contrast, areas intended for farming purposes, such as cowsheds, granges, sheep pens, hen houses and so forth were not the special preserve of agrarian trades: one bourgeois of Paris who died in 1683 kept six pigs at the back of his courtyard in the heart of Paris, on the rue de la Verrerie in the parish of Saint-Jean-en-Grève. To this end, he possessed a pigsty and a hayloft. But that was somewhat exceptional. Generally speaking, these types of buildings were rare and were to be found only on the semi-rural fringes of the suburbs.

It was in the most spacious houses, in particular those located on the edge of the city, in the suburbs or in surrounding villages, where the urban fabric was not so tightly woven, that these outlying structures are most numerous. Take the example of the Lion d'Or inn at Gonesse, a sprawling one-story building with six such structures: a bakehouse, a cellar, an attic, a stable, a hangar and a hen house. Such appendages were practically indispensable to innkeepers and *cabaret* owners, whose buildings opened on to courtyards and gardens that could also be considered as open-air additions to be used in the summer season to serve clients. Of the sixty-eight residents of Passy and Auteuil whose inventories were examined, 72 per cent were equipped with outlying structures, with an average of three per dwelling. Since they simply did not have the space, houses in the centre of the city generally were less extensively furnished with such additions than those in peripheral areas.

The cellar, and to a lesser extent the attic, are the most frequently found rooms not directly attached to the main lodgings. They are to be found in almost every dwelling, wherever it might be located and whatever the social or professional category of its occupants. One-third (33 per cent) of our deceased had a cellar. Inventories performed on an entire house often indicate the presence of several. In the home of the magistrate Jean du Tillet, for example, four cellars were listed in 1688: 'one cellar, a vault adjacent to said wine cellar, one cellar to the front, one small cellar facing the above-mentioned one'. According to a purchase agreement dating from 1669, one house on the rue Saint-Honoré was equipped with 'two large, low cradle-vaulted cellars, another large cellar above, and a vault under the courtyard ... an exit directly on to the rue Saint-Honoré'.

This arrangement on two levels seems very old and becomes increasingly uncommon in the seventeenth and especially in the following century. It was still to be seen, however, in a secondary building belonging to another great house on the rue Saint-Honoré, as described by the lease from 1670: 'two cradle-vaulted cellars separated by a wall bearing a stairway, another cellar above the above-mentioned cradle-vaults, a cellar beneath the courtyard of said house'. As is to be expected, cellars are most commonly found on the premises of wine merchants, cabaret owners and beverage sellers. At the home of a wine merchant of the rue du Temple who died in 1739, a first cellar was mentioned opening into the shop by a stairway, leading in turn into two other cellars, one behind the other. In the house of another wine merchant on rue des Fossés-Saint-Germain-l'Auxerrois, the notary listed a first cellar, followed by a second, with two others on a lower level. Those wine merchants who had no cellar in their homes might rent one in another house. This was the case with Jean-Baptiste Jolly, living in the rue Bordet in the parish of Saint-Etienne-du-Mont and renting a cellar on the rue Condé; and with Didier Hébert, residing in the rue du Faubourg Saint-Martin and renting a cellar not far from there, in the rue des Petites Ecuries du Roy.

Attics, some of which were furnished with a bed and served as sleeping rooms, were less frequent than cellars. Their presence was noted in 15.5 per cent of the households in our sample. We shall see later on how the cellar and the attic played an important role as warehouses for the various stores for the household.

Our survey of more than two thousand Parisian dwellings makes it possible for us to temper Mercier's judgement concerning housing conditions in the capital during the eighteenth century. It is true that single rooms were the refuge, as they had been for the previous century and a half, of the most modest families. That the gap between the run-down houses in the city centre, where poor wage-earners were crowded into real slums, and the newly built *hôtels* in the western neighbourhoods, where the wealthiest Parisians lived in the lap of luxury, was growing wider by the end of the *ancien régime* is also certain.

The cramped conditions of Parisian dwellings were also not exaggerated: 73 per cent of the dwellings in our data set have at most three main rooms. Despite the admittedly small size of these lodgings, crowding as revealed through the inventories was not excessive. The wealthiest classes, especially those in the world of finance, were not the only ones to benefit from Enlightenment progress. Within the strata of the middle class, those most representative of the urban population, housing conditions underwent significant improvement during the eighteenth century. Given equal or at least comparable social status and fortune, the households of merchants or trade masters in the reign of Louis XVI seemed to have acquired a definite increase in living space when compared to those living during the reign of Louis XIII. The average occupation density on the eve of the Revolution was about two main rooms for three persons. The way the number of secondary and outlying rooms burgeoned, prompted by the desire for greater privacy and comfort, also helped to contribute to expanding the habitable living area.

But it is not enough to know how many rooms our households had in order to get a clear idea of housing conditions in Paris at that time. Other elements, which we shall attempt to evaluate in the following pages, must be taken into consideration: after all, to understand individuals' life-styles, it is important to know the location and degree of specialization of rooms, and how their occupants arranged them.

How Space was Organized

As we follow the notaries' footsteps, it is not always easy to grasp the structure of these households and to reconstitute their floor plans. Because they were generally empty of objects to be inventoried, passages such as stairways or ladders, hallways, corridors, galleries or landings were almost never mentioned. In the largest and most opulent homes – town houses or entire buildings – a chest, a chair or even a clock standing in a corridor or on the landing of a stairway can offer an indirect indication of the existence of such passages. In the absence of any such clues, these internal transitions are difficult to detect, and it is not easy to discern the configuration of these interiors.

Nonetheless, the vocabulary used by the notaries contains a certain number of expressions that provide an idea of the position of various rooms in relation to one another. Like footprints for a hunter, these terms serve to guide us in our wanderings through the house. Yet however varied and numerous they may be, these spatial clues remain vague and inexact. Typical examples of the most common expressions found in the inventories are: 'next to' ('in the kitchen on the ground floor next to the carriage doorway'); 'adjoining' ('the study adjoining the bedroom'); 'contiguous', 'following', 'joining' ('in the chamber joining this one'); 'at the back of' ('in a kitchen at the back of the shop'); 'to the back' ('in a small room to the back of the said story'); 'upon entering', '*vis-à-vis*', 'in a wing', 'below', 'above'.

More exact and more complete information is to be had from leases. One dwelling is described as

> a shop in which there is a trap door to go down into one of two cellars, *vis-à-vis* a door leading on to the street, a carpenter's stairway to go up to the upper rooms, which form a little enclosure of oak planks above, over which there is a loft. Following these is a room with two windows and a fireplace, having a view and an exit via a door located on one of the courtyards.

Alas, such clear indications are never given in the inventories. The more rooms there are in a dwelling, the more difficult it is to solve the puzzle of their layout, using the inventory data alone. Such a problem disappears, of course, when examining single-room lodgings.

With this mass of information, however incomplete it may be, we succeeded in establishing some of the characteristic aspects of the layout of these urban residences. The frequency of the terms 'next to', 'adjoining', and 'following' highlights the interdependence of the various rooms, to the point that, as we originally perceive them, houses seem to be a simple succession of rooms. But it is possible that this first impression may be distorted by the valuers' propensity for ignoring internal transitions.

Another structural characteristic of these lodgings, especially in the eighteenth century, is overlapping space caused by the multiplication of annexes. In an attempt to create a little privacy or to isolate certain areas such as the kitchen, occupants installed booths, lofts, cubbyholes or niches in large rooms using wooden partitions. In the home of a counsellor to the king and *Lieutenant de la Robe Courte* (mounted constabulary) who died in 1748, we noted 'three small *cabinets* separated by partitions following the antechamber' as well as 'a small alcove installed next to the chamber'. The inventory of a master dyer and merchant, drawn up in 1746, mentions both 'a small booth formed in the shop by a small partition' and 'a small booth formed in the shop serving as a kitchen'.

In addition to these booths and partitions, there were lofts, used to lodge a maidservant or a child in a corner: 'in a loft within the bedroom: a boy's bed' or 'a loft above the dining room ... where the cook sleeps'. We shall return later to these interior arrangements that bear the marks the inhabitants left on their homes.

The most striking and fundamental structural aspect of the Parisian habitat at that time was the dissemination of rooms of the same household over several levels. This vertical organization or composition occurs in 704, or 45 per cent, of the 1570 dwellings having two or more rooms in our sample. Those with single rooms were, of course, excluded from the calculations. This vertical distribution of rooms often covered not just two, but three or even four stories. We know the distribution by level of a sample of 475 composite dwellings: the great majority,

62 per cent, were spread over two floors, like today's duplex apartments; 24 per cent were on three levels; 10 per cent on four levels, and almost 4 per cent spread over five, six or even seven levels. This arrangement is due to the narrowness of land parcels, which is the reason for these upward-stretching houses. The more rooms there were in a residence, the more they tended to be dispersed over several floors: vertical spreading is therefore a function of the number of rooms.

A few examples will help us to visualize this type of fractured, patchwork habitation which is so unusual to modern eyes. The household of a *Procureur Tiers Référendaire* (referendary prosecutor) at the Court of Parlement in 1686 filled part of a house on the rue Jean de l'Espine in the parish of Saint-Jean-en-Grève, with rooms distributed over four levels: one room and an adjoining kitchen on the ground floor, a chamber serving as study and *cabinet* on the first floor, another chamber and *cabinet* on the second floor, and an attic on the third. The home of a master barrel maker and wine handler, consisting of just three main rooms on the rue des Billettes, was inventoried following the death of the man's wife in 1694. It nevertheless extended over three levels, or four if we include the cellar: the kitchen was located on the ground floor behind the shop, and the two bedrooms were one above the other on the first and second stories.

The lodgings of a beverage seller who died in 1703 in the rue Saint-Antoine, were spread over six levels: the shop on the ground floor, a chamber on the first floor that could be used as an annexe to the shop during the day, another chamber on the second floor, two chambers on the third, a kitchen and two chambers on the fourth floor, and a chamber and closet on the fifth. In this last case, it is interesting to note the position of the kitchen in the upper stories. The same was true of a lawyer who died in 1727 in a house on the rue Saint-Séverin. There the kitchen was located on the third floor, whereas a room, a bedchamber, and a *cabinet* filled the second floor. Even more complicated was the organization of the home of a priest who died in 1730 in the rue Geoffroy-l'Asnier: a common room, two chambers, an antechamber and a small *cabinet* were located on the first floor, while the kitchen was to be found on the third story. In the household of a master locksmith residing on the rue Darnetal in the parish of Saint-Sauveur, the children were housed on the third story, while their parents' bedroom and the kitchen were on the first floor. The domestic space of one Passy resident who died in 1766, a stonecutter merchant running a *cabaret*, stood across the street from his professional premises, in a 'house or shed built during his marriage'; one room 'below' was used as a kitchen on the ground floor, there was a panelled room above and, across the street, a chamber or room that served as a *cabaret*.

To twentieth-century eyes, the structure of these dwellings appears outdated, illogical and inconvenient. Think of all the rushing up and down stairs, the effort and the daily disturbances for the inhabitants, in an age when people went out every day not only to get their food but to renew their fuel and water supplies as well!

As far as the distribution by level of the various rooms in these composite lodgings is concerned, the kitchen – usually the first room visited by the notary – was most commonly located on the ground floor, or in any case on the lowest floor in the household. However, as we have seen, it could be placed on the highest stories. The main room is often adjacent to the kitchen or the shop on the ground floor and is designated by the valuers in some cases as the 'low room' or the room 'below'. Chambers were generally to be found in upper stories; servants' quarters most often occupied the last story and were sometimes installed in the attic, unless they were placed close to their masters' bedchambers.

Cabinets and dressing rooms, which usually accompanied a larger room, and antechambers and other annexes, were distributed on all levels. *Cabinets* could be 'made by partition' not only within chambers, but in shops as well, as was the case in 1755 of a wine merchant residing on the Quai de l'Ecole, in the parish of Saint-Germain-l'Auxerrois. Lofts might be opened above chambers or even in the kitchen or the shop, with a wooden ladder installed for access. As for other separate spaces besides the shop and shopback, cellar and attic, structures such as sheds, garages, stables, woodsheds or greenhouses were often located on the ground floor of outlying buildings constructed in the courtyard.

While 45 per cent of the dwellings having more than one room in our sample reveal this vertical stratification, 55 per cent were organized horizontally. Most of these contained only a limited number of rooms, rarely more than four. These apartments, in the modern sense of the word, most certainly offered significantly improved comfort and convenience when compared with homes whose rooms were scattered all over the tenement house. They were not actually referred to as apartments, as the word at that time did not have the same meaning it does today. The *Dictionnaire de Furetière* defines the term in 1690 as a 'portion of a large abode, where one person lodges or may lodge separately with another', from the latin word *partimentum*. The 1694 *Dictionnaire de l'Académie Française* specifies that an apartment is a 'dwelling composed of several chambers, or several rooms connected together in a house'. Richelet proposed the following definition in 1709: 'Chamber. Antechamber and *cabinet*. Room, chamber, and *cabinet*'. The *Dictionnaire de Trévoux* from 1752 introduces the notion of story, which is not included in the *Encyclopédie*: 'May also be considered as a story. "He is lodged in the first or second apartment."'

Such a space with a single tenant and a logical arrangement in what would one day be known as apartments, stood in contrast to the patchwork distribution and complex organization of vertical housing. Examples of the former include a counsellor to the king, who lived until his death in 1684 with his wife, three young children and a maidservant in four rooms strung together, all located on the first story of a house on the rue de la Verrerie, facing on to the courtyard: a room, a small room 'to the side', a chamber that apparently served for both sleeping and preparing meals, and a second 'small' chamber next to it. This type of horizontal habitat was still unusual in the 1720s and 1730s. The widow of a lawyer at Parlement resided in 1743 in an apartment on the second floor of another house on the rue de la Verrerie, with a view of the street and the courtyard; her home included a kitchen, an antechamber, a small *cabinet*, two chambers and another *cabinet*. The home of a spinster on the third story of a house on the rue des Juifs in the parish of Saint-Gervais consisted in 1745 of a kitchen, an antechamber, a chamber and a *cabinet*.

In some cases, merchants might also enjoy the good fortune of having quarters located on the ground floor, on the same level as their shops. One beverage seller on the rue Saint-Paul, who died in 1759, had a chamber and a *cabinet* connecting with his shop. The same was true of another beverage seller who died in 1784, in a ground floor dwelling on the rue Culture-Sainte-Catherine that included a chamber, a *cabinet*, a small corridor and a shop. As increasing numbers of tenement houses were constructed during the reign of Louix XV with four or five bays on rectangular plots measuring 120 square metres, these horizontal-type dwellings became more common during the eighteenth century and were even preponderant in Enlightenment Paris.

Do the signs of this residential evolution appear in the results of our study? If we consider exclusively the inventories drawn up after 1750, the average number of lodgings occupying a single level is 60 per cent, compared with 54 per cent for the seventeenth century. This increase may appear to be slight when we realize the technological changes that building construction went through in the eighteenth century. However, most of these houses seem to have been built prior to the 1720s and 1730s. It was only in interiors inventoried during the last two or three decades of the century and occupied by wealthy families that our visits to the houses discover a definitely modern type of accommodation.

These homes reveal a new life-style that foreshadows the bourgeois apartment of the nineteenth century. An excellent example was offered to us in the home on the rue des Lavandières in the parish of Saint-Germain-l'Auxerrois of the widow (died 1779) of Pierre Foubert, former director and treasurer of the Royal Academy of Surgery and the king's surgeon. It contained six main rooms on the same level, with clearly defined uses – *salon*, dining room with a service room, bedchamber, kitchen, cook's and chamber maid's bedchambers, an antechamber leading into these different rooms (with the exception of the cook's room, which gave on to the kitchen), and a passage connecting the kitchen to the dining room. This could really almost be considered a modern apartment. If the servants' rooms were renovated to make children's rooms, and if modern plumbing were installed, would this not be a fine apartment, worthy of the best part of Paris, where it would be snapped up immediately? It is clear that the structure of Mme Foubert's lodgings bears witness to the enormous progress that had been made over dwellings comprising either rooms scattered over several stories or non-communicating rooms on the same level.

Rare are the indications in the inventories of an antechamber, a corridor or a hall leading into each habitable room. Such an arrangement has an advantage over rooms strung together, because it isolates various parts of the house from each other and protects the privacy of the occupants. This new structure of the Parisian home that appeared progressively during the eighteenth century already prefigures the bourgeois apartment of the nineteenth century in all but one of its aspects: in the century of Eugène Sue, servants' rooms were no longer located close to those of their masters, but were placed instead under the eaves.

This evolution in the way space was organized may also be illustrated by the example of a tenement house that one *citoyen* Clié, a cabinetmaker, had constructed in 1792 on a plot of land he owned on the rue d'Anjou-Saint-Honoré. In its structure and its interior layout, it foreshadows the nineteenth-century rental property. The façade, some 18.50 metres high and 23.50 metres wide, consisted of nine bays on five levels: the ground floor was reserved for three shops placed on either side of the carriage door; above were three full stories and one story under the eaves. Each story was divided into two apartments each covering some 90 square metres. Each apartment constituted one self-sufficient rental unit consisting of four rooms – kitchen, dining room, *salon*, bedchamber with alcove – completed by a corridor and a water closet. In all, the building housed six dwellings, in addition to six servants' rooms located on the story beneath the eaves. The Clié building, erected at the height of the Revolution, was no longer rented by the room, but by the level. It was the culmination of an evolution in the way habitable space was organized, that emerged out of the great leap forward in the 1720s and 1730s and ever increasing progress made from the 1770s.

Another structural aspect of these lodgings concerns the placement of rooms in relation to the street and the courtyard. Our information is very patchy on this point, and the restrictions to be placed on the value of a sample covering 860 rooms should be apparent. Views of courtyards are most numerous, accounting for 48.5 per cent of the whole, with street views representing 39.5 per cent. A certain number of rooms also enjoyed the advantage of two openings, and 3.5 per cent gave on to both the street and the courtyard. In all, 88 per cent of the rooms in our sample faced either on to the street or on to the courtyard. Given the narrowness of the streets and the compact dimensions of the courtyards, these interiors must have been dark and dim for the most part.

Openings on to gardens were generally a privilege of town houses, residences of the wealthy, or perhaps semi-rural habitations, and were found in only 6 per cent of the rooms. Openings on a courtyard and a garden represented 1.5 per cent, and those on the street and a garden, 1 per cent. As the valuers rarely specified the dimensions or number of windows, it is difficult to imagine exactly the size of these openings or their capacity for letting in light. Nor is an indication of curtains always sufficient to determine the number of windows in a room. For example, valuers inventoried ten red serge window curtains in the room of a painter and private valet to the King in 1663. But how can we know whether there were ten, or even five windows lighting this room?

A small number of documents used to supplement the inventories can contribute useful details about these openings. For example, an estimate dating from 1632 and referring to a house on the rue des Poulies stipulates that 'the joinery for the windows and half-windows is to be done, the first, second, and third windows to be six panes, and the others according to the appropriate height, measuring four and a half feet [1.37 metres] or thereabouts in width, and the half-windows will each be three panes'. In this estimate, as in another one dating from 1614, it is interesting to note that the lighting on the courtyard side is provided using half-windows only. A contract made in 1646 between Jacques Tutin and Nicolas Barbier concerning 'three views and bays' for the house of the latter standing on the courtyard of the former, indicates the window measurements: in the first room, a large 'bay and window' 1.14 metres wide, and another some 0.81 metres wide; a third letting light into the small room on the ground floor, measuring 0.89 metres. Nicolas Barbier is bound by this agreement to install 'iron mesh', i.e. an iron grill, and *verre dormant* or 'sleeping glass', in other words a pane that does not open. It should be noted that this last opening created a barrier to the direct entry of light. It was also common in that period that 'the lower windows of all houses are grated with strong bars of iron; which must be a vast expense', as the English traveller Martin Lister noted in 1698.[5]

The houses that went up on the rue du Sépulcre around 1670–80 presented several types of windows: the age-old sliding frame model was the most widely employed; closures for each pane were more uncommon. The frame model with two panes equipped with a catch, introduced in the seventeenth century, was becoming more widespread. This type of window was preferably installed on windows facing the street and on first-story windows. The number of panes was sometimes indicated; there could be as many as twenty-four. Only in the eighteenth century did large windows become commonplace, especially on the street side: as windows became larger and the number of wooden crossbars was reduced, the quality of room light improved. In tenement buildings, each full story was furnished on the street side with four 1.30-metre-wide windows, each of which had two panels and a catch and was four panes wide and eight panes high on the first and second stories, and seven panes high on the third floor. The less costly sliding frames began to disappear in the eighteenth century, and came to be reserved, at least among the houses in the faubourg Saint-Honoré, for shop-front windows, stairways or top stories.

The choice of materials to fill in the window frames also influenced the amount of light penetrating into these interiors. In the early years of the eighteenth century, so-called 'white' or clear glass was not the only material; oiled paper, which let in only an opaque light, was still to be found: 'oak wood frame filled with tightly sealed paper', or 'one window was filled with two panes, one with large glass panes and the other with oiled paper.' To compensate for this insufficient light, windows were supplemented by glass-paned doors and partitions in certain households. In one kitchen on a courtyard, the presence of a glass-paned door with twelve panes was noted, above which stood a frame with nine panes, and 'next to the door, a large frame in oak filled with forty-eight panes of glass'.

Clear glass, also referred to as 'French glass', was the most common material in the eighteenth century; it came from Cherbourg, in lower Normandy, where a glassworks was established in 1710 in the forest of Léonce. This glass had a greenish tint; uncoloured glass was used only for the most luxurious homes. In the second half of the century, the royal glassworks of Saint-Quirin in the Vosges region, near Saarbrücken, also supplied Paris with pane glass. We found no estimates or agreements making reference to the glassworks installed in 1694 near Paris, in the faubourg Saint-Antoine.

Despite the technical advances recorded during the eighteenth century, windows in Parisian homes had not yet attained the degree of perfection that the industrial revolution of the next century would bring. These windows were criticized, perhaps in an exaggerated and partial manner, by a Protestant woman of Huguenot descent living in Kassel, Germany, who visited Paris in 1773. 'What a horror the windows in Paris are! No, since Noah's flood they have not been washed! And what's more, badly built, with crossbars two inches wide, putty applied sloppily, yes it is a pity to see lovely houses, superb *hôtels* with massacred and dirty windows.'[6]

As we have attempted to outline in these pages, the interior structure of the

Parisian habitat that had remained unchanged throughout the seventeenth century, was deeply influenced from the 1720s on by the technical progress of the Enlightenment: space within the home began to be more efficiently organized, rooms were arranged more logically and adapted to increasing needs for privacy and comfort, and natural lighting was improved. These are the primary long-term innovations that we discover through our explorations of Parisian housing.

Room Functions and their Degree of Specialization

Whatever the amount of space available and however the home might be arranged, this was where each household carried out all its daily tasks. Our sense of rational organization, attributing a specifically delimited space to a given household activity, was not shared by the subjects of Louis XIV and did not truly begin to take root until the latter part of the Enlightenment. As we accompany the notaries moving through these Parisian interiors, we notice that rooms are rarely assigned a single purpose. This emerges through the names of rooms as well as what is found in them.

The chamber or bedchamber is omnipresent in all households. It represents the heart of the living area. Its predominance is underlined by a few figures: 71 per cent of the main rooms are chambers; kitchens (including chambers used as kitchens) and rooms (a term encompassing dining rooms, sitting or meeting rooms and *salons*) represent 17 per cent and 12 per cent respectively. There are on average slightly less than two chambers per household. In the seventeenth-century mind, the chamber had a double function: this was the room in which one slept and where one received guests. The meaning of the French term *chambre* was in fact much less specific than it is today. Period dictionaries are quite illuminating on this point: 'A chamber for bedding and sleeping. A high chamber for eating and drinking. The chamber in which one habitually receives guests', reads Nicot[7] in 1606. Furetière proposes the following definition, which was incorporated sixty years later in the *Dictionnaire de Trévoux*: 'Element of a lodging, part of an apartment. This is ordinarily the place where one sleeps and where one receives company.' However, as early as 1694, 'chamber' in the *Dictionnaire de l'Académie Française* designates the 'room in a lodging in which one ordinarily sleeps'.

The *Encyclopédie* devotes a long article to the bedchamber as such, describing its dimensions, its decoration and the position of the bed with regard to the fireplace and the windows; chambers with alcoves, chambers in niches, chambers in garrets, often intended for servants, are all described as well. It is interesting to read the *Encyclopédie*'s remark concerning the number of chairs in a bedchamber: 'It is true that the purpose of a bedchamber would seem to require fewer than any other room, and only a case of illness could attract a somewhat numerous company to a bedchamber; but it is a matter of decency for such a room to contain a certain number.' Having become synonymous with the sleeping space, the chamber is recognized by the eighteenth century as a place reserved for rest and privacy, as distinct from the room reserved for socializing.

The chamber's purpose generally correlated with the make-up of the dwelling.

In a single-room home, the chamber is a multi-purpose room, serving not only as a place for sleeping, but as a kitchen, dining room, and receiving room. In the most poverty-stricken households, it may even be used as a work place. In one room inhabited in 1677 by a schoolmaster and his wife on the rue du Faubourg Saint-Antoine, the notary inventoried nine little school benches, two writing tables for pupils, and a bundle of 'quite old' booklets. The room in which a journeyman locksmith lived in 1771 with his wife and son on the rue de la Grande Friperie in the parish of Saint-Eustache housed 'a board serving as workbench with various locksmith's tools'.

In interiors that included a kitchen or even several rooms, the chamber maintained as often as not a double function of bedchamber and receiving room. Whether in the city or in the countryside, during the reign of Louix XIV or a century earlier, the chamber appeared to be the preferred place for socializing. Around 1550 or 1560, a Norman gentleman, one Gilles de Gouberville, was accustomed to receiving his guests in his chamber at his Mesnil-au-Val manor house on the Cotentin peninsula in Normandy.[8] In Parisian homes from the seventeenth and eighteenth centuries, the excessive number of chairs counted by inventories in the chambers of the deceased highlights the importance of this room as the traditional seat of hospitality (there were frequently more than twenty, and indeed thirty were found in the home of a *Maître Ordinaire* (permanent official) of the Chambres des Comptes (court overseeing state finances) in 1759).

In the homes of well-to-do seventeenth-century families, the chamber could even take on the air of a ceremonial room: one such example was to be found in the home of a *Secrétaire Ordinaire* to the Council of State and the Direction des Finances in 1654, where a richly furnished room – other than that of the deceased – was draped with funeral hangings. In the residence of a Secretary of Finances who died in 1666, there was one so-called Italian chamber, containing twenty-four chairs and other fine furnishings, in which apparently no one slept. Chambers also sometimes contained musical instruments in a small number of seventeenth-century households.

These homes of privileged people were the site of an incipient though tentative specialization of room use as early as the reign of Louis XIV. As early as 1665, the chambers in the house of Jacques-Honoré Barentin, *Maître des Requêtes Ordinaires* in the king's household and president of the king's Grand Council seemed definitely reserved for sleeping and attributed to specific individuals; the 'girls' (i.e. the servants) shared a single room, while the chambermaid and the valet each had a room of their own near their master's. The example of the fourteen chambers recorded in the house of Jean du Tillet, who died in 1668, also illustrates this evolution of the chamber towards a private, personal space.

Progressively, this model began to infiltrate the more modest classes. In the house occupied in 1666 by a livery stable keeper, his wife and two young children, the distinction between the parents' chamber, on the first floor, and the two small children's bedchambers on the second floor is easy to make. But the chamber does not truly become specialized until the second half of the eighteenth century, as is witnessed by the more frequent use of the term 'chamber for sleeping' (*chambre à coucher*) in the notarial documents. Of seventy-five dwellings in the parish of Saint-Germain-l'Auxerrois in which inventories were made between 1768 and 1790, 49, or 65.5 per cent, possess a true bedchamber. If there were enough rooms, children would have a room separate from their parents. Aside from the deceased person's bedchamber, notaries often identify 'the boys' chamber' in a household, or 'Mademoiselle's chamber'. It is worth emphasizing, however, that this specialization of the 'chamber' as a bedroom is closely related to the size of dwellings and to the number of occupants. In fact, various physical needs and daily activities must be taken care of within the available space, which in turn determines what space there is to be allotted for specific functions.

After the chamber, the kitchen is the room most frequently mentioned by notaries. In the homes visited, 45 per cent included a kitchen, or at least a room, be it a chamber, common room, *cabinet* or antechamber, that served as a kitchen. This percentage remains almost unchanged for lodgings visited after 1750. Less than half of these interiors were equipped with a kitchen, and one-fourth simply presented a room used as a kitchen. An eighteenth-century kitchen worthy of the name is defined in various dictionaries as the place where meats were cooked and prepared, requiring a certain number of elements specified by the *Encylopédie*: 'A large fireplace for roasting ... another for soups, stoves or kettles for stews, an oven'. As these kitchen furnishings were incorporated in the walls of the house, they were of course never listed in the inventories. Their presence is, however, sometimes noted by officially appointed building experts in their reports. In 1777, the residence of a *trésorier des rentes* (government pension treasurer) of the Hôtel de Ville, located on the rue de Cléry, possessed a kitchen equipped with the following elements: 'an oven, a fireplace having a hood, with a spit and a trammel, a stove with seven burners and a fish kettle, a sink equipped with waterspouts draining into the said street'. But not all kitchens were so well equipped. Those installed in a bedchamber, a room, a *cabinet* or a shopback, probably contained as sole equipment a fireplace on which meals were prepared.

Despite our ideas to the contrary, the kitchen was not always reserved for a single purpose. When it was the only heated room in a house, it might be used as living room, or as the bedchamber for a servant or a child. In dwellings with two or three rooms, this was where the family came together to take its meals, as is demonstrated by the presence of tables and chairs. The kitchen of Nicolas de Moustier, a doctor of the Sorbonne and vicar of the church of Saint-Séverin, who died in 1699, was decorated with paintings and religious objects and furnished with a day bed. A captain at the Château de la Tournelle, who benefited in 1709 from a professional lodging, slept in his own kitchen, even though his home included a large common room (without a bed), two *cabinets*, and a bedchamber occupied by his children. In the home of a widow, visited in 1704, the kitchen was where the two maidservants slept. 'The antechamber used as a kitchen' in the dwelling of Louise Robustel, a woman separated from her husband, also doubled as a bedchamber for the maidservant in 1707. The kitchen was often used as a work space for beverage sellers, demonstrating the way in which professional and domestic activities so frequently overlapped in this period. In a sample of the lodgings of sixty-two beverage sellers, we found four kitchens that were used simultaneously as laboratories for preparing the merchandise and as shops; four laboratories and five shop rooms that functioned as kitchens, and a bedchamber that was transformed during the day into a kitchen and shop.

Areas reserved for socializing included the room (*salle*) and its derivatives, the sitting room, dining room and *salon* (excluding rooms used as kitchens, offices or chambers). These were to be found in one-third of these abodes. Most often, such rooms were a sign that the nobles, magistrates, king's counsellors, auxiliary members of the legal profession, or rich merchants who made their homes in such fairly vast residences were indeed privileged. Such rooms were practically unknown to servants, artisans or day labourers. This type of room is generally described in dictionaries as large, the most spacious in the house. It is 'the first room in a full apartment and is ordinarily larger than the others', according to the *Dictionnaire de l'Académie*, and 'a large, ornate room in which one ordinarily receives the people who come to visit or wish to discuss business', according to Richelet. The *Dictionnaire de Trévoux* also defines this main room as 'the first part of an apartment in an abode. It is the biggest room in a fine apartment.' The *Encyclopédie* adds, 'and ordinarily the most decorated'. A *Manuel de la Toilette et de la Mode* of 1776 states that such rooms are 'ornate chambers in which one receives visitors; the walls are covered in three shades of damask, and the furnishings include seats and armchairs covered in the same cloth'.[9]

These main rooms, almost always adjoining the kitchen and frequently located on the ground floor, are also sometimes designated as low rooms. Throughout the inventories, they emerge as rooms with specific functions: the family gathers there for meals, to spend the evening or to entertain relatives, neighbours and friends. The furniture consisted, as we shall see later, of tables and generally a great many chairs. With the decoration, it reflects this room's purpose as a place for communal life.

In some cases, the notaries' choice of words expresses the room's specific application. The dining room, the 'place in the house where one dines or sups', as Richelet puts it, began to find its place in noble households during the reign of Louis XIV, as a means of imitating the habits of the Court. In a sample of eighty-two dwellings inventoried between 1660 and 1720 within the parish of Saint-Jean-en-Grève, the only homes equipped with a dining room were those of the Chevalier Adrien Bancé, the *Maître des Requêtes* Messire Jacques-Honoré Barentin, and Louis Ancelin, the *contrôleur général* of the Household of the late queen. Even in the eighteenth century, dining rooms were to be encountered only in society's elite. The only mentions of them found in Paris and Auteuil between 1740 and 1770 were in the homes of the inspector of the guard of the Boulogne woods and the curé of Auteuil, out of a sample of sixty-eight inhabitants.

Dining rooms were installed in a slightly greater number of Parisian homes after 1750. They nonetheless remained the privilege of a minority. Out of 500 households inventoried in the second half of the eighteenth century, mention is made of them in only 14 per cent of the homes. The concentration of dining rooms varies from one neighbourhood to another, in accordance with the social groups encountered by the notary: 26.5 per cent in the parish of Saint-Eustache between 1770 and 1772, where their presence was found only in conjunction with inheritances of more than 5000 L; 22.5 per cent in the parish of Saint-Germain-l'Auxerrois between 1768 and 1790; but only 10 per cent in the parish of Saint-Etienne-du-Mont between 1761 and 1770. Dining rooms were practically non-existent in the faubourg Saint-Antoine during the same period. It should also be noted that in a few seigniorial households employing several servants, mention was made not only of a master's room, but of a common room as well, i.e. a dining room (*salle du commun*) intended for the staff.

The sitting room or *salon* evolved in a manner similar to the dining room, though somewhat later. The term *salon* does not appear in inventories before 1720 or 1730. It does, however, figure in the *Dictionnaire de Furetière* and in that of the Académie Française at the end of the seventeenth century, where it designates a 'large room, very high and vaulted, often with two stories or ranks of arches'. 'The fashion for *salons*', adds Furetière, 'comes from Italy. Ordinarily, one receives ambassadors in a *salon*.' Even though the term was not commonly employed during the seventeenth century, such vast rooms, also called chambers, were already reserved at that time exclusively for ceremonies and receptions in the abodes of the wealthy. Such ceremonial chambers as we spoke of earlier, or 'high rooms' located on the first floor were thereby spared disturbance from the street or odours from the kitchen; these are the rooms we discover toward the middle of the seventeenth century in the residences of such high-ranking figures as Charles de Machault, counsellor to the Council of State and Private Council and Director of Finances, or Jacques Galland, *Secrétaire Ordinaire* to the Council of State and Direction des Finances, or Louis Girard de La Cour des Bois, *Maître des Requêtes*. The use of these spaces as meeting rooms is marked by their numerous chairs, especially so-called conversation chairs or *caquetoires*, and by the requirements of games.

From estimates prepared at the time, the dimensions of such rooms seem extraordinary. One document of 1650 concerns a house on the rue du Temple and stipulates that 'a large room is to be built and constructed anew on the site and place where four bowls courts are presently located. The said room will measure eleven *toises* [21.8 metres] in length by seven *toises* wide or thereabouts ... and the walls are to be four *toises* high or more if necessary, not including the foundations.' Another estimate dating from 1632 concerning a house on rue des Poulies specifies that 'the room will stand nine feet [2.7 metres] high below the beams', and the first as well as the second, third and final stories, eight feet high. These measurements are confirmed by the heights of tapestries, which vary between two and a half and three *aunes*, or 2.3 and 3.5 metres. In the eighteenth century, such rooms, referred to as company or assembly rooms, were still rare; in fact, we counted them in only 12 per cent of the 500 dwellings inventoried after 1750. A sign of luxury, like the dining room, these were the preserve of the richest classes, members of the nobility or the bourgeoisie.

The floor plan of Mme Foubert's apartment shows a salon opening on to an antechamber, which is separated from the dining room, since the bedchamber is situated between the two. The house inhabited in 1768 by Jean Mariquet, a haberdashery merchant and bourgeois of Paris, on the rue des Lavandières in the parish of Saint-Germain-l'Auxerrois, was equipped with a dining room adjoining the kitchen on the ground floor and a sitting room on the first floor which could receive as many as twenty-three seated persons, as was demonstrated by the number of chairs inventoried there. Sieur Baudard de Vandésir, whose estate was valued at more than 50,000 L, even had two *salons* in his home, one for winter and one for summer. A former Farmer General, Lalive d'Epinay, who died in 1782, had not only a *salon* in his home on the rue des Saussaies but a billiard room as well. The *hôtel* of the Marquis de Féline on the rue de la Ville-l'Evêque included a dining room, a *salon* and a small *salon* in 1774. In the most opulent interiors, these reception rooms housed exquisite pieces of furniture, tapestries, valuable paintings and other precious objects. The sitting room of Charles-Hugues Baillot de Villechavant, *Maître Ordinaire* of the Chambre des Comptes, who died in 1744, contained riches whose value exceeded 3000 L.

Such specialized rooms, whether dining rooms or *salons*, were indicative of changing life-styles. Yet they were still unheard of among the Parisian middle classes on the eve of the Revolution, as their presence was confined to the most luxurious abodes of the city.

Did secondary rooms, especially the types most frequently cited by the notaries, e.g. *cabinets*, wardrobes or antechambers, have clearly defined functions? Were they influenced, as were the chamber and the main room, by the eighteenth-century trend towards specialization? In the *Dictionnaire de l'Académie Française*, the *cabinet* emerges as a space reserved for work, privacy or storage: 'A withdrawn place for working or for conversing privately, or for arranging papers, books or some other thing, according to the profession or temperament of the person living there'. The *Dictionnaire de Richelet* specifies that it is a 'small withdrawn space in ordinary houses which is often not enclosed by a partition' and, along with the *Dictionnaire de Trévoux*, assigns it a further purpose, namely ensuring personal comfort: 'a secret place for the call of nature'.

'Adjoining' a chamber, or located 'beside' or 'to the back' of it, or more rarely located 'beside' a main room, the *cabinet* in these interiors appears to be a space set apart from and attached to a primary room. Its multiple uses are reflected in the descriptions made by valuers of its furnishings. The *cabinet* in the house of the magistrate Jean du Tillet was a true study, as is demonstrated by the presence of a desk, wall hangings, mirrors, paintings and books. In the home of a master tailor deceased in 1680, a small *cabinet* where the deceased had 'worked by himself' had been created in the bedchamber by installing a wooden partition. Such rooms were often furnished with specific materials appropriate to a study, including a desk or secretaire, writing table, 'table writing case' or portable writing case, reading stand, book cabinets, or shelves.

It is interesting to note that libraries, as well as offices, were exceptional in these interiors, even in the homes of priests, who were the greatest book owners. Among the most comfortable classes, a preoccupation with decor and a taste for rare and precious objects made itself felt in the *cabinet* as much as in the reception rooms. The Marquise de Traisnel kept ornaments in Saxon porcelain in her *cabinet*; Pierre Catinat, counsellor at the Parlement, collected bronze figurines there. Though not a true work space, the *cabinet* seemed in certain households to serve as a place for reflection, meditation and perhaps spiritual development, if it contained religious objects. The presence of wall hangings, curtains, a day bed or comfortable armchairs contributed to creating a refuge for relaxation and privacy within these lodgings that were otherwise open on all sides and not conducive to isolation.

This eighteenth-century desire to increase the number of rooms reserved for private use can also be seen in the appearance of the boudoir, a new type of *cabinet* intended essentially for women. According to the *Dictionnaire de Trévoux*, this term designates a 'tiny recess, a very narrow *cabinet*, near the chamber one occupies, for pouting [from the French *bouder*, hence *boudoir*] unseen when in a bad mood'. The term does not appear in the *Encyclopédie*. We found the term used at least a dozen times in inventories from the 1770s involving prestigious homes. Whether found in the home of the Marquis de Féline or of the Chevalier Seigneur de La Grange in the faubourg Saint-Honoré, these boudoirs, equipped with a fireplace or stove, lighted by a window, elegantly furnished with commodes, pedestal tables and easy chairs, and decorated with over-mantels and mirrors, had nothing in common with the recess described by the *Dictionnaire de Trévoux*; they bore more resemblance to an elegant *cabinet*.

The boudoir of Seigneur de La Grange seems to have served as a music *cabinet*, as it housed a clavichord, a guitar and two music stands. *Cabinets* were also frequently use to store away a surprising miscellany of objects: pieces of tapestry, kitchen utensils, laundry, clothes, books, family documents, dishware, food, toiletry articles and so forth. These were arranged in cupboards, chests, caskets, buffets, sideboards, commodes or on shelves. A *cabinet* might also be fixed up as a bedchamber for a child or a servant.

As discreet areas within a lodging, *cabinets* could also fulfil a function as 'comfort room', enclosing commode seats 'equipped with their earthenware pots'. We found indications of two 'comfort' *cabinets* and one 'English-style' commode *cabinet* dating from the 1760s. It was not until the second half of the eighteenth century that the presence of toilet *cabinets* or even bathing *cabinets* was indicated in some few fortunate households. We should emphasize how rare this room devoted to bodily care was: it was found in only 6.5 per cent of the interiors inventoried after 1750. Whether referred to as 'comfort' *cabinet*, toilet *cabinet*, or bathing *cabinet*, such rooms were innovations brought about by the age of the Enlightenment, and a sign of changing behaviour patterns that did not really percolate to the middle classes of the population until the industrial era. We shall discuss hygiene later when we investigate the use of water in the house. From the multi-purpose room that it was in the seventeenth century, we have already seen the *cabinet*'s tendency to become specialized during the following century as a private space intended for bodily ablutions.

Another secondary room apparently devoted to the same functions as the *cabinet* (with the exception of that of work space) was the wardrobe. Sometimes referred to as a hovel or *bouge*, a term indicating a tiny, cramped space, it served the purpose of a private space for resting or doing one's toilet, or as storage. 'Small chamber adjoining the one in which a person sleeps, which serves to put away a person's dress and clothing, or to bed valets one wishes to have close at hand during the night. In bourgeois abodes, "wardrobe" refers to a tiny chamber that accompanies a large one. "Wardrobe" also refers to a commode, a privy', explain Furetière and Trévoux's dictionaries. Though the wardrobe almost always follows a chamber, it could also be located by an adjoining room or *cabinet*. It does not always seem to have had a window incorporated, which lent it an air of being simply a recess or partitioned area and not a true room. As a storage area, it was not restricted to use as a linen closet and could do duty as junk closet, like the *cabinet*. In addition to a few personal articles, the wardrobe of a spinster who died in 1746, housed horse pistols, 11g kg of 'string and tow', and a portrait of Cardinal de Noailles. When used as a servant's room, it sometimes contained trestle beds.

The presence of a 'cleanliness chair' or bidet, equipped with their earthenware pots', a tin basin, and a syringe, were signs that the wardrobe might also have been used as a 'comfort' room or a toilet *cabinet*. However, in dwellings where this last commodity was provided for, the wardrobe could also serve exclusively as a privy; in 1755, the apartment of a spinster included a bedchamber, a kitchen, a toilet *cabinet* and a wardrobe in which a commode chair, night table and commode basin with a tin 'water bowl' were to be found. As these annexe rooms multiplied and evolved toward specialization during the Enlightenment, they contributed to the advancement of privacy. In the upper strata of Paris society, specific enclosed spaces were increasingly set aside for the basic functions of daily life.

The antechamber, another annexe room often cited by notaries, is equally worth examining in some detail. The *Dictionnaire de Trévoux* uses this term for 'a chamber that lies before the master's chamber or the main chamber of an apartment, where the servants of those who come to visit must stop'. The antechamber, found exclusively in the most opulent households, presents little in the way of furnishings to distinguish it from the main room: chairs in varying quantities, tables and occasionally even gaming tables were inventoried there. Some of these rooms are decorated in good taste, with paintings, draperies and pier glasses; others are quite bare. While in town houses with many rooms the antechamber served as a waiting room, in less spacious abodes it could be used as a main room in which the master of the house received his acquaintances to converse or for gaming at a table. This room could also function as an annexe to a main room or chamber, or as a storage space, in which case it was simply a passageway. When it preceded a main room or dining room, it might be cluttered with large pieces of furniture, such as cupboards, buffets or chests intended for keeping dishware and table linen, and often contained a little 'cistern for washing one's hands'.

Whether used as a waiting area, a meeting room or a simple entry (though this last term, like the 'chamber serving as an entry', is rare), the antechamber leading into the different rooms of the dwelling, as seen in Mme Foubert's interior, represents a clear step forward in the way habitable space was organized. From the *hôtels* of the aristocracy, the antechamber slowly made its way during the eighteenth century into the city's bourgeois apartments. Though the Marquise de Traisnel was a rare case in 1746, with three antechambers, one per story, it become increasingly common after 1750 to find such rooms in the homes of Paris merchants and the bourgeoisie. The four-story home of the haberdashery merchant and Paris bourgeois Jean Mariquet on the rue des Lavandières in the parish of Saint-Germain-l'Auxerrois, where this merchant lived with his wife, four children and a servant, was laid out in this manner in 1768. The floor plan of this house shows that the antechamber on the first floor gave access to the bedchamber, which in turn communicated with the sitting room and the work *cabinet*.

The presence of an antechamber, which allows for a better arrangement of the spaces used for daily life, often goes hand in hand with the specialization of these rooms in the same dwellings after the mid-century. It is interesting to note that in both Mme Foubert's apartment and the residence of Jean Mariquet the rooms are effectively specialized: though the house of the latter is drawn out vertically, on a very narrow lot in the traditional manner, it nonetheless presents a relatively modern internal organization for the period. The dining room is located on the ground floor next to the kitchen, while the first floor contains both spaces reserved for privacy – a bedchamber and study leading into the antechamber – and a richly furnished sitting room housing twenty-three chairs. The upper stories are taken up by the bedrooms, and each member of the family as well as the servant has his or her own room.

Another example of room specialization involving domestic space as well as professional space was the lodgings of a beverage merchant who died in 1748 in the rue Montmartre. Each of its rooms was assigned a clearly defined function, such as kitchen, laboratory, bedchamber, *salon* and toilet *cabinet*. These examples reveal that by the mid-century, the evolution towards room specialization within the upper middle class was well under way. We should note that on the eve of the Revolution, private life and professional life, at least in the case of merchants and masters of artisanal trades, were still carried on under the same roof. In some of these households, however, the desire to separate private and working spaces was apparent. One beverage merchant, who died in 1760 in the shadow of the great Halles market-place, had devoted the entire ground floor of his home to his business, and the first floor to his private life.

In none of the inventories do we find an example of room specialization as far-reaching as that of the town houses in the faubourg Saint-Honoré, as seen from the reports by building experts. Rooms intended for use by servants were distinctly set apart from the private apartments. In the example of the Hôtel de Vergès, constructed at the end of the reign of Louix XV, servants' areas were located in a semi-basement which included not only the cellars but also a kitchen, a pantry, an office, a common room, two water tanks, a washroom and a coal bin. The kitchens in such residences were always located near the dining room, which was found on the ground floor. Whenever possible, servants' rooms were not too far from the private apartments; otherwise, they were installed above common areas in the courtyard. In the Vergès town house, the room 'intended for the groom, above the stable', was provided in 1782 with 'an opening, closed by a wooden trap door, for inspection of the said stable'. The lodge for the door-keeper or watchman was installed in the passage by the carriage doorway.

The ground floor of this town house was arranged into one large apartment and several small ones: the entry vestibule 'communicates to the left with a first antechamber, then a second antechamber, also used as a dining room, lighted toward the vestibule by two bay windows closed with glazed doors ... the first antechamber communicates with a second one that serves as the entrance to the garden.' Next, the salon was divided into a dining room and a bedchamber by 'glazed doors'. This last room had two subsidiary wardrobes. The rest of the ground floor was 'cut horizontally to form small apartments laid out in the following way: from the bedchamber hereabove, one arrives in a winter *salon*', then 'a room with a fireplace' which served as a chamber, with an annexed English-style 'comfort' *cabinet* and a bathing *cabinet*. Behind it stood a room with a stove for heating baths. A stairwell led on to a mezzanine arranged in 'three adjoining rooms on the same level, and a gallery above the wardrobes of the bedchamber on the ground floor ran alongside a great stairway, which provided it with light.'

The first floor was 'arranged in such a manner as to form two apartments, a main one, composed of an antechamber, assembly *salon*, library, *cabinet*, bedchamber, chamber with closets used as a wardrobe, and an English-style "comfort" *cabinet*; the second is composed of an antechamber that leads to the right into a sitting room and to the left into a bedchamber with alcove.' The antechamber of the main apartment was shared with the second apartment, and the rooms within an apartment led into one another.

Finally, on the attic storey, there were 'eleven communicating rooms, served by a corridor leading to the courtyard' and intended for the servants, as well as a 'comfort' *cabinet*. Four other bedrooms for servants' use, including that of the groom mentioned above, occupied the mezzanine of the building composing the right wing on the courtyard. This ingenious distribution of the home's various spaces, which we could almost call avant-garde comfort, demonstrates the will to order and the desire for privacy and personal well-being that characterized the age of the Enlightenment.

Despite its elite and exceptional atmosphere, this residence in the faubourg Saint-Honoré caught our attention, and it seemed most useful to follow in the footsteps of the attested experts on their visit, because this prestigious *hôtel* actually represents something of a model. The innovations it brings in terms of interior architectural design and comfort were spreading slowly, by progressive assimilation, into the bourgeois dwellings of the city, as a small number of inventories demonstrate. Nonetheless, the energy saved in terms of movement, fatigue and constraint by an intelligent and functional arrangement of spaces within the home benefited only a privileged minority. Despite advances made in room specialization, the vast majority of Parisians on the eve of the Revolution actually had neither dining room nor *salon*, neither antechamber nor toilet *cabinet*. They continued to live in the traditional manner, in multi-purpose spaces.

How Inhabitants Left their Mark on their Homes

Generally crowded, lacking in convenience, and in many cases poorly adapted to the accomplishment of everyday tasks, these homes whose interior layout we have tried to envisage often bear the marks of installations and transformations made by their occupants. Saving a little extra space, protecting the privacy of each family member or endowing a room with a specific purpose were all motivations for the changes Parisians made in their lodgings. Such modifications made by the inhabitants are not always easy to detect through the inventory. The notary provides a *post mortem* picture that captures the interior at a given moment; therefore, a second glance at the same scene, through a contract of sale, a lease or an inventory after the death of a spouse, can be instructive, since it lets us compare impressions of the same place at two different moments. The few examples we uncovered of transformations made by Parisians in their dwellings date from the eighteenth century. Such efforts go hand in hand at that time with a growing dislike of large rooms strung together, in favour of more intimate spaces and the development of functional specialization.

The homes affected by these interior adaptations might just as well belong to small artisans as to members of the nobility. One worker in a stocking factory from the faubourg Saint-Antoine, who died in 1761, had installed a partition between two chambers, made of 'nineteen bits of board serving as a partition with a door containing six panes of glass'. Then there was the case of a day labourer who lived until his death in 1786 with his wife in a single room on the rue Saint-Germain-l'Auxerrois, and who tried to create the impression of possessing an apartment with several rooms: using partitions and wooden doors, he had produced an alcove which was divided into two small *cabinets*.

At the other end of the social ladder, major transformation work was done on the town house of the Marquis de Féline in the faubourg Saint-Honoré, as is indicated by a lease from 1772 and the inventory from 1775. One clause of the lease stipulates that 'the *cabinet* following the existing boudoir will be built on the site and place of the terrace which exists at present'; this extension of the side wing of the house was not inconsiderable, as the *cabinet* was to be 'lighted by four windows'. Within this *cabinet* was installed a 'small toilet *cabinet*' which was lighted by 'a panel of Bohemian glass'. Two and a half years later, the inventory mentions a library and a small *cabinet* on the side. The Marquis de Féline wished, in all probability, to be able to retire to a place that communicated with his chamber, or to isolate himself peacefully either to work or to read. The same occupant also had a pavilion occupied by stables at the back of the garden transformed into 'two small apartments', one of which was 'intended for lodging a painter'. Lastly the marquis also interchanged an office and a kitchen, fitted with the necessary equipment, e.g. chimneys for the smoke and a 'cesspool for waters from the kitchen'.

While modifications as extensive as those performed by the Marquis de Féline were apparently rare, most of the renovations mentioned in our documents reveal a quest for isolation, privacy, and at the same time, a specialization of the rooms. In 1717, the inventory of an office holder charged with distributing stamped paper listed several alterations made by the occupant in his dwelling: 'two partitions with pine frames and glass panes, two doors of which one had glass panes, separating the kitchen from the main room, with the partition of a small *cabinet* on the side serving as a pantry, all of which the said deceased had had done for his convenience'. This office holder had also had other partitions and doors installed in his home to separate bedchambers from one another and from an office. In the homes of several modestly housed priests, *cabinets* had been created by dividing up the initial chamber: in the home of one priest from the church of Saint-Médard who died in 1701, a *cabinet* had been created in the chamber out of two frames fitted with glass panes; a chaplain, headmaster of the Collège de Cambrai, whose chamber was inventoried in 1706, had installed 'six pine planks and a door serving as a partition'; in the home of another priest, sacristan at Saint-Martin, the notary listed in 1733 a *cabinet* 'installed in the corridor'.

Other inhabitants chose to install a sleeping space in a kitchen or shop. In the home of a wood merchant in the faubourg Saint-Antoine who died in 1767, we find a loft built over the kitchen, where the servant slept. In the lodgings of a master *traiteur* (purveyor of fine foods) in the faubourg Saint-Honoré just one room had changed between the lease agreed in 1765 and the inventory of 1769: the shopback had become a main room and had been enlarged with a loft that enclosed a simple bed, no doubt intended for a helper. A pottery merchant who died in 1785 had installed 'an alcove front in pine ... a partition closing off the alcove' in his shopback.

In some cases the uses of rooms were simply redefined without building alterations. One master marble mason in the faubourg Saint-Honoré who died in 1739 had made a chamber on the rue de la Madeleine into a 'room and kitchen' and turned one of his two *cabinets* into his own bedchamber leading on to the courtyard. The house of a squire named Jean-Baptiste Dumazelle had undergone certain changes between the lease in 1778 and the inventory done in 1782: the rental contract mentions 'rooms with fireplaces on the first, second and third stories', without any specific designation; the renter therefore made the first-floor room facing the street into his *salon* and turned the other rooms to his personal use as a chamber accompanied by a wardrobe that served as a toilet *cabinet*, and an antechamber with a bathtub. On the second floor, we found an antechamber and a servant's room. What the lease identified as a servant's room on the fourth floor had become an attic on the third according to the inventory. The entire ground floor was reserved for the preparation and consumption of food and drink, and the antechamber had been transformed into an office. Apparently changes in the assigned purpose of rooms were quite frequent in this period when specialization was in its infancy. The example of chambers, antechambers, *cabinets* and other rooms being used as kitchens has already been examined.

Private spaces were not the only ones transformed by inhabitants. Work spaces also underwent modifications according to the whims of various occupants. One pottery merchant took a lease in 1745 for four shops and lodgings in a structure with two buildings on the rue du Faubourg Saint-Honoré; he created a door between two shops, 'tore out the fireplace in the last of these shops ... and enlarged the entry door to the said last shop', in order to gain a bit more space and perhaps to serve his clientele better. As for one Jean-René Galopet, who died in 1755, this furniture maker had roofed a shed in order to shelter his merchandise. It is interesting to note, in the list of outstanding debts of his household, that he owed 372 L to a carpenter and a roofer for work done on the house he occupied in the faubourg Saint-Honoré.

Seen through these various examples, the space in which these Parisians lived appears to have been rather flexible. Aside from transforming and redesignating sites, another frequent practice we shall examine later was the use of screens and folding furniture that could be moved from one room to another as circumstances required. By personalizing their homes in different ways, the occupants managed to adapt them to their own needs and to satisfy, each in his own manner, their desires for privacy and greater comfort. We can admire their ability to adapt to their housing conditions, whatever these might have been, by skilfully arranging space or furniture to fit their life-styles. Is that not what a flair for living is all about?

Was the Parisians' interest in improving the setting in which they lived out their daily lives the sign of a quest for a stable home? After examining housing conditions, the question arises of how attached these urban residents were to their homes. The inventories provide very little information on this point. Only by looking at property titles or the successive leases for a house or a family might we find more exact data, but such research goes beyond the scope of our investigation. Certain clues support our feeling that Parisians were on the whole attached to their homes, or at least to their streets and their neighbourhoods. It was not uncommon for families of drapers, furniture makers or printers and publishers to live from one generation to the next in the same house, or at least in the same street. A survey of the addresses of children who left the parental nest shows that they settled near their parents, often in the same neighbourhood or parish, sometimes in the same street, but rarely on the opposite side of the Seine. A study of movements reveals this rootedness in a street, a neighbourhood or a part of the city. When merchants had several shops, they were all very close together. Since most of the population moved about the city on foot, the notion of distance in those times was not on the same scale as it is today.

The few changes of address mentioned by the inventories usually take place within the limited perimeter of a neighbourhood, a parish, a street, a block or even a building. This overall pattern of sedentary urban life seems to be part of a desire to preserve habits, to stay close to familiar faces and to keep a clientele. Even when a household made several moves, it was rare that the family crossed the Seine. Take the example of Seigneur de La Grange, who with his wife went through at least three homes in some twenty years of married life, all on the right bank: the rue du Mail in the parish of Saint-Eustache, the rue de Cléry in the same parish, and finally the rue de la Ville-l'Evêque. A servant in the service of the Comtesse de Nogent moved five times in twenty-four years, between 1739 and 1763, but he, too remained faithful to the right bank: at the time of his marriage, he lived in the rue de Bouchera in the Marais; two years later he was still in the Marais, on the rue Saint-Louis in the parish of Saint-Gervais; a few years thereafter, he took up residence in the rue du Temple in the parish of Saint-Roch, and ended his days in a single room that he shared with his wife in the Grande Rue du Faubourg Saint-Honoré.

It may be that recent arrivals in the capital, like one son of a labourer from Cleuze-en-Genevois, lacked relatives or friends to visit and therefore shifted more easily from one address to another, and even from one neighbourhood to another, than Parisians whose roots had been in the same parish for generations. The driving forces behind such moves were a decline in living standards and a change of status caused by the death of a spouse. Faced with financial difficulties, widows in particular, whatever their social class, were often obliged to change residences, as was Marguerite Dumont following the death of her husband, the Chevalier de La Barre, in 1727. This was also the case with the widow of a lawyer at the Parlement and in the king's council; after his death in 1733, she left a house on the rue Bourg-Tibourg in the parish of Saint-Jean-en-Grève to settle in an apartment on the nearby rue de la Verrerie.

The inventories are no more eloquent about the emotions that bound a family or an individual to a home than they are on the feelings that unite the members of a same household. But a home, inherited from parents in some cases, has been the scene of both the joyful and tragic events marking the life of a family; does it not bear traces of these memories? Consider the example of a candle merchant and bourgeois of Paris who died in 1650 in the house where his first wife and three of his children had died before him; or the home in which a master builder died in 1662, which his father had built on a lot purchased half a century earlier, in 1614, on the rue de Bretagne. Though the occupants' attachment to their homes is never stated in the inventories, the feeling of security that comes from having a roof over one's head is often expressed in other notarial documents.

One master baker was concerned, as he lay on his deathbed, that his wife be allowed to stay on in the house. This is revealed by his 1657 testament: 'wishes and orders that the said Marguerite Philippe, his wife, live and have her residence in the house where he has lived, for two years, and that she should have full use of the house during those two years'. The marriage contract of Marie Guyonnet and her second husband, Pierre Brunet, a Paris bourgeois, highlights the same, truly universal preoccupation with finding a dwelling. The contract stipulated 'that the said Brunet would have residence, as long as he might live, in the first two chambers of the house where the said Guyonnet resided'. A master locksmith was no doubt attached to the family home built in 1622 on the rue de Bretagne in the Marais, where there hung the sign of the Arbre d'Or (Tree of Gold). In any case, he bought up the shares belonging to his three brothers in 1633 and became owner of the whole building. A secretary to the king, the royal household and Crown of France and its finances worried before his death in 1648 about the way his possessions would be distributed and wondered whether 'a house and its appendages, all fully owned, which he had acquired by contract of sale dated 6 September 1622, would be divided among his children after his death according to noble or common principles'.

The relationship of these seventeenth- and eighteenth-century Parisians with their homes seems indeed quite different from that of their twentieth-century counterparts. The modern Parisian tends to evaluate his or her dwelling in practical, functional terms, taking into consideration habitable surface area, kitchen and bathroom equipment, the story, and available natural lighting. Their pre-industrial ancestors had an admirable capacity, as we have seen, to work around the flaws in their lodgings and arrange them to suit their needs. They seemed to maintain a much more personal relationship with their homes, whatever degree of comfort was available (or lacking), unlike today's city dwellers in their anonymous, fully equipped dormitory apartments, whether in a low-rent block, a luxurious skyscraper, or a turn-of-the-century bourgeois monument.

As the setting for domestic life, these homes also housed professional activity and bore witness to life's milestones from birth to death. The abodes of these Parisians were not a closed, isolated world: they were open to the outside and could not be dissociated from the life of the street and the parish. Daily life in those days tended to spill over into the street through all sorts of relations with neighours, clients, merchants and tradesmen.

Close bonds were also created within a parish: great ceremonies, baptisms, marriages and funerals brought together the whole community. Mass on Sunday, and even every day for the devout, religious holidays, and processions united parish members in their faith, and brotherhoods or factory workers' assemblies did the same. Solid bonds were created in this way among individuals, who became as firmly rooted in their neighbourhoods as they would have been in a village. The warmth of households, which we are trying to rediscover in visiting these many hearths, was reflected in the warmth of the street and the parish.

4

Daily Actions in the Privacy of the Home

As we accompany the notaries through these dwellings, we discover an astonishingly rich world of objects: a varied, multiform universe that could be heterogeneous and even picturesque. This inert, frozen world in these houses stricken by death is also a fascinating place for historians, because it brings us to the very heart of the daily life of these Parisians. Aside from silverware, jewels and linen, which were most often inventoried separately, this plethora of objects of all sorts, composing the backdrop of their private life, was most often listed by the valuers room by room, as they found things. These objects were the silent witnesses to the occupants' daily actions, and to the joys and sorrows that weave the fabric of every existence. Utilitarian as they are, these objects represent the most humble, concrete and familiar actions repeated day in and day out by the inhabitants of these households.

The everyday objects that we shall analyse here, bound up in such elementary and primordial functions as sleeping, eating, relating to others, storing, or working with one's hands, are palpable artefacts of a material culture that has been lost to us and that we shall try to revive here. They have an unrivalled ability to call forth the secrets of the private life of our forebears. Though basically utilitarian, their value was not exclusively material for their owners; they might also hold memories – of a loved one, of a blessed event, of a milestone in life. It should be remembered that the society of that period had a deep respect for things and was much less eager than we are today to get rid of used, broken or outdated objects. Throughout this study of life-styles, this sensitivity towards things should be borne in mind. We shall become more aware of it as we become more intimately acquainted with these households.

Sleeping

Like a house within the house, the bed was one of two focal points in the home, along with the fireplace. A space most often closed off by curtains, it was not only a refuge for sleeping and resting, but also a stronghold against cold in these poorly heated, draughty rooms. It was also a refuge for marital intimacy within these interiors where overcrowding and lack of privacy in single rooms were the lot of many families. In an age when each individual's life began and ended surrounded by loved ones, the bed was the site of births and deaths. Having witnessed both joyful and painful events in the household, it takes us to the heart of the family's private life.

It is not only an object for comfort, as we consider it today, but a source of prestige, endowed with a symbolic and sentimental value. It is a prized piece of furniture, whose importance in the household can be traced as far back as the Roman empire. Its importance is corroborated in the inventories after death by the length and detail of the valuers' descriptions: on average, seven to seventeen lines are devoted to this item, including indications about its components, from the wood to the pillows, from the horsehair *sommier* or base to the curtains and the frame, not to mention the colour of the bedspread or the materials of which the base, the mattress, the counterpane, pillows or bolster were made.

Generally placed facing the window, and increasingly rarely in an alcove or a niche, the bed was usually the first item the valuers inventoried in a room. Present in all dwellings, it was most often to be found in the chamber, though it also showed up, as we shall see, in main rooms, *cabinets*, lofts, and even in kitchens or shops, and could be fitted into tight and unexpected quarters such as a partitioned corner, a corridor or under a stairway. The notaries naturally focused most attention on the bed of the deceased, that of the master or mistress of the household. The importance of the bed in this society is also demonstrated by the rich vocabulary used to designate its various models. We recorded some thirty specific terms for bed types (Appendix 1).

What sorts of beds filled these Parisian abodes? As far as terminology is concerned, we should specify that in addition to the meaning we now know, the term *lit* or 'bed' also meant a type of mattress made of down enclosed in ticking. The terms 'couch' or *couchette*, generally designating the wooden bed frame, were commonplace in bed inventories. The term *chalit*, however, with the same meaning, was outdated and was scarcely ever used by seventeenth- and eighteenth-century notaries.

We established one category for beds with bed curtains. Among them, the most common were couches with high or low posts. Working from a survey covering some 3000 beds described in detail, including main beds as well as secondary or day beds, we estimated that beds hung with bed curtains accounted for 72.5 per cent of the total, and those with high or low posts for 63 per cent (19 per cent for high posts and 44 per cent for low posts). The difference between these two models seems to lie in the length of the posts, also called columns or distaffs (*quenouilles*). Couches with high posts were more frequent in the seventeenth century and in the early years of the eighteenth, but they began losing ground in the 1730s to low posts. The complexity, richness and diversity of the component elements is bound to surprise the modern observer, who is accustomed to very simple beds.

The components of post beds were described minutely by the valuers. A fully dressed couch included an *enfonçure*, i.e. a structure of small laths and webbing, occasionally a horsehair base mattress covered in grey cloth, a straw mattress and one or more other mattresses, a bed (in the sense of ticking mattress), a bolster, one or two pillows, one or more covers, a foot warmer in certain cases, and a bedspread made of quilted cloth padded with wool or cotton. The valance or hangings for the bed also comprised several elements: *bonnes grâces* or narrow curtains hanging the length of the posts; a canopy or tester, panels or bands of cloth arranged horizontally around the tester to hide the curtain rods, which might be single or double; a backboard or piece of cloth placed vertically behind the bedhead; a duster or ruffle around the lower part of the bed; and lastly, curtains going around the whole bed. These ran on curtain rods or were draped: in the latter case they were fixed and could be looped and held with a tieback. These *lits en housse* or hung beds, which figured in the period engravings of Abraham Bosse in particular, were very fashionable around the 1670s.

It should be noted that not all our Parisians had beds as fully dressed, though most of them were closed. This astonishing accumulation of layers on the bed frame, this profusion of cloth and curtains composing the valance actually could be said to turn our ancestors' couches into veritable fortresses: fortresses against the cold and against draughts, thanks to the protective envelope made by the drapes; a fortress, too, against indiscreet eyes, thanks to the heavy, thick curtains that made up the valance. A safe refuge and a warm and downy nest in which to dream, the closed space of the bed appears to have been a sort of inner sanctuary within the house: in the words of the French philosopher Gaston Bachelard, it was the image of a great cradle or a maternal universe.[1]

Other couch models inventoried by the notaries, also dressed with curtains, included variants on these post beds. Distinctions between various types were often based on dimensions, or the shape of the posts, the tester, or the draperies. We found mentions of *bâtard* beds in the seventeenth century: as the term *bâtard* (in the sense of 'hybrid') suggests, these were *couchettes* with curtains, dressed like a large bed, but on a smaller scale. A few twin beds, a novelty of the early eighteenth century, were also noted by the valuers. We should also mention *couchettes* with low posts on castors, which were easy to move from room to room.

So-called column beds or turned post beds, also called 'antique', had rounded and fluted uprights, while beds with high or low posts generally had square or bevelled posts and were almost always without decoration. These beds with columns, like the common models with posts, appeared in the sixteenth century. The bed *en tombeau* (literally 'tomb-shaped') was also very much in vogue by the first decade of the eighteenth century, as were commodes and secretaires bearing the same name. These beds had posts of different heights and a tester which, instead of having a flat frame, slanted down at a sharp angle. Another post model, the bed *à l'impériale*, had been widespread in France since the sixteenth century and remained so until the end of the reign of Louis XVI: a dome-shaped pavilion, it was reminiscent of the profile of an imperial crown. Introduced under Louis XIV, the 'duchess' bed was surmounted with a dais including a sloping ceiling and curtains reaching the bottom of the bed, but since it had no posts at the foot of the bed, it was not closed.

In the second half of the eighteenth century a surprisingly wide variety of models appeared. Elegant and expensive, they were highly coveted among the well-to-do classes of the capital. The inventories attest to their presence in the finest interiors. The so-called Polish bed, which appeared in the time of Queen Marie Leszczynska, had three bedheads and four columns with a four-faceted dome. A variant on this model was the Turkish bed with three arched bedheads, considered very fashionable between 1755 and 1785. Finally, we included in this category two other types of couches encountered in the inventories: the Italian bed, a type of Imperial bed, and the Roman or canopy bed, placed against a wall, with the *couchette* sideways and the tester presented not by the small end, but by its widest side.

We grouped secondary beds into a second category, representing 23 per cent of the total. These were beds counted in addition to the bed of the master or mistress of the house and were usually intended for children, servants or visiting guests. They were simpler than those mentioned above and had no curtains. Like other child-rearing articles, children's beds, often called little *couchettes*, cradles, or wicker baskets, were mentioned only rarely by the notaries. We noted the presence of a 'child's bed with high posts, dressed with a straw mattress, a white wool blanket, two small pillows, stuffed with down, with a valance' in the home of king's counsellor Simon Plastrier in 1642.

Beds without posts often become simple couches under the notary's pen, or dressed couches described in no further detail. It is interesting to note the profusion of folding and portable beds which could, according to the circumstances or the time of day, be moved from one corner of an unspecialized room to another. Most common were trestle beds, also called *baudets* or sawhorse beds, with a portable folding frame supported by trestles along the length of the bed. These were also referred to in the seventeenth century as collapsible beds. We also noted the presence of camp beds 'whose legs and posts may be folded or removed', according to the *Dictionnaire de l'Académie Française* of 1694, 'so that the wooden frame may be made into a small package when one wants to transport it'. As for servants, some had to make do with simple straw mattresses without any frame.

The third category of beds established for our study includes models that could serve for both sleeping and sitting; these account for only 4.5 per cent of the whole. These are day beds or low beds, without curtains or a frame, placed in a chamber or cabinet for resting. In the same group are sitting room beds. A few benches for sleeping are mentioned in seventeenth-century inventories. In the 1740s and 1750s two new types of day beds began to appear: beds with two backrests, curving out slightly at each end, and the so-called English bed, with three backrests, a forerunner of the sofa.[2]

A precious source of information on the main types of beds from this period, the inventories also tell us about the varieties of wood as well as the fabrics and colours used in bedding. The wood types mentioned most frequently are walnut, beech and oak. Walnut was by far the most common, used to produce more than 50 per cent of these beds. Other varieties listed include pine, alder and varnished and unvarnished, painted or blackened wood. Curtains and drapes were made of a range of fabrics: we counted at least fifteen different types, with a certain predominance of serge, a woollen material widely used for furniture. The most common colour for this material was green, though red, especially crimson in wealthy interiors, was highly prized in the seventeenth century and persisted into the eighteenth, alongside less frequent hues including blue, yellow, brown, grey, purple and white. Other more prestigious, or in any case more luxurious fabrics noted by the valuers were blue and white leaf-print *indiennes* or calicoes, whose large patterns were used for bedspreads; oriental cotton silks with multicoloured stripes for the posts and the curtains; Abbeville damask with flower prints and striped Caux damask for the dais and the curtains; satin for mattress covers or the canopy; brocatelle in yarn and wool with delicate patterns for curtains; not to mention the silks, taffetas and other fabrics in flowered or leaf-printed cotton.

Whether discreet or luxuriant, these cloths, often embellished with braid, furbelows or fringes with bright and unusual colours, provided elegant trimmings for post beds. The descriptions made by the valuers highlight the importance attached to decorating the bed, especially in the eighteenth century. Here are a few examples: a *couchette* with low posts and 'two large curtains, two *bonnes grâces* curtains, a sloping backrest, a large bedstead and three bases, all in green serge bordered and trimmed with a green silk ribbon'; a *couchette* with low posts and draped curtains 'in green serge, including a backrest, a square tester with curtain rods, large and small sloping canopy draperies, two curtains, two *bonnes grâces*, three braids in the same serge, a courtesan in Milan lemon'; 'a low-post bed, duchess-style, with backrest and imperial in white flowered satin, drapes and curtains in green serge, counterpane in blue flowered calico with white satin bands'; a valance for a high-post bed 'with drapes and curtains in red serge, trimmed with silk fringes and trim'; 'a low-post couch ... duchess-style, curtains, *bonnes grâces*, drapes in red damask, imperial, two backrests in red taffeta embroidered in gold and silver, bedcover in calico'; a *tombeau*-style *couchette* with fixed curtains 'in Turkish blue serge, consisting of two curtains, two *bonnes grâces*, and a tester trimmed with lemon yellow braid'.

The English traveller Martin Lister visiting Paris in 1698 could not help admiring the 'crimson damask and velvet beds or of gold silver tissue'.[3] The covers on these beds were often embellished with fine ornament: we noted sky-blue silk braid on blue backgrounds, a cover in scarlet serge bordered and trimmed with white silk ribbons, a spread 'in daffodil cotton silk', another in chamois-coloured satin embroidered in gold, a tester in apricot taffeta with draperies in blue damask, a spread in crimson damask decorated with false gold braid and yellow silk cord. The rich variety of this palette, with its matching or contrasting colours, is admirable; imagine how they brightened up these dark homes with their vibrant or pastel tones. In the most refined homes, the colours harmonized with those of the chairs, the window curtains and the wall hangings, as well shall see later when discussing decoration.

Equally detailed were the descriptions of actual bed linen. The mattresses, covered with blue and white checked or striped cotton, *toile* or canvas from Montbéliard or Flanders, fustian or damask, were stuffed with wool or cotton wadding. The bolsters and pillows are always indicated to be 'in tick, stuffed with down'. Blankets were for the most part in white wool, only rarely in green or red. Other materials were used for additional covers: cotton, canvas, taffeta, flannel or ratteen. The colours, however, did not vary much: white, green, yellow, blue, and a few flower prints. Foot warmers, more of a rarity, were made of cotton, especially with flower prints in quilted cotton, satin or taffeta.

Floor-length bedspreads were made in cotton, canvas, serge, taffeta, brocatelle, damask or satin, more rarely in silk or in *calamande*. The colours tended to be bright, with a great many flowered prints, though they did not necessarily match the other covers. But harmony and contrast seemed to be most sought after between the curtains and the bedspread. Draperies in green serge might be combined with bedspreads in white or yellow canvas, or in flowered cotton; yellow silk might be matched with checked canvas, or blue serge with brown canvas.

As for the sheets, these were rarely inventoried with the beds, since they were examined at the same time as the household linen. No matter what the deceased's social class, they are often described as 'worn and threadbare', 'poor', 'in very bad shape', 'patched', 'having changed *lés*' (the *lé* was the width of a cloth from one selvage to the other) and even 'almost unsuitable for use'. Sheets might be made of household cotton, yellow cotton, canvas, common cotton, or cloth from Cretonne or Alençon. Masters' sheets were indicated as distinct from servants' linen. Their dimensions were rarely given, and children's sheets were almost never mentioned. The sale value of a sheet was usually high, varying from 10 to 50 L, depending on its condition, the type of cloth and the size. Pillowcases, also estimated with the household linen, were made of white cotton or checked or striped muslin. It should be noted that sheets were used as bolster covers, and occasionally the valuers took note that sheets and pillowcases had just returned from being washed or 'from the washerwoman'.

The inventories are not as prolix about the sizes of beds as about their components. Indications such as 'large couch', 'small *couchette*', '*bâtard* bed' or twin beds are much more common than actual dimensions. The few measurements we found involved low-post beds. The most common type was apparently either 1.14 or 1.3 metres wide and could sleep two persons. Single beds were 82 or 98 centimetres wide. The length was rarely given, though these beds were apparently shorter than modern beds, as our ancestors were shorter than us as a rule.

That mention was made in certain interiors of a stepstool with two or three steps to make it easier to climb into the bed leads us to think that the accumulation of mattresses, feather beds and covers during this period was much higher than we are accustomed to. It is interesting in that respect to read the words of an English traveller of the Cullum de Hardwick family, visiting Paris in August 1782 from Suffolk:

Beds are raised to a very inconvenient height, so that even the longest legs must use a chair; one must literally climb into bed, not that the beds themselves are so remarkably high, but they are so loaded: just under you, there is a mattress, then a thin feather bed, then another mattress, and at the very bottom, a coarse litter or sack stuffed with straw. These beds have all the disadvantages that can be produced by the sweet warmth of summer and the total negligence of their owners. Without the greatest care, the sheets are always damp: nonetheless, I must do justice to the French and recognize that they are generally cleanly, both with their beds and their table linen.[4]

Assessments made by the valuers of these beds varied considerably, even among beds of the same type, such as high- or low-post *couchettes*. The price range is very broad: from a few livres for a trestle bed to 1000 L or more for the most luxurious pieces. The value of beds with curtains tended to hover between 50 and 300 L, averaging around 100 L. Low-post beds were more expensive than high-post ones. The assessment made generally depended on their condition, on the type of wood used, and above all on the quality of the valance. Almost always the most expensive piece of furniture in the home, the bed was often the only article of value in modest households, and appears indeed to have been the poor man's luxury.

The more modest a household's income was, the more significant the investment represented by the bed. It could amount to half or more of the value of the inventoried property, as two examples suffice to show: the low-post couch of a chamber valet to the lieutenant general of the king's armies, described as 'of walnut, dressed with a frame, straw mattress, horsehair litter and a bolster in ticking stuffed with down, a wool mattress, blanket in white wool, the draperies of the said bed in green serge, with backrest and bedstead, bedspread in quilted taffeta, duster with furbelow, canopy and curtains', was valued at 400 L in 1699, while the total fortune amounted to just 811 L. A spinster, whose estate was worth only 55 L in 1770, possessed a *couchette* with low posts valued with its trimmings at 30 L, or 60 per cent of her net estate. These may of course be exceptional examples, but it was not uncommon to see a bed account for 15–30 per cent of the value of the possessions in a home, as was the case with most day labourers or floor polishers. One day labourer in the Customs left 963 L at his death in 1721, including a bed valued at 200 L with draperies in blue serge and a red quilted bedspread, backed in green.

The bed was commonly an important piece of property in the poorer classes, whatever the deceased person's trade might have been. There are abundant examples: the inventory compiled after the death of a journeyman cabinetmaker mentions a *couchette* whose value of 80 L represented a quarter of his total assets. The bed of a sergeant in the regiment of the *Gardes françaises* in the faubourg Saint-Marcel was estimated at 150 L in 1755, while the total worth of his belongings was 571 L. A shoemaker's assistant and his wife living in a single room in the 1770s owned a '*couchette* with low posts, dressed with its frame bars, a straw mattress in canvas, three mattresses in wool wadding covered with checked cloth, a bed, a bolster, two pillows in tick stuffed with down, a bedspread, a foot warmer in quilted calico, green serge drapes trimmed with silk braid', which was valued altogether at the sum of 180 L, or one quarter of their fortune.

In the most impoverished households, the master of the house had to make do with a very simple bed, whose value might be less than 20 L. The bed of a stocking manufacture worker's widow in the faubourg Saint-Antoine was described in 1762 as 'a *couchette* with low posts, a bed and bolster, a small wool mattress, an old blanket, two old curtains in green serge going around the bed' and was valued at 15 L; humble though it was, it nonetheless represented one-third of their possessions' worth of 45 L. The bed of an innkeeper was valued at just 20 L, or one-quarter of his assets at the time of his death in 1754. A modest painter whose belongings had a total value of 35 L owned 'a bed with low posts, dressed with its frame, a straw mattress, bolster in tick stuffed with down, a counterpane in old

green taffeta, the backrest of said bed in gilded, sculpted wood, a small mattress
˅ered with white cotton and stuffed with wadding, valued at 4 L'. The wife of a
ᶠloor polisher, who at her death in 1751 left only 31 L in assets, had slept
⸝ husband and a young child in a '*couchette* with low posts, dressed with
ᴴattresses, an old wadding mattress, a bolster, two old blankets, one in
˅rtains in checked cloth, the whole valued at 3 L'.
⸝eased individuals possessed the most luxurious beds, valued at
⸝   ˅verage. In the home of Louis Gervais, a master surgeon, the
valᵤ   ˅o twin beds in 1772 'composed each of a low-poster
coucheₓ   and a trestled bottom, formed of a leather mattress,
dressed witₕ   ⸝ mattresses, a bed, a bolster, a feather pillow and imperial-
style draperies composed of the backrest and canopies', and estimated their value
at 1000 L. A Polish-style bed, estimated at 1200 L, appeared in 1775 in the
inventory of Seigneur de La Grange. Another resident of the faubourg Saint-
Honoré, the wealthy Marquis de Féline, who died in 1774, owned 'a Turkish-
style *couchette* with four columns' with 'wooden castors' and a 'complete set of
draperies in three colours of damask', also valued at 1200 L. A similar type of bed
in gilded wood belonging to a squire and counsellor to the king in 1772 was
estimated at the considerable sum of 2000 L, yet its value represented less than 6
per cent of the total value of the estate.

While the most impoverished Parisians slept in humble beds and the most
well-to-do in sumptuous ones, as these last examples demonstrate, the bed nevertheless does not appear to be a generally good indicator of degrees of wealth,
except at the two extremes of the social scale. Investments in this area were not
always proportionate to the value of estates, and the ratio tended to decline as the
estate's overall value increased. It was not uncommon to find beds of comparable
worth in the households of modest master artisans or even valets and in the
homes of rich merchants or lawyers. But at every social level, the bed occupied a
primary place in the home, not only in physical terms but from a psychological
point of view as well.

The bed, highly coveted at the time of death, might be dealt with specifically
in a testament, as a recompense for the devotion of a neighbour or a servant, or as
a simple gesture of friendship. In 1730, Jean Desmoulins, the curé at Saint-
Jacques-du-Haut-Pas, willed 'to Noël Le Blond, his servant for the last twenty or
so years, the bed in which he [the servant] sleeps, the two blankets on said bed
and its draperies, with two pairs of sheets used on said bed'. This priest's gesture,
singling out one of his three servants, was an act of trust and a sign of gratitude
and indeed friendship which was still full of meaning in the eighteenth century.

One last question about beds: in what conditions did people sleep? Did each
Parisian have his or her own couch in the seventeenth and eighteenth centuries?
The question is an awkward one, because our documents remain vague about the
number of persons occupying a given dwelling. With the exception of a few servant's inventories in which no bed was mentioned since it would have belonged
to the master, these documents indicate the presence of at least one bed in every
home, and on average two or three per household. Some students have attempted
to compare the number of beds and the number of inhabitants and have
calculated the rate of bed use. The figure is generally low, especially since

couples usually shared the same bed: it was 1.25 persons per bed in the parish of Saint-Nicolas-des-Champs in the 1640s, in the parish of Saint-Jean-en-Grève during the reign of Louis XIV and in the households of musicians or singers in the eighteenth century; 1.4 in the faubourg Saint-Antoine in the 1760s, and just one person per bed in the homes of beverage sellers.

It would seem therefore that in the second half of the eighteenth century, everyone had a bed, at least in the relatively comfortable categories of the Paris population. Averages, however, have a way of masking reality, and in many abodes the comparison between the number of beds and the number of inhabitants is troubling, as the number of beds does not correspond to the number of occupants. On the subject of couples, it should be noted that in the grandest families of the nobility, the masters of the house had not only their own beds, but also their own chambers, as their social condition required: 'Monsieur's room' was separate from 'Madame's room'.

As for the children, they often slept two to a bed in the seventeenth century, or more rarely in threes, even in families not afflicted by poverty. In the home of one master hatter, a Paris bourgeois who at the time of his death in 1663 owned and occupied a house which he had purchased for the sum of 10,000 L, the bedroom contained just one high-post and one low-post bed; yet the artisan and his wife had three daughters, then aged fourteen, eleven and seven. In the home of Pierre Messière, a master builder living with his wife and six children at the time of his death in 1662, the valuers counted four beds for eight people, including one high-post bed in the deceased's chamber, one low-post bed in the tiny adjoining room, one high-post bed in a chamber used as a kitchen on the floor above, and one small couch in the hovel adjacent to that room. Here again, Pierre Messière was owner of the house he occupied, and he rented out some of the rooms. Though children in the wealthiest families all had their own beds, they nevertheless shared the same room. This was the case, for example, with the grown-up sons, aged nineteen and seventeen, of Jacques Galland, *Secrétaire Ordinaire* to the Council of State and Direction des Finances, who died in 1654. As for young children, in that period they sometimes shared their parents' bed, despite the repeated warnings from clerics about the danger of their being smothered to death. When they were older, children often slept in collapsible beds.

With the progress made in comfort during the eighteenth century, crowding in beds became more uncommon. In large families of modest means, the bed was not always necessarily an island of privacy. A few examples illustrate this point: in the home of a day labourer who died in 1740, six persons, including four children, shared three beds, one of which was completely dressed. The lodgings of another day labourer's widow, who was bringing up seven children between the ages of six and fifteen, contained only two beds in 1744; only one of these had full bed curtains. In 1761, the valuers in the home of another day labourer mention just two *couchettes* for six people, including four children. The situation of the musician Jean-Georges Bruner in 1775 was even more uncomfortable. His household, consisting of the couple and three young children, owned only one bed. As it was still quite common at the time to put young children out to nurse, we wonder in some cases whether the parents lived with their offspring or not. In practice, individual beds were becoming more and more commonplace in Paris by the 1770s. In the parishes of Saint-Etienne-du-Mont and Saint-Nicolas-du-Chardonnet, 61 per cent of the households were furnished in this manner between 1770 and 1773. In the home of a humble mattress carder living with his wife and three children in the rue de la Montagne-Sainte-Geneviève in 1770, everyone had his or her own bed.

In the wealthiest homes, valuers sometimes discovered a plethora of beds, whose number had no relationship with the number of occupants. The University of Paris's messenger to Reims possessed twenty-five beds for ten people in 1639. In the home of Marin Marais, *Ordinaire* for the king's chamber music, there were ten beds for two inhabitants. For Louis Guersan, master lute maker for Monseigneur le Dauphin, and his wife, there were six beds. Were these the beds of children who had grown up and left home, or were they intended to accommodate relatives and guests?

It was not surprising, of course, to find such a collection of beds in the estates of hotel- and innkeepers, wine merchants or beverage sellers, who offered overnight hospitality on a more or less regular basis. On the first floor of the inn run in 1751 by Denis Rousseau and Anne Bauquin on the rue de Reuilly, two chambers were fitted out with eleven beds: these were simple *couchettes* with a straw mattress, a feather bed, a blanket and a bolster. In 1733 at the Croix Blanche hostelry in the faubourg Saint-Martin there were several beds lined up in the same room, but at least half of them were dressed with serge curtains. Among the eleven furnished rooms rented out by Jean Costeroust in the rue de la Grande Friperie, only two provided their clients with a low-post *couchette* having green or white serge curtains; the others contained only simple *couchettes* with straw mattresses, a second mattress, a cover and a bolster. The inventory of a beverage seller's wife who died in 1765 mentions nine beds, each decorated differently, with bedcovers in yellow or green serge or blue or white *siamois* or even calico. Another beverage seller owned eighteen beds in 1784, and he too almost certainly took in boarders.

With the exception of the most luxurious hotels in the city or the faubourg Saint-Germain-des-Prés, or in the Palais Royal quarter during later years, inns of the period almost never offered private rooms to their clients. This lack of privacy was corroborated by the comments of several foreign visitors in the seventeenth century and even early in the next century, who were lodged in rooms with several beds. Despite improvements in housing conditions during the Enlightenment, the habit of sharing bedrooms persisted in Parisian hotels into the early nineteenth century. English visitors at the time found this shocking. An English traveller set down his thoughts about two trips made in France in 1814 and 1816 in *The Gentleman's Guide in his Tour through France*: 'It is of the greatest importance for a traveller to have a bed to himself, and a bedchamber, if he can; as it is common practice all over the continent to put three or four beds in a room, he cannot be too much upon his guard against becoming the dupe of a bed-fellow.'[5]

The increasing use of both individual beds and individual bedchambers toward the end of the eighteenth century signified tremendous gains in privacy and comfort. The dissemination of high- and low-post beds that could be enclosed by curtains marked the beginning of this evolution. As the idea of privacy itself settled permanently into attitudes and habits, and as heating conditions improved with the widespread use of stoves, beds could be simplified and stripped of their curtains. By the same token, however, they lost their status as a refuge – and a part of their prestige as well.

Preparing Meals

The place where meals were prepared – whether in a kitchen, a room used as such, or a common room – was the realm of the mistress of the house or her servant, and was always centered around the hearth. Like the bed, the fireplace was a focal point at the very heart of the household. It was not only a source of warmth and light but was also the primary space for cooking food. Because it was incorporated into the masonry of the house, it was not counted among the deceased person's inventoried belongings. But its presence is suggested by mentions of fire tools such as andirons, shovels and tongs, which were usually the first items valued in a room. A whole series of articles necessary for cooking tasks were clustered around the hearth or nearby. Some were used for cooking food, others for containing it.

Andirons were used to hold logs in place and improve their combustion by raising them off the hearth floor. They came in several models intended to bear spits. The *hâtier*, mentioned in several inventories, is a large andiron with hooks on which the roasting spits could be placed. It was generally crowned by a sort of metal basket used to heat platters and cauldrons. The *landier*, also equipped with hooks, was often confused with the *hâtier* and might be designated in inventories as 'andirons for turning spits' or 'notched andirons'. *Contre-rostiers* or *contre-hastiers*, which were large andirons with several studs for holding the spits, seem to have become rare after the 1650s. The spit, a long metal rod pointed at one end, was used to present the various sides of the roasting meat to the fire. The most common model was the hand spit or roasting spit held above the fire by the notches on the *landiers* and turned by hand. A famous engraving of 1667 by Stella, entitled *La veillée à la ferme pendant l'hiver* (Evening at the farm in winter), shows a young boy turning a spit bearing a roast set on the *hâtiers*. Meanwhile his mother, seated on the ground next to him, changes the baby, and the other family members tend to their chores.

The wheeled spit or pulley spit (*broche à noix ou à poulie*) was part of a roasting jack described by valuers as 'a roasting jack with crank, equipped with chains and cords having stone weights' or 'a roasting jack with cords, counterweights, and stones'. This was a more sophisticated machine that represented a clear improvement on the simple spit, as it made hand turning unnecessary and offered a more regular rotation, thanks to its mechanism. It became more widespread during the seventeenth century but was rarely to be found outside the most wealthy households. A companion piece to the roasting jack was the dripping pan in iron or yellow copper, which was placed under the spit to capture the juices and grease from the meats as they cooked.

The trammel, a traditional symbol of the hearth, hung on a bracket or ring with notches or teeth, embedded in the chimney wall. It was used to hang pots by their handles over the fire. The types of pots found there might include the omnipresent 'red copper kettle with its cover', the cauldrons 'in different sizes' used for cooking (or in the case of the 'dishwashing cauldron', for heating wash water), or the large cauldron called *coquemar*, or the teapot. To pick up these vessels hanging on the trammel without getting burned, a sort of iron handle or hook called the 'iron hand' was used. But the trammel was in declining use during the eighteenth century, especially by the 1770s. Only 30 per cent of the households of the parish of Saint-Etienne-du-Mont were equipped with one between 1761 and 1770; 28 per cent of those in the parish of Saint-Eustache between 1770 and 1772; 19 per cent of the inhabitants of the neighbourhood around the Place Maubert in the same period; 17.5 per cent of the members of the parish of Saint-Germain-l'Auxerrois between 1768 and 1790; and only 13.5 per cent of those in the parish of Saint-Paul between 1770 and 1774.

While some 50 per cent of the humble households in the faubourg Saint-Antoine still had trammels between 1760 and 1762, these items had almost entirely disappeared from the homes of beverage sellers, as only three inventories out of sixty-two mention a trammel. More and more, it was replaced by the *trépied* or trivet, comprising an iron ring sitting on three legs, on which kettles, cauldrons, and frying pans could be set. Towards the 1770s, 43 per cent of the households in the parish of Saint-Eustache, nearly 50 per cent of those located in the parish of Saint-Germain-l'Auxerrois, 71 per cent of the inhabitants of the faubourg Saint-Antoine, 73 per cent of Saint-Etienne-du-Mont and Saint-Nicolas-du-Chardonnet parish members, and 79 per cent of those from Saint-Paul owned a trivet. A variant of this article, called a *chevrette* or tripod, was used to hold pots directly over the coals. Another age-old cooking tool in the hearth was the grill, to be found in most interiors, however humble they might be.

A tremendous variety of kitchen utensils were to be found sitting on the hearth floor, hanging from nails under the chimney mantel, or placed on shelves nearby. Both their abundance and the differentiation in their uses are striking, even in relatively modest households. Aside from the cooking tools named above, the most common elements in the kitchen arsenal included pots of various shapes and sizes. Some were round, others had straight handles; but these were not as widely used as cauldrons or pans (*poêles*). The latter were omnipresent and were allotted to distinct uses: omelette pans, chestnut pans, jam, syrup or sauce pans. The most common of them were the 'fire pans' or 'frying pans'. The *poêlon* or casserole, also widely used, was a small pan with very high edges and a short handle.

Other utensils found in many kitchens can essentially be characterized by their diversity, as a list of the various types of spoons shows: there are eating spoons, stew, pot and casserole spoons, fat-skimming and boiling spoons, jam, tea and soup spoons. These inventories of kitchenware present all sorts of items: pot lids, tongs for pulling fried food out of the pan, skimmers, sieves, cleavers, choppers, large kitchen knives, mortars for grinding salt and spices, pestles, funnels, scales and so forth. To this collection could be added other less frequent and more specialized articles that were hallmarks of the comfortable life-style reserved for very well furnished kitchens. To name just a few examples, there were fish kettles, pie pans, capon pots, waffle irons, fruit cooking cloches, stewing or braising pots, and concave lids that held coals or boiling water in order to steam food between two heat sources – not to mention the *hugueonote*, a sort of thick, well-sealed kettle used by Protestants to cook their meat on fast days, so that no odours would give them away to their the neighbours.

Just as the shapes and uses of these items differed, so did the materials they were made in. From the instruments owned by these inhabitants, it becomes possible to trace an entire hierarchy which reveals their life-style and their degree of wealth. Indispensable tools were generally made of iron, and the kitchen arsenal of the poor was almost entirely in this metal, which was less expensive than copper. Articles in brass were not, however, entirely absent from these homes. Copper was actually used to make a great many household objects. In servants' homes during the reign of Louis XIV, fire-tending tools such as andirons, shovels, tongs and grills, as well as the trivet, stove, spit and dripping pan, were all in iron, but sieves, *poêlons*, skimmers, cauldrons and kettles were most often in yellow copper. The total value of articles in iron rarely exceeded 2 or 3 L in these households, and that of utensils in copper varied between 2 and 10 L depending on how many there were. Some andirons had copper knobs, and their value increased in consequence: from 30 sols (20 sols = 1 livre) if they were entirely in iron, their value could reach 5 L per pair with 'knobs and trimmings in yellow copper'.

The kitchen equipment of humble artisans at the beginning of the eighteenth century usually consisted of three or four iron utensils and five or six cauldrons and kettles or casseroles in copper. Brass articles became more expensive during the course of the century, and tended to disappear from poorer households, where they were replaced predominantly by iron. In the homes of day labourers after the 1750s, iron utensils were more frequent than those in copper.

Though the basic tools in any kitchen arsenal remain the same from the most humble household to the most opulent, the number and diversity of instruments increase from one rung of the social ladder to the next. Given the tendency towards accumulation that characterized the eighteenth century, the finest kitchens sometimes contained an impressive collection of copper, in yellow metal or in more costly red copper. This was the case of Seigneur de La Grange, coun-sellor to the Cour des Aides (court with final authority in tax cases), whose home in the faubourg Saint-Honoré was inventoried in 1775: twenty-five casseroles, seventeen lids, two round casseroles and one oval one, four *tourtières* or pie pans, one jam pan, seven kettles with lids, one braising pan with cover, one fish kettle, two pot spoons, one skimmer, three fat skimming spoons, one *coquemar* (a large kettle with handle) and a wash kettle, all in red copper, were valued at 222 L. Imagine those shining copper pots, with their warm, bright colours, lining the walls on both sides of the high fireplace in the exceptionally fine kitchen which was the realm of the chef, Jean-Baptiste Marchand.

More representative of the average household, the copper kitchen arsenal of a wine merchant in 1765 included three cauldrons, two *poêlons*, a sieve, a boiling kettle and a skimmer, valued together at 40 L. In addition to a kettle, a haber-dashery merchant in 1770 owned two frying pans and three iron lids, one large and one small cauldron, one large and one small *poêlon*, a skimmer and one large and one small saucepan, all in copper.

Reading accounts of these many domestic objects placed around the fireplace allows us to reconstruct the housewife's daily actions as she worked to prepare meals. As she knelt, squatted or sat on a low chair before the hearth, the mistress of the house or her servant would hold a pot over the fire, turn the spit or watch things cook. An engraving by Chenu entitled *Le Paisible Ménage* (The peaceful household) from the second half of the eighteenth century shows a woman seated this way, on a low chair before the fireplace, holding a pan over the fire; her child plays at her side, and her husband, an empty basket in one hand and a lighted candle in the other, is probably preparing to go down to the basement. In the middle of the room, a folding table is half-covered with a tablecloth, on which a flat dish and a spoon have been set.

With the appearance of new cooking methods, changes began to take place during the eighteenth century: preparing food was no longer inseparably connected with the fireplace, and traditional actions were replaced by new procedures allowing the cook to work standing up. This progress was made possible by new heat sources that began to find their places is Parisian interiors. A sort of flat dish called a *réchaud* or burner came into general use in the first half of the eighteenth century as a useful supplement to the fireplace. It stood on three legs and was equipped with one or two handles and fuelled by hot coals. Kitchens commonly were equipped with one or two burners to cook or reheat food. Certain hotel keepers had whole series of these tools: there were eight in the home of Pierre Scellier in 1744, and the same number that year in the home of Thérèse Morel, and ten in Marie-Jeanne Blondelle's kitchen in 1738. This means of cooking seems to have persisted into the 1770s, as we found a master pastry maker who had neither trivet nor trammel in his fireplace at that time, but who owned two copper burners. There were also *fourneaux* or stoves, heated with wood or coal, which the *Encyclopédie* describes as 'a structure in masonry made of brick, which is about three feet tall and in which burners are embedded that drop their ashes into a vaulted space made under the stove'.

Stoves came in several types: portable stoves with two burners, brick stoves with four cast iron burners, plaster stoves, stoves reinforced and strapped with iron, masonry stoves with two burners, and sheet-metal stoves. But this article was not yet very widespread: 20 per cent of the homes of hotel keepers, *cabaret* owners and wine merchants owned one type or another; 20 per cent of Saint-Germain-l'Auxerrois parish members had a model in brick or cast iron between 1768 and 1790; 17 per cent of the inhabitants of the Place Maubert neighbourhood in the 1770s and only three out of sixty-nine households in the faubourg Saint-Antoine were equipped with a stove by 1760. It is hard to know how valuable this piece of masonry was, just as it is difficult to evaluate the *potager*, a niche in the wall where dishes were left to simmer, since it is not described in the inventories.

Even more rare than the stove, the tin cooker, an innovation of the 1750s, was the province of the wealthy. Manufactured in stoneware and enclosed in a tin shell, these stoves could be portable or mobile. They were to be found in 17.5 per cent of the kitchens of Saint-Germain-l'Auxerrois parish members between 1768 and 1790. In the parish of Saint-Etienne-du-Mont in the 1760s, the only mentions made of such cookers by the valuers were in the homes of the lawyer

Jacques Girard de La Soisson and the doctor Jean Cabaille. Lastly we should note one more means of cooking that appeared in a small number of households during the 1770s: a portable oven, the 'country oven'. In short, new housekeeping techniques were slowly coming into practice in the 1770s, but these ancillary heat sources for cooking food had not yet displaced the age-old fireplace by the end of the century.

In dwellings with real kitchens, specific pieces of furniture were to be found in addition to the various utensils and tools inventoried around the hearth. These furnishings were generally fairly limited and were primarily utilitarian, consisting of tables, chairs and storage spaces in oak, walnut, pine or whitewood. Tables were often set on trestles or could be folded. Some were called 'kitchen tables' or, more rarely, 'chopping tables'. When made of solid wood or referred to as 'dining tables' they could reach lengths of 2.6 metres. Seats were numerous but of little value, and were almost always straw-bottomed. These included chairs, *escabelles* or stepstools, benches, footstools, *placets* (small stools), sometimes armchairs. Tables and chairs were very useful to the housewife as she prepared meals. Tables were used for cutting, preparing, and laying out food; with a seat, the mistress of the house could cook sitting down and recover from the long periods she spent bent over, red-faced as she worked above the fire. An engraving from the second half of the eighteenth century entitled *La Cuisinière surveillante* (The cook keeping watch) shows the housewife's routine in the kitchen: seated close to a fireplace at a table covered with a cloth, on which two pheasants and a knife are laid, a young woman is busy preparing a partridge. We shall discuss the furniture used to store the kitchen equipment and dishes later, in the section on storage.

A Look at the Eating Habits of Parisians

What foods were prepared with the many utensils found in these kitchens? What dishes composed the meals of Frenchmen in those days? The inventories yield very little information about the eating habits of seventeenth- and eighteenth-century Parisians, because with the exception of drink, stocks of foodstuffs were almost non-existent. Most of the pantries or small closets in walnut or oak, with their brass or *archal* wire grills, were empty; so were the salting tubs in oak, often locked with a key, which could contain a half-*minot*, or some 25 kg of salt. This scarcity of reserves should not be surprising, even in the case of inventories made shortly after the death; we must not forget that the conservation of perishable foodstuffs posed a considerable problem before the invention of artificial cooling techniques. Food merchants were to be found in abundance in any neighbourhood and indeed on almost every street. It is therefore probable that most housewives usually did their grocery shopping daily at the businesses closest to their homes, to avoid storing provisions. Despite this absence of stocks of foodstuffs, we can nonetheless get an idea of what these Parisians ate by looking at their utensils and their dishes and by examining their debts with merchants.

The most basic staple, bread, was put away in a bread box which was usually made of pine, or kept in a bread bag or the pantry. The most commonly encountered debts in the households of the deceased were for 'bread supplied'.

The sums could be large, ranging from 50 to 200 L. One painter who died in 1745 owed 243 L for 'bread supplied', while the total value of his belongings was 556 L. The average daily bread ration of Parisians tended to be high, varying between 500 and 550 grams during the seventeenth and eighteenth centuries.[6] This meant that the rising bread prices that marked the end of the *ancien régime* were all the more painful for the poorer classes, who were forced to turn to other grains and to abandon protein-rich foods for a diet based on carbohydrates. In those centuries bread was apparently rarely made at home, and bakeries and pastry shops were actually the only places where stocks of wheat and flour were inventoried in the attic: 'nine *septiers* [1 *septier* = *c.* 10 bushels] of flour' worth 10 L per *septier* were valued at 90 L in 1667 in the home of a master baker; 'four *septiers* of flour, in raw form and baked bread' were assessed at 36 L in the home of another master baker in 1676.

Given the diversity of kitchen utensils, we can imagine that diets were also fairly varied. That soups and broths were cooked is demonstrated by the presence of a great number of soup tureens, soup bowls and dishes, boiling spoons and soup spoons, broth cups, strainers and ladles. Saucepans were used to prepare gruel, the basic nutrient for young children and the poor. Proof that meat was eaten may be found in the multiple articles used for conserving it, such as salting tubs or 'hooks for hanging meat'; there were also tools for cutting, chopping, skinning and cooking it, such as spits, roasting jacks, dripping pans and grills, and utensils for serving it, including stew and roast spoons. When fresh and of good quality, meat might be roasted on a spit, grilled or salted; if its quality was less good, it was cooked as a casserole or stew in the cauldrons and kettles. Mutton and lamb were as popular as beef and veal. Martin Lister commented, 'As for their flesh, mutton and beef if they are good in their kind, they come little short of ours, I cannot say they exceed them. But their veal is not to be compared with ours, being red and coarse; and I believe no country in Europe understands the management of that sort of food like the English.'[7]

A book of recipes that was a great success at Court, *Le Cuisinier roïal et bourgeois*, attributed to one Massialot de Limoges, was published in 1691 and described nineteen ways to serve lamb and mutton, thirteen recipes for beef and twelve for veal.[8] Pork was consumed in the form of bacon or ham. One master potter in 1657 had 'half a pig in a salting tub', valued at 6 L. The cellar of a wine merchant in 1664 contained '75 pounds of salted pig bacon, valued at 5 sols per pound, and 7 hams valued at 10 sols'. Sausages and blood pudding also appeared on the tables of these Parisians, as is indicated by the presence of utensils for making sausage and blood pudding as well as pans and dripping pans for cooking them. Parisians were also very fond of poultry and game. Only in the wealthiest homes were there *chaponnières*, pots for cooking capons. Twenty-three recipes in the *Cuisinier roïal* deal with chicken, seventeen with capon and fatted chicken, nine with turkey, eight with rabbit and seven with hare.[9]

A few rare inhabitants of the semi-rural areas around the faubourg Saint-Antoine and in Auteuil owned poultry yards, with chickens, roosters, pigeons, rabbits, turkeys and ducks. Meat, poultry and game also went into the pâtés that were prepared in pie pans or terrines and, in well-to-do homes, cooked in special pâté ovens. Parisians whose fireplaces were not equipped for cooking meat had to purchase ready-roasted meats. Several of the deceased, including three painters, left debts ranging from 30 to 60 L for 'roast meats supplied'.

Though the humblest families probably ate meat only about once a week, and then only salted meat, general meat consumption in Paris stood at some 50 or 60 kg per capita per year after 1750.[10] This seems to have been the case in the seventeenth and eighteenth centuries across a broad social spectrum, as indicated by the presence of spits, dripping pans, and grills even in the poorest homes. Valuers also noted debts for purchases from butchers: one master shoemaker owed 96 L to his butcher in 1772. Here again, inhabitants of the capital seem to have been more privileged than the rest of France. Louis-Sébastien Mercier seems to be blackening the portrait of Parisian eating habits when he writes, 'The bourgeois has his soup or his gruel made with meat which is most often bad, because those who buy for the big houses, such as the town houses, pensions and convents, take all the finest morsels. Anything that is not too fatty is cooked in an unhealthy manner, and to give it some flavour, is always too heavily peppered.'[11]

Fish could be cooked in broth in a fish kettle (a utensil reserved for the very rich) or fried in a pan, fresh, smoked or salted: it replaced meat during Lent and on the numerous days of abstinence throughout the year. It came essentially from the Seine or its tributaries. Sea fish was actually reputed to be expensive in Paris and almost never fresh. If we are to judge by the recipes in the *Cuisinier Roïal*, commonly eaten types of freshwater fish included pike, carp, eel, tench and perch.

Less expensive than meat or fish, eggs seem to have been a dietary staple. 'This is an excellent and nourishing food which healthy and sick, rich and poor alike all consume', stated *La Cuisinière bourgeoise*, another cookbook from 1753.[12] Eggs were eaten in omelettes or soft-boiled, as the presence of omelette pans and egg cups indicates, and could be cooked in many other ways. With a dozen hens, certain residents of the near and outlying suburbs could enjoy extra fresh eggs most of the year. According to the *Cuisinière bourgeoise*, these also 'soothed acridness in the chest'. A teamster had one and a half dozen hens pecking away in the courtyard of his house, and a wine merchant kept twelve hens plus a rooster and a capon in his attic. A gardener in the faubourg Saint-Antoine also owned twelve hens and a rooster, roaming freely in the courtyard and garden of his home. In sixty-eight houses inventoried in Passy and Auteuil, we counted 138 chickens. In 1772, valuers found 100 eggs valued at 3 L 12 sols in the home of a fruit merchant in the parish of Saint-Nicolas-du-Chardonnet.

Hardly any trace of vegetables appears through the inventories. The attic of a vine dresser in the faubourg Saint-Antoine did, however, contain 'six bushels of peas from last year's harvest, four bushels of coarse beans, two bushels of haricot beans', worth the sum of 12 L. One Auteuil resident also grew haricot beans. Humble families from outlying semi-rural areas could improve their lot this way, with fruits and vegetables from their own gardens. We should note that lettuce, rice and chestnuts also appeared on Parisian menus, as we can tell from the presence of salad bowls, salad baskets, a few rice bowls and chestnut pans.

For cooking fat, people used butter and oil. Butter pots and pots in *tallevane*, a special stoneware for storing butter, were listed in some kitchens. More explicitly, the notary occasionally mentioned 'six pounds [$2\frac{1}{2}$ kg] of butter both salted and melted', or 'eleven pounds of melted butter'. The two main means of storing butter were salting or melting it. Some kitchens were also stocked with olive oil. Kept in pitchers, it was presented on the table in 'cruets with their cruet holders'. Salt, condiments and spices seasoned the various dishes and gave them flavour. Salt was indispensable: it was contained in salting tubs for preserving food, or in salt boxes for cooking or in salt shakers to be placed on the table. Mortars were used with pestles for grinding salt into grains. The valuers also mention vinegar cruets and barrels of vinegar. Mixed with oil and mustard (kept in *moutardiers* or mustard jars), vinegar was consumed in a vinaigrette which, like all sauces, was served in a sauce dish. Other utensils included pepper shakers, pepper mills, spice boxes, olive spoons and wooden mortars with iron or stone pestles for crushing spices and garlic.

Cheese eating left few traces in the inventories: a draining rack for cheese, some 'Gruière' cheese, and a round of Brie were the only indications we noted, to which might be added a few bills with the cheese seller, including one for 20 L for twelve rounds of Brie. Consumption of milk, another highly perishable foodstuff before the invention of pasteurization techniques, is only suggested by a few milk bowls and milk pots, including 'sixteen milk pots and seven milk pitchers' found in 1760 in the faubourg Saint-Antoine home of an animal husbandman, father of seven young children who was also raising six milk cows. Six other cows, one at the home of a teamster and five belonging to Auteuil residents, were assessed. But these are exceptions. People from the centre of town did not milk their own cows: they bought their milk from the dairyman. The wife of a painter even owed 15 L to the milkmaid for eggs and milk supplied during the final illness of her husband.

Parisians had quite a sweet tooth, to judge from the many jam pots and pans, fruit dishes, fruit and syrup pans and steamers for cooking fruits. As it was probably difficult to find fresh fruit in the city's market-places, fruit was commonly eaten cooked. The penchant for such desserts is reflected in the *Cuisinière bourgeoise*, which contains some thirty recipes for fruit sauces. When eaten raw, fruits were placed on the table in baskets. Some inventories mention debts to fruit merchants. Consider a member of the Paris bourgeoisie, a candle merchant who died in 1650. He owned a small house in a field of fruit trees and insisted that a part of the rent be paid to him in kind, i.e. in fruit: 'three baskets of cherries, each weighing ten pounds, and half a hundred pears'.

Pastries were also greatly loved, as we can see from indications of specialized cooking utensils, found only in wealthy households: waffle irons, *poupeliniers* for making popovers (a recipe included in *La Cuisinière bourgeoise*) and even an oven with a copper cover, found in 1650 in the home of Aignan de Beauharnais, the *Commissaire Général de l'Extraordinaire des Guerres*, and 'used to cook marzipan', a dessert made of almonds and jam. Sugar was consumed in ever increasing quantities during the eighteenth century. The Parisian appetite for it reached 5 kg per capita per year on the eve of the Revolution[13] and was revealed by the many references made to it in inventories, both directly and indirectly: sugar loaves, pounds of brown sugar, sugar bowls, sugar pots and sugar graters. Like salt, sugar was also a means of conservation widely used by housewives.

A great deal more information is available about the beverages consumed than about solid foods, because stocks of them were more abundant. We shall not examine the question of water here, as it is covered in the next chapter. Wine, a very widely used beverage, held an important place in several inventories. Stocking it generally required having a cellar. Though a very broad range of social and professional classes had such stocks, the poor and the badly housed did not. It was exceptional for day labourers, floor polishers and artisans to have such provisions. Wine reserves were found in 21 per cent of the interiors (wine merchants, *cabaret* and hotel owners and beverage sellers were excluded from these statistics to avoid distorting the results). This figure is lower than the 33 per cent of inventories mentioning cellars. Wine was stored in carafes, decanters, bottles, or in casks that went under the generic name of barrels, or in *queues* or *pipes* – these two types of vessels were also units of measure: a *queue* contained a little more than a hogshead or 54 *septiers*, and a *pipe* held one and a half hogsheads. The Paris hogshead, the most frequent unit of measure, contained 36 *septiers*, the equivalent of 2.88 litres. *Queues* and *pipes* filled with wine lined the walls of the best-stocked cellars, where they sat on wooden *chantiers*, large square beams that prevented moisture from rotting the casks and facilitated drawing the wine as well.

Though it was preferable to store wine in the cellar, it was also kept in other parts of the home. A half-hogshead of claret was found in the bedroom in which the archer Charles Le Riche died in 1661. In 1659 in the home of a silk merchant, two half-hogsheads of Burgundy claret were kept in the 'upper warehouse'. As for the chaplain François Guillebert, he stored 'a half-hogshead of claret of Burgundy vintage' with his wood and coal, in a closet 'on the way to the third story' of his house on the rue Sainte-Avoye. Other storage areas noted by the valuers include pantries, courtyards, attics and shopbacks. The quantities of wine reserves could vary considerably, ranging from a dozen bottles or decanters to several hogsheads or *queues*. We should bear in mind that average wine consumption for Parisians was generally high, reaching 150 litres per person annually in the mid-seventeenth century.[14]

France's most famous vintages were to be found in the cellars of these Parisians. The most prized and the most expensive were the Burgundies. Other highly reputed wines such as champagne and, at the end of the eighteenth century, Bordeaux, and sweet wines such as muscatel also filled the cellars of these houses.

High-quality wines, whose prices were beyond the reach of many purses, were served only at the finest tables. In the home of the surgeon Louis Gervais, who died in 1772, '150 decanters of red wine, Burgundy vintage' were inventoried along with 'twelve bottles of red wine from Graves and Beaune' valued together at 110 L. The superintendent of the king's music possessed 600 bottles of Burgundy worth 330 L, in addition to eighteen bottles of Bordeaux, two half-bottles of Cypriot wine, and eighty half-bottles of Malaga.

Investments in wine could be considerable. The cellar of a rich clothier merchant, who was a member of the Paris bourgeoisie, was valued at 888 L in 1716, or some 40 per cent of the value of the home's furnishings. One of the richest cellars encountered belonged to the Marquis de Champcenetz; by itself, it was worth 2752 L in 1775. The greater the number of bottles, the greater was the variety of vintages. The wine cellar of Seigneur de La Grange, counsellor to the Cour des Aides who died in 1775, was estimated at 2644 L. Burgundies were predominant in it, with more than 130 litres in casks and 300 bottles of Auxerre red wine. Wines of the south-west were represented by white wines from Graves and Bayonne. There were also white Chablis, champagnes and red Héraults. The other vintages were fortified wines from the Mediterranean including some 400 bottles of Malaga, Cypriot wine, malmsey, and Alicante. There were nine boards with holes intended for storing bottles, which were washed in 'three old buckets'. Many other fine vintages are mentioned in the inventories, some from Burgundy (Nuits, Pommard, Mâcon, Sens), others from the Loire valley (Anjou, Touraine, Vouvray, Saumur and Chinon).

Ordinary red wines from around Paris or Orléans comprised the most abundant reserves. Locally produced wines from the Ile de France were very widely consumed, especially in the seventeenth century, and were available at prices much lower than those of famous vintages from wine-growing regions. Wines from Bagnolet and Nanterre were both valued at 30 L per hogshead under Louis XIV, and wine from Asnières at 32 L per hogshead, whereas a hogshead of Burgundy was worth 45 L during the same period. Yet other local wines were produced in Puteaux, Houilles, Nogent-sur-Marne, Brie, Vilorson (near Corbeil), Vaux-lès-Melun, Cormeilles and Pontoise. The origin of the most commonplace wines was not always indicated by valuers, who simply noted whether it was red, white or claret. Apparently many Parisians did not go to market to acquire their wines, but often owned a few *arpents* (an old surface area measure, approximately 30 square metres) of vines on the edge of the capital, from which they drew their table wine. Such ordinary wines did not keep as well as the Burgundies, which had a higher alcohol content. In the 1644 inventory of Jean Amelot, *Premier Président* of the Grand Council, the valuers noted his widow's declaration that she had 'sold the wine as it had turned'.

Although three-quarters of our Parisians had no stocks of wine, this was hardly a beverage reserved only for the privileged classes who had cellars. Nothing was easier, in a city like Paris, abounding in wine merchants, than to make daily purchases. Indeed, it was quite the fashion among the common people to go to those favourite resorts of popular society, the village *cabarets* outside the tax wall. Mercier hastens to underline the difference between the refined vintages stored in the city's basements and the ordinary wine served in *cabarets*: 'Having drunk *cabaret* wine the night before, feel the extreme difference offered by the cellars of the same city. Taste the wines from Romanée, Saint-Vivant, Cîteaux, Chambertin, Saint-Georges or Graves – reds and whites; smell the wine from Rotat, Cyprus, Pacaret, Samos, Monemvasia, Madeira or Syracuse.'[15]

Other alcoholic beverages, much less common than wine, were rarely mentioned in the inventories. Outside the cellars of innkeepers and beverage sellers, there were few reserves of beer and fewer still of cider. Liqueurs and other spirits were becoming more commonplace by the end of the eighteenth century, as we learn from the presence of a few 'stoves for wine spirits', 'bowls for drinking punch', and glasses, cups or bottles for ratafia listed in the last decades of the century. A small number of stocks of brandy, ratafia, cassis, cordials, lemon and orange-flower or myrtle liqueur and Lorraine liqueur were also to be found.

New beverages, coffee, tea and chocolate, became ever more popular during the eighteenth century, and this fashion is evidenced by the inventories. Following the Court's example, Parisians became mad about coffee in the 1730s and 1740s, as is revealed by the assessments of various objects used for storing, preparing or tasting it: coffee boxes or cans, generally in tin; coffee pans, called *poêles* or *poêlons*, for roasting coffee, coffee mills sometimes described as 'having an iron crank, and a box into which the coffee falls', 'burners for roasting coffee' or coffee ovens, coffeepots, sometimes described as Levant, oriental or Marseille pots, in tin, red copper, stoneware or silver; and coffee spoons and cups. In practice, the coffee grains were roasted in a pan, then milled. Two spoonfuls of powder were poured into a pint of water that had been heated just until ten bubbles had boiled to the surface. One bourgeois kitchen in 1746 contained everything necessary: an oven, a mill and three coffeepots. The wife of a wine merchant that same year owned 'a small coffee boiling pot, oriental fashion'.

Because of the price, only the very rich could afford silver coffeepots: the Marquis de Savine had one worth 174 L in 1748. In contrast, when in copper or tin, these pots were worth just a few sols. Their volume was rarely indicated, though there were occasional mentions such as a coffeepot 'in silver on three legs, containing eight cups', or two coffeepots 'each containing twelve cups in its body'. Coffee services could be of fine quality in wealthy households: Elisabeth Gaugé, a spinster who died in 1775, owned 'four cups and saucers in India porcelain'.

Stocks of coffee were rare, appearing only in prosperous households: the Marquis de Bonnac had 192 pounds (87 kg) in 1739, valued at 345 L 12 sols, or 36 sols per pound. At about the same period, Pierre Marie de La Collancelle, a priest and doctor in theology, kept '16 pounds of raw coffee' in 'a closet built in the thickness of the wall'. In the home of Seigneur de La Grange in 1775, a closet installed next to the fireplace in the *salon* held 9 kg of 'moka coffee', the finest variety, and six 'coffee napkins'. This was the height of refinement. The richest of Parisians were not alone in indulging in this stimulant. A full 37.5 per cent of Saint-Germain-l'Auxerrois parish members between 1768 and 1790, and 33 per cent from Saint-Eustache between 1770 and 1772, owned a coffeepot. This article was even mentioned in 15 per cent of the households in the poorer neighbourhood of the faubourg Saint-Antoine between 1760 and 1762.

Tea was not nearly as widely consumed as coffee, and seemed to interest only the most cultivated levels of society. The fashion for tea, which started in the 1720s or 1730s, did, however, leave its mark on a small number of inventories: tea boxes in tin, tea canisters and bowls, teapots in porcelain, red copper, white clay or, more rarely, silver, and cups and tea services. Like coffeepots, silver teapots were generally valued at considerable sums and seem to have been luxury items. Both articles were often found in the same households, to cite the example of the Marquis de Savine, where the silver teapot was valued at 140 L. Porcelain teacups were similarly limited to the wealthiest of homes: in the office of the Marquise de Traisnel's town house in 1746, 'four porcelain teacups' as well as 'six little teacups with saucers in Japanese porcelain' and a matching teapot were to be found. Stocks of tea leaves were almost non-existent. We should nevertheless mention the English gentleman, Henry Sayers Johnson, who died in 1772 in the faubourg Saint-Honoré, who had, appropriately, a half-full tin box of tea.

If we observe the frequency of teapots in the inventories of the deceased, tea drinking at the end of the eighteenth century seems to have been fairly limited: ten households out of sixty owned a teapot in the parish of Saint-Eustache; another ten musicians' households, out of sixty-eight, owned one, as did five out of sixty homes in the parish of Saint-Etienne-du-Mont and just one out of seventy-five homes in the parish of Saint-Germain-l'Auxerrois.

As for chocolate, this drink became fashionable during the Regency of Philippe d'Orléans but does not seem to have been widely enjoyed by Parisians, judging from the tiny number of chocolate pots mentioned. Like coffeepots and teapots, these were made of tin, red copper or silver in the homes of the rich. Once again, the Marquis de Savine provides the example of a chocolate pot in white Paris silver which was worth the sum of 188 L 10 sols. Chocolate cups and graters, other evidence that this hot drink was consumed, are very unusual. We also noted stocks of chocolate in the homes of the Marquis de Bonnac – who, in addition to his coffee, also had 9 kg of chocolate worth 50 L – and of the priest Pierre Marie de La Collancelle, who owned 'four pounds of chocolate in bars' along with raw coffee and 'thirty pounds of sugar in seven loaves'.

It is tempting to think, in the light to these examples, that it was always the same households that adopted each of these new stimulants, be it coffee, tea or chocolate. Tasting these delicious beverages had not entered into the habits of most Parisians by the eve of the Revolution. Though coffee had become more commonplace by the second half of the century, tea and chocolate remained luxury goods. The French did not drink a cup of coffee or tea or chocolate as they did a glass of wine, or as nonchalantly as we do now. Meeting with close friends over a cup of coffee, tea or chocolate and delighting in savouring these exotic beverages, served with great refinement in porcelain – these civilized pleasures offer a glimpse of a new way of life, focused on family privacy and on well-being, that was developing progressively during the Enlightenment.

Sociability

Sharing a meal with family or friends, chatting by the fire with relatives or neighbours, meeting in groups to play trick-track or cards – these were the fundamental rituals at the centre of the sociability of the home. By analysing the objects related to these forms of behaviours, whether furniture, tables and chairs or dishes, we can glimpse this communal life and reconstruct these gatherings of family or friends around a table or hearth. A small number of our Parisians, almost always those living alone, did not take their meals at home – unless they had them brought in by one of the city's caterers – as they possessed no kitchen utensils or dishes. These people lived in furnished rooms or were housed by their family, their master or a religious order. Apart from this category, however, these interiors generally contained a multitude of articles associated with conviviality, from items of furniture to crockery.

After trying to imagine how food was prepared and what people ate, let us try to follow the actions of the mistress of the house as she sets the table. In what room did the members of the household eat their meals? There can be no doubt when the residence has just one room, or when there is a designated 'dining room'. In other cases, it is more difficult to know, because of the non-specialization of rooms which was, as we have seen, so common at the time. It would seem that the kitchen, almost always furnished with one or more tables, was the usual dining area in homes without a *salle* or main room. The role of that main room as social space has been discussed already, but it did not always contain a table, or there might be few chairs, whereas the chamber would be well stocked.

Perhaps the dining area also varied according to the number of guests or the season: during winter, alone with the family, the kitchen, which was the warmest room, was probably the preferred spot for eating. With guests, when the weather was fine, another room or chamber, more spacious and better decorated than the kitchen, would serve as dining area. But the place where people eat is determined first of all by the size of their abode. Setting aside a room for eating does suggest a certain spaciousness. As the number of spaces multiplied and rooms became progressively more specialized, the tendency emerged in the 1770s towards eating meals elsewhere than where they were prepared. In 37 per cent of the households inventoried in the Place Maubert quarter in this period, tableware and kitchen utensils were stored separately. The latter were to be found around the fireplace, in the room serving as a kitchen, while dishes were most often stored in buffets or dressers in the dining room, the antechamber or even the bedchamber.

The great number of folding tables (*tables ployantes*) listed in the interiors leads us to think that meals were not always held in the same place, at least during the seventeenth and early eighteenth centuries. The functions of rooms in most lodgings in this period were still ill-defined. In most of these homes, a large number of tables, of all sorts, were to be found: on average, three or four per household for our entire sample. Even in the homes of day labourers living in a single room, there were two per family. Hotel owners, innkeepers, wine merchants and beverage sellers who received customers, had on average eleven tables placed in the common rooms, kitchen, shop, *cabaret* room, café or dining room. Folding tables were the most common type: they might be defined as folding (*ployante*), on an opening frame (*sur châssis*), with folding legs, on a stand, with collapsible frame, on trestles – or they might be simple boards serving as a table. These tables, folded and stored in a corner, then set up on their legs for mealtimes only, were well adapted to often cramped lodgings, crowded with furniture. Setting the table therefore actually meant setting up the table on its legs, trestles or gussets, i.e. small consoles, before laying it. Such movable tables were often made of pine, a light-weight, easily portable wood. The function of larger tables was sometimes specified by the valuers as being for the kitchen or for dining.

The most commonly employed woods for tables were pine, whitewood, oak, walnut, beech and elm. The tabletop was not always made of the same material as the legs. A marble tabletop might be placed on a walnut base, or on a gilded wooden base. Coffee tables actually often supported a marble top. The famous beverage seller Pierre Alexandre owned sixty-six tables, all with marble tops. Bases were described as consoles, cabriole legs, as turned, square or metal-tipped, as cabled legs or antique columns. In some cases, the shape of the top was also indicated: the most common models were square or rectangular, but round and oval tables were also to be found. Their dimensions, usually designated as small, medium-sized or large, almost always remain unknown. The number of places is sometimes indicated: 'a table seating six', 'a dining table seating twelve', or, in the home of a caterer, 'eight pieces of board used as a table seating sixty'.

As early as the seventeenth century, some tables already included 'leaves, pulled out by the two ends', foreshadowing the true dining table developed by furniture makers after 1750. We found one model in 1660 in the home of Louis Girard de la Cour des Bois, king's counsellor and *Maître des Requêtes Ordinaires* of the royal household. The many tables found in these Parisian interiors tended to be utilitarian; they were plain and ordinary, and were valued at generally modest sums: less than 10 L for tables with a folding pine top. Those with marble tops were more expensive and could fetch some 30 L if they measured less than one metre. They attained values as high as 70–80 L or more if they were large and of good quality.

Around the table stood seats, numerous chairs, benches, stools or, more rarely, armchairs. There was generally a plethora of seating furniture crowding the interiors of these Parisians, whatever their social level – on average, a dozen per household. Chairs were omnipresent, invading the chamber as well as the kitchen and the common room. Most often, they were simply made and of little value. Most had straw or cane seats. A wide variety of woods were used in their production: whitewood, walnut, ash, elm, alder, beech, and more rarely pine and oak. When upholstered, chairs were stuffed with wadding or horsehair and covered with any of a diversity of fabrics, including moquette, damask, calico, serge, *siamois*, wool, canvas, or in the wealthiest houses, Utrecht velvet, satin, silk, and even Gobelin tapestries, needlework or Hungarian point. Chairs were sometimes accompanied by seats without backs, stools, and simple seats called *placets*, which were almost always cloth-covered, as well as folding seats that could be easily moved from one area to another. These seemed to become a vanishing species during the eighteenth century, along with the benches (*bancs* and *bancelles*) and step stools (*escabeaux* and *escabelles*) in whitewood or oak, which are seldom mentioned elsewhere than in the kitchen or the shop.

The prices allotted to chairs varied according to the model under consideration and the wood and fabrics used. A straw chair in the mid-eighteenth century was on average worth less than 1 L, a stuffed chair from 3 to 5 L, a stool from 15 sols to 1 L. The furniture standing around a table consisted essentially, in fact, of chairs. The notary would sometimes specify 'table chairs' or *'caquetoires* [conversation chairs] used at the table' or even *perroquets* (literally 'parrots'), which were folding chairs with backs ordinarily used with the table.

Once she had arranged the table and chairs, the mistress of the house or her servant would take the tablecloth and napkins out of the linen closet and cover the table. Table linen, inventoried in the vast majority of homes, was often of very good quality: one closet, for example, contained twenty-two dozen napkins. These articles from the trousseau were part of a wife's dowry at marriage and displayed a great variety of fabrics and patterns. Tablecloths and napkins were in plain or embroidered cotton, in plain white or with openwork, in Venetian or Flemish cotton. They might even be in Indian bombazine, in *grain d'orge*, in *oeil de perdrix* (embroidered silk-and-wool cloth), in damask or cotton damask. While the fabric was usually described, sizes for tablecloths are merely indicated as small, medium-sized, and large, and the number of places is given only exceptionally. In one inventory, we found three yellow cotton tablecloths, two cloths in cretonne, and one in *grain d'orge*, all for eight place-settings. In another were eleven *oeil de perdrix* tablecloths, three in *grain d'orge* (common-quality wool with barley-grain pattern), all for fifteen table-settings. During the seventeenth century, the tablecloth might occasionally be replaced by a Turkish rug, as it was in the home of a sophisticated city rat in one of La Fontaine's fables:

> Sur un tapis de Turquie,
> Le couvert se trouva mis.
>
> (On a rug in Turkey made,
> The host's table had been laid.)

On the table, now covered with a cloth or rug and napkins, the housewife could lay the cutlery and bring out of a buffet or cupboard the bowls, plates and other dishes kept for table use. Plates, some of which were specifically for soup or dessert, supplanted bowls in the eighteenth century. Neither were often described by the valuers, who in most cases simply noted succinctly, 'pots, platters, plates and other utensils', or 'pieces not worth further description'.

The material, however, was generally specified. During the eighteenth, and even more so during the preceding century, everyday dishware was in tin. This was assessed by weight, and bailiffs differentiated between articles in 'ringing tin' (*étain sonnant*), worth from 20 to 30 sols per kilogram and those in common pewter, which was less valuable, at between 15 and 20 sols per kilogram under Louis XIV. The term 'ringing tin' was used to designate a metal that had been remelted and planed several times; through these successive operations, it became more resonant. Common pewter was new tin alloyed with 15 per cent lead and 6 per cent yellow copper. Lists of objects in common pewter are never given in the inventories; only the indications 'utensils in common pewter' or 'pots, platters and utensils in common pewter' appear repeatedly in the notaries' writings. According to indications given by valuers, dishes in ringing tin included plates, bowls with handles for soup, table pitchers for water and wine, salt shakers and mustard jars.

Earthenware, even for the most common articles, did not begin to appear on Parisian tables until after 1720. Ceramics had not yet become part of daily life for most people before then, and objects in earthenware, such as pots, platters and cups, were used as decorative ornaments around the fireplace. The development of pottery factories, however, had a snowball effect on Parisian interiors beginning in the 1720s and 1730s. Plates and other earthenware items were fragile but inexpensive, and they made their way on to tables. They could be counted by the dozen, even in fairly modest households, as the inventories of a certain number of painters revealed: Louis Boucher, whose total fortune in 1750 amounted to 640 L, owned twenty-four pieces of earthenware; François Leroy, who died in 1746, left behind 1500 L, including seventy-seven items, 'platters, terrines, plates, salad bowls, as well as saucers'; and the wealthy Gilles Thevenot, whose fortune was more than 8000 L in 1748, had forty-eight earthenware plates. This ceramic material was specified as common or fine. In the home of another master painter who died in 1744, seven platters and thirty-six plates, 'partly cracked in common earthenware', were found, while 'twenty pieces of earthenware both fine and common' were inventoried in 1730 in the home of André de La Rivière.

Only occasionally are the colours of this pottery given. The master painter Isaac-Simon Rebour owned two platters, two plates and a salad bowl in blue and white earthenware, as well as twelve plates in white earthenware, in 1734. The eighteen plates belonging to Charles Go in 1724 were in white earthenware. In 1729 in the home of the painter of the Duchesse d'Orléans two pots in 'Flemish earth' kept company with twelve plates in 'Holland earthenware'. This new type of dishware, in brown or white clay or in stoneware, was much less expensive than silver or tin. It was produced, for the most part, by pottery shops in Normandy and the Ile de France, or in the Parisian factory at Pont aux Choux, founded in 1743, or, towards the end of the century, in the rue de la Roquette factory near the Bastille.

As tinware vanished from tables after 1750, earthenware became omnipresent in every home, making it possible for even the most modest households to accumulate a more diverse range of dishes. In addition to plates, complete table services also had to include platters, soup tureens, sauce dishes, ewers, salad bowls, egg cups, jars, fruit plates, terrines, water pots, *rafraîchissoires* (literally 'refreshers' or coolers), sugar bowls, cups and saucers and so forth. But as ceramic items came into more general use, notaries began to value them in batches and were content to note briefly, 'a bunch of pottery not worth describing', or perhaps 'twenty-four pieces of earthenware and pottery platters, plates and other household utensils not worth further description'.

Services in porcelain were rare, belonging only to the most affluent households. Various sorts, including Sèvres, white and blue, Saint-Cloud, Rouen, Holland, China, Japan and India porcelain, are mentioned. It is interesting to note that porcelain from Saint-Cloud won the admiration of Martin Lister, who confessed in 1698 that he 'saw the pottery of St. Cloud, with which I was marvellously well pleased, for I confess I could not distinguish betwixt the pots made there, and the finest China ware I ever saw', though he added, 'They sold these pots at St. Cloud at excessive rates.'[16] In the home of Seigneur de La Grange, the wealthy counsellor to the Cour des Aides, china services from Chantilly, Dresden and Japan were stored in the closets of the office, no doubt destined for table use. In less opulent homes, where people owned only a limited number of china pieces, these objects remained essentially decorative, to be displayed on the mantel or perhaps used only for drinking coffee or tea.

What about silver? A great many households from all social categories possessed dishes in silver, but to what extent was it present on Parisian tables? Owning a complete silver service including plates, platters, containers of all sorts, cutlery and cups was a luxury which only the most opulent could afford. Simon Plastrier, counsellor to the king in his council and *Maître Ordinaire* of the royal household before his death in 1642, must have made daily use of his silverware, valued at more than 3000 L, as he had no other dishes. The same was certainly true of François Gaudart, whose luxurious silver service, inventoried in 1698, included two dozen plates, two salt shakers, two ewers, a vinegar cruet and a candy box, not to mention the cutlery. The silver belonging to the Chevalier Bancé, estimated at 14,300 L in 1689, and that of Louis Ancelin, *contrôleur général* of the household of the late queen, worth 13,200 L in 1694, showed forth their magnificence on the tables of their famous owners, whose social rank prohibited them from eating off tin, which was reserved for commoners. In the following century, the tables of people like Charles-Hugues Baillot de Villechavant, the Marquise de Traisnel or François Francoeur were also decked with luxurious silver, including both plates and stemware (stemmed drinking vessels) which must have sparkled in the evening candlelight, creating a dazzlingly beautiful setting.

Among the affluent, sumptuous dining was part and parcel of an elegant lifestyle. But such refined dining and arts of sociability, copied from the Court, did not percolate to the middle classes of the population. In bourgeois and business families, neither platters nor plates nor stemware were in silver. In fact the only silver that appeared on their tables was the cutlery and tumblers. In more humble households, the cutlery was made of tin. Furthermore, though the use of eating spoons had become general by the sixteenth century, it should be recalled that the fork appeared much later. Forks are mentioned in small quantities in seventeenth-century inventories, as it was frequent practice at the time to eat one's meat with one's fingers. Louis XIV himself used his hands to eat his poultry stew. Only in the eighteenth century did the fork come into regular use among the bourgeoisie. Knives were even less widely used than spoons and forks, and their rarity raises a question: did each guest bring and use a knife he or she carried about at all times, as was done in the countryside? Or were one or two knives placed on the table to be used by all? The handles are sometimes described, and ivory, horn, shell and especially silver are among the materials mentioned by the valuers.

Once the housewife had laid out dishes and cutlery, she would set drinking glasses as well as pitchers of water and wine on the table. Glasses were made in distinctive shapes and materials and were designated by several terms: goblets, tumblers, *vases*, or *tasses gondolles*, i.e. 'gondola cups', which were described as 'drinking vessels, long and narrow without stem or handle, so named because of their resemblance to Venetian gondolas', according to the *Dictionnaire de Trévoux*. Drinking vessels could be stemmed, cut, in tin, in silver, in glass or, more rarely, in crystal. Finally, the mistress of the house would pour wine and water into the tin or earthenware pots, carafes or decanters of common glass or crystal.

Though the inventories furnish a profusion of detail on the array of objects for table use, they tell us nothing of how meals took place. Perhaps pictures can come to our aid here. Although Abraham Bosse devoted himself exclusively to figuring the lower nobility and the rich Protestant bourgeoisie in the age of Louis XIII, it is interesting nonetheless to have a look at two of his engravings, respectively entitled *La Bénédiction de la table* (Saying grace at table) and *L'Esprit en la virilité* (Spirit in virility), both of which show family meals. The first print has a father and mother, seated side by side at a large rectangular table and surrounded by their nine children. Hands clasped, they are reciting grace together. Another child, standing at the end of the table, and a servant join in the collective prayer. The practice of reciting the *Benedicite* before beginning a meal certainly persisted until a late date, at least in the more Christian households – consider the famous painting by Chardin from 1740 on the same theme.

In Abraham Bosse's engraving we can see the plates set before each family member, as well as platters heaped with food in the middle of the cloth-covered table. The glasses, however, are lined up on a sideboard, and the carafes of drink are set in a cooler standing on the floor. The practice at that time among the well-to-do was actually for each diner to drink, one after another, and to return his empty glass to the valet who had served it. It was only towards the 1760s that the habit grew up of leaving glasses and bottles on the table. And in the second Bosse engraving, *L'Esprit en la virilité*, we can actually see the servant standing behind the master's seat, holding a glass in one hand, with a bottle standing on the ground. This scene portrays a father and mother seated opposite one another, surrounded by their three daughters and the girls' tutor. In the room where the table has been laid stands a *couchette* with curtains, decorated above the posts with four bouquets of feathers – a reminder that rooms were far from having specialized uses at that time, even in well-to-do households.

Besides the ceremony surrounding meals, the inventories also highlight other aspects of sociability. Furniture for receiving guests includes not only dining tables and chairs but also the armchairs and other seats placed along walls or around the fireplace in the main room or chamber. Once again, we must emphasize the abundance of chairs in these abodes, averaging a dozen per deceased individual, as we saw earlier. This demonstrates how important social life was in these homes. In all social and professional groups, the number of chairs was almost always much greater than the number of occupants. Although the case of Seigneur de La Grange, who owned 173 chairs for ten inhabitants and thirty-nine rooms (including servants' quarters) is clearly an extreme example, that of the widowed Mme Ollivier, who piled ten chairs and five armchairs into a single room on the rue d'Anjou where she lived alone, does not seem exceptional. The two primary rooms in the home of another solitary occupant, a master lute maker and merchant, contained respectively fourteen and twenty-one seats. Day labourers and typeset handlers, most often housed in single rooms, had an average of eight chairs per household. In these modest interiors it was most common to find straw chairs, though armchairs were not completely absent: we found seven in the home of a customs porter from 1754. Painters possessed on average fifteen seats in their lodgings, or ten if they lived in a single room. In the faubourg Saint-Marcel, rooms with fireplaces held an average of ten chairs.

Based on a sample of 7000 seats inventoried during the seventeenth and eighteenth centuries, we calculated that of every 100 seats, sixty-three were upright chairs, twenty-three were armchairs, and fourteen were of various types, either stools or folding seats without backs, or benches or sofas. It should be noted that in the first half of the seventeenth century, the distinction between armchairs and other chairs (often designated as 'with arms') was not always clear. In households in the parish of Saint-Nicolas-des-Champs between 1635 and 1649, armchairs represented only 16 per cent of all seats. Older models such as *escabeaux* and *escabelles* (stepstools), *formes*, *selles* (or saddles), *bancelles* (benches), antique chairs or chairs with arms still persisted in that period. We also found so-called *chaises à vertugadin*, i.e. 'bustle' or armless chairs, on which women dressed in flounced robes or bustles could sit comfortably. Though there were no real armchairs in these households, there was nevertheless a great number of seats. One priest in 1634 had arranged six walnut *vertugadin* seats in his chamber, six walnut stepstools, and a chair with arms covered in green serge. The main room of one bourgeois of Paris contained not a single armchair in 1657, though the man was not poor. The eleven seats inventoried included six *placets*, two folding seats, one chair with arms and two small chairs. The main room of Pierre Gargan, king's counsellor and *Intendant des Finances*, was also empty of any armchairs at the same date, though it held twelve tapestry-covered chairs and twelve stools.

During the reign of Louis XIV, however, armchairs, henceforth distinguished from chairs, became a fashion that permeated all classes of society. In 1665, in the home of a master mason, we found six high-backed chairs that could be called Louis XIII style, four armchairs, one small chair, and six *caquetoires* or 'conversation' chairs. This last category, highly popular in the seventeenth century, designated low chairs, used to 'seat oneself near the fire, where one chats at leisure', according to Furetière. The Louis XIV-style high-backed armchairs to be seen in interiors in this period were solid and sombre articles, with massive lines and no sculpted or added ornament. Nevertheless, their wood was sometimes gilded or varnished, and in the most affluent homes, a taste for decoration can be seen in the quality of fabrics used in the upholstery – brocade, velvet, damask, needlepoint tapestry – and in the colours used, matching those of the curtains on a bed or window. Backless, cloth-covered seats remained in vogue at the beginning of the eighteenth century, no doubt because women's dresses were still full.

Around the same period, valuers noted a few sofas and settees. According to the *Dictionnaire de Trévoux*, the sofa was a 'type of day bed with a back and two arms which has recently come into use in France'. One settee was described in the same manner in the early years of the eighteenth century: 'a large walnut settee six feet long, padded with horsehair and bordered with needlepoint tapestry with a small mattress and two bolsters having a white embroidered silk satin background and a tapestry compartment, the back and two arms covered with the same satin and similarly embroidered', estimated at 150 L. The so-called *confessionnal* armchair, a wide high-backed armchair with upholstered wings, also dates from the reign of Louis XIV and was encountered in a few homes. A related model, the *commodité* armchair, is defined by Furetière as 'a well-stuffed chair with a lectern for reading and writing and a trammel for raising or lowering the back as one desires, in which one may sleep and lean back'. This is not to be confused with the commode chair or armchair equipped with a ceramic bucket or a basin.

Still other types of seats were to be found in these early eighteenth-century interiors: 'queen' armchairs or chairs, which were straight-backed, and *ruelle* armchairs, which were narrow so that they could fit into the small space by the bed. The latter were reserved for guests coming to visit a sick person or a woman in childbed. *Ruelle* armchairs, to be found exclusively in the chamber, apparently fell out of use after 1750. The chamber of one master painter in 1736 contained 'four *ruelle* armchairs, in sculpted, arched wood, stuffed with horsehair, covered with tapestry, and two similar stools'.

The armchair rose to its triumphal status in the furniture world during the reigns of Louis XV and Louis XVI. With the progress in the arts of wood-working and cabinetmaking that began under Louis XIV, production developed and models became more diverse. Straight and stiff lines yielded to light, gracious forms. Curved and sinuous shapes inspired by the drawings of the Berains, father and son, and by *ornemanistes* or ornament designers from the Regency, woods gilded or delicately stained with varnishes, and the subtle harmony of fabric colours and wood tones all conferred a great elegance upon these chairs.

Elegance was enhanced by greater comfort. Pomp and ease went hand in hand, and these new models encouraged the art of sociability. The most comfortable of them was the *bergère*, or easy chair, which made its appearance around 1725: this long, gondola-shaped armchair had a rounded, stuffed back, wings, armrests, and a seat padded with a *carreau* (square cushion) or a little feather mattress. Some easy chairs were called 'confessional'-style. Some twenty years later, just before 1750, the *cabriolet* was created, an elegant chair or armchair with an arched back and curved legs. These new and highly fashionable seats were inventoried in the most affluent households, those enjoying one or more reception rooms at the end of the century: the composer Duni owned an easy chair, twelve *cabriolets*, and twelve *chaises à la reine* (queen chairs) in 1775. In 1787 the rich furnishings possessed by Francoeur included, among other items, twelve easy chairs, four *cabriolets*, six queen armchairs and one 'confessional' armchair. In the dining room of Seigneur de La Grange stood four *cabriolet* armchairs, as well as a dozen chairs, and in the sumptuous and tasteful *salon* next door were twelve *cabriolet* armchairs, covered with needlepoint tapestry, and two others in Utrecht velvet, in addition to eight large queen armchairs and a three-place settee. These last nine articles were all covered with Gobelins tapestries 'representing flowers and animals'.

Other decorative and comfortable seats found their places in the loveliest residences, such as the settee and its variants, the ottoman and the sofa – names evocative of the Orient, whose attraction persisted throughout the century – the chaise longue, the *veilleuse* (a long settee) and the day bed. These seats, which lent themselves to resting, reading and relaxing, were also well adapted to gallant conversation. Indicative of an attention to comfort and a taste for luxury, these were valuable pieces of furniture, part of the preserve of the rich. In 1764, the composer Jean-Philippe Rameau owned a two-place settee. A lawyer at the Parlement, who died a bachelor in 1772, possessed an ottoman in his company *salon*, a *veilleuse* in his bedroom and a small day bed in his dining room. In the residence of Seigneur de La Grange, the *salon* on the ground floor furnished with the three-place settee was not the only room containing such an item, as the *salon* on the second floor held another of the same type, in addition to more than twenty-one other seats.

As for the types of wood used in manufacturing these various types of seat, they differ little from those used in dining table chairs, except for the omission of pine or poplar, which were reserved for very ordinary furniture. We should emphasize the predominance of walnut, a wood easy to tool and sculpt, followed by beech, which was highly regarded by chairmakers because of its elastic texture. Ash, alder and elm all seem to have been less common. The valuers seldom give any indication as to how the wood was actually worked, though there are occasional indications on the question, such as notes that the wood on chairs, armchairs or stools had been turned or carved. The mention of *capucine* style often appears in the notaries' writings to designate seats with wood that was simply turned and not cut according to a certain calibre or moulded. Unlike chairs, armchairs rarely had straw seats, but models with caned seats were very much in vogue in the first part of the century.

In discussing dining table chairs, we have already named the various fabrics used to cover seats. Though the range of cloth was wide as far as the elegant furniture from the second half of the century was concerned, there was a marked preference for four of these fabrics: damask, moquette, Utrecht velvet and needlepoint tapestry. As we shall see later when examining the question of decor, the richness of these coverings, the choice of sober or bright colours to harmonize with other furnishings, and the use of flower or leaf prints or stripes were all signs of an aesthetic development that characterized the Enlightenment.

Other furniture and objects, such as gaming tables and parlour games listed in the inventories by the notaries, demonstrated how Parisians socialized. Playing cards, trick-track or draughts in the family or with neighbours or friends was a popular distraction. Such diversions, however, were only for the most privileged classes, who had leisure time. By means of the gaming tables and various games assessed, the inventories tell us how many households could afford to enjoy these pastimes in their own homes. In the seventeenth century and the early years of the eighteenth, parlour games were still rarely seen in Parisian interiors, as they are mentioned in only 8 per cent of our households. Furthermore, their variety is limited: there are decks of cards, piquet, quadrille, *ombre*, three-of-a-kind, or again, trick-track and draughts. Only rarely do the notaries in that period mention other types of games: one snakes-and-ladders game, one backgammon board, two billiard tables, and one game of *boules*. So-called gaming tables, with no further description, were used for cards and were most often described as 'in walnut, covered with green cloth'. The Marquis Charles de Barbezières owned such a table in marquetry with cabriole legs in 1709. Trick-track boards were generally valued with their fifteen pieces, their cups and dice, and the boards and pegs.

Games were most often inventoried in the main room, or perhaps in the *cabinet*, as in the home of Pierre Gargan, *Intendant des Finances*, who kept 'two trick-tracks, one covered in Chinese-style wood' in 1657. Game owners belonged almost without exception to society's elite, and the richest even owned several types. The affluent bookseller Frédéric Léonard had a complete trick-track, with pieces and cups, in what was called the 'games room' in his home in 1706, which contained 'two tables covered with green serge, a game of *boules* at standing height, in mall form, covered with green serge, and thirteen ivory *boules*', as well as 'an octagonal table for the game of *portique*' (a type of roulette). Another room on the first floor held a large billiard table in green serge with its 'balls and cues'. In all, this was a true gaming den for which we found no equal, even in cafés and beverage-sellers' establishments. A passage from the *Roman bourgeois* by

Furetière evokes these gatherings of gamers held by the aunt of the bourgeois wife Lucrèce in the world of men of law: 'Just after having dined, we set out on the table two decks of cards and a trick-track ... When she [the mistress of the house] had won, she had a pie and a *poupelin* (puff pastry) brought in with a glass of home-made jams, which she offered as collation to the company, that took the place of supper.'[17]

Parlour games became increasingly popular during the eighteenth century. This is when they became widely used and reached the middle classes, such as merchants and masters of urban trades, while maintaining a stronghold in the wealthiest households. But such superfluous furniture as piquet tables were also occasionally found in the homes of day labourers in the 1740s and 1750s. According to our count, objects used for games of all kinds were to be found in 22 per cent of the households visited by notaries between 1720 and the 1790s. The range of games noted by the valuers was much broader than in the previous century. In addition to cards, trick-track, draughts and billiards, there were dominoes, chess, dice, skittles and games with pucks or barrels. In most cases, tables were referred to by the card games for which they were intended: the most common, the quadrille table, was square, intended for four players; then came piquet tables, for two players. Three-of-a-kind, a sort of poker played by two to five players, was hardly a great favourite of Parisians, if we can judge by the small number of pentagonal tables found for its practice.

Most of these tables, generally located in common rooms, were made of cherrywood or beech and were covered with a green (or less commonly red or blue) cloth or carpet. Some folding tables or 'sliding' tables (*à coulisses*) were worth less than 10 L. Others with a more luxurious and elegant appearance, such as the little quadrille table with its cabriole legs and amaranth inlays found in the company room of a wine merchant in 1753, were worth as much as 100 L. Around these tables stood chairs: the company room of another wine merchant who died in 1784, held two quadrille tables accompanied by eight chairs covered in sateen straw. In the residence of yet another wine merchant, Jacques Merlin, a little piquet table covered with a green cloth in the company room was surrounded, in 1765, by three armchairs with feather cushions and needlework tapestry.

Portable games, assessed in their boxes, seemed in large measure to be luxury objects, according to the notaries' descriptions: one quadrille game had four tiny boxes and cards in mother of pearl; a game of trick-track in ebony, with ebony and ivory pieces, silver cup and dice cup in a leather pouch, was estimated at 32 L. This last game belonged to a notary at the Châtelet (headquarters of criminal justice in Paris) in 1744. A draughts board 'accompanied by its twenty-four pieces in ivory and ebony', and valued at 12 L, was found in 1747 in the home of a gold and jewellery merchant. Billiard tables, which needed a spacious abode, were as rare in Parisian interiors during the Enlightenment as they had been in the century of Louis XIV. A master buttonmaker who died in 1751 had one table 1.22 metres long, covered in green cloth, with two balls and two cue handles. A haberdasher in the faubourg Saint-Antoine who died in 1760 had installed a billiard room in a shed leading on to the garden of his home. Finally, we must have a look in the home of the former Farmer General Lalive d'Epinay on the rue des Saussaies in the faubourg Saint-Honoré in 1782 to see a 'small billiard table in oak wood covered with an old green cloth, three ivory balls, nine handles and cues', and well lit by 'six candelabra in tin and their whitewood supports'.

Only in the most affluent households did the company gathered around the masters of the house have a choice of several games. One cloth merchant in 1751 possessed two painted and varnished quadrille boxes, as well as an ebony trick-track game composed of a board, ivory and ebony dice and a horn cup. A lawyer at the Parlement also had several games to offer in 1770: 'a trick-track on its table, accompanied by its ivory and ebony wood pieces' and a game of draughts. As for the rich Seigneur de La Grange, in 1775 he could offer his guests eight gaming tables, including two piquet tables, two quadrille tables, and four trick-track tables in the ground-floor antechamber of his house.

The time that many households today spend passively watching television, our ancestors spent in communal activity. People were apparently in the habit, in those times, of gathering in groups, as the abundance of seats attests – around a table to eat together, or near the hearth to spend the evening in pleasant conversation. Among the most well-to-do, company gathered around a game. We can picture the human warmth, the animation, the atmosphere of delight and sharing that these sociable habits introduced into homes before death knocked at the door. Was not the simple pleasure at being together the best antidote to life's everyday hardships in a world so deprived of ease, where the threat of sickness and death of loved ones was always lurking close at hand?

Storing Belongings

Where in these Parisian lodgings did people store the different objects of the interiors that we have discovered with the notaries, be they kitchen utensils, dishes, linen, clothing or other articles? How did our forebears in France solve the age-old problem of where to put things away? From the various types of furniture mentioned by valuers, we can try to see how things were stored and how these habits evolved.

Just as we were surprised at the profusion of tables, and even more so by the numbers of seats belonging to these Parisians, so the plethora of storage furniture piled into each home, and even into each room, is remarkable. There was an average of six pieces of such furniture per household, both during the reign of Louis XIII and on the eve of the Revolution. These figures apply no matter what the type of housing or the occupant's degree of fortune. This average takes into consideration not only large pieces of furniture – trunks, closets, buffets – but also containers such as bread bins, salting tubs and pantries, as well as storage surfaces such as shelves. While the position of this furniture remains unknown, the great amount of space it occupied is beyond question. The chamber of a rich hosier in 1723 held six closets and three trunk-chests. In the chamber of one of the king's tapestry manufacturers at the Gobelins works in 1730 stood five closets and two chests. An orange merchant, living in 1755 with his wife and child in lodgings with three chambers and a kitchen, had packed his chamber with one large and one small commode, one closet in walnut, one small closet or bookcase, a set of drawers in cardboard and two small closets in whitewood, in addition to a bed, a cradle and two chairs. Though we do not know how big these rooms were, it is easy to suppose that with such an accumulation of furniture, there was not much space left to move around.

The chest (*coffre*), or trunk-chest (*coffre-bahut*), was omnipresent during the seventeenth century in these Parisian interiors. An object of generally mediocre quality but easy to move, a chest could be placed anywhere in the home. Most often, it was covered with black leather and equipped with a lock and key. It could take on a variety of forms, round, rectangular or square. The prefix 'trunk' was attached to it when its cover was rounded, as it then bore a resemblance to a trunk. Valuers sometimes actually described it as 'in the form of a trunk' or 'trunk-fashion'. Some chests were placed on stands, such as one 'square trunk-chest covered with black leather placed on its stand in walnut'. When crate-shaped (*caisse*), chests could also be used as seats. Mentions of safes called *coffres-forts* ('safe-chests') or caskets containing papers, jewels or silver were rare.

Practically all the households inventoried in the seventeenth century and in the first decade of the eighteenth were furnished with at least one chest, in which linen and dishes were stacked. The chest was a symbol of constant travel and removal, reminiscent of an age when the Court was itinerant, and was gradually supplanted during the Enlightenment by the closet, a symbol of stability – though it did not simply disappear from eighteenth-century homes. As a traditional piece of furniture of peasant origin, and practical also because of its mobility, the chest (inherited, perhaps, from a grandfather or great-grandfather) was something people remained attached to, especially in the poorer classes.

In households that did not have the means to purchase one or more closets or a fashionable new article such as a commode, the chest continued to occupy an important place. Its value was in fact often lower than that of a closet, of the order of 5 to 10 L. In contrast, a walnut closet could fetch from 20 to 50 L. The sole piece of storage furniture that one journeyman baker possessed in 1723 was 'a square trunk-chest standing on its legs in walnut wood'. In the home of a *cabaret* owner who died in 1725, the chest was, with the exception of the bed, the only piece of furniture in the chamber. It served not only for storage but also as a seat and a table. In the middle classes of the population, chests often co-existed with closets. The chamber occupied by a pork butcher and his family in 1723, for instance, contained a trunk-chest worth 5 L and a closet worth 60 L. The same was true of a grain merchant in 1724; in her lodgings there was a large closet in walnut with two doors, with a value of 45 L, and a large square trunk-chest covered in black leather, valued at 8 L.

By the 1740s and 1750s, however, the chest began to disappear from chambers and rooms, at least in the wealthier classes, and was relegated to the kitchen, where it was reserved for specific uses. We found an oat chest and a bread chest in 1738 in the home of a hotel keeper, and two chests intended to store dough in the bakery of a hotel keeper in Gonesse who died in 1755. Chests of these types may be classified with the salting tubs, pantries and bread bins sometimes listed in kitchens, offices and shopbacks, especially in those semi-rural homes in the suburbs or surrounding villages. By the 1750s and 1760s the chest had become a vanishing species in all Paris interiors. Even in the faubourg Saint-Antoine, less than 20 per cent of the households still owned a chest or chest-trunk by 1760.

In place of the traditional means of storing, done without sorting, by simply piling things together, the closet substituted a more logical and methodical system. Already at the beginning of the seventeenth century, the closet had its place along with the chest in a number of households. It was present, for instance, in 77 per cent of the residences inventoried in the parish of Saint-Nicolas-des-Champs between 1635 and 1649. It was often described at that time as taking the shape of a large pair of closets, i.e. with double doors 'in walnut wood with four wickets (*guichets*) closed with keys and two sliding drawers (*layettes*)'. This article almost always included wickets, also called shutters (*volets*) or flaps (*battants*), which were small doors, of which there were usually one or, more commonly, two pairs set in the main doors, as well as one or two drawers and in some cases balusters, i.e. small columns that widened in the middle and were used to hold up a shelf. Closets might be decorated with a cornice that could be used to display delicate objects in earthenware or porcelain. To judge by the valuers' descriptions, the shape of the closet evolved little during the seventeenth and eighteenth centuries. A solid and massive piece of furniture in walnut or oak or, more rarely, in beech or pine, the closet – unlike the chest – generally appears to have been an article of fine quality, representing one of the key items of furniture in the home. It often figured in the dowry of a young wife. Usually, it stood in the deceased person's chamber and housed a range of objects, beginning with personal effects such as clothes or household linen.

Its contents often seem heterogeneous and scarcely denote a concern for organization, as our survey of priests' households at the beginning of the eighteenth century revealed. In the home of a professor at the Collège d'Autun who died in 1704, the valuers found one closet containing eleven small books, plus clothes, shirts, long-johns, bathrobes, nightcaps, socks and slippers, not to mention a pillowcase. A 'large closet with two locking doors' in the home of another priest in 1705, also held an accumulation of all sorts of things: liturgical vestments such as cassocks, cappa magnas, albs and surplices, as well as personal and household linen, a toiletry kit, two spoons and a tin saltbox, plus some books. Concurrently with the chest, the closet therefore seems to have perpetuated a taste for multi-purpose furniture, in many cases taking on the appearance of a junk closet.

The actual terms used by valuers to designate closets assigned them specific functions: the 'library' model was equipped on top with brass wires and two small curtains; the 'pantry-type' also had an upper grill in brass wire, to allow air to circulate; the dish closet contained several shelves. We should also mention a model in the shape of a cabinet, containing many more drawers than was customary. Finally, the expression 'bottomless closet' or 'closet front' was used to designate a closet 'set into the wall', 'in the wall', or 'enclaved' which was placed in a masonry excavation made in a wall not far from the fireplace – a sort of cupboard, in short.

As the chest went out of favour, this created an opportunity for the closet, which found its way into the great majority of households during the eighteenth century. Only the most impoverished families did not own one, making do, as we have seen, with a chest as their only storage furniture. Closets were present in 83 per cent of day workers' and floor polishers' lodgings between 1721 and 1761. Its average value in these modest interiors was 24 L. In the home of a day labourer who died in 1738 we counted six closets. The following year, three were found in the home of another day labourer. For humble people, whose belongings were often worth less than 500 L, the closet was a sign of wealth, often representing more than 10 per cent of their estate. The room of a poor painter who, at his death in 1711, left behind just 282 L in possessions, held a large closet valued at 35 L and another smaller one, much less valuable, estimated with a chest-trunk at 3 L 10 sols. The value of these closets could vary widely, depending on the wood, the size and the shape of each model. While those in whitewood were worth just a few livres, and never more than 15 or 20 L, large articles in oak might be valued at 80 or 90 L.

Because of its great volume, its inside shelves and its drawers, a closet provided a large storage capacity. But its height, measuring 1.67–1.82 metres, could require a ceiling height not available in every home. This is why owners were often obliged to amputate the upper section, and the remainder, called a *bas d'armoire* or 'closet bottom', kept only the lower two wickets of a four-wicket closet, making it resemble a buffet. These closet bottoms, less costly, appeared frequently in interiors, where they were often the only storage furniture, unless accompanied by a complete closet or a chest.

The buffet, another piece of furniture intended for storing dishes or food reserves, was similar to the closet bottom but less common. In general, these were low pieces, in oak or occasionally walnut or pine. One was described as 'a buffet in oak measuring $4\frac{1}{2}$ feet, with two flaps and a marble top, valued at … 36 L'. Such marble tops were exceptional. The buffet might include two sections or be topped with shelves. The buffet belonging in 1751 to the day worker Edmé Gradot, for example, had two sections and consisted of 'a chest in the form of a trunk in black leather and was fitted above with two flaps set with brass wire and below with two solid flaps, all of which could be locked with a key'. It was assessed at 24 L. Often encountered in modest homes, the buffet had its place in the kitchen or the shopback as well as in the common room.

Cupboards known as *vaisseliers*, present in a small number of households in the eighteenth century, were small buffets generally topped with shelves for storing dishes. Variants on the cupboard included the dish dresser (*dressoir à vaisselle*), the dish buffet (*buffet porte-vaisselle*), and the cupboard-closet bottom.

Decorative pieces of furniture, found only in the wealthiest milieux, could also be used for storage. The cabinet, introduced as early as the sixteenth century, was a sort of buffet with several doors and drawers used to contain precious belongings such as silver, jewels or papers. Often made of an exotic wood such as ebony, its value could be considerable: for instance, the 'German-fashion cabinet in ebony with six drawers' owned in 1642 by the king's counsellor Simon Plastrier was worth 300 L. As the notes of valuers demonstrate, a cabinet could be formed in a single body or might have two sections stacked one on top of the other. In the latter case, the bottom might be a simple pedestal or, like the top, a true small closet with wickets and drawers – a cabinet 'fitted on the bottom with two flaps and two drawers and on the top with ten drawers and one flap', or perhaps a cabinet with 'nine drawers and a wicket on a pedestal with cabled columns'. During the eighteenth century, cabinets might be decorated with chinoiserie motifs, according to the fashion of the day. The wife of a wine merchant had such a cabinet in 1753, 'painted Chinese fashion'. Because it generally constituted a luxury element in the furnishings, this item was preferentially located in one of the main rooms of the house, or in the cabinet room. By the end of the eighteenth century, however, it was completely out of fashion, displaced by the secretaire and the bureau, which enjoyed great popularity at that time, as we shall see later.

The commode, which appeared at the end of the seventeenth century, was an article of prestige, reserved for society's elite, until the 1720s or 1730s. In two town houses belonging to members of the nobility at the turn of the century, we found a commode in varnished wood and another in marquetry. This item of furniture, whose dimensions were smaller than those of the closet, was adapted to a style of home more intimate than in the previous century. Enjoying an enormous success from the reign of Louis XV on, it gradually found its way into every household. Baptized with a name meaning 'convenient', the commode was just that, taking up little more space than a chest while providing a comparable volume and a much better-organized means of storage.

It came in the most varied forms: the Regency or *tombeau* model was seen most frequently, with its short legs and three large drawers one above the other; the top drawer might be replaced by two half-drawers side by side. Other models were called *ancienne* or wardrobe-style. The commode could be distinguished above all by the luxurious types of wood used in manufacturing it. It might be simply built, generally in walnut or much more rarely in oak or beech, or it could be an elegant piece of cabinetry with veneer or marquetry in exotic wood. In fact, the use of rare and expensive woods in its construction differentiated it from other pieces of furniture: rosewood, purpleheart, *palissandre* (a superb, dark wood from Guiana), wood from the Indies, mahogany. Marquetry might also be done in purpleheart or even shell. With its ornaments in copper or bronze, shape like hands, handles, apples, or knobs, its keyholes, and its top in marble from Languedoc, Brittany or Aleppo in colours varying from white to Campagna green, wine or speckled with red, the commode was an elegant and refined piece of furniture exhibited with pride in reception rooms.

Though the commode eventually found a place in every social class, the most luxurious and costly models remained the privilege of affluent households. A haberdasher who died in 1720 owned a model in violet wood decorated with copper, including three drawers, one of which was divided in two, with a value of 100 L. The commode of another merchant haberdasher and bourgeois of Paris, built in *palissandre* with little copper figures and a marble top, was estimated at 50 L in 1740. In the home of a former chief clerk of the Constabulary of the *Maréchaussée* in 1773, we found 'a Regency-style commode in *palissandre* wood with two large and two small drawers, decorated with hands, keyholes and ferrule in coloured copper with marble top', valued at 72 L.

In the more modest classes, the commode – made of local wood and bare of any ornamentation – did not reach such prices. The one found in the home of a floor polisher in 1751 was in 'walnut wood with two large and three small drawers locked with a key' and was worth 16 L. In another floor polisher's home that same year, a commode 'with three large and two small drawers locking with a key' was valued at 18 L. The value of these simply made pieces, belonging to day workers or floor polishers, did not vary widely and generally did not exceed 20 L. Some 43 per cent of these hard-working souls owned commodes between 1721 and 1761. The day labourer Pierre Faveret even had three in 1738. A certain disorder seemed to reign inside these pieces of furniture, as in closets, to judge from the example of one sub-deacon in the diocese of Paris, an abbé at the Abbey of Saint-Etienne-de-Vaux, who stored pictures, a shaving bowl, a sugar grater and a stoup in the same commode.

During the eighteenth century, no other article of decorative furniture enjoyed the same universal success as the commode. Chiffoniers, corner cabinets or *encoignures*, secretaires, bureaux and bookcases were rare on the whole and were itemized in only a limited number of homes among the wealthy bourgeoisie. The chiffonier, also called a *chiffonnière*, was composed of superposed drawers and varied in height (depending on the number of drawers) though it was generally narrow. An eighteenth-century invention, it was originally intended to store embroidery and sewing work. This elegant article, combining the storage methods of the commode and the secretaire, was not widely represented. It might be in veneer, decorated with copper mouldings.

The corner cabinet, shaped like a small triangular closet, was usually fitted with a single door and was designed to stand in the corner of a room. Models often came in pairs, surrounding a commode in the same style. In the home of our former chief clerk of the Constabulary of the *Maréchaussée*, for instance, there were 'two corner cabinets, rosewood, with double wickets, with their marble tops, valued at the sum of 362 L', accompanied by the commode in *palissandre* described above. These small pieces of furniture, more decorative than functional, were also to be found in musicians' homes: in the home of the organist of the Petits Pères in 1753 were 'two corner cabinets with double doors' and 'two corners with marble tops'; in 1755, in the residence of a Music Ordinary at the king's chamber and chapel 'a corner cabinet in veneer' was found; 'two corner cabinets in cherrywood' stood in the home of Rameau in 1764, while the Italian composer Egidio Romualdo Duni had 'two corner cabinets and four corner shelves' in 1772.

The secretaire, intended for writing, and protecting papers from prying eyes, came on to the scene towards the mid-century and took various shapes: *tombeau*, sloping, closet, and 'commode-shaped'. Sometimes decorated with ornaments in gilded copper and topped with marble, it was equipped with a leaf-door that, when folded out, was used as a writing table. The secretaire was furnished inside with pigeonholes, drawer compartments, and a writing case with an inkstand. In a few homes it was accompanied by a safe and was generally placed in a chamber or cabinet. Woods used included walnut, veneer, rosewood, violet, *palissandre* and mahogany. Rameau possessed five secretaires in veneer, rosewood and *palissandre*, as well as two *serre-papiers* (or 'file cabinets') used for storing documents. Of the two secretaires owned by the composer Duni, one was closet-shaped, in rosewood, and the other tomb-shaped, in violet wood.

Other furniture connected to the arts of reading and writing, such as bureaux and bookcases, were found in increasing numbers during the eighteenth century, but of course they involved only a limited number of households generally belonging to intellectual circles. The bureau seemed to be used both as a storage unit, with two to six drawers, and as a work table. Furetière defines it as 'a table equipped with drawers or shelves, where business people or scholars write and put their papers'. Some priests possessed several bureaux that stood in the different rooms of their lodgings: one canon who died in 1720, for example, had three bureaux, one located in his chamber, another standing in the antechamber and the most luxurious model in a *cabinet*. We also found two bureaux in the home of a doctor of the Sorbonne in 1706, and another two in the home of Jean Desmoulins, curé of Saint-Jacques-du-Haut-Pas in 1732, and in other homes as well. The drawers of these pieces of furniture were sometimes real catch-alls. In the bureau drawer of the Abbé Louis Fornier, one valuer unearthed 'three old pairs of black wool stockings, a toiletry set, a comb case, a carpet in green cloth, two wigs, four pairs of cloth socks, four pairs of knitted buskins and three pairs of muslin stockings'.

These bureaux varied considerably in value, according to the wood used – walnut, marquetry or commercial wood, more rarely oak or blackened pear with copper ornaments. The bookseller Frédéric Léonard owned several, whose value ranged in 1706 from 30 to 50 L. But a luxurious model like the one 'in marquetry with copper scales, having several drawers', which belonged in 1709 to the Comte de Chemerault, attained the value of 100 L. A lawyer at the Paris Parlement possessed five bureaux, including one in *palissandre* worth 60 L, in 1728. In this same house stood three bookcases, including a large book closet in walnut wood with eight doors, estimated at 80 L.

Often those who owned bureaux owned bookcases as well. Though it was exceptional for priests to have a library room, they usually stored their books in appropriate furniture, called book closets or library closets. The most traditional model had two sections: a lower part with two solid leaves and an upper section that was glazed or screened with brass wire backed with curtains.

While the chest, like the closet and later the commode, typified general-purpose storage furniture, decorative furniture and pieces used for intellectual pursuits touched only that fraction of the Parisian population that was culturally or economically privileged. Such pieces constitute an element of social differentiation. Made by Parisian cabinetmakers in the eighteenth century, these prestigious furniture novelties bear witness to the exquisite and refined decorative tastes of the era of the Enlightenment. While they provided additional storage spaces, these elegant pieces of marquetry were placed in the most refined interiors, where their function was clearly more ornamental than functional, and they became part of the backdrop for reception rooms.[18]

Dwellings in which the quantity of furniture was not sufficient for storage needs were also equipped with shelves, often described as dish shelves, or planks for placing dishes, or book shelves. Shelves in pine, whitewood or more rarely in walnut, put every corner of these cramped lodgings to use for storage purposes. They sometimes were installed above a closet bottom and were most frequently found in the kitchen. Despite the multiplication of furniture pieces in the eighteenth century, shelves were still very widespread in humble abodes, even after the 1750s. Assigned multiple uses, they were to be found in 60 per cent of the households in the faubourg Saint-Antoine in 1760–2. In some households, sets of drawers were also recorded.

In an age when, as we have seen, meal preparation required the housewife to work close to the ground, storing objects on the floor – especially kitchen utensils or foodstuffs, which were kept around the fireplace – seems to have been a common practice, at least in less well-equipped homes. Engravings from the period illustrate these habits centred around the use of the fireplace for cooking. One eighteenth-century engraving by Laurent Cars, entitled *La Bonne Mère* (The good mother), shows a mother busy watching her children and cooking; on the ground, we see a coal burner topped with a casserole containing a large wooden spoon. Pierre Aveline's 1735 engraving *La Belle Cuisinière* (The pretty cook) portrays a young woman carrying eggs in her apron and preparing a meal: various vegetables lie on the ground near the fireplace, in which a cauldron hangs over the fire.

As new styles of cooking were adopted that allowed the cook to work standing up, this habit of storing objects on the floor slowly began to vanish. And as the chest was replaced by the closet, a similar transformation took place: instead of working on all fours to store things, people began to store vertically, with the upright storage furniture that could be as high as a standing person could reach. These shifts in storage habits, which we have tried to grasp through the objects used for them, were labour-saving, more comfortable, and more logical, a tribute to the spirit of the Enlightenment.

Professional Life in the Privacy of the Home

This world, rich with such a variety of objects that the notaries help us discover, demonstrates the close-knit relationship in that period between working life and private life within the home itself. Workers in what Peter Laslett has called 'the world we have lost' did not in fact 'commute' to their workshops, their shops or offices; their professional activities often took place under the same roof as their family life, or at least close by, in the same street or neighbourhood. While some trades, such as those of the butcher or the washerwoman, required adapted sites set apart from living areas, others largely invaded domestic space. The non-specialization of rooms which was, as we have seen, so commonplace, often went hand in hand with this trespassing of work space into lodgings. In the homes of poorer artisans who practised a trade that took little space, these two types of space overlapped.

Through the professional tools and merchandise valued, the inventories are especially revealing about this interpenetration of professional and family domains. This aspect of daily life which today seems so surprising, apparently affected a wide range of social and professional groups. Concrete examples taken from different fields of activity will help us grasp this behaviour which was so typical of *ancien régime* society.

In the food and drink business, trade masters had specific sites whose size varied according to the activity they practised, which could include manufacturing, distribution or both. At least two rooms on average were devoted to the master baker's trade in the eighteenth century: flour was often stored in an attic; in the bolting room the flour was remilled, and the bakehouse contained the instruments used for preparing bread in the kneading trough and the oven. Last of all, the bread was sold from the shop. Despite their specialization, these areas were not always distinct from the living area. In certain cases, the latter spilled over into the work space, which was necessarily important for most trade masters. Sometimes, the shop and even the bakehouse were used as the family kitchen. Occasionally there were even beds, usually reserved for shopboys, in these professional areas. In the home of Master Pouget in 1743, the shop served as both a bakehouse and a kitchen and contained a bed.

Beverage sellers, most of whom not only sold their goods but also received their clients in their drinking rooms, were also generally well provided with commercial space. As with bakers, they demonstrate this overlapping of private and public spaces. The kitchen sometimes opened on to the shop, or might be a simple alcove in it, when the two were not one and the same. In the home of a wine merchant who died in 1775, we found a '*boutique* used as a kitchen', furnished with a counter and tables, but also with all the utensils necessary for preparing meals. Another wine merchant in 1755 had a shop and a *cabaret* used as a kitchen. Among the café owners, the kitchen was the room most often used as a 'laboratory' for the preparation of food and drink for clients, as the valuers noted: 'kitchen used as laboratory'. This area, where the merchandise offered to clients was prepared, was also sometimes said to be 'used as a kitchen'. Consider the modest café owner who, in 1720, opened his bedroom during the day as a shop room.

In the decoration field, painters rarely worked in a room specifically designated as a 'studio', 'laboratory' or 'chamber used to mix colours'. Most of them, unless they worked outside their residence, carried on their activity within their lodgings. Claude Patin, for example, who died in 1744, had painted in a room 'serving as a kitchen or studio'. From the inventory's indications alone, it is often difficult to determine where these painters without studios worked. Their tools were most often kept in their chambers. Those of Robert Bourgeois were found in the chamber and the kitchen. Other tools were to be discovered in a main room, a *cabinet* or an outlying building. Jacques Bisson, who lived in 1737 in a single room, had stored his tools in a cellar; another artist's tools were found in a pantry in the courtyard; and the merchandise and tools belonging to Gilles Thevenot and 'used for his profession' were inventoried in several chambers 'used as a warehouse on the first floor of the building at the back of the courtyard'. These craftsmen seemed, then, to mix their work intimately with their daily life.

This interpenetration reappears among master carpenters and cabinetmakers, even though they were on the whole well provided with professional space: 82 per cent of our sample worked wood in a shop sometimes extending into a shopback, a shed, a workyard or, more rarely, a workshop. Because of the space taken up by their tools, these artisans needed a great deal of space, and often stocked the finished furniture orders in the rooms of their homes. Valuers commonly took note, for example, of 'merchandise found in the chamber on the first story'. In the home of master furniture maker Jean Boucault, who in 1737 possessed a shop

and a small storage room, the inventory listed merchandise found in the basement and even in the bedroom, where in addition to his own furniture, there
were twenty-four armchairs, six armchair frames ready to be covered, and six
chairs. In the dwelling of another master cabinetmaker, two chambers had been
requisitioned on the first floor for stocking ninety-eight pieces of furniture,
including thirty-six tables, eight pedestal tables, twenty-four armchairs, twelve
chairs, nine stools, a bed, and eight bedsteads. Not all master woodworkers had
so much space. Claude Didon lived in 1716 with his wife and two children in a
single room which served simultaneously as shop, chamber and kitchen, and held
three workbenches. Pierre Durand also had to make do, for himself, his wife and
a child, with a chamber-shop, while his apprentice slept on a *couchette* up in the
attic.

In the area of textiles, haberdashery merchants constituted a sort of merchant
aristocracy and often enjoyed clearly distinct professional spaces which were
separated from their private apartments even if they were located in the same
building and were contiguous. The typical home of a rich haberdasher and
bourgeois of Paris around 1740 included a shop, a warehouse, a kitchen, and a
dining room on the ground floor, a storage room and *cabinet* on the first floor,
the master's quarters on the second floor, including antechamber, common
room, main chamber and children's chamber, and another chamber preceded
by a small room plus storage space on the third floor, then three small rooms for
employees on the fourth.

Among clothiers and ribbon merchants, whose lot was generally less comfortable than the haberdashers', intermixing of workspace and private space seemed
to be the rule. Master clothier and ribbon merchant Jérémie Le Prestre dwelled
in 1668 in two chambers, one of which was used as a kitchen, on the third floor of
a house. To the practice of his trade he had devoted another chamber on the floor
above, in which the inventory listed 'twelve high-warp weaving looms equipped
with their tools', six spinning wheels of different types, 'a spindle, a pair of
reels', and lastly, 'two pairs of scales in yellow copper, furnished with their
iron beams and a spade weighing sixteen marks, also in copper, and an assay bal-
ance'. The partitioned corner of this room contained a low-post *couchette* as well
as three mattresses and was used as a bedroom. Although he had a workroom,
Jérémie Le Prestre stored his merchandise, worth 2090 L, in one of the chambers
of his lodgings on the third story. In 1751, another master clothier and ribbon
maker stored his merchandise in all four rooms of his home. Workers in the
service of a master did piecework in their single rooms, like the journeyman
gauze- and ferrandine-weaver whose ferrandine loom and tools were valued in his
chamber.

In the clothing sector, hosiers who, like drapers, were solely merchants, had a
work space that was distinct from their private apartments. Craftsmen, however,
often practised their activities within their homes. In the home of a master gar-
ment tailor in 1668, 'a tiny closet' next to a 'gallery' used as a kitchen contained
not only a *couchette* but also a 'bench used for said trade'. Master Delpèche, also a
master tailor, used his antechamber in 1721 as a workroom. Another tailor from
the same period practised his trade in his kitchen, where there were two
workbenches on trestles. The same went for a master haberdasher and button-

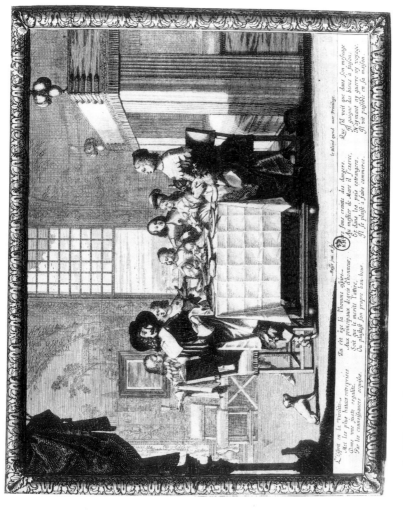

1. *L'Esprit en la virilité* (The spirit of virility), by Abraham Bosse. A table next to a bed, before the birth of private life. Circa 1630. Bibliothèque Nationale prints, Oa 44, pet. fol., p. 22 (photo: BN).

2. *Auditus. L'ouye* (Hearing), by Abraham Bosse. Before musical instruments became widespread in Parisian households. Circa 1630. Bibliothèque Nationale prints, Oa 44, pet. fol., p. 28 (photo: BN).

Tu charmes nos trauaux,&nos inquietudes. LA NVIT   Puisque le Soleil mesme eʃt bien ʃe cacher ⁴
Belle nuit qui nous faitz, ʒouir d'vn doux repos!   & repoʃer tandis, que ʃa ʃœur fait la ronde,
Tu ʃoulages nos corps,&les rend plus diʃpos   chacun a ʃon exemple peut au lit ʃe coucher,
&donne a nos eʃpritz le plaiʃir des eʃtudes.   &prendre du repos, comme cest œil du monde.

3. *La Nuit* (Night). Post bed and light. Circa 1660. Bibliothèque Nationale prints, Oa 45,
pet. fol., p. 76 (photo: BN).

Femme, de qualité s'habillant pour Coure, le Bal

4. *Femme de qualité s'habillant pour coure le bal* (Woman of quality dressing to go to a ball). The torments of the toilet in the age of the revocation of the Edict of Nantes. Bibliothèque Nationale prints, Oa 52, pet. fol., p. 151 (photo: BN).

5. *Le Déjeuné* (Lunch). Coffee colonizes the city. Mid-eighteenth century. Bibliothèque Nationale prints, Db 28 III, in-fol. (photo: BN).

6. *Le Paisible Ménage* (The peaceful household). In a modest household, items are stored on the ground and cooking is done at floor level. Second half of the eighteenth century. Bibliothèque Nationale prints, Ef 3, in-fol. (photo: BN).

Peint par Ant Dieu .   *Gravé par C Duflos .*

Madeleine en quittant le monde et ses douceurs | *S'est acquise un tresor de supremes bonheurs*
Pour vivre en solitude et faire penitence . | *dont elle jouira avec pleine asseurances .*

Se vend a Paris chez Baxin rue de St Severin devant l'église aux armes du Roy . Avec Privil.^{ge} de sa Majesté

7. St Mary Magdalene. Represented in a quarter of all images of saints, a symbol of penance and ecstasy, in the slightly sentimental tone of the eighteenth century. Bibliothèque Nationale prints, Db 10, in-fol., p. 25 (photo: BN).

8. St Genevieve. The patron saint of Paris continues to protect the Christian people of her good city. Bibliothèque Nationale prints, Da 35, in-fol., p. 140 (photo: BN).

maker, whose kitchen held two oak workbenches and two spinning-wheels in whitewood.

Whatever their trades, many other artisans tended to their tasks in their family setting, as the following examples show: one master musical instrument maker who died in 1632 had only a chamber-shop, in which were valued, among other things, the tools of his trade – saws, planes and so forth – as well as merchandise and rolls of strings for viols and lutes. One mirror merchant who occupied a chamber and a hovel in 1679, had installed in the latter room 'a workbench in pine wood with a table' and two other 'tables used for said trade'. Eleven mirrors as well as 'two reams of paper' were inventoried there. In the home of a master enameller who decorated thermometers and barometers, the kitchen was set up as a workshop: in addition to an oak counter, tools, a workbench, a bellows and merchandise, it held 'two large double barometers bordered in gilded wood, twelve large thermometers, three single barometers, five small thermometers, figures and tubes of enamel and glass, three packages of tubes of glass and enamel ... thermometer glass'. One master cooper lived in the 1670s in two chambers, one of which housed his work tools, 'a reel, two spinning-wheels, and tournettes'. In the home of another master cooper and wine handler, the shop in 1688 represented the focal point of the household, and the couple's bed dominated the shopback.

As for the hospitality trades, we have already emphasized how difficult it is to distinguish between rooms set aside for private life and those assigned to receiving clients. These spaces were in fact closely intermingled, as the valuers' notes indicate. It is common to find a room in innkeepers' and *cabaret* owners' establishments used both for serving customers and as a kitchen. The *cabaret*, a space that opened on to the outdoors, seemed to be the focus of semi-public and semi-private life, where the occupant spent a good deal of his existence, mingling with the crowd of clients. The latter most certainly had their place at the same table as the owner and his family. Unlike the artisan's stall or the small businessman's shop, both scenes of simple trade relations, the hotel, the inn and the *cabaret* were by their very nature places for extended socializing, offering bed, board or both to passing clients. Areas intended to protect family privacy are scarcely visible through the inventory's data. This field of activity is where the overlap between actions linked to family life and those related to business is most striking and, apparently, most commonplace.

Merchants and artisans were not alone in practising this intermingling of work and family so characteristic of daily life. The same habits reappear among the professions referred to today as liberal or intellectual. Men of law and scholars actually worked on their cases and received their clients at home. One bailiff and valuer of movables who died in 1703 had an office at home which consisted of a *cabinet* equipped with a bureau. The *cabinet* of a *Procureur-Tiers-Référendaire* at the Cour de Parlement in 1686 was larger, with tables, shelves and books. This office holder was helped by two clerks whom he lodged in his attic, set up as a chamber.

Finally, we can visit Louis-Claude Plastrier, Sieur de La Vernade and a notary at the Châtelet, in 1744 in his office on the ground floor of a house on the rue Saint-Antoine, where he was the main tenant. The office itself, heated by a cast iron stove 'of medium size' was furnished with a beechwood bureau and a walnut table with drawers locking with keys, an oak bench and straw chairs for visitors, as well as a closet with four flaps. This man of law also had a file cabinet (*serre-papiers*) in walnut for classing his files. A carpet in green cloth and a tapestry in blue wool with yellow fleurs-de-lis added a decorative note to this austere interior. This office communicated by a glass door with a *cabinet* furnished with a fireplace over which stood a double pier glass and a 'pendulum clock with bells'. The furniture consisted of a bureau with cabriole legs and a walnut armchair, both covered in morocco leather, six cane chairs, an ebony writing desk with gilded copper trimmings, and a bookcase-type shelf. Green taffeta curtains brightened the room, which housed, among other things, 340 books 'dealing with different practical subjects'. It is impossible to know if these two rooms were used solely as the notary's work area, or if they occasionally also served as a family space.

We have cited these few examples from the widest range of professional categories in order to highlight how in the pre-industrial era, there was no true break, as there is today, between working life and home life. The movements of the merchant in his shop, of the craftsman at his stand or of the ministerial office holder in his office blended almost habitually at that time into the everyday life of the household. Through unity of place, they became part of the most humble and ordinary actions of daily life. It would be inappropriate in these pages, devoted to private family life, to undertake a study of the working world as seen through notarial documents (e.g. inventories of businesses, tools and professional instruments and apprenticeship contracts). We have simply focused our attention on the relationship that grew up between working activity and domestic tasks in day-to-day life.

While unity of place was the primary factor in the interpenetration of these two realms, it was not the only one. Because spouses or children frequently participated in the trade practised by the father of the family, this also helped to strengthen the bonds between the worlds of profession and family. Though almost all our documents are silent about women's work, it is certain that many wives collaborated more or less actively in their husbands' trade, as is suggested by the numerous examples of widows taking over their deceased spouse's business. All the while tending to household chores or watching the youngest child, wives often lent a hand in the shop or workshop, and did so all the more easily since it was usually only a few steps away. The collaboration of sons or sons-in-law emerges through the comparison of their trades with those of the father. This continuity in trade from one generation to another and marriages between families within a same trade were commonplace practices in that age.

As Peter Laslett has demonstrated for England, the artisan's or shopkeeper's household, be it in London or in Paris, was both a centre of family life and a working community. This was perhaps one of the predominant features of the vanished world of the pre-industrial age.

5

Elements of Convenience in the Home

The notion of comfort (in the modern sense of creature comfort) was unknown to our ancestors, and the term *confort* did not have the same meaning in seventeenth- or eighteenth-century France, or even at the beginning of the nineteenth century, as it does today. For Furetière, it was 'an old word meaning help'. The *Dictionnaire de Trévoux* repeats this definition and adds the synonyms 'consolation, relief, encouragement'. This ancient meaning survived till later, since in the 1822 and 1835 editions of the *Dictionnaire de l'Académie Française* we can still find an entry for 'comfort' which reads, 'help, assistance (old)'. It is not until Littré's *Dictionnaire* of 1863 that, in addition to the traditional definition, we find the modern meaning: 'Everything constituting material well-being and facilities in life. This meaning was given to the French word 'confort' in England, whence it came, thus transformed, back to us.' Then came the noun *confortabilité* and the adjective *confortable* as applied to lodgings. Following in the wake of the industrial revolution, the notion of comfort or convenience came across the Channel from England, which in that area was several decades ahead of France.

In contrast, the term 'well-being' (or *bien-être*) had acquired its present meaning by the eighteenth century. Associated by Furetière with 'birth and education', it designated the 'situation and state of a person who lives comfortably and who lacks nothing, according to his condition' in the *Dictionnaire de Trévoux*. Supplying the most elementary needs of the human body, such as warmth, light and water, all essential to maintaining good health and indeed life, is the first condition for well-being. How did Parisians deal with all these problems of heating, lighting and water supply before the progress of the industrial revolution brought about fundamental changes in life-styles? Thanks to the wealth of information they provide, the inventories let us respond, at least partially, to these questions.

Heating

The fireplace was the place where food was cooked and the centre of gravity for sociability, but it was also the primary source of heat and could serve, in addition, as a means of lighting. A very symbol of domestic life, fire was synonymous with the hearth and home in the language of the times, and the fireplace, because of its multiple uses, was an essential pole of attraction in the home. Though it is never described in and of itself, its importance in the valuers' eyes emerges through the care they take in inventorying its elements, in detail and before anything else in a room: andirons, shovels, tongs and, more rarely, bellows, all of which are sometimes covered by the general term 'fire' (*feu*). The value of these accessories was small on the whole and rarely rose above some 4 L.

Other items besides these traditional instruments sometimes hint at the presence of a fireplace in a room: a screen or fire-screen able to withstand the heat of the flames; a *devant* or front, which might consist of a painting or a panel blocking the opening and preventing cold air from coming in, mentioned for a fireplace not in use. A rug placed before a hearth, ornamental pieces of earthenware or porcelain lined up on the mantel, a mirror or pier glass placed above the cornice, and candlesticks were all used as decorative elements. The fireplace was sometimes framed in a mantelpiece of beech, oak, painted wood or marble, and it could be equipped with two shutters to close its mouth and stop draughts. There was also the *garde-feu*, a mobile grid in iron or brass placed before the hearth; *garde-cendres* (fenders) were used to catch cinders; the grill, connecting the andirons, held the brands; the damper or bell was used for extinguishing the fire; and finally, the cast iron plate or fire-back protected the back of the hearth and stored heat.

Using these different objects, we proceeded to count the number of fireplaces in each dwelling and each room. This yields an average of approximately two fireplaces per household throughout this period, and one fireplace for every two rooms. While one-room dwellings were almost always equipped with a fireplace, the most spacious residences were proportionately very badly furnished, as a few examples from the early years of the eighteenth century reveal: in one merchant hosier's immense household occupying two buildings, the valuer mentioned only four fireplaces for twenty-one rooms.

When winter temperatures reached record lows, as they did in 1709, freezing temperatures must have reigned in these buildings which contained not only all those rooms, but numerous passages, *cabinets* and small storerooms as well. The fine home of the rich bookseller Frédéric Léonard was equipped with just seven fireplaces for nineteen rooms. A fur merchant occupied nine rooms in a house in which we counted only three fireplaces. From one dwelling to another, the number of fireplaces could vary considerably. The estimate for a house on the rue des Poulies, dating from 1632 stipulated that

> there should be made five fireplace mantels to be used, one in the common room and the others in the four chambers, which shall be in plaster and rubble, ornamented with a skirting above and below, fitted with their hearths which shall be in masonry with large tiles of terracotta, the mantels to be coated as is the custom, the said mantels being four and a half feet wide.

Thanks to progress in hearth technology, heating conditions began to improve significantly in recently constructed homes during the 1720s, with the adoption of multiple-hearth flues.

In one tenement building constructed during the reign of Louis XV, every room had a fireplace. Louis-Sébastien Mercier noted, in fact, that 'today, the chambermaid has her fireplace, the tutor has his fireplace, the butler has his fireplace'.[1] A number of inventories drawn up during and after the 1730s make mention of these dwellings so well supplied with heat sources. A parishoner from Saint-Roch lived, around 1760, in a fifteen-room house that held fourteen fireplaces. Six-room lodgings in the same neighbourhood were frequently provided with five hearths. A day labourer who died in 1738 rented thirteen rooms, each with a fireplace. By mid-century, certain hostelries also had a fireplace in almost all their rooms: at Louis Filliet's hotel, nine were counted for ten rooms in 1751. Another twelve were recorded for the fourteen rooms belonging to a hotel owner, Marie-Jeanne Blondelle, in 1738, and fourteen hearths were distributed among the sixteen rooms in Thérèse Morel's establishment in 1744. But the degree of comfort could vary greatly from one establishment to another, even late in the century. The inn run by Jean Costeroust in 1775 possessed heat sources in only two rooms – the shop and one chamber. The other fourteen rooms, essentially furnished rooms, were often crowded with three *couchettes* and were without fire. In the luxurious residences of the faubourg Saint-Honoré, there was in almost every case one fireplace per room. The only rooms without one were most commonly wardrobes, or rooms heated by a stove.

Although fireplaces were to be found in every room of these new buildings, older houses were much less well provided. This has an impact on the results of our study: taking into consideration only inventories made after 1750, we obtain an average of two fireplaces for three rooms. Yet even on the eve of the Revolution, the lodgings of our forebears in Paris, did not, on the whole, have as many fireplaces as they did rooms, because only a small portion of them were of recent construction. The majority of the houses visited then by the notaries probably dated from before the reign of Louis XV, as we have already seen, and therefore remained untouched by technological progress in the area of heating. Traditionally the rooms with fireplaces were the kitchen and the chamber of the deceased. The common room was also often brightened by the presence of a fireplace, but other rooms were heated only more rarely. Those used by servants, as well as outlying rooms, were almost never heated. There were exceptions, however. The estimate for a house in 1620 actually provided for 'a fireplace in one of the wardrobes of the said chambers, where it shall be placed for the best'.

As the numbers of fireplaces grew during the eighteenth century, their heating efficiency improved as well. Instead of gaping fireplaces with wide vertical conduits, buildings constructed after the 1720s substituted a narrower and deeper hearth with a lower mantel and curving chimney. Oblique conduits were adopted and became widespread before the middle of the eighteenth century. These had two advantages: they drew better and smoked less. The vast fireplaces with straight chimneys in the older houses were in fact a wretched method of heating, with a low calorific yield of 6–12 per cent and a nasty tendency to smoke. At the beginning of the eighteenth century, the use of metal plates to increase the reflective surface and reduce heat loss was still rare, even in prosperous interiors. Such heating technology or *mécanique du feu*, to use the expression of the times, was increasingly employed during the 1770s. Blondel offered several models for estimates in his *Cours d'Architecture*, published in 1771. The ironwork model provided that 'for each fireplace in the apartment there shall be furnished five fittings in cast iron plates of a size appropriate to occupy the entire edge as far as the mantelpiece'.

Furnished in this manner and equipped with curved stacks, fireplaces gained in efficiency and could sometimes even be used to heat two adjoining rooms. The presence of such fireplaces, designed according to the new technology, is attested in the inventories by mentions of mirrors or pier glasses installed above the mantel, whose shape was now lower and narrower. With its painted panels, its mirrors, and its decorations in earthenware or porcelain, the eighteenth-century fireplace blended into the decor of the room, where it was becoming one of the essential elements, as we shall see.

Despite progress made in its operation, the open fire nonetheless remained a mediocre means of heating, as the German traveller Volkmann emphasized during his stay in Paris from 1787 to 1788: 'For a German accustomed to a moderate temperature, fireplaces are not pleasant ... Too near the hearth, you are burned and your eyes sting; elsewhere, you freeze.'[2]

In Germany and the northern countries, another means of heating, the stove, was preferred. This article appeared towards the middle of the century in Parisian homes: before the 1740s and 1750s it had reached less than a fourth of all households inventoried, and it did not truly begin to rival the open fire until the 1760s. Long scorned for safety reasons or rejected out of simple prejudice, its success came late. There seem to have been psychological barriers hindering its acceptance, if this well-known passage from Mercier is any indication: 'What a difference between a stove and a fireplace. The sight of a stove deadens my imagination, saddens me and makes me melancholy. I prefer the sharpest cold to that dull, lukewarm, invisible heat; I like to see the fire; it brightens my imagination.'[3]

While we may grant that the author has exaggerated somewhat, this opinion would seem to translate the attachment Parisians had to the traditional actions, ceaselessly repeated from generation to generation, connected with the presence of a fire in the hearth – the motions of fire-tending and gestures of sociability which, as we have seen, brought together family and friends around the fireplace. According to Volkmann, 'the French readily say that fire keeps company, because they spend much time making it.' The German visitor, accustomed to the stove, added disdainfully, 'Anyone who can't find a better way to occupy his time should truly be pitied.'[4] That the open fire remained the primary means of heating in most households in the 1770s was due to its symbolic value more than to its calorific contribution: only 40 per cent of the households in the parish of Saint-Germain-l'Auxerrois between 1768 and 1790 were fitted with stoves, 35 per cent of those in the parish of Saint-Eustache from 1770 to 1772, and 17 per cent of those in the parishes of Saint-Etienne-du-Mont and Saint-Nicolas-du-Chardonnet during the same period.

Yet this new means of heating offered the advantage of being economical: the cost of a stove, 10 to 20 L on average, was within reach of almost any purse, its calorific yield was higher than that of a fireplace, and its fuel consumption lower. Yet both modest families and the wealthy came late to this means of heating which had been introduced in countries like Germany, Switzerland and the Netherlands as early as the sixteenth century. A journeyman furniture maker in the faubourg Saint-Antoine used a stove as his only heat source in his chamber in 1760, and in the home of a day labourer and his wife in 1770 the common room was heated by a stove. In many cases, this item was accompanied by a fireplace and seemed to be used to meet peak demand. In interiors consisting of several rooms with an insufficient number of fireplaces, stoves would be used to heat rooms without hearths, such as the dining room, the antechamber, the *cabinet* and occasionally a chamber. But in fine reception rooms, the fireplace retained its charm and prestige, and could not be replaced by a stove.

One such apparatus was inventoried in the dining room of the priest Nicolas Le Bègue in 1772. That same year, another was noted in the antechamber of the surgeon Louis Gervais and in the *cabinet* of a journeyman rope maker. Its efficiency did not go unnoticed by the rich Marquis de Féline, who expressed this wish in the lease of his town house in 1772: 'In the dining room shall be a stove to fill the empty bay located between the first antechamber and the dining room and to heat these two rooms; this stove shall be covered with a marble shelf.' The stove also frequently found its place in shops, especially beverage sellers' establishments.

The results of our investigation prove that Mercier was right when he said of stoves, 'They have the flaw of making us shivery; they have their place only in antechambers, in places where we eat and in the cafés where the idle go to shelter their lack of occupation and to take refuge from the cold.'[5] Of sixty-two beverage sellers' inventories, forty-six, or 74 per cent, mention a stove, and this article was listed in 80 per cent of the shops. The 26 per cent of beverage sellers who did not own stoves either died in the first half of the century or did not have shops. The first such item was listed by valuers in 1748 in the inventory of a beverage seller, Jacques-Georges Gouget. In the abodes of hotel- and innkeepers, *cabaret* owners, and wine merchants, where specific rooms were also set aside for receiving clients, the stove had found its way into 37.5 per cent of the households. In 1765 in the home of one wine merchant, two stoves supplemented the five fireplaces counted in the dwelling. That same year, in the residence of Jean Lanson, another wine merchant, two 'rolling' earthenware stoves were inventoried. In the house of yet another wine merchant who died in 1784 the three fireplaces available to heat ten rooms were supplemented by three cast iron stoves, whose number doubled the available heat sources.

What did these stoves look like? The models inventoried were made of various materials: cast iron, sheet metal, earthenware, or glazed, varnished or marbled clay. A stove might be square or round, or even bell-shaped. It was sometimes mounted on castors and was always fitted with sheet-metal pipes.

Despite the increasing numbers of better-designed fireplaces and the use of one or more stoves in many Parisian households during the second part of the eighteenth century, the problem of heating had not been fully resolved in pre-revolutionary Paris. Though it is well established that the capital was more advanced than the countryside and provincial cities, its inhabitants nonetheless seem to have been inadequately equipped to face the deep cold of those dark winters of 1693, 1694, 1695, 1709 and 1740. But of course, among hyper-sensitive modern Parisians and other city dwellers who have lived all their lives in over-heated apartments, there is a tendency to judge according to late twentieth-century standards of comfort.

To strengthen their defences against the cold, our ancestors had several tricks, using various accessories filled with coals as supplementary heat sources. Most common of all were braziers or *braseros*, or foot-warmers in clay or metal with openwork. To warm the bedcovers, there were copper warming pans, found in more than half the households, or bedwarmers called *moines* or 'monks' and hot-water bottles. There were also wicker baskets for warming linen, fitted with a metal heater or a cauldron and kept, like the many irons for ironing, next to the fireplace.

Wall hangings, or wood panelling in the homes of the rich, thick window and bed curtains, door curtains and folding screens were not employed solely for decorative purposes. They gave protection from draughts and retained the little circulating warmth provided by the flames in the hearth. Finally, wearing warm clothing indoors and in bed was another defence against the cold. In most of the wardrobes examined, the inventories list dressing gowns, nightcoats and nightcaps. Jean François de Guénégaud, *Maître Ordinaire* at the Chambre des Comptes, possessed 'a dressing gown with blue and yellow background lined with squirrel, trimmed with silver and gold ribbon', valued at the high price of 150 L. The dressing gown of a *Commissaire Ordinaire des Guerres* who died in 1658 was described as being in 'silken serge lined with lambskin' and was valued at 25 L. A notary who died in the same year made up for insufficient heating at night by donning 'a nightcoat in crimson velvet lined with lambskin', worth 10 L. A master baker also kept a 'lined nightcoat' in his wardrobe in 1659. Only when the stove began to be introduced into interiors, after 1750, did Parisians dare remove some clothing when they came inside. They could also remove the bed curtains from their beds without fearing that they would shiver all night long. As the stove became widespread, it set in motion a transformation of habits and lifestyles that foreshadowed the nineteenth century.

What sort of fuels were used to feed these heating sources? When present, stores of wood and coal listed by the valuers provide an answer. But the majority of these households were empty of any fuel, as only 35 per cent had such stocks. This absence of reserves in so many homes may seem surprising. It was in no way related to the season in which the inventory was drawn up, and in any case, whatever the outside temperature might have been, food had to be cooked, which meant that a fire had to be kept going every day of the year.

This deficiency could be explained by the time that elapsed between the death and the notary's arrival. Above all, however, it seems to be due to the lack of space for storing such bulky materials. In fact, we know that only one third of these lodgings had access to a cellar, and almost as many more Parisians lived in single rooms. The costliness of wood and its constantly rising price during the eighteenth century kept poorer people from buying in great quantities. Fuel supplies were most frequent and most abundant in well-to-do hosueholds. Numerous households probably acquired their fuel day by day. From a guide for foreigners in Paris published in 1716, we learn that supply yards selling firewood were to be found in various places, at the Porte Saint-Antoine, the Porte Saint-

Bernard, and the Grenouillère; new wood, fascines and faggots could be bought on the Quai de la Tournelle, the Quai de l'Ecole and the Quai de la Grève. Waste wood could also sometimes be purchased in the ports and in yards, where it was cheaper than other wood. As for coal, it was available on the Place de la Grève.[6]

In homes stocked with fuel reserves, these were generally kept in outlying rooms, primarily the cellar, followed by the attic, the woodshed, the workshop, the loft and sometimes the courtyard. Wood and coal might also be kept in small quantities in the occupied rooms, as the valuers noted: 'in a small closet, a half-quarter of a *voie* of new wood [a voie weighed about 1250 kg] ... in a small cabinet used as a kitchen, twenty logs of new wood and eight faggots ... in a small chamber, a quarter of a *voie* of wood and four *boisseaux* [bushels] of coal dust'. In the home of a Guardian of the Royal Treasury and member of the Paris bourgeoisie who died in 1748, a curtain from Bergamo 'serving to hide wood and coal' was listed in the antechamber.

Different sorts of wood were used for heating. The variety is never specified – though it was apparently usually oak, and less commonly beech, hornbeam or even lime, which was particularly used by bakers. But the form taken by these stocks is almost always noted: floated wood, transported by river, was the most commonplace. It came from Burgundy, and more specifically from the mountains of the Morvan region which, from 1726 to 1787, supplied on average 250,000 *stères* (a stère = 1 cubic metre) of floated wood per year, or half the requirement of Paris.[7] 'The wood that makes the Parisians' soup', wrote Mercier,

comes from forty leagues away without wagons or boats. Thrown into the streams, it descends as far as the rivers; industrious hands then put together those long, floating masses whose pieces are perfectly bound together. It is another job to tear these rafts apart. Men, muddy amphibians living hip-deep in the water, all dripping with dirty water, carry all that wet wood, piece by piece on their backs, that is to be burned the following winter.[8]

This log-floating operation actually included several successive steps. Marked with the wood merchant's sign, the logs were set afloat in streams in no kind of order. Then, following the stacking operation, they were left to dry for six to eight months. Once dry, they were formed into trains. A train consisted of several stumps joined by rounds, and resembled a sort of raft some forty-five metres long, on which two or three men rode. To make it easier to float these trains, dams were constructed to create reservoirs, and narrows to make the water rise. Some two years passed between the time the logs were floated and their arrival in Paris. 'The wood brought by the river', Mercier continues, 'and stacked in piles as high as houses, will disappear in the space of three months. You see it in square or triangular pyramids, which block your view of the surroundings: it will be measured, carried, sawn and burned, and all that will remain is the square.'[9]

Floated wood could be distinguished from new wood by its poorer burning quality, as its two immersions in water made it porous. It price was also lower than new wood: a *voie* of floated wood was worth 10 to 12 L toward the mid-eighteenth century, whereas a *voie* of new wood fetched 12 to 16 L. The latter sort was brought by boat without being dumped in the river, and was then cut into logs. Many other adjectives were used by the valuers to designate heating wood: burning wood, cut in a certain manner to make it easy to fire; sawn wood; cordwood, cut in 144-cm logs; the *cotret* or fascine of short brushwood, in pieces or sticks tied together at both ends with ties called *hares*; the *falourde*, a bundle of thick branches made of cut poles or thin floated wood; and finally wood shavings.

While 'wood consumption has become frightening' in the Paris of the 1770s and 1780s, according to Mercier, coal was far less popular. As he says, 'Hard coal, despite the perfection it has attained recently, has as yet been adopted only by smithies.' In spite of its lower cost (5 to 6 L per *voie* by the mid-eighteenth century) and its superior calorific yield, coal was much less widespread than wood and seems to have been used only as a supplementary fuel, for operating burners, foot-warmers, or *braseros*. Its presence was noted only in households also stocked with provisions of wood. The inventories never specify whether the fuel is hard coal or charcoal. The coal sold in Paris may have come from deposits of lignite that were mined during the eighteenth century in the lower Seine valley, near what is now Les Mureaux. As for charcoal, the best producer was the upper Nivernais region, because of its beech forests.[10] Despite its excellent qualities, hard coal seemed to inspire a certain wariness: it had a reputation for being dangerous and creating a danger of suffocation. It also smoked and gave off an acrid smell.

Though the quantities of fuel found in Parisian homes varied from one household to another, they were rarely abundant. The amounts were expressed in *voies*, a measure equivalent to about two *stères*, or two cubic metres. As an indication, one *stère* of wood could be used to make ten fires. Large reserves of these bulky materials were noted exclusively in the homes of the very rich and those with very spacious abodes. 'Thirty *voies* of cordwood plus two thousand faggots valued at their just price of 390 L and 110 L' were stocked, in 1660, in the home of Louis Girard de La Cour des Bois, king's counsellor and *Maître des Requêtes Ordinaires* of the royal household. An auditor at the Chambre des Comptes in the same year stored 'eight *voies* of new cordwood' worth 90 L in his home. Only the privileged classes had the means and the space to warehouse such quantities of fuel. Mercier seized the occasion in March of 1783 to underline rich people's extravagant consumption, which they pushed to the point of causing a wood shortage:

> The kitchen, the antechamber, the *salon*, and twenty private rooms in the same house devour wood. One forgets what it costs to bring the wood. What does it matter, to a man with one hundred thousand livres in independent income, to burn two hundred *voies* of wood pointlessly? Does he know that by being prodigal in this way, it is as though he bought and destroyed the air he breathes? This means that a great many humble households must make do with two *voies* of wood – the rich man has burned their portion.[11]

In the vast majority of households, fuel reserves were no larger than a quarter, a half, or three-quarters of a *voie*. In bakers' households, their trade obliged them to have more substantial stocks, which reached on average five and a half *voies*. Other measures used by the notaries include the cord, for wood, equivalent to two *voies*, and the bushel (*boisseau*) or the hogshead (*muid*) for coal. Fascines and faggots were sold by four-and-hundred and were assessed at 4 to 5 L per hundred early in the eighteenth century. The smallest of wood stocks consisted of a dozen boards and a few faggots and logs, enough to keep a fire going for one day.

Though heating conditions for Parisians in this period seem very rudimentary to the twentieth-century observer, it is important to recognize that at the very least they had improved significantly by the second half of the eighteenth century, to the point of having a heat source in almost every room. We should also emphasize that in the fight against the cold, Paris seems to have been strongly privileged in the age of the Enlightenment; the inhabitants of the rest of France, especially those in the countryside, did not benefit from such a profusion of heating devices.

Lighting

When we imagine Parisian dwellings from this period, or at least those in the centre of town, the picture is sombre, even in broad daylight when the sun was out. Though the inventories remain mute as to the number and size of openings in these rooms, natural light appears to have penetrated only with difficulty into most of these interiors, because of the height of surrounding buildings and the narrowness of streets and courtyards. Only houses opening on to gardens – which were rare on the whole, as we have seen – and new buildings constructed after the 1720s or 1730s, with greater amounts of window area, could really take advantage of daylight and sunshine.

With progress made in glass manufacturing techniques during the eighteenth century, large glass panes did begin to replace the squares of canvas or oilcloth or tinier panes, thus improving lighting quality. But while it was possible to live by the sun in summer, how did these Parisians manage in late autumn and in winter, when darkness fell in mid-afternoon? In rooms with fireplaces, the fire in the hearth served not only as a means of cooking and heating, but also as a light source. Though the glow of the flames was sufficient to brighten a conversation by the fire or a meal shared by family members, it was certainly not enough to read or write by or to do needlework.

Our visit to these Parisian households shows us the different lighting methods available to their residents. Though the numbers could vary considerably from one residence to the next, lights were on the whole fairly abundant: the average, which remained steady throughout the seventeenth and eighteenth centuries, increasing slightly after the 1750s or 1760s, was five per household. Like all averages, this figure masks some wide disparities. A number of homes, and not always the poorest ones, seemed to make do without any light sources whatsoever. Could this reflect an omission on the part of the notary? Or did the inhabitants, perhaps single people, get by with plain candles, without holders? Or, in the case of servants, did the lights belong to their masters or lodgers? In contrast, other dwellings, especially those with several rooms, contained a profusion of lamps: we counted twenty-eight in the home of the royal messenger of the University of Reims in 1639, and twenty-two owned by a spice merchant in 1649. The home of Frédéric Léonard was lit in 1706 by thirty-two lights, and that of a haberdashery merchant had twenty-three in 1708. Forty-four lights were assessed in the home of the Marquise de Traisnel in 1746, and thirty-four in the abode of a wine seller in 1755.

Certainly these examples come from wealthy families living in spacious residences. But the average number of lamps per room, which amounted to three for every two rooms, does not actually seem to have been much higher than in more humble dwellings containing fewer rooms. Good lighting was not always a privilege of the rich. Day labourers, for instance, did not differ in this from higher social categories, as they too possessed an average of five lamps per household. In fact, in the home of one such worker who died in 1738, the notaries found about twenty. It was not uncommon to find single rooms equipped with four to six lights. The second figure is relatively high and represents the average number of light sources found in households of the faubourg Saint-Antoine around 1760.

These instruments were in most cases valued with batches of other objects, and their price varied depending on what they were made of. The most ordinary objects, however, were only of nominal value: the three candlesticks and two holders mounted on one fireplace were estimated at 2 L 10 sols. Prices for candlesticks could range from a dozen sols to 8 L. Individuals of little wealth, like day labourers, attempted to imitate the rich by indulging in better lighting.

Light sources came in two types, mobile and fixed. The former were more common and presented a range of models. We found that the majority of lights in kitchens were of this type. As the only room in the house in which a fire burned all year long for cooking, this was where each family member came in the evening to light his or her candle with an ember from the hearth. The kitchen therefore appears to have been the usual place for storing lamps. This would explain why other rooms were completely void of lights at the time of inventory, since every candlestick in the house would have been brought to the kitchen first thing in the morning.

Based on a sample of more than 8000 lamps, both mobile and fixed, we calculated the frequency with which different lighting articles were listed in inventories (see Appendix 2). The candlestick, with one or two branches, is far and away the most commonplace, representing 63 per cent of the sample. It was most often made of yellow or silver-plated copper, or of red, gilded, bronzed or coloured copper, of *potin* or cock metal, an alloy of lead and copper rinsings, of iron, or – more rarely – of silver, pewter or wood. It is described with its candlerings, little hollow cylinders in which the candle was inserted. These were the most elementary means of holding a light; they were also the cheapest, and the first that any household acquired. In the humblest homes, a candlestick was the single source of light, as was demonstrated by the one yellow copper candlestick found in the miserable dwelling of an innkeeper in 1754, or in the chamber and kitchen occupied in 1749 by a *cabaret* owner, his wife and his children. Some of these candleholders had specific uses that were noted by the valuers, e.g. 'shop candlestick', 'counter candlestick', '*cabinet*' or 'office', 'bedside' or 'toiletry candlestick'.

The torch (*flambeau*), or candelabrum for large candles, accounts for 15 per cent of the lighting sample and generally had its place on dining or gaming tables.

When the model differed little from a candlestick, it was often made of copper; when in silver, its value was assessed with articles of dish- and glassware, and it was a symbol of wealth, inextricably linked to a certain standard of living. The Marquis de Savine owned twelve candelabra, including two 'with girandoles having two candlerings', worth 417 L, and four other 'round' and 'sculpted' holders valued at over 790 L. A preserve of well-to-do households, the candelabrum apparently had an aura of prestige about it, as is revealed by the inventory of a priest, one Jean-Baptiste Duhamel de Saint-Lambert, secretary of the Royal Academy of Sciences, who died in 1706. The cleric's family indicated to the valuer that the two silver candelabra standing over the fireplace did not belong to the deceased; rather, they had been 'lent by his nephew, so they said, because he liked them'. In addition to its functional purpose of providing light, a silver candelabrum also played an ornamental role, simply because it was a pleasure to look at.

Other kinds of lighting were much less frequently inventoried in these interiors. The *martinet*, a flat candleholder in yellow copper or iron, fitted with a long handle so that it could be held out to light the user's way, was sometimes encountered in shops or modest households. One market porter who had a shop at the wheat port in 1740 used four *martinets* in it. The two-room lodgings in which a coach driver lived in 1734 were lighted by a single iron *martinet*. A master carpenter in the faubourg Saint-Antoine also possessed just one lighting device at his death in 1761: a yellow copper *martinet*.

Lamps were used only rarely (accounting for 3 per cent including *lampions*, a variety of oil lamp). Fuelled with oil, they generally stood on a base in cock metal or pewter. They might include four, six or eight reservoirs in cock metal, tin or pewter, surrounded by a glass sleeve. They had the disadvantage of giving off a smell as well as smoke, and had to be meticulously tended, which involved watching the oil level and pulling and trimming the wick as the lamp burned.

Intended for more specific and uncommon uses, lanterns (2 per cent) in tin with glassed openings were used to illuminate a shop, a stairway, or a cellar. They could be permanently hung from the ceiling, using a structure in gilded bronze, and fitted with glass panes and candles. The 1744 inventory of Charles-Hugues Baillot de Villechavant, *Maître Ordinaire* of the Chambre des Comptes, mentions one 'stair lantern with its pulley', estimated at 30 L.

A few Parisians made use of simple candleholders (1.5 per cent) that took the form of a small candlestick without a stand, consisting of a ring or a handle to hold it. Finally, two other types of mobile light were used on occasion: the night-light (*veilleuse* or *veilloir*) and the girandole (1 per cent). The former, made of tin, bore similarities to the lamp or lantern and provided light, as its name suggests, during the night. The girandole, a sort of candlestick with several branches, was sometimes decorated with crystal lustres and was not only a light source but an ornamental object as well. Its presence is noted by valuers only in the most luxurious interiors. Two gilded girandoles with crystals, worth 150 L, and two others in gilded copper, were counted among the numerous lighting instruments belonging to Frédéric Léonard. The two girandoles belonging to the Marquise de Traisnel were described as 'in gold-leafed copper, trimmed with rock crystal almonds' and were valued at 120 L.

These portable lights made up more than 90 per cent of the light sources in the homes of our Parisians. Their very mobility meant that they could be used in any room or building of the household, making it easier to move about after sunset. With the exception of silver candlesticks and candelabra, owning such an article was not a sign of wealth. Furthermore, their variety actually contributed to cultural development: having light at night meant being freed from the sun's rhythms and gaining time to work, read, write, and therefore to learn. These portable points of light had the advantage that they could be used where they were needed, on a table, a commode or a mantelpiece. The very purpose of those tiny, elegantly shaped *guéridon* (pedestal) tables that began to appear in the most refined interiors during the eighteenth century was to raise a light high enough to illuminate part of a room and make it possible to read. This high, narrow piece of furniture consisted of a large stand and a very small round or octagonal surface. Some of the loveliest models were marquetry-covered with copper patterns. The most ordinary ones, of little value, were 'in blackened wood, Chinese fashion'.

Though a great convenience in daily life, plain candle stubs or roving candleholders nonetheless presented a real fire hazard (even though the holders were most often in metal, which was preferred to wood). The account of Jean-Gaspard Dolfuss, an envoy from the city of Mulhouse sent to Paris in October 1663 with an escort of eight persons for the renewal of the treaty of alliance between Louis XIV and the thirteen Swiss cantons and allied cities, is telling. The traveller, who stopped at the Hôtellerie de Flandre near the rue Sainte-Marthe, in the small rue des Petits-Champs, told how fire broke out at 3 a.m. on 13 November in the room next to his:

> A young man ... had stayed up drinking and gaming in his chamber ... with the waiters of the house; he had leaned his candle against the wall, and it fell over during his sleep and set his straw mattress on fire. The neighbours were alerted by the smell of burning straw and gave the alarm. Two foreigners, lodged in the next room, woke up and broke the door down; the wall, the bed, everything had already burned.[12]

Few and far between in the seventeenth century, fixed lights began to spread in the following century, with the fashion for mantelpiece candleholders, especially among well-to-do people. Representing 9 per cent of all light sources in these households, such holders, with one, two or even three branches in gilded or coloured copper, stood in the finest room in the dwelling, one on each side of the pier glass. They might be embellished with ornaments in porcelain, crystal or enamel. The success of these fittings was closely related to that of the mirrors, which increased the brightness of the room by reflecting light. In 1746, the Marquise de Traisnel owned a 'pair of single-branched copper holders with leaves and flowers painted in enamel, trimmed with candlerings in gilded moulded copper', worth 15 L, as well as 'two holders with two branches, in English crystal, trimmed with copper candlerings' valued at 12 L. When in plain copper, these holders were within reach of any purse: two small mantel candle-holders with coloured copper candlerings were worth 50 sols.

Of great rarity, chandeliers or *lustres* (0.5 per cent) were true luxury items, to be found only in the homes of the very rich. They seem to have marked the height of refinement in the home of Jean-Jacques de Beauharnais, *Commissaire aux Requêtes* at the palace, where, in 1646, 'a chamber chandelier to be hung from the ceiling, with twelve branches, made by Robertet' was described. It weighed 43 marks, 6½ ounces in silver and was worth the considerable sum of 1720 L. Twenty years later, when the home of Roland Gruyn, a *Secrétaire des Finances*, was inventoried, the valuers used the term *lustre* to designate the two hanging lights, one with eight branches, in crystal, valued at 400 L, and the other with six branches, also in crystal, valued at 80 L. More commonplace in the eighteenth century, the *lustre* nonetheless remained a showpiece with its crystal pendants, where the light of the flames danced with a thousand sparkles. This is how the article owned by the Marquise de Traisnel appeared: a '*lustre* with six branches, with a frame in gold-leaf, trimmed with almond drops in rock crystal', worth 300 L.

The assessment of these lighting appliances often included that of various accessories: sconces, the *binet* (a small piece of metal with a point in the centre, placed inside the candle ring to hold the candle so that it could burn all the way down), and the *garde-vue* (a sheet of paper, cardboard, metal, porcelain or frosted glass used as a lampshade to prevent the light from blinding one's eyes). Wick-trimming scissors, inseparable from their scissor cases, were omnipresent. Candle snuffers in the shape of metal cones in cock metal or copper were noted in a few households and were used to put out the flame. As for tools to light these flames, they are mentioned only exceptionally. In the home of an abbé, a lighter 'in the shape of a pistol' was kept in the bottom of a commode.

There is simply no comparison between the abundance of light sources and the tiny quantity of reserves of candles and oil inventoried by valuers: indeed, only 4 per cent of our households possessed the latter fuel, and these were the richest, where there were actually large numbers of lighting appliances. The largest stocks of oil could reach weights of up to 100 pounds (45 kilograms) or more, at a rate of 5 to 7 sols per pound. The Chevalier Jean de Choisy, *Chancelier* and Keeper of the Seals to the late Duc d'Orléans, even had a store of 500 pounds in 1660. In that same year, we found 100 pounds of oil in the home of an auditor at the Chambre des Comptes. The same weight in moulded candles, worth 32 L, was mentioned in 1744 in the estate of Charles-Hugues Baillot de Villechavant, *Maître Ordinaire* of the Chambre des Comptes. Such considerable reserves of candles seem to have been exceptional, as the most common stocks were generally no larger than 14 kg. A lawyer at Parlement owned 11 kg of tallow candles in 1648; one of the king's counsellors, an intendant of finances, had a stock of 6 kg in 1657; a cloth merchant, some 9 kg valued at 60 L in 1705; a hotel-keeper in 1744, 14 kg and so forth. Candles might be stored in boxes or crates, as the valuers sometimes noted: two candle boxes in whitewood containing 14 kg of moulded candles were found in a cellar; a pine crate containing 2½ kg of candles, worth 2 L 10 sols, lay in a lawyer's basement.

Wax candles were much more expensive than tallow ones and appear only rarely in inventories. Only the wealthy could afford to keep stocks of them: 15 kg worth 24 L 16 sols, were found in the home of a counsellor and secretary to the king in 1648; 20 kg estimated at 49 L 10 sols, in the home of a counsellor at Parlement in 1657.

These limited reserves of tallow and wax candles lead us to wonder whether the valuers simply omitted to mention them if they were present in insignificant quantities. The practice was probably to buy supplies day by day. If a Parisian's candle went out and, for lack of sufficient stocks, left him in the dark (as in the nursery song 'Au clair de la lune'), he could always refresh his supplies easily 'at the Halle, on Wednesdays and Saturdays at the free candle market, where candles are sold at better prices than by chandlers'. According to the *Guide des étrangers dans la ville de Paris*, 'there are also candle factories in the Saint-Antoine and Saint-Laurent faubourgs and elsewhere, and the tallow market is held every Thursday on the old Place des Veaux.'[13] The practice of making moulded candles from tallow at home does not seem to have been widespread, to judge from the negligible number of moulds inventoried.

Though the most impoverished households were quite literally forced to trim their wicks and make do with the glow of burning logs in the fireplace like their country cousins, the great majority of Parisians, whatever their social level, had several means of lighting. Possessing abundant, diverse and beautiful light sources, however, remained a privilege of the very wealthy. Only in their luxurious interiors did the lamp become an actual fixture, and therefore attain the rank of decorative element. From a useful object, it evolved into a pleasant one. Our contemporary world, both inside our homes and in the urban environment, has been so transformed by the revolution in lighting early in the twentieth century, with the introduction of gas, petrol and electricity, that we can hardly appreciate the prestige that light enjoyed in traditional societies. But we can imagine the sumptuous illuminations at Versailles or other princely residences, or the bright lights that appeared on the major holidays in the capital. By its dazzling brilliance, light possessed a power of attraction that was all the greater for those Parisians who lived in semi-darkness, even in daytime, in much of the city's housing. The fashion for mirrors which reflected the sparkle of lustres, wall-mounted candleholders, and girandoles with their many branches highlights the growing taste for light during the eighteenth century.

This progressive extension of artificial light in rooms went hand in hand with a growth in the penetration of natural light, through larger openings and improved glassmaking techniques. During this same period, light began to brighten of the streets of Paris as well, thanks to measures taken by the city authorities. New procedures came into use for lighting public roads, beginning with street lamps from 1745 to 1766, then oil lamps, which replaced the eight thousand candle lanterns in 1770, and finally Quinquet lamps with glass chimneys in 1783. Furthermore, to improve air circulation and sunlight in the streets, the regulation of 10 April 1783 set out a coherent policy for public streets by correlating street width and building height. In the eyes of contemporaries, Paris on the eve of the Revolution was beyond doubt the city of light, the *ville lumière*.

Water and Hygiene

Accustomed as we are to our super-equipped homes where we need only turn a tap to have torrents of water, we can hardly imagine how precious this liquid was to our ancestors. Can we understand the daily struggle involved in getting supplies, storing and consuming it? The inventories do not offer much help in satisfying our curiosity in this area. Nevertheless they do tell us about the types, capacity and currency of the various containers intended for storing water and for its various domestic uses, such as drinking, cooking, housework and personal cleanliness.

The cistern or *fontaine*, immortalized in the works of artists like Chardin, contained the main water supply for the household. Most often, it is described as being in red copper, with a lid and a tap, standing on an oak base. Models also sometimes appear in hooped wood, lead, earthenware or stoneware. Though this was an essential article for storing water, cisterns were inventoried in only 68.5 per cent of these homes. A voluminous vessel, whose capacity was rarely less than a *voie*, or 30 litres, it was generally to be found in the kitchen, or occasionally in the shop. Its volume varied widely from one model to another: the most common size held 1 or 2 *voies*, but some were found containing 6 *voies*, i.e. 180 litres or more. Working with a sample of 650 cisterns whose volume was indicated by their valuers, either in *voies* or in buckets (or *seaux*, the equivalent of a half-*voie* or 15 litres), we calculated the amounts of water that a dwelling would have had available. The largest group of households, 32 per cent, was equipped to store 2 *voies*, or 60 litres; 25 per cent had the capacity to stock 45 litres; 17.5 per cent from 75 to 90 litres; 16 per cent could store no more than 30 litres, and 9.5 per cent, 130 litres or more. The average capacity per household amounted to some 65 litres.

The value of these cisterns varied according to their size. A sampling of values estimated in the mid-eighteenth century ran from 1-*voie* cisterns valued at 18– 20 L and 2-*voie* cisterns worth 25 L, to 4-*voie* cisterns at 30 L and 5-*voie* ones at 40 L. If it was sand-lined in order to filter the water and thereby improve its quality, the cistern was even more costly: a sand-lined cistern in red copper, holding 2 *voies*, with lid and tap on an oak stand could fetch 35–40 L. Wicker-covered stoneware models, which became widespread among the poorer classes in the eighteenth century, were more modestly priced: 'a cistern holding around 2 *voies*, in wicker-covered stoneware, with a cock-metal tap, on a turned alder base' was worth 12 L. Cisterns were expensive, and were found with large volumes or in number only in affluent households. One exceptionally large cistern, holding fifteen buckets, or 225 litres, stood majestically in the kitchen of Jacques Galland, *Secrétaire Ordinaire* to the Council of State and the Direction des Finances in 1654. In 1740, in the kitchen of the home of the Maréchal de La Fare, the inventory listed a sand-lined cistern in red copper with a lid and tap, standing on its wooden base, valued at 80 L, and another cistern in red copper, holding about two *voies* and estimated at 28 L. One wine merchant possessed two cisterns with a total storage capacity of nine *voies* or 270 litres.

Many other receptacles noted by the valuers could contain water, either in the absence of a cistern or as a supplement to it. These included buckets in red copper, iron, earthenware or simply in rimmed or hooped wood, or coopered or bushelled buckets, tubs, basins, rimmed barrels, wooden pans or stoneware pots 'for water' or 'serving as a cistern'. These various portable utensils, unlike the voluminous cisterns, were no doubt intended not only to store water, but also to carry it back from the well or water fountain to the dwelling for daily consumption.

Where did the water come from that was kept in these various containers? Very rare were the references in inventories to a well, like the one noted in the valuation of the possessions of a doctor of medicine and king's *Professeur* in 1646: in the dispensary was 'a copper pulley used for the well, the bolt and the iron handle used for the cord: 40 sols'. However, other documents involving these Parisians, such as trade or sale contracts or leases, can provide us with information on the possible presence of a well in a courtyard. At the time it was acquired in 1655, the home in the rue Saint-Martin of the widow of a sworn wood moulder who died in 1678 included 'a courtyard in which, in addition to the above-mentioned hostel building, there is a well'. The same was true of the home of a master baker, inventoried in 1680 and described in the 1669 contract of sale as having a 'courtyard behind the said main building, with a well in it'. We know that each house in the rue de Sépulcre possessed a well, but one was spoiled.

Wells could be either private, i.e. for the use of a single house, or common to two or three houses. For instance, the house purchased in 1632 by Marie Guyonnet and her first husband, Georges Masselin, had 'a courtyard where is a common well'. Whether private or common, wells gave daily experience of communal life to their users. One master baker had the usufruct of only a quarter of the courtyard and well attached to the house he had acquired in 1694. But these wells were often dry or polluted, and their water was notorious for its mediocre quality, which could even prove dangerous. Despite precautions taken when constructing them (such as lining them with leaded terra cotta), in practice wells were not always protected from infiltrations from septic pits, which were also dug in the courtyard.

The problem of wells polluted by infiltrations from septic trenches was a source of frequent litigation among neighbours, duly recorded in reports by building experts. Even the inhabitants of the fashionable faubourg Saint-Honoré were not spared these problems of neighbourly nuisances, as one example will demonstrate: the experts summoned in 1790 by the Marquis de La Vaupalière, plaintiff against the dowager Vicomtesse de Breteuil, whose town house stood adjacent to that of the Marquis, stated,

We had water drawn from the well using the pump, and we recognized that it was thick, muddy and very foul, and in such a state that we could not examine inside the well, which is hermetically sealed. Hence we ordered Monsieur de La Vaupalière's master builder to raise the stone covering the well and to hold open the doors of the *cabinet* in which it is located, so as to let the mephitic air evaporate, so that we might proceed with the operations which formed the object of our mission.

Parisians could also take water from municipal fountains, of which there were thirty-five in the middle of the seventeenth century and sixty-five a century later, according to Abbé Expilly, who adds, 'There should be ten times more.' The water distributed came from the Seine, the springs of the Pré-Saint-Gervais, and from Belleville. The aqueduct of Arcueil, rebuilt early in the seventeenth century to bring spring water from Rungis, drew the admiration of the English traveller Martin Lister in 1698, for whom the 'Aqueduct of Arcueil ... by the by, is one of the most Magnificent Buildings in and about Paris, and worth going to see. This noble Canal of hewn stone conveys the water 15 miles into Paris'.[14] The fountains supplied the different neighbourhoods of Paris, and the water from aqueducts and pumps was redistributed through terra cotta or wooden pipes.

Inhabitants of certain parts of the city were luckier than others. Those in the Temple neighbourhood, for instance, had five public fountains available, at Sainte-Avoye, Paradis, l'Echaudé, les Vieilles-Haudriettes and Blancs-Manteaux, supplied by 'the northern springs', i.e. Belleville and Ménilmontant. Water supplies to the Louvre neighbourhood were provided by the well-known Samaritaine pump, built under a span of the Pont Neuf by the Fleming Jean Lintlaer in 1608, which poured twenty inches of water a day, or 400 cubic metres, into a reservoir situated in the cloister of Saint-Germain-l'Auxerrois. The Porte Saint-Jacques or Observatoire water tower, endpoint for the aqueduct of Arcueil, supplied water to the Luxembourg neighbourhood. Two pumps were set up in 1672 under the Pont Notre Dame that drew 3000 cubic metres of water. Despite the measures undertaken by the city authorities in the seventeenth and eighteenth centuries to equip Paris with numerous fountains that would serve both as public utilities and as ornaments for urban design, the capital had a chronic water shortage. Demand from the population grew in the second half of the 1700s, and several projects were proposed in the era of the *Encylopédistes* to palliate this dearth, though not all came to fruition.

The plan developed in 1762 by a member of the Académie Française named Deparcieux to convey water from the river Yvette by canal and by aqueduct failed for financial reasons. The brothers Vachette installed pumps in 1771 on boats on the Seine to draw water into reservoirs built on the Place de la Bastille, the Place du Palais Bourbon and the Quai de la Conférence. This water was sold to waterbearers at 2 sols per barrel of approximately two hogsheads. The real pioneers in the field, however, were the brothers Perier, who followed the example set by English engineers by installing a means of bringing water into the home, which represented a bold innovation at the time. Their water supply company, a *société capitaliste* (or joint-company), was founded in 1778 with a capital of 1,440,000 L divided into 1200 shares. In 1781 and 1785 it installed two fire pumps, one at Chaillot and the other at Gros Caillou, to produce the water its Parisian subscribers needed. In 1785 the company absorbed the competing business run by the brothers Vachette, and it was brought under the financial and political control of the government in 1788, becoming the Administration Royale des Eaux de Paris. Despite the reasonable price of 50 L per year for a hogshead of water per day, the brothers Perier were distributing only 900 hogsheads a day in 1788.[15]

The main purveyors of water in Paris were the slinged water carriers who sold the liquid door to door at 2 sols per *voie*, or 3 or 4 L per cubic meter, not including tips or extra charges for climbing stairs. 'Twenty thousand water carriers', wrote Mercier, 'carry two full buckets, morning and evening, from the first to the seventh storey, and sometimes higher. If a bearer is sturdy, he makes some thirty trips a day.'[16] Debts to water carriers are sometimes mentioned in inventories: one member of the Paris bourgeoisie owed 20 sols to the water girl for 'a month of her salary' at his death in 1707. Carriers also supplied passers-by with water, as William Cole saw in 1765: 'I have seen People on the Pont Neuf, with a large Copper Vessel on their Backs, with a Cock to it, selling drinking water to the Passengers.'[17] In wealthy households, the servants were sent to draw water from the well, the river or a fountain. Water consumption was estimated at twenty litres per Parisian per day by Deparcieux around 1760. Around 1775, according to the economist Victor Riqueti Mirabeau, the figure was ten litres.[18]

What was water used for in the households of our Parisians? Along with wine, water was a common drink. It was served on Parisian tables in water pots made of pewter or earthenware, or in carafes and decanters of thick glass or crystal, as we have already seen. But the Seine's water, which most of the city's population drank, was considered unhealthy, especially for those unaccustomed to it. Martin Lister commented in 1698 that

> the River Water is very pernicious to all Strangers, not the French excepted, that come from any distance, but not to the Natives of Paris, causing Looseness, and sometimes Dysenteries. I am apt to think, the many Ponds and Lakes that are let into it to supply the Sluices upon the Canal de Briare, are in part the cause of it. But those who are careful of themselves purify it by filling their cisterns with sand and letting it sink through it, which way clears it, and makes it very cool and palatable. As for the Spring Water from the Maison des Eaux, it is wholesome in this respect, and keeps the Body firm; but it is very apt to give the Stone, which the People of this Town are infinitely subject to.[19]

Fifty years later and more, travellers had a similar view of the poor quality of the Seine's water. For William Cole, it

> is as thick and muddy as the Channel of the Severne which comes up to Bristol: so that to drink such water is not practicable: besides they say it is very unwholesome, Creates Gravel, and is very purgative, especially to Strangers: so that they carry clear Water about in Pails and Vessels, and sell it by the Quart or Gallon, at a very extravagant Price.[20]

According to the German Volkmann, the Seine's water was a silt-laden, reeking dumping place for all sorts of refuse. It gave foreigners diarrhoea. Water from the river Yvette, in contrast, was thought to be very clean.

English and German travellers were not the only ones in the age of the Enlightenment to believe that Paris water could be detrimental to the health of its inhabitants. Having become of scientific interest to students of hydrology and geology, it was analysed by chemists like Antoine Laurent de Lavoisier in 1783. Water was also a source of preoccupation for doctors late in that century who were convinced there was a close relationship between health and the environment. It should be noted that in the same period, by decision of the Parlement in 1780, executed six years later, the cemetery of the Saints-Innocents, the great Parisian necropolis, was permanently closed for health and hygiene reasons and was transferred to the edge of the city at Montrouge.[21]

The same concern for hygiene stimulated the idea among the enlightened public that the waters of the Seine should be treated. Complementing the desire to increase the amount of water distributed was the desire to improve its quality. On the tip of the Ile Saint-Louis a hydraulic machine was installed to purify the

Seine water, which was then transported by wagon in barrels bearing the king's arms. Purifying fountains, invented by the Sieur de Charancourt, an engineer in the city of the same name, were set up on the Quai des Miramiones, at the wheat port, and on the Quai de l'Ecole.[22] The most well-to-do Parisians owned sand-lined cisterns in order to remove impurities. The curé of Saint Séverin, Jean Pinel, even used a water-filtering stone in 1751. It was in 1745 that one Sieur Marque had the idea of replacing the layers of sand with porous sandstone, which he called filtering stone (*pierre filtrante*). On this matter, Mercier wrote,

> We must purify water from the Seine at home, in order for it to be light and salubrious. We drank water twenty years ago without paying much attention. But since the family of gases and the race of acids and salts have appeared on the horizon ... we have thought about what the chemists announce ... We have begun to analyse water, and when we drink a glass today, we think – something our careless ancestors did not do.[23]

Water was also used for preparing meals, essentially to cook vegetables. All sorts of vessels, like the *coquemar*, a big kettle with a hook, the *marabout*, a large boiling kettle, the *bouilloire*, which we would call a tea kettle, and the cauldron were used to boil water in the hearth. Other housekeeping uses for water become apparent only through a limited number of objects found in a few interiors: for doing the dishes, there were cast-iron *chaudières* or dishwashing kettles, cisterns for washing glasses, and tin drying racks; for cleaning clothes, we found washbasins, tubs, wash *chaudières* in copper, wooden buckets, wicker baskets, wash pots, *rouleaux à savonner* (lathering rollers), as well as iron rods and some horsehair cord, inventoried in a courtyard for washing and drying laundry. Given the scarcity of these clothes-washing tools – with the exception, of course, of the few homes of washerwomen in our sample – it appears that the practice of washing one's own laundry at home, or at least the large items, was not as well established in town as it was in the countryside, where greater amounts of space and water were available. This work fell to the washerwomen, who often lived in the suburbs, near the Seine, especially around Auteuil or Passy, as is indicated by the lists of their customers' debts: 7 L due to the washerwoman from one bourgeois of Paris in 1707, or 53 L 10 sols owed by a master painter and gilder in 1721 to a washer of household linen in Boulogne.

Furthermore, certain declarations recorded by the notary highlight the washerwoman's role in cleaning the household's laundry: 'which laundry the said widow declared she had received from the washerwoman since her said husband's death', or 'next, the laundry which the said widow declared had been returned from the wash after the seals had been fixed', or 'the said Sieur Martin declared that he had taken the laundry ... from the washerwoman that she had been given to wash.' Though equipment for washing laundry was often absent in these dwellings, articles for ironing were more frequent, such as irons, platens for drying laundry, and tables and covers for ironing it. In the area of domestic chores, it is important to emphasize that housekeeping articles are apparently absent in many lodgings. Was this actually the case, or was it more probably a sign of negligence on the valuer's part, given the scant worth of such objects? We found few mentions of horsehair brooms, dusters, brushes, mops, rags and washrags.

Were these inhabitants as zealous in cleaning their lodgings as they were in sweeping before their houses, as required by police regulations? Such *ordonnances* ordered citizens to 'have swept regularly before their houses, courtyards, gardens ... as far as the gutter, and half the roadway, every morning at seven o'clock in summer and before eight o'clock in winter, and to pick up garbage and refuse beside the walls of their houses and make a pile of it so that the city cleaning services may remove it'. According to the 1663 regulation, residents were to 'throw at least two buckets after sweeping on the pavings and gutter situated before their houses'.[24] But these measures were not always carried out, and the city's streets – especially the narrowest arteries in the city centre, which received almost none of the sun's beneficial disinfecting rays – were unclean and became virtual cesspools when the weather was wet, according to testimony from contemporaries.

What role did water play in bodily hygiene? We can attempt to answer this question by looking at the toiletry articles inventoried in these Parisian households. Articles used for washing were rare in the eighteenth century and were the preserve of the upper layers of society. One lawyer at the Parlement, a member of the parish of Saint-Nicolas-des-Champs, owned 'a round basin in silver, for handwashing' in 1648; two members of the Paris bourgeoisie living in the same neighbourhood at about the same time each possessed 'a little cistern for handwashing'. Only a privileged few could devote a toiletry corner to body care in the wardrobes adjoining their chambers. In the home of one Ordinary Purveyor to the King in 1645 we found not only a little copper bowl standing on a wooden base, but a burner for heating water as well. A painter and chamber valet to the king in 1633 possessed 'a square table with a white and red marble basin, valued at 120 L' hidden behind a screen. 'The half-bath in red copper with its lid and its tap on a wooden chassis, valued at 12 L' and inventoried in a recess in the home of the wealthy *Secretaire des Finances*, Roland Gruyn, was the height of refinement in 1666. Among the linens of the deceased were found 'three small curtains used around the bath', worth 6 L.

This example seems quite exceptional for the seventeenth century. Even though the first modern bathtubs, with their elongated shape, appeared as early as the reign of François I, bath-taking was very rare in the sixteenth and seventeenth centuries. People were highly distrustful about the idea of water touching the body at the time, since it was believed that the water infiltrated the organs and weakened them. The evil effects of bathing were described thus in 1655: 'Baths, except for medical purposes in cases of pressing necessity, are not only superfluous but also very damaging to humans. The bath debilitates the body, and because it fills it [with moisture], makes it susceptible to the influence of bad qualities in the air ... Baths fill the head with vapours.'[25]

The use of water for hygienic purposes was therefore limited, during the century of Louis XIV, to washing the face and hands. Cloth towels 'for washing hands' are sometimes mentioned by the valuers. In the first half of the eighteenth century washbowls, generally accompanied by water pots, cisterns for washing hands, and basins made a tentative entry into the city's merchant bourgeois milieux. That an invitation might be offered to tend to such cleansing, perhaps before sitting down at the table, is revealed by the presence in a room, a chamber or a vestibule, of an earthenware or copper washbowl, standing on a walnut base, or of a little earthenware cistern on a similar base or an iron console, sometimes defined as 'for washing hands'. Relatives of these washbowls, such as basins – sometimes in silver – and buckets were also occasionally assigned specific functions: basins for washing hands or for lathering, shaving basins, large basins for heating water, in red copper with iron legs, or large buckets for footwashing, in earthenware.

Bathtubs made very slow progress until 1750 and remained the hallmark of an aristocratic elite. Even though he did not have a specific toilet *cabinet*, the Marquis de Bonnac did possess a red copper bathtub in 1739, worth 40 L, which was installed, oddly enough, in a greenhouse at the back of the garden behind his town house on the rue de Grenelle. When he died in 1737, the priest and Sorbonne doctor Louis Lebesgue de Majainville was the owner of a coopered bathtub, which was also inventoried in an unusual place, in his wine cellar. An officer of the Duc d'Orléans also kept a bathtub worth 8 L in the basement of his home in Passy, in 1740. The practice of daily or even weekly baths could hardly be said to be a regular habit. Finally, the Marquise de Traisnel and the Marquis de Savine, who died in 1746 and 1748 respectively, could enjoy the luxury of a bath in their steamrooms.

As progress in room specialization continued and the toilet *cabinet* and the bath *cabinet* made their appearance after the half-century mark, a change came to be felt in people's attitudes toward using water for their bodily hygiene. Though to certain minds it was still of dubious usefulness, water was no longer the focus of as many prejudices as it had been in the previous century. Not that toiletry articles for such ablutions had become commonplace: water pots and washbowls appear in only 21 per cent of the households visited after 1750, and cisterns for handwashing in 11 per cent. A few large basins were designated as being 'for footwashing'.

It is interesting to note the appearance in the wealthiest homes of a new item, the bidet. This item, very likely introduced in France from Italy in the eighteenth century, consisted of a wooden seat and a basin. It is most often described as being made of walnut, with a basin or vase in earthenware. Bidets were to be found in only 7.5 per cent of these interiors.

The bathtub, which had come to occupy a room of its own in the finest homes, remained the preserve of a social elite and equipped only 3 per cent of the homes. It was almost always made of red copper, and could be worth a substantial sum, as the following example shows: in the bathroom of a master surgeon, which was located next to his bedroom in 1770, there stood a large bathtub, with a reservoir and a tap, in red copper, 'its cylinder fitted with sheet metal and lead pipes for conducting water'. The whole installation was worth 200 L. Another master surgeon who died in 1763, owned a bathtub in red copper with a cane seat. The type of bathtub made of zinc was much simpler, like the half-tub or sitz-bath (a sort of vat with a seatback and two handles) that belonged in 1771 to Sieur Baudard de Vandésir, *Trésorier Général* for the Colonies.

Note that among the above-mentioned bathtub owners, there were two master surgeons. That members of the medical profession should be equipped to go through certain cleansing motions would seem to be symptomatic of the changing attitude towards hygiene. Immersing one's body in water was no longer considered to be harmful to one's health. Though the practice remained outside the realm of experience of the vast majority of Parisians, bathing was slowly making its way into society's upper levels. The architect Jacques-François Blondel counted five bath *cabinets* in 1750 for seventy-three town houses in the capital. In other words, at mid-century less than one *hôtel* in ten had a special bathing space. A similar survey conducted in 1801 and covering sixty-six town houses built since 1770 mentions twenty bath *cabinets*: from 6 per cent, such spaces were now to be found in 30 per cent of the most luxurious dwellings.

Though the improvements in heating made possible by the adoption of the stove were more propitious to these new hygienic practices, bathing was still restricted to a few privileged homes, because of both the difficulty in acquiring enough water – especially hot water – and the cost and complexity of such sanitary installations. Taking a bath was not simply a way of cleaning oneself. It was a pleasure of the rich that was both refined and sensual.

The beauty and luxury of the decor in bathrooms in the wealthy faubourg Saint-Honoré are stunning, as recorded in the detailed description given by a building expert in one of his reports: at the Hôtel de Vergès in 1782, the bath *cabinet* located on the ground floor, just behind one of the chambers, was 'tiled with black and white compartmented tiles, had a ceiling with a cornice around its circumference, and was lighted with a bay window fitted with a frame containing large panes of Bohemian glass' with

jalousie blinds opening in two parts ..., all the interior circumference is decorated with story-high pilasters in lattice-work, including the cornice, which similarly represents lattice-work, and the back of the niche enclosing a copper bathtub with a fresco painting represents standing nymphs holding a vase and flowers in the corners; between the lattice-work panels, there are six painted cartouches, four of which represent pots of flowers, and two, busts of women; water is brought to the bathtub by two solid copper taps, one for cold and one for hot water.

This town house was supplied by water tanks, two of which were located on the basement level, another above the stables in the building facing on to the courtyard, and the last on the first floor of the main building, on a landing that led off the great staircase.

The bathroom of the Count de Vauvineux on the rue d'Anjou was only slightly less luxurious, as described in 1787:

Lighted from the courtyard by a bay of windows, the room is tiled with tiny tiles in fine sandstone and little black tiles with a band around the edge; the high ceiling is surrounded with a cornice ... the circumference of the said room is decorated with earthenware tiles up to standing height, surrounded with bands of marble in turquoise blue, the skirting is in yellow marble; in the part arranged for the bathtub (in tinplated copper) stands a lead basin fitted with a pipe carrying the dirty water out to the terrace ... a water heater, in red copper with a brick furnace, heats a lead-lined oak water tank located on the mezzanine ... lead pipes carry the water to the bathroom above.

These splendid bathrooms were of English inspiration, and were already, at the end of the age of the Enlightenment, fitted with all the elements of modern comfort. They marked a major milestone when compared to the lovely *hôtels* of the Marais, from the reign of Louis XIV, which at best were equipped with a basin and a pot of water in a wardrobe. But once again, such hygienic practices, though indicative of the growth of a new awareness, affected only a small minority of the Paris population.

Even in the second half of the eighteenth century, water was hardly used for bodily hygiene in the majority of Paris households. Cleanliness was considered a matter of personal linen and of appearance. Fashions in dress, the degree of whiteness of lace, hairstyles and perfumes were the criteria for cleanliness. During the reign of Louis XIII, Dr Louis Savot wrote that his contemporaries had no use for steam baths, 'because the linens we have help us to keep our bodies clean today'.[26]

The very term *toilette* did not presuppose the use of water in the definitions offered by the *Dictionnaire de Furetière* or the *Dictionnaire de Trévoux*. Rather it designated the 'linens, silk rugs or other cloths that are spread on the table for undressing in the evening and dressing in the morning', or 'the square on which rouges, pommades, essences, beauty spots and so forth are set. For men, it consists of a case in which combs and brushes are kept.'

These articles were rare in the seventeenth century. On several occasions, inventories done in and around 1640 note the presence of 'night boxes' in chambers, which were intended to store clean linen, combs, brushes or mirrors. A lawyer at Parlement possessed such a box 'in red velvet with a lock, having a cushion (*charlotte*) in red velvet trimmed with a silk fringe (*mollet*) and a small open-work dust cover (*crépine*)'. Lists of toiletry articles and toilet tables, with all the accessories used to care for women's faces and coiffures, were more frequent during the eighteenth century, though they were still to be found in only 9 per cent of these Parisian homes. Toiletry articles laid out in a bedroom or in the adjoining *cabinet* were signs of luxury that bore witness to a certain degree of refinement and sense of decoration: the *toilette* in white serge trimmed with striped muslin that was found in 1735 in the home of a merchant hosier was decorated with *plottes*, or jars of powders and creams, that were covered in red damask bordered with gold ribbon, as was the mirror frame. The whole set was valued at the considerable sum of 120 L, and went with matching chairs and a matching bed in red serge with white silk decorations. In the home of a cloth merchant who died in 1751, the toiletry articles were painted 'in the Chinese fashion', on a black background. The set included two comb boxes, a *vergette* or small brush, five powder boxes for *plottes*, for beauty spots and for roots, a matching mirror and two toilet candlesticks in silver.

The wife of a wine merchant in 1753 kept her toiletry kit, which consisted of a mirror, two powder jars, a casket and a brush – all painted 'in the Chinese fashion' – in an antique case similarly decorated, which stood in a small toilet *cabinet* next to her chamber. The toilet *cabinet* was also the room in which a spinster in 1738 chose to install a table covered with a muslin toilet (in the sense of an embroidered cloth) and a finely worked toilet cloth on which were arranged nine little jars for powder, sponges, beauty spots and the like, a small mother-of-pearl casket, three crystal vials with silver ferrules and stoppers, a *vergette* brush, two small, silver-plated copper candleholders, and a mirror with a Chinese-style varnished frame.

Toilettes like those described by the valuers are to be seen on engravings of the period as well. Van der Bruggen, for example, made two prints in 1685 entitled *Femme de qualité à sa toilette* (Woman of quality at her *toilette*) and *Femme de qualité s'habillant pour coure le Bal* (Woman of quality dressing to go to a ball). In the first engraving, the woman is seated before a rectangular table covered with a rich rug with embroidered trim. On the table is placed a mirror with a stand, as well as two square boxes containing pots of pommade, jars of rouge and beauty spots, brushes and combs. The second engraving shows a round table with two legs, covered with a rug, on which a mirror with a stand has been placed, in addition to a rectangular casket, a comb, boxes and pots and a pin cushion.[27] This list of all the little things composing a toilet could be extended with other articles, both masculine and feminine, that are mentioned more rarely by the valuers, such as soap boxes, boxes or 'heads' for wigs, spittoons, generally in silver, ear picks, toothpicks and instruments for tooth care. The latter were apparently exceptional and were found in 'a little casket in black shagreen' inventoried in the home of a spinster, one Marie-Anne Blanquet, in 1746.

Most of the toiletry articles for men's use were shaving instruments: basins, shaving bowls or plates or 'face grooming' bowls (*bols à faire le poil*), razors, whetstones, shaving linens or moustache curling irons. Shaving plates, made of earthenware, porcelain or red or yellow copper, appeared in only 10 per cent of eighteenth-century households. With these utensils, razors were often to be found, but were less commonplace, as they were used by barely 7 per cent of our Parisians. Several razors were sometimes mentioned in an inventory: one master painter in 1737 owned four, while the English gentleman, Sayers Johnson, was particularly well furnished, as befitted his standing, with 'three razors with shell handles and a leather razor strap' in addition to a 'shaving basin in earthenware' and a soap box. The wine merchant Jean Lanson, at the time of his death in 1765 kept a case with four different razors in his *cabinet*, along with a whetstone, two files, two pairs of scissors, a knife that could be closed with a spring mechanism, and a silver-trimmed vial. Almost totally absent from Parisian interiors during the seventeenth century, these shaving instruments seem hardly more prominent in the following century, if their presence in the inventories is any indication.

Despite the growth of the practice of shaving at home, the barber's shop, a true social centre in this 'world that we have lost', had not yet been deserted by inhabitants of the capital at the end of the eighteenth century, as indications of debts owed to barbers and wig merchants attest: these often included debts 'for beard', for a 'month of beard' or 'remaining beard', or for a 'wig made and furnished by the said merchant'. In the most prosperous households, men had themselves shaved by their servants, or better still, had the barber come to their homes, which explains the presence of shaving bowls and linens in certain interiors despite the absence of razors. In the home of the former Farmer General Lalive d'Epinay, five shaving cloths were returned from the wash in 1782.

Among all these toiletry articles, the most common, from the reign of Louis XIII to the end of the *ancien régime* was the mirror. More than half the households – 53 per cent – possessed at least one. This piece of equipment, a sign of concern with external appearance, was to be found in all social categories; indeed, some families possessed two or three. With a value ranging between 7 and 20 L, these objects generally comprised a small mirror held in a wooden frame of walnut or rosewood which might be painted, varnished or, frequently, gilded or painted red. Sizes are rarely given, though we did find models measuring 25 by 20 cm, 20 by 15 cm, and 35 by 25 cm. This abundance of mirrors in comparison with other toiletry articles highlights how much emphasis was placed on external appearance, as dictated by the rules of propriety at the time.

Hygiene, however, seems to have been excessively rudimentary, if we can judge by the type of toiletry objects found and their limited numbers. However great the progress made in personal hygiene by the second half of the eighteenth century, it remained limited to a tiny minority of Parisians who lived in the lap of luxury. Only when water supplies became industrialized could these practices of personal cleanliness develop within the middle classes of the population.

Closely connected with hygiene were the 'conveniences' intended for satisfying the call of nature. The descriptions in the notary's hand tell us about the private actions of our forebears. Privies or lavatories are almost never discussed in the inventories, as they were generally the common property of several occupants in the same building or, in town houses, did not contain anything to be valued. As early as 1374, a royal ordonnance had declared that all owners of buildings in the city of Paris and its faubourgs should have 'sufficient latrines and privies in their houses'. This order was renewed several times over the course of the centuries that followed. A decision by the Parlement in 1538 even announced that 'those who may have excused themselves from having cesspools dug for their houses' would be punished 'exemplarily'. The set of general regulations for the cleaning of the city of Paris, dating from 1663, devotes one article to denouncing the absence of privies in certain houses.

We have been able to discover the number and location of these conveniences through works estimates, leases and other documents drawn up by building experts. The five houses studied on the rue de Cléry were all equipped with such *cabinets*. Half of these buildings had only a single *cabinet*, while the residential buildings had several. When these facilities were located on the ground floor, they were installed either in the courtyard or under the stairs. In the upper stories they opened on to the stair landing or the end of a corridor. In older houses consisting of two buildings connected by a gallery, the 'privy seat' or *siège à privé* was to be found in the gallery on the first floor. In most of the houses on the rue du Sépulcre, these facilities were located in the upper stories. When only a single privy was present, it was generally placed in the highest stories, on the mansard story, half-way between the attic and the garret, or on the fourth or fifth story.

Some homes on this same street had lavatories on two levels: one house had them on the second and fifth floors, another on the fourth and in the garret of the sixth floor. These *cabinets* were often located one above the other, overhanging the courtyard. Lighted by openings in the walls, they were tiled, sheltered by their ceiling, and closed with a wooden door that was held shut with a bolt. The commode seat was connected to the cesspool by clay pipes, usually made of varnished terracotta, or occasionally lead or cast iron, that formed the flushing column.

The cesspool in the courtyard was covered by a stone slab called a *tampon* that was fitted with a ring. Despite the many precautions taken, the contents of these cesspools did sometimes seep into a neighbouring house or threaten to contaminate a well, as we saw earlier. These annoyances were usually due to negligence on the part of the owners, who had little inclination to engage in regular, costly emptying operations. The inventory of one painter lists debts owed to a cesspool emptier: the wife of the deceased declared that 'the succession of the communal estate owed the Sieur Lefèvre, master cesspool emptier, 25 L for half the emptying he had done of the cesspool at the house on the rue Cassette in 1727'.

As a new degree of sensitivity developed, the horrid state of the lavatories was denounced in enlightened circles. Mercier echoed these concerns when he wrote,

> Three-quarters of all latrines are dirty, horrible, disgusting. In this regard, Parisians have accustomed their eyes and their noses to uncleanliness. Architects, hampered by the cramped locations of houses, have thrown their pipes about at random, and nothing can be more astonishing to a foreigner than to see an amphitheatre of latrines perched one above another, adjacent to the stairway, next to doors, alongside kitchens, and emanating the most fetid odour from every corner.[28]

English-style *cabinets*, in which water was introduced as the only possible means of flushing out the nauseating odours, were still exceptionally rare in pre-revolutionary Paris. Among all the inventories, we found only one such system, in the home of a rich spinster who died in 1790 in an apartment of several rooms in the parish of Saint-Germain-l'Auxerrois. Like bathrooms, these English *cabinets* required both water and space, which made them a hallmark of the wealthiest families, those living in town houses or grand residences constructed or renovated in the last decades of the eighteenth century. When one section of the Hôtel d'Argenson in the faubourg Saint-Honoré was rebuilt by Lemoine in 1782, specifications were given for reservoirs to be installed above the toilet *cabinet* and the English *cabinet*, located in a tiny room that formed a mezzanine between the first and second stories. In the Hôtel de Vergès, the lavatory was contiguous with the bathroom and was

> tiled with black and white marble tiles in compartments with bands around the edges, oval-shaped, with wainscoting ... one story high, all painted in white marble. The seat is in wood, similarly painted in marble, the basin inside is in marble, and the said seat is fitted with taps having gilded copper knobs. Above the seat, an oval bay fitted with a frame holds a single glass pane ... within the bay is an iron cross with spear-shaped struts forming a star.

Across from the seat was 'a basin supported in a stand in the shape of a shell, all in marble; above, a swan-neck tap with its knob, all in gilded copper'.

At the Hôtel Leblanc on the rue de Cléry, the English-style *cabinet* was decorated with aquatic animals and birds painted on the walls. A niche housed an 'English seat with stone basin, taps, water spouts, the valve and taps in copper ormolu'. Another niche contained a marble basin in the shape of a shell with a drainage pipe and a tap. This *cabinet* also contained wooden closets holding shelves. In the most refined households, the desire for decoration and aesthetic pleasure penetrated even these most private rooms. In the great majority of Parisian houses, however, the latrines were those repulsive *cabinets* described by Mercier, who seems not to have exaggerated the sombre reality.

To avoid having to visit these spots and climb up and down all those stairs – and because there were not enough of them – a number of occupants had conveniences installed in their own quarters. Most commonly, these were seats, chairs, armchairs or *placets* which were specified as being for cleanliness or commodity, or as having a 'pierced' seat. These were found in 30 per cent of the households. Chamber pots and commode basins were listed in inventories in only 16.5 per cent of lodgings. The seats were generally stuffed with horsehair or straw and were covered with morocco leather, panne, velvet, carpet or even tapestry. A framework was built out of walnut, oak or beech. The most comfortable of these devices might have castors and a cushion: 'one commodity armchair, a commode seat with castors and its cushion, all in velvet', was assessed at 18 L. The receptacle, an indispensable element of these seats, was called a bowl, vase, pot, bucket or basin, and was usually made of earthenware or tin. We noted the presence of these commode seats in various rooms of the home, with a preference for the chamber, the *cabinet* or the wardrobe, though they were also to be found in the main room, the kitchen, and even in the *salon* and the antechamber. The pots, called chamber pots or night pots, and the convenience basins, also called bed basins, were made of tin or earthenware and were generally relegated to more discreet corners. The wealthiest families possessed several such objects, although the examples of Jacques-Honoré Barentin, *Maître de Requêtes* and president of the Grand Council, who had as many commode seats as there were members of his household in 1665, or Pierre Audiger, a king's counsellor equipped in 1784 with seven convenience armchairs, are exceptional cases.

It is hardly surprising that the libertine members of the age of the Englightenment all ranked high on the list of owners of both commodity and toiletry articles. One such figure whom the notaries introduce to us was particularly well equipped: Marie Geneviève Rainteau de Verrières de Furcy, a resident of the faubourg Saint-Honoré who died at the age of forty-five in 1775, entertained such eminent figures as the Maréchal de Saxe, Marmontel, Lalive d'Epinay, and the Duc de Bouillon; through her marriage to the Maréchal de Saxe, she was George Sand's great-grandmother; and her wardrobe, located behind her chamber, housed not only a night table and a clothes closet, but also a 'cleanliness seat' (*chaise de propreté*) with an earthenware basin and a tin syringe 'covered in red morocco', a second 'cleanliness seat' with 'basin and tin syringe', and two toilets.

Despite their primarily functional purpose, these convenience furnishings also could demonstrate a clear concern for elegance, as can be surmised from some of the valuers' descriptions: a commode armchair in light-tan damask, three commode chairs and a commode armchair in walnut upholstered in red panne, others covered in tapestry or carpet in bright violets, blues, leaf-printed reds or red and green. Few Parisians could experience the privilege enjoyed by the Marquise de Traisnel of using a chamber pot in Dresden china.

As our look at the home of a courtesan shows, these sanitary installations were fairly frequently accompanied by tin syringes, sometimes stored in cardboard or leather cases. These syringes were intended for enemas or other hygienic use. We also noted bloodletting bowls, some of which were in silver. Enemas and bleeding, both medical techniques that call to mind scenes from Molière, were commonplace practices at the time.

Though the notaries sometimes neglected to value insignificant objects 'not worthy of valuation', their inventories nonetheless provide a sufficient amount of detail to paint a picture of the hygienic habits of the time. Only in the most privileged levels of society did people develop the habit of seeking privacy for the performance of their natural functions and for washing their bodies with water. In the pre-revolutionary dwellings of Paris, so-called English-style installations, and even wardrobes or *cabinets* set aside for the calls of nature were few and far between. Most households had no private corner where the inhabitants could go for this purpose. In those times, nobody was offended by having to use a commode seat in common view, or urinating in the ashes of the hearth, or by chamber pots emptied out of windows – nobody, that is, except English travellers and the members of an enlighted elite. Changing attitudes towards hygiene did begin to materialize in the last decades of the century. But privacy – like the use of water, a prerequisite for any other progress in cleanliness – did not win its place until the nineteenth century, and then thanks to new technologies like the steam pump that were developed during the industrial revolution.

6

Home Decoration

In the course of our treasure hunt for objects in the company of the notaries, we have discovered not only the traces of a material civilization, but also decorative elements that reveal the artistic tastes of Parisians in this period. While everyday objects are used for the requirements of bodily existence and fulfil needs, objects of art embellishing the home represent deliberate choices prompted by aesthetic or cultural desires. Whether devoid of artistic value or signed by the greatest painters, engravers and woodworkers of the age, such objects enhanced the setting of daily life. Placed in a room of the home to offer simple visual pleasure, they added a happy touch of colour and light to these often cramped and gloomy interiors, creating a more personal atmosphere. Their materials – essentially wood and various sorts of fabric – and the wide range of colours used in them bestowed warmth and a feeling of well-being on the restricted physical comfort of the dwellings.

Investment by wealthy households in decoration might be slight, while in some cases people of modest standing longed to adorn their humble abodes with a few lengths of tapestry and a small number of cheap paintings. In the home of Pigeon de Saint Paterne, a lawyer at Parlement whose total estate was worth 8600 L in 1770, there were no tapestries, curtains, mirrors or other decorative elements. In contrast, in 1715 a *maître d'hôtel*, Vincent Patault, owned a so-called 'Flanders green' tapestry in seven sections backed with canvas in 15-*aune* bands that was assessed at 330 L, as well as two paintings, a small statue of Louis XIII on horseback with an ebony stand, and a grandfather clock in a marquetry case in ebony and horn, standing on a console decorated with marquetry and shell.

Paris, the capital of the arts and of good taste in eighteenth-century Europe, won the admiration of foreign visitors. Some of them made note in their diaries of the beautiful interior furnishings of houses to which they were invited. True, these English or German travellers belonged to the intellectual and social elite of their own countries and did not mix with the man in the street. The milieux in which they were received were home to the very people who worked hardest at imitating the Court and the princely households, and thereby set the tone in the city and determined what was fashionable. Martin Lister in 1698 could not speak highly enough of the richness and cleanliness of the furnishings, finishing within side [interior decoration] and furniture answer in riches and neatness; as hangings of rich tapestry, raised with gold and silver threads ... cabinets and bureaus of ivory inlaid with tortoiseshell, and gold and silver Plates in a hundred different manners: branches and candlesticks of crystal: but above all most rare pictures. The gildings, carvings and paintings of the roofs are admirable. These things are in this city and the country about, to such a variety and excess, that you can come into no private house of any man of substance, but you see something of them; and they are observed frequently to ruin themselves in these expenses. Every one, that has any thing to spare, covets to have some good picture or sculpture of the best artist ... Here as soon as ever a man gets any thing by fortune or inheritance, he lays it out in some such way as now named.[1]

As the French Revolution approached, the luxuriousness of these Parisian dwellings was denounced by Louis-Sébastien Mercier:

Once a house is built, nothing is done yet; you have met just a quarter of the expenditure. Then come the cabinetmaker, the tapestry maker, the woodworker and the rest. They are followed by the mirrors ... The inside takes three times as long as the construction of the town house ... The furnishings are given an over-abundant and unsuitable magnificence. A superb bed that resembles a throne, a carved dining room, andirons fashioned like jewels, a toilette in gold and lace, are surely signs of puerile ostentation.[2]

Though the notaries do not mention ornaments carved or painted on the walls, ceilings or floors, above doors or incorporated into the building itself, with their frequently detailed descriptions they do help us to visualize the decor of those rooms in which our Frenchmen lived out their lives. Tapestries, painted images or engravings, mirrors and decorative furniture or curios were the main items with which Parisians liked to surround themselves. In addition to the diversity of materials, shapes and patterns, the range of colours was also infinitely varied. Whether simply made or intricate, whether revealing artistic qualities or not, the interplay among all these elements endowed each interior with a personal, engaging quality. Certainly the furnishings of these different abodes must have presented some similarities, but the English writer Horace Walpole, son of the prime minister Robert Walpole, was surely exaggerating when he wrote to Anne Pitt on 25 December 1765,

I have seen but one idea in all the houses here; the rooms are white and gold, or white; a lustre, a vast glass over the chimney, and another opposite, and generally a third over against the windows compose their rooms universally. In the bedchamber is a piece of hanging behind and on each side of the bed; the rest of the room is stark naked. Now and then there is a piece of tapestry or damask opposite to the windows; but surely there is nothing in which they so totally want imagination as in the furniture of their houses!

How far can we believe a writer who notes, a few lines later, 'In short, their whole system of habitation is to me absurd'?[3]

It hardly seems important whether these objects were so similar from one interior to another, whether they were humble or precious, as long as they were filled with meaning. Once acquired by their owners, they effectively became reflections of the artistic or cultural sensibilities of an age. Received through legacies or inheritances, they represented the memory of loved ones, handed down from generation to generation. These articles were the object of pious respect and were kept, even when old, worn, broken, threadbare, patched or worm-eaten, as these frequently used terms in descriptions from the period attest. Based on the elements that the notaries hold up for us to see, what kind of image can we create of the decor in these Parisian interiors?

Tapestries and Other Wall-coverings

In addition to its role of protecting against damp walls and draughts and preserving circulating heat, which we discussed earlier, tapestry also had a purely ornamental function. This type of hanging was very much in vogue during the seventeenth and eighteenth centuries, as 75 per cent of our Parisians used tapestries to decorate their interiors. Despite the arrival of new fashions in wall coverings, such as printed cloth or wallpaper, even after 1750 70 per cent of these inhabitants continued to use tapestries to cover the walls of their dwellings. The rooms most commonly trimmed with such hangings were the chambers, common rooms (*salles*), salons, and antechambers, but could also include *cabinets*, kitchens and shopbacks. Though the valuers did not always give exact indications as to the number of pieces or dimensions of the tapestry, they did list the many varieties, which they designated in different ways: according to type, e.g. Bergamo tapestry; according to the region where it was made, e.g. Auvergne or Flanders; according to the technique, e.g. needle-stitched, or high or low warp; or according to the pattern, e.g. Hungarian point, greenery, with figures, and so forth.

Bergamo tapestries, which represent more than 50 per cent of the valuers' notings, were the most widespread and the most common. Coarse in appearance and generally large enough to go all the way around a room, these tapestries were produced on looms, somewhat like cloth, using various sorts of spun materials, including flock silk, wool, cotton, hemp, and cow or goat hair. Its warp was usually made of hemp, which meant that the fabric was very solid. It drew its name from the Italian town where it was invented.

The first French Bergamo manufacture was opened in Lyon in 1622. Eventually several French cities began manufacturing it, especially Rouen and Elbeuf, though Lille, Roubaix and Amiens were also producers. Some valuers make note of 'Bergamo tapestries in the Rouen fashion'. This type of hanging was also imitated in England, and we found one mention of 'Bergamo from England'.

Because of its reasonable price, Bergamo tapestry enjoyed great popularity among the modest classes. At prices ranging from less than a livre to 10 L per *aune* (1.15 m), depending on its condition or pattern, this material was within the budget of servants and day labourers, who covered the walls of their single chambers with it. It is interesting to note that among the poorer classes, these tapestries are often specified as being old or worn: 'eight small pieces of old Bergamo tapestry measuring 2 *aunes* approximately, worth 25 sols', or '7 *aunes* of Bergamo tapestry in very bad condition: 40 sols'. Indications were sometimes given about patterns: we found self-coloured bands, large bands covered with birds and flowers, stripes with birds, with flowers, with Hungarian point (i.e. with chevrons), or with scales, making reference to an imitation of fish scales. The term 'Rouen tapestry', commonly used by the valuers, is simply another way to describe Bergamo. Whatever city was given as its origin, the value was comparable: a width of 18 *aunes* from Rouen was estimated at 30 L. According to the *Dictionnaire de Furetière* and the *Dictionnaire de Trévoux*, 'poor people's tapestry is from Rouen or Bergamo, made of wool and cotton thread and worked like cloth. These tapestries were sometimes said to be 'from the gates of Paris' because they were 'sold retail in different *boutiques* and stores near to the gates of Paris', as the *Voyageur fidèle* informs us.

Other tapestries inventoried by the valuers were generally significantly more expensive and belonged to more comfortable households. Auvergne tapestries, sometimes called Aubusson or Felletin from the names of the cities where they were manufactured, enjoyed great popularity among Parisians. The workshops of these cities in the province of Marche, founded as early as the fourteenth century by Flemish weavers, grew tremendously in the reign of Louis XIV: the royal manufactures of Aubusson and Felletin were established respectively in 1665 and 1669. Prices for these hangings were high.

A *procureur* of the Grand Council possessed an Auvergne tapestry 18 *aunes* wide valued at 600 L in 1668. In the home of François Auger de Combault, who died in 1706, an Auvergne tapestry measuring 17 *aunes* in six sections, on which the four seasons were represented, was valued at 350 L. Another Auvergne tapestry decorated with human figures and inventoried in the same household, was worth only 100 L because it was 'most old'. The production of the Auvergne manufactures usually figured greenery, that is to say, 'tapestries with landscapes in which green dominates', according to Furetière, and were highlighted with animals, birds or hunting scenes. These were always worth at least 100 L, and could reach as much as 300 L for an average size of 12 by $2\frac{1}{2}$ *aunes*, or a little more than 14 metres wide and 3 metres high. A chamber in the home of a master painter and gilder in 1721 was hung with 'approximately 12 *aunes* of Auvergne greenery tapestry in five sections lined in bands, worth 180 L'. In the home of a painter to the Duchesse d'Orléans, the walls of one chamber were hung with 'four pieces of tapestry in Auvergne greenery without lining, valued at 210 L'. We also noted the presence in many interiors of modest, very worn Auvergne greenery in smaller dimensions, like that found in the home of a spinster, measuring 10 metres wide by 2.40 metres high, worth only 30 L in 1708. Aubusson tapestries could be purchased in Paris on the rue de la Huchette and in that quarter, states the *Voyageur fidèle*.

Even more lovely and more costly were Flemish tapestries. Since the Renaissance, centres in Brussels, Antwerp, Audenarde, Bruges, Valenciennes and Lille had been highly reputed, and they shipped a part of their production to Paris. Once again, the rue de la Huchette was the place where one could procure these works, in a shop specializing in the sale of Flemish tapestry. In the home of Frédéric Léonard, one *cabinet* was decorated with an 8-*aune* long Flanders tapestry in three sections with figures depicting the *Triomphe de l'épousée* (*The Triumph of the Bride*). It was valued at 600 L in 1706. Jean-Noël de Barbezières,

Comte de Chemerault, possessed a Flemish greenery tapestry measuring 10 *aunes* in four sections, worth 450 L. Some exceptionally valuable Flanders tapestries belonged to particularly luxurious households: one from Brussels, 24 *aunes* long by 3 *aunes* high, with the story of Aeneas was valued at 3000 L when inventoried in 1744 in the home of Jeanne Lefèvre d'Ormesson, wife of the Marquis de La Bussière, a *Président* of the Parlement. Another Brussels tapestry in eight sections portraying the history of Venice, measured 24 *aunes* in length and 2¾ aunes in height and was valued at 2500 L in 1735 in a room in the home of Jeanne Lefèvre de La Barre, widow of the Chevalier d'Ormesson, *Maître des Requêtes* and *Intendant de la Généralité* in Soissons. Owning such works of art was not just the exclusive privilege of the robe nobility. In 1751 in the home of a rich draper, an 18-*aune* Brussels tapestry whose theme was 'inspired by Teniers' was noted and valued at 2000 L.

Productions from the royal manufactures of Beauvais and Gobelins, founded respectively in 1664 and 1667, were luxury items reserved only for the very wealthy. These are mentioned only rarely by valuers. Charles-Hugues Baillot de Villechavant, *Maître Ordinaire* of the Chambre des Comptes, possessed six pieces of Beauvais greenery with figures in 1744, worth an estimated 1200 L. Hung in his company room, they measured some 21 metres. The same room held a sofa and eight armchairs covered in Gobelins tapestry 'representing subjects from fable' and worth 600 L. Two Gobelins tapestries appeared in 1668 in the inventory of Jean du Tillet, king's counsellor, one in eight sections representing the story of the gods, worth 800 L, and the other in three sections portraying greenery, valued at 500 L. We also noted another Gobelins tapestry with small figures, in four pieces measuring 12 *aunes* in width by 2½ in height, valued at 800 L.

Two other tapestry factories are mentioned a few times by the notaries: one in Nancy, an important regional tapestry-making centre as early as the fifteenth century, as was the town of Saint Mihiel, and one in Avignon both specialized in producing common and inexpensive tapestries.

In most cases, neither the origin nor the style of the various tapestries listed is given, and the valuers find it sufficient simply to note the stitch – Hungary, English, Turkish – or, more frequently, the pattern: greenery, greenery and figures, greenery with birds or flowers, with figures, with 'beasts and small figures', with landscapes and so on. Greenery tapestries whose patterns were inspired by flora and fauna were predominant. Little description is ever given of those with figures. The few themes recorded fell into several basic categories: the Old Testament, portraying the story of Esther, the story of Rehoboam, of chaste Susannah, or the history of sin; mythology, with the story of Aeneas, the story of the gods, Diana or Ariadne; history, featuring the story of Cleopatra and Mark Antony, the story of François I, the history of Venice; or a battle, or allegories such as the four seasons, or genre scenes such as shepherdesses or hunters. The theme of the 'two pieces of tapestry painted on fustian' valued at 36 L in the children's chamber of a master painter in 1716 was well suited to the room's purpose, since it represented children at play. Figurative tapestries were generally the most costly. The same went for high-warp or *haute-lisse* tapestries, so called because they were woven on vertical looms. In 1725 in the home of Marguerite Lefèvre de La Barre, widow of the Chevalier Sieur de Quincy, a high-warp tapestry was listed that portrayed the history of François I in seven pieces measuring 20 *aunes* by 3, without any indication of where it had been produced. It was assessed at 400 L.

Tapestries were not the only coverings found on the walls of these interiors. A few leather hangings were mentioned: one of the rooms in the dwelling of the widow of the Chevalier de Beauregard was trimmed, in 1672, with gilded leather on a green background. Some of the rooms in the home of Frédéric Léonard were also hung with gilded leather of no great value. In the home of a merchant draper and Paris bourgeois, the *cabinet* was lined with embossed leather. This type of hanging, very fashionable during the *grand siècle*, had not completely disappeared by the second half of the eighteenth century, since the dining room of a squire was hung in 1772 with sixteen sheets of gilded leather covered with figures, and the bedchamber of a used clothing seller of approximately the same period was trimmed with several pieces of boiled leather.

The fashion for cloth wall coverings made its way into many interiors during the eighteenth century. A great diversity of materials was used in these hangings: Caux damask, Abbeville damask, satin from Bruges, velours, brocatelle, *siamois*, silk moiré, carpet, calico or *indienne*, cotton canvas, and painted twill. Less costly and more cheerful, these wall coverings were sometimes printed with bright colours that introduced a note of fantasy and novelty, and they began in the 1760s and 1770s to compete seriously with traditional tapestry. The manufacture founded in 1759 by Oberkampf in Jouy-en-Josas contributed to increasing the distribution of printed cloth. During that period, the use of such fabrics often went hand in hand with a concern for aesthetic unity. The walls of the salon of one *Maître Ordinaire* of the Chambre des Comptes were decorated in 1770 with crimson damask framed in rods. The window curtains and the coverings on the chairs in the room, including the wing chair, eight armchairs and two other chairs in carved and gilded wood, were all in the same fabric. Formerly produced in the Orient, this material, made entirely of silk, had been manufactured in Lyon since the seventeenth century.

Such concern for harmonious room decoration, while more highly developed in privileged milieux, could be found to a lesser degree in the most socially diverse households. In the home of a chaplain to Monsieur (the King's brother), the walls of the common room as well as the oak, claw-legged chairs were upholstered in 1751 with stripped moiré. At the Saint-Séverin presbytery in 1751, the same brown serge trimmed the walls of the assembly room as well as thirty chairs, two armchairs and a couch. Wall coverings in blue and white *siamois* with matching curtains in the same material embellished the single room in which a tailor's boy died in 1772. *Siamois*, a silk and cotton fabric introduced during the reign of Louis XIV by ambassadors from Siam, was later manufactured in Rouen. Like the *indiennes*, it was sometimes said to be 'from the Gate', and it highlighted the sway that the Orient, with its ritual, its colours and its technology, held over the decorative arts in Enlightenment Paris. In the home of the master instrument maker Louis Guersan, valuers in 1770 noted wall coverings in calico and *siamois* from the Gate.

In the final decades of the century, tapestries actually began to disappear completely from some luxurious interiors, supplanted by wall-covering fabrics.

For example, the valuers who inventoried the home of Jean-Philippe Rameau in 1764 noted six *aunes* of calico, seventeen *aunes* of *siamois* 'from the Gate', and six *aunes* of canvas. Different types of wall fabrics were to be found in the home of François Francoeur, the superintendent of the king's music, in 1787: crimson damask bordered with gilded rods in the *salon*, crimson and white striped silk moiré identical to the fabric of the bed coverings in the chamber, and painted canvas in the other rooms. These wall fabrics were in some cases sumptuous items of great value, reaching the prices of the finest *haute-lisse* tapestries. In 1725 Marguerite Lefèvre de La Barre, for instance, owned not only the tapestry representing the story of Françqis I, but also a rich hanging in brocatelle, a brocade silk material, portraying the seven wonders of the world and valued at 2000 L.

We also noted another, original type of wall covering, apparently very rare: woven rushes, like those that covered the chamber of one master baker in 1753.

The fashion for wallpaper, especially that produced in the faubourg Saint-Antoine by the famous Réveillon manufacture in the years before the Revolution, does not find an explicit echo in the inventories. Mentions made of it were still fairly rare, and they usually involved paper that was glued to cloth which was in turn hung on the walls. The question that arises, then, is to what degree wall-paper hung directly on the walls would have been included in the evaluations made. In the home of Marie-Geneviève Rainteau de Verrières de Furcy in 1775, the walls of the antechamber were covered with 'fifteen widths of paper with a white background used as wall coverings in said room and some two hundred feet of moulded rods painted grey', while those of the bedchamber were covered with 'twenty widths of grey and crimson *tontisse* [fabric on paper] measuring $2\frac{1}{2}$ *aunes* high and some 240 feet of carved and gilded wood'.

In the most affluent households, wood panelling replaced the traditional tapestries. In addition to its ornamental role, it helped to save heat, as d'Aviler explained in his *Cours d'Architecture* in 1691: 'Woodwork makes spaces dry and warm and in consequence healthy and habitable shortly after they have been built ... Wood panels can also be used to correct defects in rooms such as a slant or an enclave caused by a chimney pipe.'[4] However, because it was built into the wall, this woodwork was almost always ignored by the valuers. A lease from 1772 tells us that the salon of the Marquis de Féline in the faubourg Saint-Honoré 'will be newly panelled'. We know from a works estimate that the apartment of a draper included varnish for the panelling as well as for the closets and insides of windows. In the home of a hosiery merchant in 1735, the mantel with two pier glasses in the dining room was not valued because it was built into the woodwork of the room. The company room of a cabinet maker in the faubourg Saint-Antoine was walled in 1760 with pine woodwork described as 'the woodwork trimming the two sides of the room in which had been installed a glass door on each side, with six panes on the window side, all in pine wood, the whole valued at 24 L'.

Wood-panelled rooms were to be found essentially in the most fashionable homes, as the documents drawn up by building experts reveal. Panelling could be of two types, depending on the size of the room: wainscot panelling, covering the lower half of the wall, was used in spacious rooms, and could be combined with wallpaper or printed cloth: in the Hôtel de Vergès in the faubourg Saint-Honoré, the remaining surface up to the cornice was covered with 'China paper coverings glued on to canvas', or 'hangings of painted French cloth depicting flowers, birds, landscapes and attributes of the arts or of gardening'. Full-length panelling, covering the entire wall surface up to the cornice, was often kept for smaller rooms, such as *cabinets*. But the *grand salon* of the town house belonging to *Président* d'Aligre on the rue d'Anjou was decorated 'with high panelling with large frames, panels and pilasters, ornamented with trophy sculptures representing the elements in their different attributes and ornamented with shells and rock work from which acorns hang'.

So the range of mural coverings gradually broadened during the eighteenth century, at the expense of woven or embroidered tapestries, and revealed greater diversity. The omnipresence of these materials in the households of the deceased is in marked contrast with the small quantities of door and floor coverings: 15 per cent of our Parisians protected themselves from draughts and noise by using door curtains, and only 10 per cent sought to resist the dampness of their floors by laying down carpets. While door curtains and rugs were present in only the wealthiest homes, window curtains, on the contrary, were in general use and were inventoried in 65 per cent of all habitations. These curtains, generally described with their iron rods and copper rings, were made from a variety of fabrics: cotton canvas, calico, serge, *camelot*, twill, *siamois*, damask, taffetas, or muslin. They were often of the same height as tapestries, commonly measuring $2\frac{1}{2}$ *aunes*. Generally, they came in pairs. The chamber was the primary room in the house to be fitted with window and door curtains. Then came the main rooms, then *cabinets*, and last of all kitchens. Half-curtains covering only the lower part of the window, to offer protection from sunlight and especially from prying eyes, did not seem to be in very frequent use in the last decades of the eighteenth century.

Rugs, which were rare outside bourgeois households, were sometimes referred to as being from Turkey or Persia, or after the style of those countries, or in *gros points* (like tapestry). They could be in moquette, or woven in thick wool with the pile on one side, or made of rags, serge or satin. One Turkish rug was valued at 40 L in 1730 in the home of a master musical instrument maker. Exceptionally, mention was made of rugs manufactured in the Savonnerie workshops, established during the reign of Henri IV in the former Chaillot soapworks and later incorporated into the Gobelins manufacture. Only the very rich could afford these articles. It is interesting to note the unusual rug found in 1772 in the bedchamber of a squire and secretary to the king: it was a large bearskin. There are also a few so-called fireplace rugs, which were placed before the hearth.

Two other decorative elements, folding screens (*paravents*) and screens (*écrans*), were sometimes designed to harmonize in more refined interiors with the wallcoverings and curtains in the room. Placed 'in chambers, near doors, near the fire, around beds to protect and fend off the wind', according to the *Dictionnaire de Trévoux*, *paravents* are described as having four, six, eight or even twelve panels, 'painted Chinese style', or covered with painted cloth and lined with calico, or perhaps with old sheets, flowered moquette, taffeta or damask. Partitions might also be used with screens, which were placed before the fireplace as a protection against the heat of the flames. Screens might be presented as 'tapestry in Turkish needlepoint in a frame and on a walnut stand' or perhaps in walnut wood, trimmed with a panel covered with tapestry on one side and taffeta on the other.

This desire to coordinate the different decorative fabrics in a room highlighted an aesthetic concern. By the Enlightenment, this preoccupation was no longer limited to the homes of the nobility, as it had been in the previous century, but began to appear in various social settings. Three representative examples demonstrate this change. In the chamber of a master painter in 1721, the bed covers, the armchairs and the curtains were all blue, with the same sky-blue silk trim. In the home of an innkeeper, curtains in red calico with little white bouquets were associated with a calico wall covering of white branches on a red background. The bed trimmings of a spinster who died 1775, as well as the wall coverings and the curtains in her chamber, were all of 'blue and white striped *siamois*'.

Whether intended to trim walls, doors, windows, chairs or the bed, these decorative fabrics are astonishing for their great variety, which is highlighted by the rich vocabulary the notaries use to designate them (see Appendix 3). We were able to list some forty terms in common use by valuers – terms which are in most instances unknown today in a world invaded by synthetic fabrics. As we shall see later on, the range of colours describing these materials is no less impressive.

In these interiors which, as late as the second half of the eighteenth century, generally enjoyed neither abundant heating nor great amounts of light nor a sufficient water supply, the luxury of fabrics is indicative of an incipient desire for comfort and an increasing concern with embellishing the domestic environment. As a barrier against cold, dampness and draughts, but also as beautiful materials and sources of colour, these textile coverings contributed in many dwellings to creating an atmosphere of well-being and warmth.

Painted Images and Engravings

Hanging paintings or prints on the walls of a home is more than just a way of embellishing one's environment; it also creates a personal touch. To what extent did the images found in the most varied interiors express the feelings and tastes of the inhabitants? The more insignificant their commercial value, the more laden with meaning these images apparently were for their owners. After all, humble devotional engravings bore witness to the religious fervour of their owners, and modest family portraits were a sign of attachment to loved ones, living or dead. Paintings representing allegories or scenes from mythology or history were indicative of a certain humanist culture whose roots lay deep in antiquity. However, when these images are true works of art belonging to rich individuals, or are part of a collection, it becomes more difficult to determine which works simply manifest the fashion of the day or a desire for ostentation and which have sentimental value.

Unfortunately, our curiosity about these choices of imagery is rarely satisfied by the information provided by the notaries. Often the fact that the subject or title of a picture or print is not identified signifies that the monetary value of the object was small. The less valuable objects were, the less effort a notary would make to describe them, tending instead to focus on their supports or frames, which could be more valuable than the image itself.

Our investigation of home decor reveals how omnipresent images were in the majority of Parisian households. Over the whole of our sample, 66.5 per cent of the inhabitants possessed paintings or prints. This proportion reaches 71.5 per cent if we consider only the interiors visited after 1750. The number of images found varies greatly from one dwelling to another, and can range from a single object to several hundred. The average is some seven or eight per household. But collections contribute to distort these results, although we excluded the largest ones from these figures. Though these figures are relative, it is important to note that the average falls to five if we consider only the households inventoried during the seventeenth century. Like ordinary household objects, the number of paintings and engravings in Parisian interiors tended to increase during the eighteenth century. While the taste for pictures had reached a number of social categories as early as the first half of the seventeenth century, it was constantly growing and becoming more popular during the Enlightenment: only 27 per cent of all servants owned paintings or prints in the seventeenth century, whereas by the middle of the following century, 64.5 per cent of all day labourers decorated their humble abodes with them. By the 1770s, 88 per cent of the inhabitants of the faubourg Saint-Antoine decorated their homes with an average of nine images.

How did this taste for painting become so widespread throughout all social levels in the eighteenth century? From its foundation in 1673, the Académie Royale de Peinture et de Sculpture contributed to making known the work of its members and recognized artists by organizing public showings at the Louvre: thirty-six were held between 1673 and 1791. The earliest of these Salons were held in 1673, 1699 and 1704. The event was not repeated until 1725, and it became annual from 1737 to 1743 and from 1745 to 1748, then biennial from 1748 to 1795. Twenty-six of these exhibitions were held during the reign of Louis XV alone. Generally opening on 25 August, the feast day of St Louis, the Salon ran for some three weeks, and admission was free. We know that 220 works were presented to the public in 1763, 432 in 1765, and around 480 in the following years until 1790. These exhibitions produced not only catalogues, but also – beginning in 1737 – reports published in *Le Mercure* and other newspapers and reviews of the period. Though the most famous Salon critic of the eighteenth century, Denis Diderot, eclipsed all the others with his *Salons* published from 1759 to 1781, he was neither the first nor the only art critic of his age. Two of the greatest Salon critics of the century were Lafont de Saint-Yenne and Saint-Yves.[5]

Exhibitions rivalling those of the Académie were organized from 1751 to 1774 by the Académie de Saint-Luc. As for second-rate painters, looked down upon by the official artists, they showed their works every year at the Place Dauphine.

Public sales of paintings were held irregularly and rarely until 1730, then began to increase in number during the 1740s, growing from a frequency of five per year between 1750 and 1760 to fifteen a year between 1761 and 1770, and culminating at more than forty in 1773. By the mid-century, catalogues of these sales, as well as those published by Gersaint and Mariette, the most famous art dealers of the city, provided increasingly methodical and detailed notes describing the canvases, some by named artists, some anonymous. The number of collectors grew accordingly: some 150 were counted between 1700 and 1720, and 500 between 1750 and 1790.[6]

This expanding interest in artistic production did not escape the observant eyes of Enlightenment writers. Pons-Augustin Alletz noted in 1761, 'The taste for these Arts has won over, so to speak, all the estates',[7] and ten years later the Abbé Laugier remarked,

> The fashion is for taste in paintings. This taste, less dominant than it was, is, however, still sufficiently general to give rise to the vanity of wanting to do likewise. You go to see pictures the way people go to the boulevard, without any other motive of preference than the sheeplike intention to do as others do. You say you like pictures, because you buy some in every style and at every price; but that is only a vain luxury. In your home, these paintings are true superfluities that show nothing more than your opulence. The same is true of the study where they are kept, and of your library full of books which you never read.[8]

The popularity enjoyed by painting during the eighteenth century was accompanied by an explosion of engravings, which offered the advantage of distributing art works that would otherwise remain unknown. As Dezallier d'Argenville wrote in 1727, 'Prints have a singular merit: like so many trumpets of fame, they carry everywhere an idea of the good paintings and drawings done by great masters, of which we would be deprived without their help.'[9] The engravings sought by the public were above all those reproducing paintings that were in fashion, whether classic or modern. In this way, 750 prints during the century, from the hands of numerous engravers, reproduced Watteau's paintings. We know that making engravings as a hobby was highly fashionable, as is seen by the example of Mme de Pompadour or the diplomat and collector Lalive de Jully.[10] 'In our day', Mercier judged, 'a ridiculous abuse is made of engraving.'

In the inventories following a death, the valuers do not always distinguish clearly between paintings and prints, and we have not attempted to separate the two genres. We found mention of 'engraved pictures' in their gilded and sometimes sculpted wood frames, under clear glass, 'reliquary pictures', and 'prayer pictures'. Nor can we learn from these documents how long a given picture had belonged to a family, whether it had been handed down by inheritance or legacy, or purchased by the deceased during his lifetime. Notations like the one appearing in 1746 in the inventory of Louise Madeleine Le Blanc, Marquise de Traisnel, are exceptionally rare: 'A painting on canvas representing the reigning king Louis XV, of which His Majesty had made a gift to the late Monsieur Le Blanc, Minister of War, which the family considers a respectable memorial'. Paintings could be purchased at the Saint-Germain fair, one of the most important commercial centres for works of art. Established at the beginning of the seventeenth century, it opened every year on 3 February and lasted some two weeks. Merchants selling prints or paintings in tempera or oil set up their stands, called *loges*, with a counter and wooden shutters to ensure they could be closed effectively.

Most of the paintings and engravings inventoried seemed to have had little value. But it is not always easy to obtain a clear idea of their price, since they were usually valued in groups. Here are a few examples of prices found at different periods: towards the middle of the seventeenth century, four paintings on canvas, 40 sols; the portrait of Cardinal de Richelieu painted on canvas, 30 sols; a small picture of Jesus painted on wood, 40 sols; during the first decade of the eighteenth century, two paintings on canvas, 40 sols; fifteen paintings on canvas, 3L 60 sols, four paintings on canvas, 35 sols; thirty prints and forty-three paintings on canvas, 112 L. In 1764, two paintings done on canvas, one oval and the other square, representing two portraits, one of a man and the other of a woman, were worth 3 L with their frames. Most of these images, worth scarcely more than a livre, were therefore accessible to people of modest social position.

The more privileged households – financially and culturally speaking – contained high-quality works with a significantly greater market value. The study of Madeleine Séguier, widow of Anne Jacquelin, *Intendant* of the king's buildings, was decorated around 1640 with a picture on copper figuring the *Marriage of Thetis and Peleus* assessed at 26 L. In the home of Jean François de Guénégaud, the *Maître Ordinaire* of the Chambre des Comptes, a canvas of Leda was valued in 1643 at the considerable sum of 1600 L. Louis Ancelin, *contrôleur général* of the household of the late queen, possessed a fine portrait in 1694, valued at 200 L. A painting by Sébastien Bourdon entitled *The Flight into Egypt* and belonging to Jacques Andry, a draper, in 1715 was estimated at 160 L.

Collections containing more than fifty works, not including prints, were to be found in a small, specific group of households. In such cases, the valuers usually called in specialists to value the works. It should come as no surprise to find numerous pictures in the homes of painters. Sauval remarks that 'in the lodgings and houses of painters you see an infinity of pictures piled and stacked on top of each other'.[11] Eighty paintings were counted in 1663 in the home of the widow of a painter and chamber valet of the king. The widow of one of the king's *peintres ordinaires* possessed 119 paintings worth 1780 L, or an average price of 15 L per painting, in the early years of the eighteenth century. In the workshop of master painter François Leroy, ninety-two paintings were inventoried in 1746, and sixty-six were found in the chamber of another master painter, Paul Jouette, in 1734. Were these the works of these painters, on exhibition in their lodgings, hung on the walls or stacked on the ground? No indication as to the signatures is given to settle the matter. In the home of François Leroy the notary specified that a portrait had been begun and that one canvas was 'mounted on its frame and pencilled'. In another painter's home, some 'fifty-seven small study pieces painted both on board and on paper', and 'a portfolio filled with several small drawings and studies of flowers painted on paper' were found. These details reveal in both cases that the works inventoried had been done by the deceased artists. Were these paintings actually merchandise, intended for sale, rather than decorative items? Because of its value and despite the more limited number of items, it is also worth noting the collection belonging to Magnus Bodasse, a Dutch master gold beater and amateur painter: his twenty-six paintings were valued at 800 L, or 30 L per painting, at the beginning of the eighteenth century. One of these canvases, *St Peter's Denial*, worth 15 L, was painted by its owner. Imbued as they were with Latin and humanist culture, the Dutch could be rightfully proud of their school of painting, and they were great art lovers. Their investments in this area were much larger than those of the French during the seventeenth century.

Painters aside, the principal owners of collections were nobles, magistrates, lawyers, Parisian bourgeois and merchants. In the home of the widow of the Marquis de Fontaine Martel, seventy pictures were listed and valued at the considerable sum of 5122 L. Louis Ancelin, the above-mentioned *contrôleur général* of the household of the late queen, owned 103 pictures whose total value was estimated at 1429 L. Antoine Coulier, a lawyer at the Parlement, was the rich owner, upon his death in 1721, of a collection of 107 paintings and prints. The widow of another lawyer in 1743 possessed thirty-seven pictures, of which nine were family portraits, valued at the tidy sum of 102 L. We know that by the seventeenth century, collectors also counted members of the Parlement in their ranks, and the most prestigious magistrates of the eighteenth-century Paris Parlement, blessed with vast residences, formed a welcoming public for works of art.[12] But the few Parisians in our sample who belonged to the robe nobility apparently preferred to invest in books instead of paintings. It is indeed widely recognized that cultural priority among men attached to the Parlement was given to libraries.

Several Parisian bourgeois and merchants also figure among these collectors. The home of Charles Rossignol, a member of the Paris bourgeoisie who died during the first decade of the eighteenth century, was filled with pictures. Perhaps the master of the household was himself an amateur painter, as is suggested by the presence in one room of two sketched out canvases, 'three canvases in a package', and thirty-eight wooden frames. The total of 262 paintings was valued at some 1300 L. The collection belonging to the Parisian bourgeois Jean Trolieur, who died in 1728, consisted of seventy-three paintings, including a whole range of portraits. The collection of the mathematician Pierre Turpin, another member of the Paris bourgeoisie, consisted in 1754 of not only seventy-five paintings inspired by various sources, but also an impressive series of 3910 prints and drawings, stored in boxes, estimated at the relatively trifling sum of 95 L 18 sols. The cloth merchant Jacques Andry, mentioned earlier, possessed a collection of 100 paintings and prints valued at 1475 L and stored on the fourth floor of his home in 1715. The musician and Parisian bourgeois Jean Dun, who died in 1745, had a collection of thirty-one works of varying worth, which were examined by two painters from the Académie, Charles Coypel and Jacques Dumont (called Le Romain), who set their value at the significant sum of 4604 L, which represented approximately 75 per cent of the estate of the deceased.

Though acquiring a true collection necessitated both a certain level of income and a certain amount of space, it was not necessarily restricted to a specific social class. Personal taste seemed to play a greater role than financial means in many cases. There were actually modest eighteenth-century households that turned out to have more pictures than the general average. In such cases, engravings, which were significantly less expensive than paintings, predominated. When the wife of a stone-cutter died in 1771, leaving behind only 447 L in her estate, her fortune included fifty-eight prints under glass and seventeen paintings on wood, valued at the modest sum of 12 L. In the home of the wife of a master furniture maker, we counted a total of thirty-five images in 1755, including paintings on canvas, one painting on copper and prints under glass. A chamber valet, who lived in 1734 in two rooms, covered his walls with thirteen paintings and prints. In the home of a servant whose combined worldly goods were worth only 230 L in 1737, the valuers inventoried twelve engraved paintings under clear glass.

Whether they were images of great value or little worth, the sole picture in a household or one piece in a large collection, these paintings and engravings had been acquired for the subjects they presented, for pleasure, and not because of the artist's reputation. The names of the painters and engravers are almost always unknown today. They actually seemed to be of little importance to art lovers of that period, or at least during the seventeenth century and into the first half of the eighteenth.[13] There were, however, collections in which the experts called in by the notary gave the names of the most celebrated artists.

The Italian school was heavily represented among the works belonging to the musician and collector Jean Dun: there was a painting on wood of *St John the Baptist* by Andrea del Sarto, *Abraham and Hagar* by Fra Bartolommeo, a *Virgin and Child* by Jacopo Bassano, *The Death of Phaethon* by Veronese, and a *Flight into Egypt* by Giovanni Benedetto Castiglione. Each of these paintings was valued in 1745 at the sum of 100 L. There was also a small painting by Carracci, found in 1774 in the home of the Marquis de Féline, figuring the dead Christ on the Virgin's lap, valued at 300 L.

The works of the Flemish school in Jean Dun's collection included four works signed by Paul Bril: a view of Italy, worth 400 L, and a view of Loreto and two landscapes, one of which was glued on wood, worth 50 L each. There was also a landscape glued on a wooden support, worth 20 L and painted by the brush of Vincens Leckerbetien, also known as Manciolla. Magnus Bodasse possessed a *Virgin and Child* by Jordaens, valued at 50 L, and Jacques Andry had three paintings by Teniers.

Several paintings from the French school were also identified in Jean Dun's collection: a view of Normandy worth 40 L by Pierre Patel, called Pierre Le Bon; a spinning woman with several animal figures by the Le Nain brothers, assessed at 80 L; *Theseus and his Mother* by Poussin, one of the most valuable pieces in the collection, worth 800 L; and *The Samaritan Woman* by Nicolas Pierre Loir, valued at 120 L. Another canvas by Poussin was inventoried in the residence of the Marquis de Féline; it showed another episode from the epic story of Theseus and was valued at the substantial sum of 1000 L.

Jacques Andry possessed a *Flight into Egypt* by Sébastien Bourdon in his collection, valued at 160 L. The master painter Nicolas Marion decorated his chamber in 1749 with ten prints 'painted by Boucher', showing 'the king, the queen, and Monsieur the Dauphin and children'. The Treasurer General of the Colonies, Sieur Baudard de Vandésir, owned fourteen prints of French ports, attributed to Joseph Vernet. More numerous than paintings by the masters were the copies or works painted by other hands in the style of the great artists of the Italian, Flemish and French schools. Magnus Bodasse's collection, for instance, included a *Virgin* done in the manner of Correggio, valued at 20 L, and a blind man holding a bow, done in the style of Raphael, valued at 60 L. The widow of the painter Charles Goy had a *Christ* done in the style of Raphael, worth 3 L, and

Jacques Andry owned a *Holy Family* of the same type. In the home of the Marquis de Féline, 'a landscape representing a wolf tearing apart a sheep, in the taste of Tempeste' was valued at 300 L.

It was Flemish painting, however, that seemed to have had the greatest success with the Parisian public. We know that a large colony of Flemish artists had settled in the city during the seventeenth century. In the collection of Magnus Bodasse was noted a painting of the five foolish and five wise virgins by a pupil of Rubens, valued at 40 L; a *Magdalene in the Desert* by a pupil of van Dyck, worth 20 L; and six other paintings, in the style of Paul Bril, including the *Four Seasons*, in four pieces, worth 200 L, and two canvases done in the manner of Teniers. Copies of Teniers and other so-called 'Flemish' paintings were mentioned in other households. These were usually genre scenes. Among the copies of paintings from the French school listed by the notaries were *The Marriage*, in the style of Poussin, found in the home of Jacques Andry, and a *Christ carrying his Cross*, copied from Lebrun.

Though the notaries rarely gave any attention to the artist or the style of these works, they generally provided a meticulous description of their physical aspect, especially the support and the frame. Wood and canvas were easily the most usual supports. Though the two were both equally widely employed before 1600, canvas became twice as widely used after that date as wood. This change became more and more evident during the seventeenth and eighteenth centuries. Of 1253 indications of painting supports noted for the period from 1775 to 1830, 1149, or 92 per cent, were canvas, and only sixty-six, or 5 per cent, were on wood, and thirty-eight, or 3 per cent, on various other materials. Among these, paper had all but disappeared by the beginning of the seventeenth century. Nonetheless we found 'three paintings on illumination paper' in the home of the wife of a haberdashery merchant in 1636. In contrast, prints and drawings, which were more common, were almost always done on paper, vellum paper or board, as the notaries sometimes specified. Other supports included copper, which occurred with increasing frequency, Limoges enamel, which came back into favour in the seventeenth century, marble and, much more rarely, ivory, alabaster, plaster, glass and slate. There were also a few pictures embroidered on silk or satin.

The material for the frame, also called a chassis (*châssis*) or border (*bordure*), was indicated in most cases: 'a painting on canvas with trim and frame in gilded wood', 'six small paintings on copper with their pearwood borders' and so forth. These frames, which often had a greater market value than the image itself, were subject to careful attention from the valuers, whereas it was far from certain that the subject of the picture would be specified. Intended to highlight the painting or engraving by contrasting or bringing out its colours, the frame was a decorative element in and of itself. The most widespread type was in gilded wood, which could be carved, smooth, or '*à filet*', forming a thin band. Other types of wood mentioned included blackened pearwood, brown, painted or *capucine*-style wood and oak or cedar. In the most luxurious interiors of the late eighteenth century, canvases to be placed over doors were set in a woodwork frame. Hung over a mirror, they were built into the pier glass. It should be noted that framing was used not only for paintings, but also for engravings. These were usually trimmed with borders in gilded wood, that were less rich than those around paintings:

free of any sculpting, they were described simply as a 'band of gilded wood' or, more rarely, of darkened or painted wood. By the end of the eighteenth century, most prints were observed to be under clear glass.

On the subject of the shape and size of these pictures, information in the inventories is exceptionally rare. Only indications such as 'small', 'medium' or 'large' give us an approximate idea of their size. Smaller formats were the most numerous, since they were best adapted to the usually fairly limited space available in Parisian lodgings.

As for the painting techniques used in these images, they also apparently failed to interest the notaries. While works 'painted in oil' were the most common, tempera, whose price was lower, was also widely used. A whole section of the Saint-Germain fair was reserved for the sale of such works. This type of painting was done using colours that were diluted with water and glue or with water and egg yolks. A few pastels are also mentioned, like one in the home of the painter Adrien Blain, where in 1729 'a picture painted in pastel, covered with clear glass' was found. Finally, we should not forget the small number of 'miniature paintings'. As for the technique used in engravings, such as line engraving (*taille-douce*), burin or etching (*eau-forte*), almost no description is ever given.

What is most interesting about this exhibition of several thousand images of all different sorts that we discover in wandering through these Parisian habitations are the iconographic subjects. A religious engraving, a portrait of the family or of a king, or a landscape are not simply neutral objects. Rather, they express the cultural and artistic sensitivities of their owners. Was it through ignorance, negligence or a simple lack of interest that the valuers indicated the subjects of these pictures, drawings and prints in only 55 per cent of the cases, as we calculated using a sample of more than 11,500 images? The result in any case is that the themes of 45 per cent of these works remain unknown, to the great disappointment of twentieth-century historians. There are too many paintings and engravings 'not worth any description' or 'representing different … or diverse subjects' with no further detail, or simply described as containing 'human figures', 'various figures' and so on, with no thematic notes, to make a serious statistical study possible.

Despite these gaps in our documentation, a quantitative study of the distribution of those subjects identified by the notaries is called for. This is how we proceeded with a survey of more than 8000 images which were identified. The great majority featured religious themes, which constituted 52 per cent of the images represented in our sample. There was a great diversity of profane subjects, but two categories stand out: portraits, accounting for 21 per cent, and landscapes, 15 per cent. Other subjects are less frequent: still lifes, 3.5 per cent; genre scenes, 2.5 per cent; mythology, 2 per cent; history, 1 per cent; allegories, 0.5 per cent; animals, 0.5 per cent; and finally various subjects, 2 per cent. We shall analyse the religious subjects later on, when we deal with the issue of spirituality. In the secular realm, it is important to emphasize the fashion for portraits in Parisian interiors during the seventeenth century, and even more so in the following century. As La Font de Saint-Yenne wrote in 1747, this was 'the type of painting most abundant today, the most cultivated, and the most flattering to very mediocre brushes'.[14]

In the seventeenth century portraits seemed on the whole to be reserved exclusively for the well-to-do, especially office holders and members of the Parlement, who were intent on exhibiting the figures of the king, the queen, members of the royal family, or other important personalities or political figures in some place of honour within their homes. The Chevalier Jean de Choisy, *Chef du Conseil, Chancelier* and keeper of the seals of the late Duc d'Orléans, possessed a set of eighteen portraits of Henri IV, Louis XIII and Louis XIV, members of the royal family since Maria de' Medici, Richelieu and Mazarin. Louis Ancelin's collection included fourteen portraits of the king. A priest and former counsellor to Parlement owned portraits of Henri IV, Louis XIV and the king of Spain. The age of the Enlightenment brought about a tremendous growth in this fashion for portraiture, which finally spread into all levels of society. An examination of the subjects of 1500 images inventoried after 1750 shows that portraits account for 30 per cent of the whole, to the detriment of religious subjects, which had lost ten points and represented only 42 per cent. Parisians who were connected with the king's service by their social standing or their function were no longer the only ones who owned a portrait of the sovereign. Merchants and masters of the urban trades also expressed their faith in the monarchy by hanging a court portrait on the walls of their chambers or sitting rooms. The widow of a master button maker had collected five paintings and three prints of all sorts in her chamber in 1748, including a portrait on canvas of Louis XIV and a print featuring 'the reigning king and the queen'. In the home of the widow of a beverage merchant who died herself in 1775, there hung a portrait of Louis XV 'in his youth'.

In addition to the figures of sovereigns and members of their families, portraits of ministers, celebrities of the day and famous men also found a place even in the most modest Parisian homes. Thanks to their low price, which made them an easily distributed form of propaganda, prints were accessible to almost every purse. We noted portraits of Louvois, of the Duc de Villeroi, Monsieur de Belle-Isle, Monsieur d'Argenson, the lieutenant general of the police, the Cardinal de Noailles, of Bérulle, the archbishop of Paris and many others. Louis Guersan, the master stringed instrument make to the Dauphin, possessed a portrait of Boileau in 1770. Charles Baton, former musician to the late queen, possessed a print of Benjamin Franklin in 1784. In the home of the musician François Devienne the valuers in 1790 found a collection of fifty-four prints featuring portraits of artists of the period who are unfortunately not identified. It came as no surprise to find a portrait of the composer and violinist Jean-Baptiste Lully in 1709 in the home of Boutelou, a member of the royal academy of music, or a print of the French composer André Campra in 1743 in the home of a music master.

Also very much in vogue during the eighteenth century were family portraits. They are almost never included in the assessment of the estate; with rare exceptions, they are simply mentioned 'for memory'. Still uncommon in the France of Louis XIV, they won the favour of all social strata in the following century. As testimony to a concept of family that bound together the members of a same family unit or lineage, the purpose of these portraits was to perpetuate the memory of loved ones, just like our photograph albums today. They represented the dead relative with wife or husband, ancestors, descendants or collateral family members. The interior of one master enamel artist was decorated with a painting of the artisan and his wife, and another of his daughter. A hotel keeper in 1751 possessed a portrait of himself. Nor should it come as a surprise to find five portraits in the home of a figure as famous as Rameau, four of which represented himself, and one of which represented his wife. It may seem ostentatious for the master of the household to have his own portrait on display for general admiration. But it was apparently the fashion at the time to have one's portrait painted. In the home of one master painter, we noted the portrait of a 'young child', and in the home of another painter, that of his father and mother. A spinster had portraits of her sister, her brother and her nephew.

Portraits could be signs of respect and admiration for the monarch or the great figures of the day, or signs of affection for close relatives. They could also express bonds of friendship or fidelity: in the home of Jeanne Dameron, nurse to the Duc de Bourbon and first chambermaid to the Duchesse de Bourbon, there were two oval paintings in 1710, representing her masters, the duke and duchess, held in gilded wooden frames. They were valued at 6 L.

Unfortunately many of the portraits belonging to our Parisians are not identified. Frequently we are merely told that they are family portraits, or portraits of a man, a woman, an old man or woman, a knight, a priest or a chaplain, a young boy, a sleeping child or two small children. Were these family members that no one participating in the inventory was able to identify?

While the more or less official portraits of famous people were generally hung for all to see, in the antechamber or in a common room, family pictures tended to be dispersed throughout the house, though there seems to have been a slight preference for the chamber. The value of these familiar, silent witnesses to daily life, present even in the most humble households by the eighteenth century, was first and foremost sentimental. One touching example was that of a former *officier des vivres* (quartermaster), who died in the depths of misery in 1748, with a total estate of 31 L. He possessed three portraits: his own, one of his wife and 'one of their deceased daughter'. These made up the sole decoration in his poor dwelling.

Most of the landscapes ornamenting the dwellings of these Parisians were not described, and the term 'landscape' was used with no additional details. When any more specific indications were given, they frequently identified seascapes or views of sea ports, such as the port of Marseille or the port of Nice. The work of the famous painter Joseph Vernet contributed to the success of this genre during the second half of the 1700s. We should note that between 1753 and 1762, this painter prepared an important series of canvases depicting the ports of France, to fulfil a commission from the King. Reproductions of these works began to appear in engravings by Cochin and Lebas in 1758, at an average price of 6 L per print for subscribers, and 9 L thereafter. These series were immensely successful; indeed, fourteen of these prints adorned the home of Sieur Baudard de Vandésir.

Rustic landscapes, often of Flemish inspiration, sometimes figured with descriptions such as 'landscape with hedged fields', 'landscape by night', 'lightning behind a landscape', or 'cows in a landscape'. This was an age marked by the sentimentality of Jean-Jacques Rousseau, which drew its inspiration from the spectacle of natural beauty, and landscapes hanging over doors and pier glasses were highly fashionable at the end of the century in the most refined Parisian interiors.

Other secular subjects were much more rare. Still lifes most commonly represented flowers and fruits, and these, too, were found over doors and pier glasses. Genre scenes, inspired either by the Flemish school, especially Teniers, or by the French school as illustrated by Watteau and Chardin, offered some variety: these included village festivals such as weddings and balls, a mill with washerwomen, or scenes set in landscapes, such as hunts, shepherds and shepherdesses, rustic diversions, travellers, bathers, or even scenes from domestic life, such as a Flemish lunch, a kitchen, a man holding a child, a woman making gruel, children playing, musicians or dancers.

Mythological subjects were on the decline during the eighteenth century. These pictures tended to deal with such divinities and members of antiquity's pantheon as Jupiter, Juno, Minerva, Apollo and the Muses, Diana, Venus and *putti*, Mercury, Cupid, Bacchus, Pan and the Sirens, Pomona or Andromeda.

Historical painting was uncommon, even though art critics considered it to be the greatest of all genres. As Saint-Yenne wrote,

> The painter-historian is the only painter of the soul; the others only paint for the eyes. He alone can bring into play that enthusiasm, that divine fire which makes him conceive of his subjects in a powerful and sublime manner. He alone can form heroes for posterity, through the great actions and virtues of famous men that he presents for us to see, not in a cold rendering but actually seeing the events and the actors.[15]

Most of the historical subjects noted by the valuers concerned battles – the battles of Alexander or those of modern times, such as the siege of Tournai or the French crossing the Rhine in view of the Dutch army. We also noted the following themes: Nero and Agrippina, the Turks descending on a sea port, a feast for Henri III served by Venetians in a wood, and the king going to Parlement.

Allegories were rare. Those we noted included the four seasons, the four elements, the five senses, as well as various virtues, such as charity, prudence and justice, in the tradition of Cesare Ripa's *Iconology*. A few paintings and prints portrayed a diverse array of animals, and these too were placed on walls or above the doors and fireplaces of our Parisians. The menagerie included dogs, a cat holding a bird between its paws, a dog and two cats, horses, sheep, roosters, chickens, birds and fish.

Under the 'miscellaneous' heading we have included architectural views such as the Vatican, the Coliseum, the façade of the Louvre, the church of Notre Dame de Lorette, the rue Saint-Laurent, and various ruins, as well as literary subjects inspired by La Fontaine's fables, Ovid's *Metamorphoses*, *Don Quixote*, the *Roman comique* and Molière's plays. We also included the small number of maps we found in these interiors, such as one example showing the port of Marseille.

This survey of the main subjects of the images that embellished these homes highlights how eclectic their owners were in their artistic choices. It was not exceptional, even in the most humble households, to find a set of small images of little value, dealing with the most varied subjects. This situation was illustrated by the case of a master furniture maker who, upon his death in 1684, left behind fifteen images: a portrait, a village wedding, three pictures of flowers, and ten pious images. The widow of a master button maker in 1748 had collected five paintings and three prints of various types in her chamber. These included portraits of herself and of the king, pious images of Judith, Noah's ark and St Mary Magdelene, animals and rustic figures. The neighbouring room was decorated with three paintings and sixteen prints, also representing a sampling of genres: there were portraits of the Turkish ambassador and his son, still lifes of fruits and flowers and an allegory of the four elements. The notary's way of listing a succession of such diverse subjects, for example 'Louis XIV and a vase of flowers' or 'St John and Minerva', may make us smile. It would seem that the choices of images made by these Parisians were not at all dependent on criteria of aesthetics and unity, but rather on more sentimental and cultural motives.

Mirrors

In their desire for better living, which was also often a quest for useless and superfluous things, eighteenth-century Parisians seemed to accord a special place to wall mirrors in decorating their dwellings. By setting up a play of lights that seemed to expand space, these mirrors embellished interiors, that were often badly lit and excessively cramped, with a touch of wonder and enchantment. Their success carried them across the boundaries of all social categories. More than 70 per cent of the households inventoried from the end of the seventeenth century were furnished in this manner.

Mirrors began replacing tapestries, paintings and prints as they invaded the walls of numerous Parisian dwellings of the period. The favour they enjoyed was striking even to contemporaries, and the art critic La Font de Saint-Yenne reproached their owners with 'exiling from their apartments the most beautiful of the arts', namely painting, and especially historical painting. 'These mirrors', he wrote,

> which form pictures in which the imitation is so perfect that it equals nature itself in the illusion it creates before our eyes, these mirrors that were fairly rare in the previous century and are extremely abundant in this one, have dealt a mortal blow to that fine art and have been one of the principal causes of its decline in France, by banishing the historical subjects that had created its triumph from the positions they held and by taking over the decoration of *salons* and galleries. I must admit that the advantages of these mirrors, which are great, deserve in many respects the favour they have won with fashion. They pierce walls and enlarge an apartment by adding a new one to it; they give back the rays of the light they receive, be it daylight or candlelight. How could man, the born enemy of darkness and of everything that can occasion sadness, help loving an embellishment that enlivens and enlightens him, and that fools his eyes without fooling him as to the real pleasure he receives?[16]

So that author expressed the underlying reasons for this passion for mirrors.

The massive introduction of mirrors into Parisian households during the eighteenth century was closely related to the growth of the royal manufacture of

Saint-Gobain, founded by Colbert. As production costs fell and technology improved, mirrors were no longer luxury objects reserved exclusively for society's elite. Instead they became accessible to the broadest possible public. They even graced the modest homes of servants, day labourers and artisans in the faubourg Saint-Antoine. In the wealthiest residences, numerous mirrors could be found in each room, set between windows or above fireplaces the better to capture and amplify light. This profusion drove Mercier to write, 'Oh! Who can calculate the cost in workers' harsh sighs of these mirrors which we place everywhere, and which form the primary luxury of our homes? ... And where do we not put them? In alcoves, in stairways, in wardrobes.'[17]

With the exception of toiletry mirrors, these mirrors appeared in two forms: mobile, framed in a border; and fixed, set in a pier. The former owed their beauty not only to their brilliance and their size, but also to the way they were framed, as was the case with paintings and prints. We identified several types of frames, some simple, square or round, oval or rectangular, depending on the shape of the mirror, as well as other less common models with capitals, sometimes referred to as 'Dauphine' style beginning in the 1770s. Even more rare were the models decorated with a curtain or silk trim, like one mirror measuring 66 by 20 cm 'in its border and capital in sculpted gilded wood', draped with blue taffeta curtains trimmed with a little braid in fine gold. Valued at 100 L, it was found in 1712 in the home of an *officier plancheyeur* and *metteur de planches* who was night guard at the gates of the city. We also found examples in blackened, browned, painted, white or varnished wood. They type of wood, when it is mentioned, is usually walnut, ebony or cedar. Other materials, such as gilded copper, gilded bronze, enamel, black leather or glass, are less frequent.

The value of these mirrors depended not only on the quality of their frames, but above all on their size. Sizes actually varied considerably, ranging from some 20 cm high to more than a metre. The most widely used mirror models were about 30 cm high and included a single-pane mirror. But when size required it, they might be made up of several juxtaposed mirror panes, as the techniques for manufacturing large sections were still poorly understood at the time. The values of mirrors also had quite a range, from a few livres to several hundred. Investment in mirrors often represented significant sums in the eighteenth century, especially for relatively modest households.

To cite an example, a chamber valet who died in 1710 possessed 'a mirror in glass 24 to 26 inches high and 16 to 18 inches wide in its mirrored border decorated with plates of gilded copper, valued at 30 L'. In the same year, a mirror measuring '36 inches high by 24 wide in border with its mirrored capital, decorated with little borders and plates of sculpted gilded wood' was valued at 80 L in the home of Jeanne Dameron, nurse of the Duc de Bourbon. A mirror measuring 50 by 7 cm in a border of sculpted wood, inventoried in 1721 in the home of a day labourer, was estimated at 50 L. The lodgings of a master painter were decorated in 1731 with a large mirror, formed of 'a single mirror 2 feet 5 inches high by 1 foot 11 inches wide, in its border, also mirrored, its capital the same, the whole with ornaments in gilded copper, valued at 80 L'. Many households did not make do with a single mirror, but hung several on the walls of their abodes.

Less widespread than simple framed mirrors, pier glasses came into increasing use, especially after the 1750s, when fireplaces with lower mantels became more commonplace. The term 'pier glass' could also be used to designate 'mirrors that are ordinarily placed between two windows', as the *Dictionnaire de Trévoux* specified. The smallest among them measured 63 cm high and were made of a single mirror. But they could often attain significant dimensions, larger than 70 cm and sometimes reaching more than 2 metres. In such cases they were composed of two or three mirrors, with the largest models including as many as six. Held in a gilded wood frame or set into a parquet painted green or marbled, or more rarely grey or white, with pilasters or patterns sculpted in gilded wood, these pier glasses occupied a privileged place in the home, above a fireplace. They were sometimes placed between two candle branches or two windows. Mirrors placed between windows might be crowned, as we have seen, with a painting of a landscape or a still life.

Their value was generally greater than that of simple mirrors, and was rarely less than 20 L. This was the value attributed to a pier glass over a fireplace in a very simple model consisting of 'two mirrors measuring 21 inches high by 14 wide each, in a border with parquet' found in 1761 in the home of a master saddler and carriage maker from the faubourg Saint-Antoine. In the common room of a master painter who died in 1731 was inventoried 'a fireplace pier glass with two mirrors each approximately 1 foot 8 inches wide by 1 foot 4 inches high in its small border of gilded wood, with two candelabrum branches in copper, also gilded, valued at 24 L'. A wine merchant had decorated his company room in 1784 with a large pier glass approximately 2 metres high by 1.50 metres wide, valued at 160 L. In 1771, the wife of a wood merchant possessed a pier glass between two windows comprising three mirrors, the first '33 inches high, the second 23 inches and the third 24 inches, the whole 26 inches wide, in its border of sculpted and gilded wood' valued at 80 L. Pier glasses made up of two, three or four mirrors, measuring more than two metres high, could be worth as much as 400 or 500 L. Although the pier glass gradually made its way into the middle classes of society, its novelty, its size and, above all its price meant it was still much less popular than the simple mirror, even by the end of the century.

This abundance of mirrors discovered in these households manifestly demonstrates how the tastes of the Parisians changed during the eighteenth century. The rise in the number of mirrors and pier glasses used as decorative elements was accompanied by a decline in the use of tapestry. In some rooms, the surface area covered by mirrors was considerable. Though the example of the company room of Baillot de Villechavant, *Maître Ordinaire* of the Chambre des Comptes – adorned with three pier glasses each having three mirrors and with one fireplace pier glass covering 9.76 square metres – was an exception, it was quite frequent to find decorative mirrors covering up to two square metres in rooms such as the *salon* of a merchant goldsmith in 1744, or the chamber of the wife of a former office holder of the king in 1747.

The decline in the use of tapestry was borne out in the respective investments made by the deceased in hangings and in mirrors. In the homes of musicians and stringed instrument makers, the ratio between these two types of outlays, which had been clearly biased in favour of tapestries during the first three decades of the century, slowly began to shift by 1730, and the difference had spread to one to five in favour of mirrors by the 1770s. This ratio even reached one to seven in 1770 in the inventory of Marie-Jeanne Zeltener, wife of the stringed instrument maker Louis Guersan, where the value of the mirrors was estimated at 438 L. The estimated value of the mirrors alone in the home of François Francoeur in 1787 totalled 1587 L; there were 900 L worth of mirrors in the *salon* alone, and 347 L worth in the bedchamber, with others scattered throughout the apartment, and even in a study. The prestige of mirrors was even further heightened by the fact that they represented a luxury that had formerly been reserved for the great and was henceforth accessible to the popular classes. These mirrors were simply a response to a desire for gaiety and an attention to appearance which developed in this period. By reflecting light and space, they constituted a decorative element that seemed to invite festivity and amusement. After all, did not those haunts of pleasure called cafés, most of which were decorated with a multitude of pier glasses and mirrors, make a substantial contribution to the spread of this fashion?

Knick-knacks and Decorative Objects

The decor of a house included not only mural ornamentation, but also all sorts of essentially superfluous articles, sometimes set on a shelf over the fireplace, or standing on a piece of furniture. The rare knick-knacks to be found in the seventeenth century were simple items, but they became highly fashionable and much more numerous during the Enlightenment. The most commonplace items as early as the age of Louis XIV were mantelpiece decorations. These consisted of collections of pots, vases, glasses, cups, bottles, urns and so forth, mostly made of earthenware, or more rarely of porcelain or crystal, which were lined up on a shelf above the hearth.

These ornaments, to be found in the homes of merchants or trade masters as well as in the most affluent milieux, were generally arranged in groups of at least ten items, and larger collections could include more than twenty pieces. The collection found in the home of a monastic priest in 1716 consisted of twenty-eight pieces of earthenware and enamelled glass. Often set on small stands in gilded wood, these objects, which caught the eye thanks to their highly visible position above the fireplace, seemed intended for display rather than for use. Some pieces were collectors' items, like the tea service in Japanese china inventoried in 1720 in the home of a canon. Others seemed to be luxurious dishware, including vinegar bottles, gondola vases in porcelain or crystal bottles. As a result, the fireplace often gives the impression of being a display case for fine objects whose owners took pleasure in displaying them for all to see.

Though they always corresponded to the social standing of the household, these ceramic ornaments presented little variety on the whole, and actually seem to have been fairly stereotyped and without great value. Exceptionally, highly prized items were assessed separately by the valuers, but these appear only in the richest homes. The inventory of the Marquise de Traisnel in 1746 offers some fine examples: she had two saucers and two cups with handles in Dresden china, four tiny varnished saucers and a cup from Japan, as well as an old porcelain pot-pourri from Japan, which were worth 400 L altogether. Usually intended to decorate the fireplace, these objects sometimes spilled over to find a place on a table, a console or on top of a closet, a cabinet, a buffet or a desk. In the home of the former curé of Charenton in 1707, the valuers found 'five objects in earthenware as decorations on a table', and in the home of another priest who was *procureur* of the Collège de Cambrai, there were a few earthenware pots on top of a closet. In the dwelling of the Abbé Louis Fornier in 1722, numerous ceramic articles and various objects were exhibited on a console, on a closet and on shelves. We should also mention the 'liqueur cabinet platters garnished with cups and saucers' in earthenware or Japanese porcelain, or painted Chinese-style, often arranged on tables in even the most modest dwellings, as part of the decoration.

The taste for flowers in the eighteenth century can be perceived through the presence of a few flower vases in earthenware, porcelain, glass, or crystal, as well as the existence of flower or bouquet baskets. These were often trimmed with thin braid. The wife of a certified salt measurer in 1709 possessed 'a basket in which there were artificial flowers'.

As by-products of the introduction of tobacco, from the end of the seventeenth century lovely little snuffboxes could be counted among these knick-knacks. Eleven were listed, in all sorts of materials and original shapes, in the home of a lawyer at Parlement in 1707. The simplest models were in silver, like the one belonging to a sergeant in the regiment of the Gardes Françaises, who owned one in 'very thin silver' in 1755. They could also be covered with tortoiseshell, like the 'tortoiseshell snuffbox studded with little gold nails, with a hinge in gilded vermeil' that belonged in 1728 to Marin Marais, *Ordinaire* of the king's chamber music. A spinster, who was a lingerie merchant, in 1773 also possessed 'two small round snuffboxes in board, one painted red with a little flower encrusted with gold, and the other painted water green colour with little birds, both of them lined with tortoiseshell'. And there were others, trimmed with ivory and silver, or mother-of-pearl, or dogfish skin. Round, chiselled, tomb-shaped or shell-form, they came in various shapes.

Other bibelots listed by the notaries showed a greater diversity. Most numerous were figurines, sculpted in a wide variety of materials: plaster, bronzed plaster, gilded copper, bronze, marble, wood, earthenware, porcelain, wax and so on. These were often busts: 'two busts of antique figures', 'two busts of children in bronzed plaster', and 'two small busts in white marble' were some of the items found. When these statuettes were not anonymous, they sometimes portrayed royal effigies: 'an equestrian figure in bronze of Henri IV' was inventoried in 1744 in the home of a counsellor to the Parlement; a small statue of Louis XIII on horseback standing on an ebony base was found in the home of a *maître d'hôtel* in 1715; and busts of Louis XIV and Louis XV were inventoried in the home of a counsellor to the king and *Lieutenant de Robe Courte* in 1748. In the residence of Louis Gervais, the master surgeon, a bronze bust of the man himself could be admired in 1772. Some of these items represented animals, like the ones owned by Antoine Lambin in 1747, who had a horse and a bull in bronze.

Though of little value, knick-knacks of this type were found in only a minority of households. Even more rare, but much more intriguing, were the fanciful trinkets such as sea shells, grottoes made of shell, bits of coral, a crystal pyramid, marble or glass balls or pagodas in porcelain. A *procureur* at the Châtelet in 1672 owned a veritable roomful of curiosities which held a multitude of objects representing the baroque taste of the age: an ivory head, a bronze of Apollo, three figures in bronze, two grotesques, a little box covered with leather containing six medals, a little gold box decorated with a woman's head, a box featuring a Turk's head, a little enamel vase, two glass balls, a rock made of shells with a water tube, nine sets of feathers from small birds of different colours in a box, a unicorn's horn measuring some six feet long in an ebony case, a unicorn's tail, and one round and one oval medal, one of which showed Cardinal Richelieu, among other trinkets.

In addition to this decor composed of various trifles, there were also the instruments for measuring time, including different sorts of clocks that were both ornamental and useful. Though they were assessed at rather high amounts, ranging from 25 to more than 200 L, these objects were nonetheless to be found in almost 40 per cent of all households after the 1750s. The pendulum-driven clock or *pendule*, usually enthroned in the middle of the mantelpiece, occupied a privileged place in interior decoration. This new fashion actually irritated Mercier, who wrote, 'People put a pendulum clock on every mantelpiece; they are wrong; what a lugubrious fashion. There is nothing so sad as to contemplate a pendulum: you see your life slipping away, so to speak, and the movement warns you of all the moments that are being taken away and which will never return.'[18]

As late as the reign of Louis XIV, this instrument, in the shape of a wall clock with a marquetry case highlighted with gilding or ebony, was still considered a luxury. But it became more widespread during the eighteenth century and eventually emerged as a commonplace object. It was not exceptional to find several in the same household. The wife of a wine merchant possessed more than three watches and two pendulum clocks in marquetry cases in 1753. In the home of another wine merchant who died in 1784, the valuers listed three pendulum clocks as well as two watches.

As it gradually made its way into all the different levels of the population, the pendulum clock began to play an increasingly important ornamental role in the rooms in which it stood, whether raised up on the mantel, or standing on a piece of furniture, or hung on the wall. It began to display greater variety in its decoration, and was enhanced with sculpted patterns and colour. It might be described as chiming on the hour and the half, as a repeating clock (*à répétition*), or with an enamelled copper face marked with the hours, the minutes and, more rarely, the seconds, but it was always housed in a case that demonstrated a certain degree of refinement and imagination: there were marquetry cases with gilded copper figures, coloured copper, copper, bronze, silver or pewter ornaments. These cases might also be in oak, black ebony, pearwood or gilded, silver-plated, enamelled, copper-plated wood, tortoiseshell or horn painted green – and the list goes on. They sometimes stood on a console in marquetry or a base in varnished or gilded and carved wood, or one decorated with copper or bronze ornaments. We should note that, unlike paintings, which were almost always anonymous in the inventories, most of these pendulum clocks, as well as the watches, were signed by the watchmakers who manufactured them.

Rarer and more rustic than pendulums were clocks with cords and lead weights, which were described in their cases of oak, gilded iron or pine. Such clocks, generally estimated at less than 50 L, were real pieces of furniture with a sober and massive presence, and were placed in the kitchen and the shop as well as in the chamber. They did not have the same decorative value as pendulum clocks. In the same way barometers and thermometers *en cartel*, i.e. in their housings, had an ornamental function in addition to their practical usefulness.

These many little things, tell-tale signs of cultural level, personal tastes or a desire to keep up with fashion, all contributed to decorating a dwelling. Whatever their market value, or their artistic value, may have been, these objects of all sorts radiated the fanciful refinement of their shapes and the delicacy of their construction, and conferred an intimate charm on these interiors that was in tune with the age of the Enlightenment. The most opulent homes enriched their decoration with elegant and costly furniture as well, including commodes, secretaires, chiffonniers, corner cupboards, desks, pedestal tables and fine seats that suited a new demand for comfort and intimacy.

By the beauty of their wood and the grace of their lines, the creations made by eighteenth-century Parisian woodworkers were truly luxurious furnishings. They were produced through the collective labour of several trades: the carpenter (*menuisier*) built the frame of the piece, the woodworker (*ébéniste*) put on the veneer and applied the marquetry of rare woods, the painter-gilder or the sculptor applied the gilt, varnish and mouldings, and finally the upholsterer prepared the covers and upholstered the seats. Because they came from distant lands and were costly, exotic woods like rosewood, *palissandre* or mahogany, which were kept for manufacturing such decorative furniture pieces, were generally applied in a thin veneer on a frame of native wood such as oak, pine or poplar. Marquetry and veneering were the fundamental techniques for decoration, in addition to painted ornamentation, Chinese-style varnishes, gilding, and table tops in marble from the Ardennes and Flanders (for ordinary quality) and from the Pyrenees, Provence or Italy (when the best quality was required). The nuanced shades and the grain of the woods and marbles, like the gilding on copper plating, blended in with the rich colour scheme of furnishing fabrics to form a harmonious whole in the finest interiors. As for colour, it is so important to the decoration of these dwellings that it deserves to be considered on its own.

Colour

This was a world of colours: bed curtains in green serge, in red or crimson damask, in pale blue *calamande* with white and sky-blue ribbons; seat covers in red velvet with yellow stripes or in blue and white *siamois*, in flaming *satinade*, in violet velvet; wall hangings in brown serge, in striped brocatelle with a flower print, or in moiré silk with white and crimson stripes; door curtains in checked cloth, in green and grey striped *camelot* moiré; curtains in white canvas. The pageant unfolds before our eyes as we read the notes taken by the valuers, and we are struck by its richness, its variety, and its harmonies. In order to designate these many colours, the notaries used a vocabulary that was rich, precise and image-provoking all at once, thereby revealing the importance of these aspects of interior decoration. We drew up a list of more than eighty mentions of different colours as applied to interior furnishings, including indications of shades such as pale blues or frog greens, and fifteen different sorts of grey (see Appendix 4). We did not, however, count the patterns with several colours, the green and white stripes, the red and white checks, the blue and white flowers, the bouquets of roses and so on.

This proliferation of colour was a contribution of the age of the Enlightenment. Indeed, the palette of colours used by upholsterers and decorators in the previous century was much less varied. Of 257 indications noted for the period from 1635 to 1649, the repertory includes only a dozen different colours. Later, new statutes governing the dyers' trade, and above all inventions by chemists contributed to making a greater range of colours possible. In an *ordonnance* issued by Colbert in 1671, colours were divided into two groups: those which were *grand teint*, or colour-fast, and those which were *petit teint*, whose colouring tended to be less reliable. The second category carried the day in the eighteenth century.

In addition to dyes for *grands teints*, such as mignonette or 'yellow grass' and madder for yellows, *guède* (woad) and pastel for blues, and cochineal for carmine, a 1737 regulation drawn up by the chemist Dufay authorized the use of such products as indigo, campeachy wood, soot black, walnut stain, curcuma and annatto. In 1740 the chemist Barth invented the Saxony blues, and in 1747 the Prussian blues made with ferrocyanide. Mordants such as alum, tin, copper, iron, zinc, bismuth and chrome were used to obtain variations on the colours and tones produced. Whereas 79 tones were used in tapestries made around 1680 to designs by Charles Le Brun, hangings made in the middle of the following century used 364 tones, and by 1780 they used no less than 587.[19] This bursting, overflowing abundance of colours and tints during the eighteenth century made its most marked contribution in the area of decoration.

What were the colours that won the popularity contest within the Parisians' daily environment? During the reigns of Louis XIV and Louis XV, two colours – red and green – were predominant. Based on a sample of 3360 indications of plain colours, these two tones, including the various shades of red, crimson, cherry, vermilion and scarlet, comprised 64 per cent of all notations. Until around 1715, red held a slight edge over green, with 29.5 per cent versus 28.5 per cent, if we consider only the 1255 indications given during the reign of Louis XIV. In the following decades, however, green gained a clearly preponderant position, since it accounted for 41.5 per cent of all mentions, while red declined to 26.5 per cent. Instead of a bright, aggressive colour (which was nonetheless considered to be a noble and distinguished hue in its crimson form), contemporaries of the age of the Enlightenment seemed to prefer the softer, more restful and earthy colour of green.

It is interesting to note that reds tend to disappear from the canvases of painters of the period such as Watteau, Fragonard, and Greuze, who favoured the use of more delicate shades. The *Encyclopédie* echoed the spread of this taste:

Green is just the right mixture of clear and sombre to please and strengthen the sight instead of weakening or troubling it. Hence the fact that many painters have a green cloth hung near the place where they work, on which to throw their glance from time to time, and to relieve them of the fatigue caused by the brightness of the colours. All the colours, says Newton, which are most brilliant, dull and distract the minds of animals that see; but those which are the most dark do not give them enough exercise, whereas the rays which produce in us the idea of green, fall on the eye in such a just proportion, that they give animal minds all the play necessary, and by this means they arouse in us a very agreeable sensation. Whatever cause it may please you to attribute to it, no one can deny the effect, and this is why the poets award the title of 'gay' to this colour.

It is equally interesting to note the breakthrough made by blue in the eighteenth century, moving from 1 per cent of all mentions to 10.5 per cent. To replace sober shades, including blacks, browns and violets, the age of the Enlightenment turned to pastel tones, such as various sorts of greys, pale hazelnut, rose, apricot or sky-blue. These light, delicate colours, often used for trims, ribbons or fringes on bedcovers, curtains or seat covers, provided an answer to the need for light and refinement which we have seen emerging in all the decorative elements used during this period. As a greater range of colours became available, various associations of colours could be made: white was commonly used with blue, red, green or yellow, but we also found yellow associated with green, blue or red. The spreading trend in favour of checks, stripes such as the *siamois* 'with large green and white stripes', and printed fabrics in the second half of the century worked to the detriment of plain-coloured fabrics, whose monopoly seemed to have been broken. Two-tone stripes and checks (mainly in red and white, but also in blue and red) were great favourites with Parisians. The numbers of patterns with bouquets of flowers, leaf prints and birds, inspired by the natural world, also began to multiply with the development of printed fabrics, engendering silver flowers on yellow or green backgrounds, green flowers on yellow or white backgrounds, 'gold and silk flowers' against crimson, and others. As these prints became part of the scenery, a fanciful note made its way into Parisian interiors.

As a corollary to this new aesthetic sense, a desire began to emerge, in fine residences but also within some modest dwellings, to make all the shades of furnishing fabrics harmonize within the same room. Curtains, bedcovers, seat covers and wall hangings in the chambers of the deceased were all matched – as we have seen in a few examples – creating a refined appearance that was a pleasure to the eye. In 1773 a treatise on colours and varnishes published by a spice merchant, expressed the age's new sensitivity to harmony in colours when it stated,

The painted background or the general colour should be white, soft grey, water green, lilac ... Sometimes occupants paint their apartments because of the furnishings; then the dominant colour of the apartment must be the dominant colour of the furnishings and the colour for highlighting must be the dominant colour spread throughout the furnishings ... If the furnishings are of a single colour, the painting of the apartment will not be harmed by gilded or gold-coloured mouldings.[20]

In the finest residences, ornamental furniture made of precious woods was another participant in this orgy of colour. Exotic woods like rosewood, with the colour of autumn leaves traced with red veins, *palissandre*, also called violet wood because of its colour, black ebony or costly mahogany, which was still little used, with its reddish grain – all these were eagerly sought after in the eighteenth century for the richness of their natural colouring and the variety of their grains. Gilded or 'coloured' copper ornaments sometimes highlighted the tones of these elegant pieces of furniture, like the 'small commode in violet wood having two large and two small drawers with knobs and keyholes in coloured copper and a top in Aleppo marble' or the 'small bookshelf closet in *palissandre* wood with keyholes in coloured copper'. Some furniture was painted, for example, a wooden desk painted black, a corner cupboard painted yellow, or an antique cabinet painted black and standing on a base painted red. Another widespread fashion of the eighteenth century was painting in contrasting colours: for example, we found two armchairs and three cabriole-legged chairs painted grey, with contrasts done in gold, as well as a wooden buffet painted white and highlighted with red.

This widespread enthusiasm for colours, which had earlier been considered as a luxury and a privilege reserved for aristocratic circles, marked one of the eighteenth century's triumphs. Like mirrors, colours in home furnishing had finally become accessible to almost all social categories. It would be most interesting, though outside the scope of the present work, to compare these colours with those used in clothing. We already know that while men of the poorer classes around 1770 wore dull and sombre-coloured clothes, women of modest background eagerly chose dresses with bright, light colours, or patterns with stripes and checks.[21]

This explosion of colour in the eighteenth century cannot be attributed solely to progress in dyeing technology. It seems also to be related to a phenomenon of sensitivity. The growing taste for colour, like that for increasingly precious furniture, for brilliant mirrors or for fanciful wall hangings, came in the wake of the Enlightenment, as part of a quest for greater comfort, for happiness and for sensual pleasure. These all carried interior decoration to its highest level.

7

A Look at Spiritual and Cultural Life
as seen through Household Objects

'Man shall not live by bread alone, but by every word that proceedeth out of the mouth of God', said Jesus to the Devil during his temptation in the wilderness. To what extent did Parisians put the word of Christ into practice and welcome the gift of God into their homes? A great deal of attention has been focused in these pages on the physical setting of the daily lives of the Parisians, through the many objects which were involved. But what can we learn from the notarial documents about the spiritual aspirations and the intellectual preoccupations of the inhabitants of these houses? Unlike wills, and especially autograph wills written, dated and signed by the testator, the inventories do not reveal the secrets hidden in the hearts and consciences of the deceased. Nonetheless they provide clues, through the books, images and pious objects listed by the notaries, as to the religious convictions and practices of the deceased. It is equally possible to approach the intellectual life of these Parisians by examining the secular books and other cultural artefacts, such as musical or scientific instruments, that they owned.

Whatever their value or their number within a household, these cultural objects, free of any material utility, were as full of meaning as works of art, because they represented personal choices. Some of these artefacts might, of course, have come from legacies or gifts, but on the whole, they can be considered as incontestable evidence of piety and culture. On the other hand, the complete absence of devotional books and objects in a household does not furnish absolute proof that its inhabitants did not know how to read or that they were oblivious to any religious feeling. Though this study is based on a quantitative analysis, we shall attempt to use the factual data contained in the inventories to shed light on the actions and behaviour of everyday religious and cultural life within the home.

Books

Excellent work has already been done on the libraries in Parisian homes,[1] and it is not our intention here to perform an exhaustive analysis of the books belonging to some 1200 households, which would weigh down this study and bore the reader. It is nevertheless appropriate to know who among these Parisians possessed books, how many volumes they had, what their favourite subjects were, and in particular what share of their collections was devoted to religious works. Books were to be found in 42 per cent of the households in our sample set, a relatively low percentage when compared with the high level of literacy among Parisians and the important role of the capital in the field of printing and bookselling. However, if we restrict these book counts to the years after 1750, we reach a rate of 51 per cent. These figures cover both owners of individual books and those with libraries holding several hundred or thousand works. It should be noted that these results are much higher than the 22.68 per cent calculated by Michel Marion for the mid-century. This difference can be explained by the specific studies devoted to priests and to lawyers. Despite these rather inflated figures, however, books did not enjoy as great a degree of popularity with Parisians as images in the seventeenth and eighteenth centuries.

Both books and images are cultural indicators. However, unlike images, books were not necessarily a sign of wealth, with the exception of those found in considerable libraries which required a minimum amount of space and material comfort. The taste for reading also required sufficient lighting in the home, and this activity could not be developed among those who had no leisure time. The time that artisans, who worked all day in their workshops or stalls, could spend reading was certainly very limited. At best, in the evenings or on Sundays, they might occasionally open a devotional book or an almanac. It therefore comes as no surprise that the homes without any books were not only those of the most impoverished and least literate, but also of those who worked hardest, such as merchants, master craftsmen, servants and day labourers.

We should note that studies of book ownership based on inventories are often troublesome for historians. The absence of any written material in the home of a deceased person belonging to the upper strata of society, for example, necessarily poses a problem. How can we explain that while men who belonged to the Parlement or were jurists had richly furnished libraries, there were lawyers who did not own a single book? How can it be that not a single work was listed in the home of Frédéric Léonard, who owned a bookstore, inventoried separately, which was worth more than 150,000 L? As for nobles without books in their Parisian homes, did they perhaps have collections of rare books on their country estates? Of course we know that these gentlefolk were not always cultural paragons! All these questions remain without answers, unless the decision is made to examine each individual case separately. As a result, we can say that although the socio-professional range of book owners was very diverse, so was that of non-owners.

The number of works inventoried could vary considerably from one household to another, and it ranged from a single book to 6000 volumes. On this point, we should emphasize the potential gaps in the inventory: the valuers often deliberately ignored books or brochures of little value, such as almanacs, calendars, or small in-12 or in-32 volumes from the *Bibliothèque Bleue de Troyes*, which were scarcely worth more than one or two sols. These amusing little volumes, distributed by pedlars, were probably as widely read as devotional books, at least in the working classes, where they met with tremendous success. In the long run, the number of books belonging to Parisian households increased continuously. The tendency to accumulate, which applied to all household goods during the eighteenth century, whether utilitarian or decorative, made no exception for books. Progress in literacy, a thirst for knowledge, and the intellectual curiosity of contemporaries of the age of the Enlightenment also contributed to this growth in book ownership. It is interesting to compare the average number of books per household in the parish of Saint-Nicolas-des-Champs between 1635 and 1649 with that for the faubourg Saint-Antoine in 1760 or 1762. The rate almost doubles, rising from 17 to just over 30, although there are considerable disparities from one home to another. In one household a few books would be found in a corner, sometimes where they might least be expected; in another there might be several hundred or thousand volumes carefully lined up in a bookcase inside a study. These are indications that there were two different types of reader: the occasional and the habitual.

But just what use did these Parisians make of their books? A book owned is not necessarily a book that has been read. The valuers' notes shed little light on this question. When sets of books were 'missing volumes and not worth describing', and were valued at insignificant sums, had they come to be in that state because they were used daily, or because they were old and abandoned? It is tempting to imagine that the few threadbare books found in modest households, tucked in among the linen or the dishware, were more likely to have been read than the superb collections of gilt-edged volumes bound in leather and carefully arranged in a library. No doubt a great many of these works were never opened. A book, and especially a beautiful book, was in fact a prestige article, a sign of a certain financial and cultural position, and, like ornaments and works of art, it could be present merely for show. It nevertheless seems that certain library owners, such as priests, lawyers and doctors, consulted their books fairly regularly. For them, these were the tools of their trades. If we could know where these texts came from, it would be more possible to judge their utility. Had they been purchased by their deceased owners, or received in a legacy or as a gift? In the first case, they would certainly represent the tastes of their owners. In the second, they would have been accepted but not chosen. From the inventories, however, we have almost no means of discovering the origins of these works.

Among book owners, we can distinguish between those who possessed real libraries, filled with hundreds or thousands of volumes, on the one hand, and those who had less than a hundred works. The former, whom we shall examine first, constitute some 25 per cent of all book owners, or one reader in four. What social categories did they belong to? Two social groups predominate: ecclesiastics and representatives of the various legal and medical professions, who together accounted for 62 per cent of all library owners, or 31 per cent for each category. Nobles, magistrates and king's counsellors take third place, accounting for 17 per cent of the total. Other professional classes are only scantily represented: merchants and bourgeois of Paris, 8 per cent; members of the military, single women and miscellaneous, 6 per cent; accountants and financiers, 3 per cent. As for craft masters and artisans, journeymen and servants, their numbers are so small in the ranks of library owners that we did not classify them into separate groups: they comprise 4 per cent of the total. The vast majority of these fine book collections, then, belong to the social and cultural elite, while among the working classes of the population, the number of written works almost never exceeds a few dozen. When very considerable libraries had to be valued, a bookseller was often called in to help the valuer with the inventory of these many volumes.

As an example, it is interesting to examine the contents of a few of these libraries, in order to appreciate the intellectual concerns and the central interests of their readers. Because of gaps in the inventories, however, our vision of the tastes of these Parisians in terms of reading material remains very fragmentary. From one inventory to another, the proportion of titles or even subject matter actually noted down (e.g. devotional, history) is very uneven, but is generally low, ranging from 50 per cent to less than 10 per cent.

Very frequently, formulas such as 'a packet of — books', with no other description than the format, or 'a packet of small books' are used, without any indication of their number or dimensions, or simply 'so many books dealing with various and sundry subjects' or 'so-and-so many 'books, including two history books'. When the volumes are small, for instance in-12 or in-16, it is even more rare to see the titles mentioned. When books were valued in batches, the bookseller would choose one or two titles in order to give an idea of the general contents of the packet. This resulted in a system of classification by genre in which the same or very similar titles were persistently used, and the reader's personality can scarcely be discerned. Under such conditions, there is every reason to fear that even the finest library would be reduced to a sort of stereotyped average by this type of classification by literary genre based on the use of what we might call 'touchstone titles' such as *Histoire de France* by Mézeray, or *Opera varia theologica* by Maldonat. Of course this procedure does highlight at least one reality: it designates the works that had received the widest circulation. At the same time, though, it threatens to conceal other, rarer and less well-known titles that could have provided better indications of the tastes and the true personalities of their readers. Despite these reservations, however, looking at libraries still can teach us much about the spiritual and intellectual life of these Parisian households.

Let us begin with the libraries of ecclesiastics. Books were omnipresent in the households of priests, and they played a significant part in the valuation of their estates. Whether born during the reign of Louis XIII or a century later, whether of humble or wealthy origins, clerics often invested a considerable share of their financial resources in books.

Some of these ecclesiastical Parisian libraries are interesting to look at. One Jean Desmoulins, born in 1650 in the parish of Saint-Etienne-du-Mont to a family of members of the Parlement of Paris, became curé at Saint-Pierre-aux-Boeufs on the Ile de la Cité before being called to Saint-Jacques-du-Haut-Pas, and was a doctor in theology at the University of Paris. At his death in 1732, he left a sizeable library of 2347 volumes. A survey of the various titles, though very incomplete, reveals the traces of the humanist culture acquired by a man of the cloth in that period. He was, however, an exceptional figure and, at 82, was still 'sound of body, memory, and mind', as the notary emphasized in his will. Half of the volumes inventoried had large formats: there were 591 in-folios and 442 in-quartos. Among the 340 titles indicated, 171 were in Latin. Many of the works existed in two or even three copies. Was this form of accumulation the result of inheritance? Religious works occupied a fundamental place in this library. There were many editions and translations of the Bible: *La Sainte Bible* by Lemaistre de Sacy, *La Bible* by Diodati, *Le Nouveau Testament* by Father Amelote, *Biblia Sacra* by François Vatable, *Biblia Hebraica*, and *Biblia poliglotta* by Le Jay among others.

While Jean Desmoulins was apparently a man of tradition who drew much of his knowledge from ancient Latin texts, he was also attuned to his times. His interest in the religious debates taking place around him and in other controversies is manifested by the titles of other books he owned: *Ordination des prêtres anglicans*,[2] *La Lutte religieuse contre les Luthériens*,[3] *La Démonomanie des sorciers* by Jean Bodin, and many other books on topics including schismatics, Richerism and Jansenism. Highly conscious of his responsibilities, Jean Desmoulins possessed numerous treatises on marriage, and one document called *Traité de l'éducation des enfants*.[4] The shelves on legal matters were also well stocked, containing works on both civil law and canon law. A few art books. dealing with great artists from the end of the fifteenth century to the first half of the seventeenth, such as Leonardo da Vinci, Philibert Delorme and Annibale Carracci, were also found in this collection. Though the series of literary works was fairly classical, including authors such as Rabelais and Boileau, it also contained one book of Confucius and two other volumes on oriental countries. Furthermore, this ecclesiastic took several journals and reviews, including the *Journal de la République des Lettres*, which may have contributed to the remarkable open-mindedness he displayed about the problems of his times. Unlike many other priests, who kept their books anywhere within their abodes, Jean Desmoulins possessed a room which he transformed into a proper library.

Nicolas du Moustier, a doctor of the Sorbonne, winner of a prize for eloquence from the Académie Française in 1675 and vicar at Saint-Séverin, died in 1699. He left a library of 680 volumes, in which religious works were predominant over any other genre. In addition to his sacerdotal functions, which made him the principal assistant of the curé, there is every reason to believe that Nicolas du Moustier was responsible for teaching the catechism, to judge by the composition of his library: in addition to countless catechisms and breviaries, there were also a few useful complementary works, such as a *Vie de Jésus* by an unknown author, an *Affaires de morale*,[5] a *Méthodes de confession*,[6] and *La Sonde de la conscience*[7] among others. The quality and the wealth of this material, which was, so to speak, technical and professional, revealed how great an importance this catechist and spiritual director attached to his work. A doctor of the Sorbonne, he also possessed a solid religious culture, in so far as can be judged from the contents of his library: seventy-five titles, or 33 per cent of all his religious books, are patristic works. On the other hand, books on spirituality are much less numerous: though the works of some of the best-known Spanish mystics were listed in the collection, there are no treatises on prayer or piety. Both St Augustine and St Thomas had their place in this library, next to the sixteen volumes of the *Bible de Port-Royal*. Nicolas du Moustier also took the *Journal des Savants* in order to keep himself well informed.

The less sizeable library of Luc Aubry, sacristan at Saint-Jacques-du-Haut-Pas, contained 294 volumes in 1725. Consisting to a large extent of small formats, it held 199 in-12 and in-14 books and may have been composed of works more recent than those in the previous two examples. As the brother of a curé with a parish in Senlis, and apparently without family in Paris, Luc Aubry was no doubt of more modest origins than the average parish priest in the capital. Unlike Parisians belonging to the world of office holders, he had not even a small collection of legal works, unless we take into account a single book on law. Audry's library was made up of theological works and religious histories. Among the latter figured not only the twenty volumes of the *Histoire ecclésiastique* by the Abbé Claude Fleury, but also the ten volumes of the *Histoire de France* by Mézeray, as well as the six books of the *Histoire de l'Eglise* by Antoine Godeau and the six volumes of the *Histoire des Conciles* by Jean Hermant. The collection also included several other multi-volume editions: the seventeen volumes of *Essais de morale* by Pierre Nicole and the four volumes of *Vies des saints* by Adrien Baillet. Such a collection indicates that Audry's culture was of recent acquisition, and that he sought out authoritative voices to confirm it.

Though each of these libraries has its own distinctive character, like many other libraries of parish priests, they reflect not only personal sensibilities, but also the pastoral preoccupations of these men, confronted with the difficulties of their evangelical tasks. These libraries reveal how concerned these clerics were with deepening their faith, by reading the Bible, especially the French translation by Lemaistre de Sacy which was the most widely owned version, and studying Latin texts; and by theological reflection based on the writings of St Augustine and of the Spanish Jesuit Maldonat. Traditional patristic literature, however, with the exception of St Augustine and certain scholastic texts, was fast losing ground. The works of St Jerome and St Thomas were scarcely ever cited, with the exception of isolated volumes. Could it be that anthologies, such as the *Bibliothèque des auteurs ecclésiastiques* by the Jansenist Louis Dupin, were replacing these older texts?

One clear exception was the library belonging to a distinguished and high-ranking member of the clergy, Pierre Deblanges, a doctor and *sénieur* of the Sorbonne, vicar general to the bishop of Coutances and prior at the queen's chapel at Sainte-Geneviève. At his death in 1706, he left 109 patristic titles in a collection of 359 identified religious works. In this library of 1167 volumes, of which 750 titles were listed, the works of the great fathers and doctors of the western and eastern churches were to be found: the full set of the *Summa Theologica* and the *Commentaries on the Epistles of St Paul* by St Thomas, stood side by side with the works of St Augustine, St Jerome, St Gregory the Great, Tertullian, St Gregory of Nazianzus, St Basil and St Cyprian.

The presence of missals, books of the hours, brevaries, lives of the saints, Imitations of Christ and other works on spirituality, especially those by Spanish mystics such Luis of Granada, St Theresa or Father Rodriguez, demonstrates what a place these men created for prayer and meditation in their lives. There were even collections of sermons on the shelves of these priests, including those by Bourdaloue and Massillon, or more rarely by Bossuet, as well as *Homélies* by Father Séraphin, *Instruction des prêtres*,[8] and *Le Guide des Pécheurs*,[9] all most useful books for accomplishing their ministry and works that could in a sense be considered tools of their trade.

Whether inventoried during the reign of Louis XIV or as late as the mid-eighteenth century, most of these libraries bore the marks of the religious context of the times. It is interesting to note that many of them contain works by Jansenists or by authors with Jansenist leanings, such as Nicole, Saint-Cyran, Arnauld, Pascal or Jansen. Other works mentioned include the *Catéchisme de Montpellier*, *Logique de Port-Royal*,[10] *Cas de Conscience*,[11] and *Vérité de la religion*.[12]

History in general was the second most important focal point for these priests, though their collections tended to be oriented toward religious history with histories of the Jews, the people of God, of the synods, the popes, the Church, the League, heresy and so forth. Among other volumes in Pierre Deblanges's library, there were works by Father Mainbourg published between 1673 and 1678, including *Histoire de l'Arianisme*, *Histoire de l'Hérésie des Iconoclastes*, *Histoire du Grand Schisme d'Occident* and *Histoire des Croisades*. Mention was also commonly made of books dealing with antiquity, Cicero, Caesar and the Roman empire, as well as the history of France as written by various authors, including Mézeray of course, and also Father Daniel, *Président* Hénault and Henri de La Popelinière. There were also histories of England and Holland.

Great works of literature occupy only a limited place in these libraries: the valuers noted a few ancient authors, such as Plutarch, Cicero, Sallust, Livy, Virgil, Horace and Ovid, but the place of honour was reserved for classical writers of the sixteenth and seventeenth centuries like Erasmus, Rabelais, Ronsard, Montaigne, La Fontaine, Molière, Racine, Boileau and Dancourt. A certain number of dictionaries were also to be found: in addition to the *Dictionnaire historique et critique de la Bible* by Dom Calmet, there were reference works by Moreri and Furetière. Since most of the priests in our sample died during the reign of Louis XIV, we were unable to find any trace of the *Encyclopédie* in their inventories, or of other Enlightenment literature.

Though it was uncommon to find scientific works among books in general, they were not totally absent from the libraries of ecclesiastics. In fact, in the inventory done in 1720 of the priest Nicolas Lequel de La Marre, they even filled more space than theology and history. Out of 1362 volumes, of which only 15 per cent of the titles were listed, we counted at least seventy works in the scientific area, almost entirely devoted to medicine. These included not only Hippocrates' writings but also *La Médecine des pauvres*.[13] Another scientific library was inventoried in 1706 in the home of Jean-Baptiste Duhamel, a former professor of philosophy at the Collège Royal, who had left his chair in 1694 with a pension of 400 L. He had previously been prior at Saint-Lambert and secretary of the Académie Royale des Sciences. In his library of 358 volumes, 13 per cent of the works dealt with scientific subjects, divided fairly equally among medicine, botany, magic, physics and mechanics. In his will, this former philosophy professor, who had published a *Theologica theoretica et practica*, displayed such preoccupation with the publication of two other works of his writing, *Histoire latine de l'Académie des Sciences* and *Philosophie*, that it would seem he had become completely absorbed in his functions at the Academy of Science. Though he had taught philosophy, works on this subject and on great literature represented only 5 per cent of the titles in his collection.

Almost seventy years later, in 1772, Nicolas Le Bègue, a priest with a *licence* degree in law, also proved to have a strong interest in science. His library contained Buffon's *Histoire naturelle* as well as works on geometry and architecture. Nor was law completely absent from these clerical libraries, though it was represented only by a limited number of titles, such as works on the *Corpus juris civilis*, canon law, or *Coutumiers*, i.e. collections of customs, unwritten laws and forms of procedure.

In looking at the libraries of these Parisian priests, most of whom were born during the reign of Louis XIV, it becomes apparent that these were learned men and in some cases scholars, who had received solid theological training in the seminaries that developed out of the Catholic Reform. The interest they show for history, the sciences or other disciplines remains personal and never seems to overshadow their preoccupations as men of God. Their knowledge of holy scripture, their pious aspirations and their desire to fulfil their pastoral duties are all reflected in the range of religious works in their libraries.

It is also worth noting that the size of these personal libraries had nothing to do with the spaciousness of these clerics' lodgings, as a few examples will show. Jean Minet, a professor at the Collège Duplessis, and François Chaudon, vicar at Saint-Jacques-du-Haut-Pas, respectively managed to pile 236 and 320 volumes into their two-room homes. Pierre Billet, a *receveur* (tax collector) and former rector of the university, had collected 1000 volumes in the three rooms he occupied in 1720. As for Nicolas Lequel de La Marre, who was discussed above, and the Abbé Guillaume Parisot, they owned 1362 and 4309 volumes respectively, with which they each shared their two-room homes. We can imagine how little space was left for them to live in, invaded as they were by books. Generally speaking, these books were stored in book closets or on bookshelves suited to this purpose. They were usually said to be valued 'in the quarters occupied by the deceased'. In short, books were to be found everywhere in the house: whether in the chamber, the antechamber or the kitchen.

Even when they were gathered into a single room, this space was rarely furnished for reading. In the home of Paul de Curduchesne, a doctor of the Sorbonne, abbé, and counsellor to the Cour des Comptes of Montpellier, the 142-volume library valued in 1718 had been stored in a room containing neither chair nor lectern. It was also used as a wardrobe. Nicolas Lequel de La Marre kept his books in the same room as his stock of firewood. Even in large residences, a library room was rare. Canon Jacques Belin lived in 1720 in a house with some ten main rooms and several annexe rooms, yet he had scattered his 234 volumes throughout the house. This non-specialization of rooms was therefore not necessarily related to a lack of space, but to the simple fact that specialization had not yet become customary.

Those members of legal professions who owned libraries were almost exclusively lawyers at the Parlement. This category includes the 343 volumes inventoried in the home of the wife of Louis-Claude Plastrier, Sieur de La Vernade, a notary at the Châtelet who died in 1744. The libraries of jurists were rich and well diversified, and were generally organized along two lines: one was the specialization demanded by their functions, and the other was more personal, focusing on various subjects depending on individual tastes. This phenomenon emerges clearly through a look at the composition of some of these libraries. André Chauffourneau, a lawyer at the Parlement who left behind several hundred books when he died in 1707, had a remarkable collection relating to his profession, including all the *Coutumiers* of the different French provinces. The core of this library consisted of classical Greek and Latin authors such as Plato, Aristotle, Seneca, Pliny and Livy. Other entries were surprisingly diverse: books of philosophy, heraldry, dictionaries, twenty volumes of collections of gazettes from 1674 to 1693, and of course devotional works such as the New Testament translated by Lemaistre de Sacy and a copy of the *Histoire de l'hérésie*.[14] It is interesting to note that a great many of these books were in Latin.

A former lawyer at the Parlement, François Réversé, who died a year earlier, possessed several hundred books in Latin and French, valued at the considerable sum of 4862 L. Legal works were particularly abundant. But like the most cultivated members of society, imbued with antique and humanist culture, this lawyer clearly had a very inquiring mind. Medical works stood side by side on his shelves with volumes of history and literary works. Like his colleague André Chauffourneau, François Réversé displayed a clear predilection for antique authors in all areas, including Thucydides, Virgil, Tacitus, Pliny, Sallust, Ovid, Aesop, Horace and Martial. The only contemporary writers represented were the historians François de Mézeray, Antoine Varillas and André du Chesne, and Corneille and Molière. There were relatively few religious works.

The library of more than 300 volumes left in 1742 by Catherine Garanger, the wife of a former lawyer at the Parlement, contained an important series of legal works dealing with customs in Paris and the provinces, with jurisprudence, and with legal settlements, as well as several treatises: the *Traité sur les hypothèques* by Henri Basnage, *Traité des monnayes* by Jean Boizard, and *Traité des Aydes* by Pierre Asse. In addition, the library contained collections of edicts and declarations by the king, *arrêts*, *tailles* (direct tax levies) and so forth. Those writings dealing with religious matters took an essentially legal approach, like *Institution du droit ecclésiastique* by the Abbé Fleury, *Histoire du droit canonique et du gouvernement de l'Eglise* by Brunet, and *De l'Estat et gouvernement de l'Eglise* by Simon Vigor. However, there were also copies of *Traité de la fréquente communion* by Arnauld, *Traité de l'amour de Dieu* by St Francis of Sales, and *Traité de la perfection du chrestien* by Cardinal Richelieu, whose *Instruction du chrestien* also figured on the shelves. There were no Bibles or other strictly devotional works.

A few works of history and geography proved that the library's owner had a certain interest in how the world was made: in addition to the history of France as told in *Démêlés de Boniface VIII et de Philippe le Bel*,[15] a *Mémoire de ce qui s'est passé en France depuis 1605 jusqu'à 1635*,[16] the memoirs of Cardinal de Retz, *Histoire du prince de Condé*,[17] *La Vie de Colbert*,[18] and a *Testament politique* by Louvois, the history section also included an *Alphabet d'Espagne et de Portugal* by du Val,[19] a *Description de la Livonie*,[20] *La Saxe galante*,[21] *L'Etat de la Suisse*,[22] a *Mémoire sur le gouvernement de la Hollande*,[23] *La Vie de la reine Elisabeth*,[24] and *Histoire de Charles XIII roy de Suède* by Voltaire. Great literature and the sciences were sparsely represented. Unlike libraries of the previous generation, works in Latin – with the exception of texts from the Council of Trent – were absent here, as were writings from antiquity. Only two ancient authors, Theophrastus and Petronius, and a single work of ancient history, *Voyages de Cyrus*[25] were mentioned.

Still more impressive than the libraries of lawyers were those of certain nobles, magistrates, king's counsellors and office holders of the royal household, which displayed a remarkable wealth and diversity. Through a study of 160 libraries belonging to eighteenth-century members of the Paris Parlement, François Bluche has unveiled the vast and relatively enlightened cultural background of its magistrates.[26] The inventory of Jacques Amelot, the *Premier Président* of the Cour des Aides who died in 1668, offers an example of a fine seventeenth-century magistrate's library. Religious books held an important place in it, as did works on controversial issues, such as *Les Libertés de l'Eglise gallicane*,[27] *Le Mystère d'iniquité* by du Plessis-Mornay, and *Réponse au Mystère d'iniquité*.[28] There was also an ample selection of law books, the tools of this magistrate's trade, including the *Corpus juris civilis* and treatises by Charles Loyseau. There were also foreign-language dictionaries in Latin, Greek and Hebrew, and a work entitled *Hieroglyphica Egiptorum*. Amelot was a humanist who read the works of Erasmus, Marsilio Ficino, and Lorenzo Valla. He even manifested a certain attraction for occult traditions, as is suggested by the presence of a book on the cabbala. His interest in history and geography seemed to reach out to all lands and all times. In addition, this library also contained thirty-six copies of diplomatic and political texts and memoirs, including five volumes on the peace signed at Münster, the *Journal de Monseigneur le cardinal duc de Richelieu*, and one volume on the *Etats de la noblesse de 1614–1615*.[29]

The library we discovered a century later in the home of François Francoeur, superintendant of the king's music, who was a member of the cultural elite of his age, was at the opposite extreme from that of Jacques Amelot. No religious books, no works from antiquity or even from the Renaissance appear among these 1091 volumes. This was a resolutely modern library, containing only seventeenth- and eighteenth-century writings: a library for a contemporary of the Enlightenment. The musician Francoeur left behind a reputation as a libertine and a man of intrigues, and he had a clear predilection for great literature and amusements. Indeed, such works made up the greater part of his library with their 506 volumes. In particular, there was a large collection of plays in French, Italian and English. Did Francoeur read these with the intention of using them in composing operas in collaboration with Jean-Ferry Rebel? Among the playwrights mentioned were Pietro Metastasio, Evariste Gherardi, Antoine Houdar de La Motte, Corneille, Molière, Quinault, Regnard and Dancourt. Madame de Sévigné, Scarron, Piron, Voltaire, Rousseau's *Nouvelle Héloïse* and the Abbé Prévost's *Mémoires et aventures d'un homme de qualité* all found their place in this library. Other titles included *Histoire amoureuse des Gaules*,[30] *Sacrifices de l'amour*,[31] *Amusements des eaux de Spa*,[32] *La Vie et les aventures de Robinson Crusoé*, *Histoire de Tom Jones*, and *Don Quichotte*. The valuers also listed the works of Paradis de Moncrif, who cooperated as librettist with Francoeur and Rebel on some of their operas, including *Zelindor, roi des silphes*.

Along with his taste for literature, Francoeur also showed a notable preference for history, since he owned 368 volumes classified in this category. Not only were there traditional manuals such as *Abrégé chronologique de l'histoire de France* by Hénault, *Histoire du règne de Louis XIII* by Le Vassor and *Histoire universelle* by Pufendorf, there was also a striking number of memoirs by important figures of the times. The valuers listed eighteen different authors, including Sully, Bassompierre, Madame de Motteville, Berwick, Villeroi and Villars. This collection was completed by the correspondence of Henri IV, Louis XIV, Bussy-Rabutin, Madame de Maintenon and many others. The musical section of this library, recorded in less detail than the previous areas, contained 180 volumes, among which figured fifty operas by Lully, fifty various operas and eighty trios and other music. As mentions of composers' names were rare, it seems plausible that a fair share of these works had been composed by Francoeur himself, even though the words 'by the defunct sieur' did not appear in the inventory.

Among the ranks of these owners of well-endowed libraries there were also a certain number of individuals who had practised a medical or intellectual profession. Like most of his colleagues from the previous generation,[33] Pierre Hometz, a doctor at the Faculté de Médecine of Paris and *Médecin Ordinaire* to the king, was a cultivated man whose library was well stocked in all areas when he died in 1666. While his professional books accounted for a hundred or so volumes, including the works of Hippocrates, religious works were also abundant. There were two Bibles, thirty-six volumes on theology, twelve devotional works, several lives of the saints, writings of St Gregory, St Jerome, St Augustine, St Cyprian, and St Bernard, works by Arnauld and *De la pénitence publique* by Pétau. The shelves of philosophy and great literature contained works by authors from antiquity, including Plato, Aristotle, Theocritus, Seneca and Horace. The works of du Bellay, Montaigne's *Essais*, and ten volumes of comedies also found their place there. History was less well represented, though it did make an appearance: works mentioned included volumes on Roman history, a book by Plutarch, a history of the Council of Trent and a history dictionary.

The library belonging to the Parisian bourgeois, Pierre Turpin, master of mathematics, proved to be more technical when it was inventoried in 1754. It nevertheless has a certain interest, since it serves to highlight the curiosity about science that spread to all quarters during the Enlightenment. Though only a very small number of the volumes in his library were identified, we know that Pierre Turpin possessed not only anthologies on mathematics, but also books on medicine and architecture, as can be judged from the following list: fifty-seven in-octavo volumes which included the writings of Avicenna, twenty-eight in-quarto volumes, including Euclid's *Elements*, twenty-one in-quarto volumes which included a *Traité de Mathématiques*, forty-four in-twelve volumes, including *Traité des Fièvres*, thirty-eight in-quarto volumes including *Eléments de Géométrie*, thirty-four in-folio volumes, including one on architecture entitled *Fortifications de villes*, and seventeen in-folio volumes, which included Belidor's *Architecture hydraulique*. Nor does the cultural background of this master of mathematics seem to have been limited to the sciences, since he also owned more than a hundred books of history.

Though the most voluminous and diversified libraries belonged to the intellectual elite of Parisian society, members of the middle categories of the population, such as merchants and masters of the urban trades, did also occasionally manage during the eighteenth century to build up collections of several hundred books. This was the case with Noël Pincemail, a hosier and bourgeois of Paris, who at his death in 1751 left behind 396 volumes devoted almost exclusively to religious subjects; the same went for Pierre Bourdeau, a haberdasher, who in 1768 possessed 200 volumes ranging from history to literature, morality and pious readings. Finally, it is interesting to examine the case of a library of 208 volumes, estimated at 115 L, belonging to Pierre Allain, a modest women's hair-dresser who died in 1755, leaving a total estate worth 918 L. The glimpse of his library provided by a few titles shows that this artisan was interested in history, and especially in the history of France and of the Jews; in poetry, notably in Ovid's works; and in geography. It seems worth noting that no devotional books appear among the titles listed. The presence of libraries, however small, even in households of popular society, confirms what Louis-Sébastien Mercier observed: 'People certainly read ten times more in Paris than they did a hundred years ago.'[34]

Three out of four Parisians who owned books possessed fewer than 100 volumes. From one inventory to the next, the actual number of books might range from a single volume to a few dozen. It was rare to find single books in households, and indeed it became exceedingly rare in the eighteenth century. There are nonetheless a few examples: the only book owned by a master cutler who died in 1680 was a volume on the lives of the saints. In the home of the wife of a master furniture maker visited in 1709, there was simply a book of the hours, bound in black shagreen with a gilded clasp. Another lone book entitled *Des écrits des saints* was left behind by a master painter upon his death in 1720. While widows like Louise Catrix and Jeanne Guerin in 1704 had only three or four books, including the Bible and the New Testament, masters of urban trades, servants and day labourers almost always owned at least six or seven volumes. The average number of books counted in the homes of artisans in the faubourg Saint-Antoine around 1760 was high, ranging from eleven to sixty-three. Master painters during the first half of the eighteenth century possessed an average of fifteen volumes.

Whether they died during the reign of Louis XIV or Louis XV, these small-scale book owners generally displayed a clear preference for pious works, which were often their only reading material. This was the case of a chambermaid in 1714, who owned twelve small pamphlets of prayers and meditations, as well as a parchment-covered volume of the life of St Theresa, the whole valued at 3 L. A painter who died in 1723 owned just nineteen volumes, all devotional works, stacked on a shelf, while a journeyman cartwright in 1770 had 'ten volumes, devotional subjects'. In the dwellings of day labourers and floor polishers, all the valuers usually found were 'books dealing with devotion', to cite their expression. No titles were indicated. Sometimes one or two titles would be identified within a batch of books: in the home of one day labourer, for example, there were twenty-four volumes on the Holy Virgin, Jesus Christ, the Adoration, and other subjects, plus a life of the saints and the spiritual works of Luis of Granada. In the home of the widow of another day labourer, valuers in 1744 repertoried a life of the saints in two volumes, a *Misères de l'homme* in-quarto,[35] and thirty-one volumes, including a *Semaine sainte*.

This predilection for pious books was not limited to the poorer classes. At her death in 1730 Madeleine Letellier, widow of the Chevalier Germain-Christophe de Thumery, Seigneur de Boissise and *doyen* of the *présidents des enquêtes* (examining magistrates) of the Parlement of Paris, left behind forty devotional books. She attached great importance to them, as the following lines of the will written in her own hand indicate: 'Let my books not be sold, but rather shared among my children ... the reading of good books should be the food of the soul.' Of course not all owners of devotional books displayed such exemplary piety as this woman who wanted to strengthen the faith of her children through proper reading material. But it is worth emphasizing the sharp predominance of religious material over other subject matter, a predominance which increased inversely in relation to the number of volumes inventoried.

Certainly households which owned exclusively secular writings were not unheard of: there was the case of a spinster in 1708, whose fourteen volumes dealt with 'antiquities of Paris' and other subjects. But these are exceptions that prove the rule. The religious volumes held by these small-scale owners were different from those filling the shelves of large libraries: there were no works on theology, religious controversy or Church history. Much more frequent were the holy scriptures, and of these, more often the New Testament, or works on the imitation of Jesus Christ, lives of the saints, anthologies of prayers, psalms, missals, books of the hours, *Exercices spirituels*, an *Année chrétienne* or a *Semaine sainte*. Only rarely were the authors of such books mentioned.

When there were more than fifty-odd volumes, these devotional works were sometimes supplemented by entertaining books or works on history. One bourgeois of Paris had collected ninety-one books valued altogether at 66 L at the time of his death in 1704. In addition to pious writings, there were dictionaries and works by Molière. One master furniture maker had developed a real little library of 100 volumes in 1761, comprising 'books both bound and covered with parchment, dealing with subjects of devotion, history and others, in very bad condition, the whole valued at 30 L'.

From time to time, books were discovered in the abodes of merchants, masters of the urban trades, and artisans which related to their professions. Books as tools of a trade were in fact not exclusively reserved for priests, lawyers, doctors and musicians. For example, in the home of a master stonecutter in 1643, 'works of architecture, *La Géométrie pratique*, a book covered with parchment entitled *Le Premier Tome de l'architecture* by Philibert Delorme' were listed. The inventory of the widow of a merchant draper and Parisian bourgeois in 1742 listed *Le Parfait Négociant*, with a subtitle explaining that the book provided 'general instruction on everything concerning trade in all sorts of merchandise, not only in France but in foreign countries', by Jacques Savary. Such professional influences on the constitution of libraries is equally apparent among many master painters: Jean Legendre owned three volumes in 1709 'concerning painting'; in the workshop of Jacques Lehonte, master painter and painter to the king's armies sixteen books were found in 1722, including a 'Bible and books of prints and coats of arms'; among the twenty-one volumes belonging to Pierre Julien in 1726, there was 'a volume dealing with sacred paintings about the Bible' as well as a collection of prints.

Despite its gaps and its lack of detail the inventory compiled after death does provide an idea of the books that Parisians owned. Though they were absent in 58 per cent of the households in our sample, and though their numbers were very limited in many homes, the total quantity of books, piled into what were often cramped lodgings, was considerable. They accumulated as a result of personal acquisitions or legacies passed on from one generation to the next. As seen through this study, books were neither rare articles nor signs of luxury in seventeenth- and eighteenth-century Paris. As progress in distribution during the Enlightenment brought printed materials even to the working classes, books actually became common consumer articles, though not massively so.

While a look at the titles of these writings seems to reveal a broad diversity, this variety is only apparent. In actual fact, the same titles appeared over and over, whether in the field of theology, history, literature or law. The tastes of these readers seemed on the whole to be quite classical and traditional. Parisians, especially elderly people, preferred to read and reread books they had inherited from their parents, or which they had acquired during their youth, rather than to discover the latest publishing fashion. This explains the rarity of the *Encyclopédie* and of the works of Voltaire and Rousseau in the libraries of the deceased, even as late as the 1770s or 1780s. These pre-revolutionary generations of readers whose books are inventoried by the notaries seem to be scarcely moved by the philosophical ideas of the Enlightenment. In most of the households of our sample that had access to written culture, it was religiously oriented works, and often those with Jansenist leanings, that overshadowed most other types of literature, even after 1750.

This preponderance of religious subjects becomes undeniable in libraries containing less than 200 volumes. Of the books listed in the faubourg Saint-Antoine around 1760, 67 per cent dealt with religious subjects. In the neighbourhood around the Place Maubert devotional works ranked far ahead of any other type during the 1770s in households owning fewer than 200 volumes (these represented 64 per cent). But the figure drops to 17 per cent in libraries composed of more than 200 volumes. This abundance of pious books bears witness to a profound aspiration of their owners to strengthen the role of faith and prayer in their lives by meditating on the holy scriptures or commentaries upon them, and to edify themselves by reading about spirituality or the lives of the saints. The mental outlook of the age apparently attached a certain prestige to devotional books, and all the more so to the book of the word of God. This prestige, like that of crucifixes or rosaries, surely came from the sacred character of these works. Although new ideas made their way throughout the enlightened elite to which men like Francoeur belonged, devotional literature remained practically the only reading material for vast numbers of households in the middle strata of the population. Indeed, like religious processions and external signs of religious attachment, the presence of these works would seem to be an indicator that a great many Parisians remained faithful to Christianity, and that a communal sense of piety continued to exist. Only the shock of the Revolution, bringing a train of anti-religious laws in its wake, would be strong enough to shake this faith.

Other Cultural Artefacts

In this world in which the printed word was not absolutely omnipresent, oral communication played a significant role in passing on knowledge. Unfortunately, such communication leaves no trace for the historian. The pre-eminent position of books as vehicles for knowledge stands out even more sharply in the inventories when we realize how rare other cultural artefacts were in these Parisian homes and how their numbers were confined to a very limited group of households.

The only place in which musical instruments were to be found in any abundance was in the homes of musicians. Just as priests and lawyers needed their books in order to perform their duties, so musicians could not do without their instruments. We should nevertheless emphasize that out of the 142 inventories done on musicians and instrument makers during the seventeenth and eighteenth centuries, 17 per cent make no mention of any musical instruments. Is this absence, which seems unthinkable, simply to be blamed on the quality of our documents? Or had these objects disappeared just before or after the death of their owners? Did some musicians merely rent their instruments? In any case, the quantity of musical instruments inventoried in the homes of these musicians and instrument makers was great.

The second group, who were called *facteurs*, or in the eighteenth century, *luthiers*, were by the very nature of their trade involved in making and selling musical instruments. Upon their deaths they sometimes left an impressive number of instruments in their workshops – which might equally be referred to as shops, warehouses or chamber-shops. Jean Des Moulins, the king's instrument maker, owned nearly 300 instruments in 1648. We counted some 2916 instruments distributed throughout nineteen homes of instrument makers during the eighteenth century, for an average of 153 instruments per shop. In the home of the master stringed instrument maker Nicolas Bertrand, who died in 1725, 114 violins, five cellos, five basses, fifty-three viols, and 106 guitars were inventoried. The inventory of Marie-Jeanne Zeltener, wife of Louis Guersan, who was the famous master *luthier* to the Dauphin, attested in 1770 to the presence of 493 violins, four violas, two cellos, twenty basses and contrabasses, 128 viols, sixteen guitars, and five mandolins.

With the numerous small technical advances achieved by the *facteurs* of the late seventeenth century, these various instruments became increasingly refined during the age of the Enlightenment. Notable progress in the area of acoustical research during that period led to mechanical inventions that could modify existing sounds or create new ones.[36] The development of high-quality instruments went hand in hand with a growing demand on the part of both professional and amateur musicians. Instruments inventoried in the workshops of their makers were not all 'fashioned by the said deceased'; some of them came from foreign manufacturers, as the valuers often indicated: two English violins, twenty-nine Tyrolean violins, sixty-four violins from Lorraine, two German violins, one Italian violin, and another by Amati, of the well-known family of stringed instrument makers in the Italian city of Cremona. There were also a bass and a viola from the Tyrol and four mandolins from Naples.

Whether they were produced in Paris or in another country, instruments of all different sorts began arriving in ever increasing numbers in the shops of merchants after 1750, supplying the market of the capital as well as international demand. Playing the double role of artisans and merchants, these eighteenth-century *luthiers* struggled to satisfy a growing clientele, not only by improving the quality of their merchandise, but also by offering special terms of trade. Consulting the 'papers' category of the inventories reveals that certain instrument makers kept instruments which they had produced available to clients for rental. Given the often surprising number of such instruments, it would seem that the market for rentals must have been at least as flourishing as that for sales. At his death in 1756, the master instrument maker Pierre-François Grosset left behind 'a bundle of seventeen documents which were acknowledgements by various individuals that they held different instruments in rental that belonged to the said Sieur Grosset, against the sum stated'.

These instrument makers of the age of the Enlightenment were true artists endowed with great skill, who contributed to the spread of musical culture. Yet they did not seem to play any instruments themselves, not did the members of their families. It was actually very unusual to find instruments for personal use by them or their wives or daughters in their homes. Only the clavichord maker François Descourbes possessed an old clavichord in 1751, valued at the modest sum of 20 L.

Musicians and composers, the primary clients of these *facteurs* and *luthiers*, were also sometimes well equipped in the eighteenth century with musical instruments of all types. The chamber of Nicolas Gigault, the organist at Saint-Nicolas-des-Champs, was packed in 1701 with four spinets, three clavichords and a monochord, as indicated in the inventory compiled after the death of his wife, Anne Aubac. Though an organist, this musician also possessed five violas and a bass viol. This offers further proof that in that period, the viol was still a basic instrument for music making, as was the clavichord. Louis Marchand, former organist to the king, owned seven spinets, three clavichords and a monochord as well as other stringed instruments including a viol, eight guitars and three flutes.

It may come as a surprise to see so many relatively bulky keyboard instruments in dwellings with a limited number of rooms. Of course spinets were not very deep and could be easily leaned up against a wall. It was harder to make space for clavichords, at least the long ones or those with one or two keyboards, inherited from the seventeenth century. The instruments signed by Antwerp's famous *facteurs*, the Ruckers, were decorative pieces of great value, famous for their musical quality as well as their ornamental beauty. The organist Charles Noblet, a member of the Académie Royale de Musique, owned two clavichords in 1769, each worth 240 L, one of which was built by the Ruckers. Organists could practise playing the organ in a church, but at home, for reasons of space and finances, they turned to the clavichord. Most of these organists, including Nicolas Gigault, were also teachers, which meant they had to have several instruments available for their personal use and that of their students. The presence of an 'organ case with two keyboards' was indicated in 1784 in the home of the organist of the Prémontrés de la Croix-Rouge. Another organ was inventoried in 1764 in the home of a music and dancing master. In addition to organists, other clavichord owners included composers and various other musicians. The valuers identified a Ruckers clavichord in the home of Francoeur in 1787, valued at 240 L, as the model belonging to Charles Noblet had been. The instrument on which Egidio Ramualdo Duni probably composed his comic operas was a clavichord valued at 120 L. As for Jean-Philippe Rameau, the most illustrious musician of the age, he made do with a miserable old and broken-down clavichord estimated at 24 L.

The clavichord was the most popular instrument in professional musicians' households and those of music lovers. It was nonetheless imbued with an aristocratic and refined aspect. As a result, during the Revolution it was 'deposed', so to speak, by the less old-fashioned and more bourgeois piano-forte. We found just a single model of this modern instrument, listed in the home of the musician François Devienne during the inventory of his wife in 1790. It was an Erard pianoforte in mahogany, worth 320 L, which was found in the company of a violin, a viola and a bassoon decorated with silver, instruments worth 200 L.

Keyboard instruments were very much in vogue during the eighteenth century, and stringed instruments also seemed to be great favourites throughout that period, if their number in the inventories of musicians is any indication. The violin had been the most popular instrument in the previous century, but after the 1750s it made a breakthrough in the world of French musical sensibility and won a nobler place for itself on the concert stage. In 1706 the musician Louis Allair possessed only one 'broken-in violin', and the music master Pierre-Augustin Lepeintre had a single violin with a bow in 1737; another music master, Etienne Chauvet, had four instruments in 1754, and ten years later, the musician and dancing master François Gauvillier also owned four. Though viols became more rare after 1750, that was the decade that saw the first cellos appear: at his death in 1755, Jean-Baptiste Stuck, known as Baptistin, *Ordinaire* of the King's music, was the owner of 'two violoncellos with bows and cases, valued at 120 L'. Woodwinds were less commonplace than these stringed instruments or keyboard instruments. Among them, flutes were found most frequently, such as the German flute in boxwood belonging to a musician and dancing master in 1761. There were also musettes and bassoons: one Chinese musette with silver keys in the home of Etienne Chauvet in 1754, and three old bassoons in the home of Louis Allair in 1706.

As we have already seen in the Francoeur household, these instruments were sometimes found together with works of music, a number of which were composed by their owners. The 696 volumes of Jean-Baptiste Stuck's library included 400 works of music, valued at 280 L. Among them were six volumes by the Italian composer and violinist Corelli, eight volumes by another Italian violinist, Mascitti, and 380 volumes of vocal music, cantatas, Italian airs, operas, *Te Deums*, vespers and symphonies 'both by the defunct Sieur Baptistin and by others'. As for the library belonging to Jean-Philippe Rameau, the 609 works of music it contained were written exclusively by the deceased.

Outside these professional settings, the practice of playing an instrument was very uncommon in Parisian society in the seventeenth and eighteenth centuries. If we exclude musicians and musical instrument makers, only 4.5 per cent of the deceased left behind a musical instrument. Though public concerts presented on the feast day of St Louis or following a Te Deum drew multitudes of Parisians according to accounts by contemporaries, musical culture involved only a very limited number of amateurs. What musical instruments were found in these interiors? Which ones seemed to have enjoyed the greatest popularity? Out of 150 instruments whose presence was identified by the inventories, 58.5 per cent were stringed instruments, 24.5 per cent were keyboards, and 17 per cent woodwinds. More than a third of the stringed instruments were violins. In the household of a merchant brewer who died in 1740, two violins, with a music stand in purpleheart wood from which to read music, were inventoried in the chamber of the deceased. One priest assigned to the church of Saint-Séverin possessed a violin with bow at the time of his death in 1751. This very popular instrument was usually estimated at less than 10 L. Though they began going out of fashion in the eighteenth century, the alto viol and the bass viol were still the most frequently observed stringed instruments after the violin. When he died in 1751, a deacon in the diocese of Paris owned two bass viols, an Italian one with its fingerboard and strings, and another with a bow in violet wood and horsehair. In his library, 'the works of Marais for bass viol' were noted. In the home of the wife of a cloth merchant, a viol was found in 1720 with bows and a walnut music stand, as well as five music books. There were eleven basses to be counted in the household of the widow of a master writer in 1705, which were described as 'both high and contra basses'.

Other stringed instruments were less widely represented: 'one guitar, dismantled, with its case' was mentioned in 1666 in the inventory of a squire and *maître d'hôtel ordinaire* to the king. The wife of the bookseller Léonard owned two guitars in 1706, one of which was from Italy and was 'worked with inlay'. The guitar, like the violin an instrument for popular music-making, generally had an average worth of little more than 6 to 7 L. The lute, which fell into disuse in the eighteenth century, was to be seen in only a tiny number of households during the reign of Louis XIV. It was described as being 'accompanied by its broken case' in the home of a *gentilhomme ordinaire* of the king's chamber in 1668. Instruments such as dulcimers, hurdy-gurdies, theorbos, harps or mandolins were exceedingly rare. A 'hurdy-gurdy featuring the name of Meline of Paris with its leather case', estimated at 18 L, was inventoried in 1774 in the estate of a *maître maréchal*. Another one 'equipped with its crank and its wooden case covered in black leather' was found during the same period in the home of a squire and former infantry captain. This had been an instrument of popular musical culture during previous centuries, but it earned a place of honour in high society between 1760 and the Revolution. The theorbo, a sort of large lute, had become unfashionable by mid-century, though it had not yet completely disappeared by the end of the reign of Louis XIV, since 'two very old theorbos with their cases and bows' were listed together with the eleven basses belonging to Catherine Mondon in 1705. This collection which was valued together at the modest sum of 20 L, was almost enough to equip a chamber orchestra.

Larger and more costly than these stringed instruments, keyboard instruments were a privilege reserved for a tiny number of fortunate amateurs. Unlike violins or guitars, the clavichord was an aristocratic and prestigious instrument, not within reach of every purse. In several cases this instrument could actually be used as an indicator of social standing, as the following examples show: a 'spinet clavichord six feet in length' valued at 150 L in 1657 in the home of Pierre Gargan, king's counsellor and *Intendant des Finances*; another model valued at 75 L in 1666 in the residence of Roland Gruyn, *Secrétaire des Finances*; the beautiful clavichord owned by Anne Delaleu, the wife of a haberdashery merchant, which was described as having two keyboards and legs in black varnished wood, manufactured by Jean Rucheere of Antwerp, and valued at 240 L in 1708; or Lalive d'Epinay's instrument, worth 720 L in 1782.

Close cousins of these clavichords, spinets were often estimated at fairly low values, but this did not mean they were popular instruments. The model with walnut legs belonging in 1646 to Philippe du Val, *médecin professeur* to the king and doctor at the medical school, was valued at just 100 sols. However, another model, with pearwood legs, was estimated at 50 L at about the same time. One instrument worth 15 L was noted in the home of a bourgeois of Paris in the first years of the eighteenth century. Anne Delaleu, wife of a merchant haberdasher, and Marie-Anne des Essarts, wife of the bookseller Léonard, played both the clavichord and the spinet. In the home of the first of these ladies, the spinet was described in its walnut case, with column-shaped legs; the second instrument was said to be from Flanders. The pattern of the inventories seems to show that spinets became increasingly rare over the course of the eighteenth century.

The organ, an instrument for church music, appears unexpectedly in four households. In three of these, the instrument was said to be German. The inventory of a priest from the diocese of Coutance in 1736 mentions an 'imperfect and dismounted' organ case described with its bourdon, its vox humana and its pipes out of place, and the throat of its bellows detached. As for pianofortes, the only mention made of a model belonging to an amateur was that owned by Lalive d'Epinay in 1782. Built by an English artisan, it was in mahogany and was worth 240 L.

Woodwind instruments were less well represented than keyboards or strings, but they did have their amateurs among Parisians. This category included mainly flutes (*flûtes traversières*) and recorders (*flûtes à bec*). These instruments evolved toward the mid-seventeenth century and were to be found exclusively in households inventoried during the following century. They were sometimes made using exquisite materials, like one flute in rosewood with gold joints, or another in ivory and wood from the Indies. Other woodwinds also appeared among the belongings of the deceased: there were three musettes, one of which was decorated with silver and another with ivory, two oboes, two fifes, one flageolet, one bassoon, as well as one hunting horn and one trumpet. A silk merchant and Parisian bourgeois who died in 1659 must have adored woodwind instruments, since he had the choice of playing an oboe, either of two fifes, or a small flageolet. The hunting horn identified belonged to a bourgeois of Paris in 1665, and the bronze trumpet, which the valuers described as old, belonged to another bourgeois of Paris who died in 1668. To this list of musical instruments we should add the *serinette*, a sort of barrel organ that worked mechanically. We found this instrument in two households: the widow of a master spice seller even owned two in 1771, that 'played eight airs on two cylinders, valued at the sum of 200 L'.

How were the owners of these musical instruments distributed among the various levels of society? A small poll based on seventy inventories indicated, as the examples above have shown, that musical instruments were not the exclusive province of the nobility, since merchants and Parisian bourgeois head the list of owners, with 24 per cent, one point ahead of nobles, magistrates and king's counsellors, who take second place, comprising 23 per cent of the total. They are followed in decreasing order by masters of urban trades, 16 per cent; clergymen, 11.5 per cent; members of legal and medical professions, 10 per cent; and accountants and financiers, 8.5 per cent. Last of all, we lumped together a carter, a *maître d'hôtel*, a coachman and two spinsters in a final category of artisans, servants and spinsters representing 7 per cent of instrument owners. It appears, then, that these amateur music lovers were drawn from all ranks of society. But whatever their status, they were always people who were both fairly well-off, since they could afford inessential pleasures, and culturally advantaged. As we know, playing a musical instrument requires not only a certain amount of free time but also a degree of instruction in order to be able to read music. It was often the wife or daughters of the household who were the primary users of these instruments, simply because they apparently had more time than their menfolk, who were occupied with their businesses or trades.

Though the practice of music during the eighteenth century did not become truly a popular pastime, it did extend into a broader range of social strata. Finding a musical instrument in the household of a merchant or master of a trade became less unusual in that period than it had been in the previous century. In fact, a hierarchy of instruments developed which corresponded to the social standing of their owners. Nobles preferred keyboard instruments to 'common' instruments like the violin or the guitar. After all, the clavichord was a symbol of aristocratic society under the *ancien régime*, just as the piano became a symbol of the bourgeoisie in the nineteenth century. That women like Anne-Thérèse Delaleu and Anne des Essarts, the wives of affluent merchants, played the clavichord was merely symptomatic of their desire to climb the social ladder. This instrument was also inventoried in 1784 in the home of a rich master baker who inhabited an eight-room house in the faubourg Saint-Honoré and left behind an estate worth more than 10,000 L after his death. The presence of a clavichord in these families of businessmen and artisans during the last century of the *ancien régime* can be read more as a sign of social success, revealing a desire for ostentation, than as a true indication of their love of music.

Only a tiny minority of the deceased seemed to have been exposed to musical culture. But interest in the sciences seems to have been even less prevalent, if the contents of the notaries' assessments serves as a guide. Scientific curiosity did make itself felt in a few dwellings through the presence of specialized books or scientific instruments. Yet the progress made in the sciences and the broadening scope of scientific knowledge, especially after the 1730s, were reflected in only a very few inventories. As has already been noted, it was exceptional to find any mention of copies of the *Encyclopédie* or *Dictionnaire raisonné des sciences, des arts et des métiers*. However, since Diderot's work was published between 1751 and 1780, it does arrive late in relation to our study.

Mathematics, to which the Jesuits paid particular attention in the teaching at their *collèges*, aroused the curiosity of several of our Parisians. At the time of his death in 1734, the chamber valet Claude Piau possessed 'a compass and several little mathematical instruments' as well as a case with 'four instruments for mathematics'. In 1746, in the homes of Marie-Anne Blanquet, a spinster who was a true scientist, and of a bourgeois of Paris, the valuers found a compass and a square, carefully stored in a black leather case. The sworn architecture expert Charles-François Lebrun possessed not only these instruments, but also 'a half-circle in copper, used to draw plans' in 1747. But in this case, these were the tools of his trade. Finally, the Marquis de Féline, too, accorded a certain interest to mathematics.

Astronomy and meteorology also seemed to exercise a great power of fascination on these Parisians. The so-called *multiplicateurs sensoriels* (enhancers of the senses) which had been invented in the seventeenth century simply in order to observe the sky, were refined and improved during the Enlightenment and became *salon* objects, as did weather instruments. In the home of the Marquis de Bonnac in 1739 could be seen a thermometer and a barometer in sculpted and gilded wood, as well as a telescope and a microscope trimmed with copper, valued at 20 L. Claude Piau was captivated not only by mathematics, but also devoted his free time to star-gazing, using his telescope. The *salon* of one wealthy Parisian bourgeois in 1770 held a telescope and a globe, in addition to a barometer and a thermometer. The Marquis de Féline possessed three telescopes in 1775, and Lalive d'Epinay had a long-view and a telescope in 1782. One of the interesting cases among our deceased was Marie-Madeleine de Dorlodot de Vermanchamp, who died in 1772, and whose husband was the Navy astronomer Charles Messier, who discovered thirteen comets and observed more than forty, thereby earning for himself the nickname of 'the comet ferret' bestowed by Louis XVI. The *précepteur* of the Duc du Maine wrote in 1775 in his *Instruction sur l'histoire de France et romaine* about one of these comets discovered in 1770: 'It could be seen by the naked eye though very far from the earth; it is the eleventh [comet] that this astronomer has discovered in twelve years.'

The vogue for travel on the Continent in the eighteenth century, the taste for exoticism and for expeditions to far-off places, and of course the efforts that geometers and surveyors began to make around 1750 to improve the network of roads all contributed to stimulate the Parisians' interest in geography. In a small number of households, globes, books, planispheres and, above all, maps revealed how this science was blossoming. Augustin Bogillot, the director of a printing press who was responsible, by virtue of his trade, for disseminating new knowledge, left behind two copies of *Méthodes de géographie* upon his death in 1748. In the same year, the Marquis de Savine, lieutenant general of the king's armies, kept twenty-five maps in the closet of his office. Of course they may have had some professional value for him. Such was not the case with the wife of a haberdasher, who also had 'three geography maps glued on canvas with tube and roller in black wood'. In other inventories, we found indications such as, 'two medium-sized maps with their tubes and rollers, valued 20 L', or a compass, a small sphere, a planisphere and various globes of the Earth or the heavens, 'including a celestial globe on black wooden legs'. Around 1770, we also noted two geographical dictionaries by Baudrand and La Martinière.

Whether these diverse scientific objects dealt with mathematics, astronomy, meteorology or geography, they are often grouped together in the same households, as these few examples have demonstrated. Though they sometimes played an ornamental role as part of the decor in a reception room, they were primarily indicative of the curiosity shown by an enlightened Parisian elite about scientific and technical progress, and of a thirst for new knowledge. Diderot's description of a still life by Chardin entitled *Les Attributs des sciences*, which was exhibited at the 1765 salon, illustrates the excitement the age of the Enlightenment felt for science: 'We see, on a table covered with a reddish carpet, going, I believe, from right to left, some books set on their edge, a microscope, a bell jar, a globe half hidden by a curtain in green taffeta, a thermometer, a concave mirror on its stand, a spyglass with its case, map rolls and the end of a telescope.'[37]

Devotional Images

In a world where the written word could touch only a minority of the population, images, and especially religious images, intended to educate and to edify, had considerable impact on the minds of their beholders. Eminent historians such as Victor-Lucien Tapié[38] and Michèle Ménard[39] have elegantly emphasized the educational role of religious iconography in altarpieces. It should be noted that the subject matter – not only of painted and sculpted representations in retables, but also of the numerous prints in circulation – was determined by men of the Church, who closely surveyed their production and their conformity with post-Tridentine doctrinal orthodoxy. Indeed, during the age of Catholic reform, ecclesiastics such as the Jesuit Louis Richeome and the Sulpician Jean-Jacques Olier had a decisive influence on this religious iconography, which became in a sense the equivalent of a catechism through images.

With the technical progress made in the field of line engraving on copper plates, which henceforth replaced xylography, or engraving on wood, the trade in religious imagery in Paris expanded significantly in the first decades of the seventeenth century. It should also be noted that in the same period, engraving merchants, who had clustered during the previous century around the rue Montorgueil, began setting up shop near the university and its bookshops in the vicinity of the rue Saint-Jacques. Some of these merchants, who often handled the burin and the point themselves, founded dynasties, such as the famous Mariette, Bonnart and Audran families. These printers of line engravings did a major part of their business in devotional images, as can be seen from the catalogues of the Bibliothèque Nationale print collections. Most of the pious engravings owned by the deceased persons in our study probably came from workshops in the rue Saint-Jacques.

Paintings and prints on religious subjects were inventoried in about half the households in our sample. This proportion seems to remain at almost the same level until the 1770s, and it does not really begin to decline, under the anti-religious influence of the Enlightenment, until the eve of the French Revolution, in years beyond the period covered by our study. As an indication, some 52 per cent of the images valued in Parisian homes in our study dealt with religious themes, but the figure is only 42 per cent after 1750.

What social categories displayed this preference for pious imagery? One study, based on a sample of 610 religious images and 942 secular ones, found in 148 households during the first half of the eighteenth century, demonstrates the predominance of devotional images in the homes of individuals of modest social status. In contrast, secular images are proportionally much more abundant in the homes of the nobility and members of the legal professions. This same study reveals that the average value of religious images, 3.3 L, is at least one livre less than the average value of secular ones, i.e. 4.5 L. But even among religious images, there is great disparity in value from one subject to another. It is hardly surprising that pictures with unspecified subjects were estimated at only 20 sols on average: the subject was not described because it was simply not worth describing. Such images were never valued individually. Instead, they were grouped into packets, which probably contained a high proportion of cheap prints in small formats, like those of religious brotherhoods. Images of the Crucifixion and the saints, very common, were worth 2 L and 3 L respectively. Other subjects relating to Christ or the Virgin were valued at between 3 and 4 L. Rarer themes from the Old Testament were of greater value and might reach 8 L: since they presupposed a greater knowledge of sacred texts, they lent themselves to larger works in the historical genre. Various themes such as the Trinity or the Seven Sacraments, which were uncommon, were estimated at more than 4 L. It would seem, then, that the frequency of a subject was inversely proportional to its value.

What were the major iconographical subjects of these images? We have already emphasized the lack of precision in the inventories on this point. It should be borne in mind that we know the theme of only about three out of every five religious images inventoried. Expressions such as 'devotional picture' or 'pious image' are common. It so happens that these images, unidentified because they were often of little value, were frequently the ones found in the most modest households. Take the example of a master vinegar maker who owned 'eleven devotional pictures on canvas' in 1643, or the day labourer who, at his death in 1732, left sixty religious images and a single secular one.

Nevertheless, we have been able to establish a sample of almost 2000 identified images, making it possible to obtain an idea of the distribution of iconographical themes. The single most common one is Christ, appearing in some 33 per cent of these images. Then come the Virgin and the saints, with 30 per cent under each heading. Episodes from the Old Testament are much less frequent, at 5 per cent, and there were 2 per cent of various subjects. This iconography, reflecting the devotional focus on the figure of Christ in the post-Tridentine tradition, is echoed in the pious invocations found in wills from the same period. About half of these images of Christ represent the Son of God in his human suffering, the Redeemer who died to save mankind. The inscription written below a Christ on the cross flanked by the Virgin and St John in an engraving by Denis Landry recalls this mystery: 'Christian, Jesus died so that you might live.' Among the scenes from the Passion, the Crucifixion and the Descent from the Cross are the main themes. Indeed, we noted that in engravings showing domestic scenes, especially those by Abraham Bosse, there is almost always a picture on the wall of Christ on the cross.

We also observed how important phrases such as 'Son of God' and 'Passion' were in testamentary language.[40] The preamble of most wills began with the sign of the cross, 'in the name of the Father, and of the Son and of the Holy Spirit', followed by formulas stating that the testator 'recommended his [or her] soul to Jesus Christ, Saviour and Redeemer', or appealed to the merits of the death and passion of Jesus Christ. It must not be forgotten that the image of Christ in agony, whether painted, engraved or sculpted on a wooden cross, was present on the chamber walls of these Christians, who turned a last gaze upon it as they yielded up their souls. Though Christ's final struggle was the most frequently represented scene from the mystery of the Redemption, standing as it did for the state of salvation, other episodes from the Passion story also figured in the homes of these Parisians: Christ being whipped, Christ wearing the crown of thorns, *Ecce homo*, Christ bearing his cross, Christ on the Mount of Olives. These stations of the cross provided illustrations of how the Son of Man lowered himself to save sinners. The image of Christ crucified reappeared in paintings of the Holy Shroud or the Holy Face. Though the cult of the Holy Sacrament was growing in the seventeenth century, pictures of the Last Supper or the Eucharist were rare. But perhaps this devotion to the body of Christ was simply illustrated through small images whose value was nominal and which were not worthy of description: images distributed to the members of brotherhoods of the Holy Sacrament or to children learning their catechism. Equally rare were portrayals of Christ in glory, be it the Resurrection, the appearance at Emmaus, the Ascension or even the Transfiguration.

More than a quarter of these Christological subjects were simple figures of Our Saviour, without any further detail, or of the Saviour holding the globe of the world. Inseparable from the mystery of the Redemption was the mystery of the Incarnation, illustrated by portrayals of the infant Jesus and of scenes from his childhood, i.e. the Nativity, the Adoration of the kings, or much more rarely, the Adoration of the Shepherds or the Flight into Egypt. These images accounted for just over 15 per cent of Christological subject matter. Exalted by Bérulle and the French school of spirituality, this devotion to the infant Jesus was a means of paying homage to the humility of God made man and of celebrating the joy of his coming into the world. Paintings and engravings dealing with the public life of Jesus and his evangelical teachings were much more rare, constituting less than 10 per cent of Christological imagery. They tended to feature the baptism by John the Baptist, Our Lord and his apostles, the Wedding at Cana, the Resurrection of Lazarus, the meal in the home of Martha and Mary, the woman at the well or the temptation in the desert. The only parable mentioned was that of the Prodigal Son, which symbolized the sacrament of penance.

The abundance of images figuring the Virgin Mary bears witness to the profound belief held by the deceased in her powers of intercession. We should note that almost 90 per cent of the testators stated their trust in the prayers of the blessed Mother of God. Among these images of the Virgin, 76.5 per cent showed her holding the child Jesus in her arms, or present in his company or that of an angel or St John. We have classified the Mariological theme with representations of the Holy Family, whose cult had been honoured by the Council of Trent. Jesus surrounded by Mary and Joseph appeared in 11.5 per cent of the images devoted to the Virgin. This earthly trinity served to represent not only a simple exaltation of family life, which was perfectly appropriate within the reality of the home, but also a symbol of the heavenly Trinity as well. Scenes from the life of Mary were few and far between, with the exception of the Annunciation, a part of the mystery of the Incarnation, which accounted for 8.5 per cent of the occurrences. The Visitation, Pentecost, the Assumption, the Virgin's *dormition*, or 'going to sleep', and her coronation are all occasionally represented, accounting altogether for 35 per cent of all images of the Virgin. It is interesting to note that we did not find a single mention of a sorrowing Virgin. This theme, a favourite in the late Middle Ages, continued to appear frequently between 1580 and 1630, when it was referred to as Notre Dame de Pitié, or the Pietà.

Alongside the intercession of the Mother of God stood a whole galaxy of saints, whose portraits are also present in these homes. We know that the testators called upon their mediation, either naming specific saints or collectively designating the heavenly host or all the saints in paradise. Some of these intercessors were especially revered. Images of St Mary Magdalene, for example, constituted almost a quarter of all those representing saints. An incarnation of penance and ecstasy, she was one of the most popular saints of the period. In paintings and engravings, she is generally shown as a penitent woman with long flowing hair, her eyes filled with tears as she prays before a crucifix in the solitude of the desert. Surrounded by a skull, a book, a perfume jar and sometimes by the attributes of her sin – a jewel chest, a mirror, a necklace – she is a moving illustration of the great power of expiation. She was painted by all the most famous artists of the 'century of the saints', including Philippe de Champaigne, Simon Vouet and Charles Le Brun. The portrait done by the last of these artists, and reproduced in thousands of copies as an engraving by Nicolas Bazin, shows the saint in an attitude of penance, wiping her tears with a corner of her robes and kneeling before a table on which have been placed a parchment and two bottles of perfume. At her feet lies a jewel box with necklaces scattered around. The engraving by Bazin is accompanied by four lines of verse:

> Madeleine pleurante, en proye à la douleur,
> Se dépouille de tous ses charmes,
> Le croirait-on! C'est en quittant ces armes,
> Qu'elle sçait vaincre le Sauveur.[41]

> (Magdelene weeping, preyed on by pain,
> Strips herself of all her charms,
> Who would believe it! By abandoning these arms,
> She is able to win the Saviour.)

An engraving by Audran, done after a painting by Antoine Dieu, shows Mary Magdalene stretched out on the ground on a straw mat, with a book, a crucifux and a perfume jar nearby. In her left hand, she holds a skull that rests against her knee, and her eyes are raised to heaven, where a concert of angels appears. The painter has chosen to illustrate a verse of the Gospel according to St Luke which follows the parables of the lost sheep and the lost silver piece: it portrays 'the joy of heaven at the conversion of sinners', according to the caption under the engraving, and the words of Jesus in the margin reinforce the message: 'I say unto you, there is joy in the presence of the angels of God over one sinner that repenteth' (Lk. 15: 10).[42]

Though much less frequent than Mary Magdalene, St Peter generally headed the list of saintly figures on altarpieces in Brittany and the Maine region and was the second most venerated saint in Parisian households. This domestic cult surrounding the leader of the apostles seems to have been less an expression of homage to the first pope and father of the Church than one honouring the repentant disciple of Christ. Almost all the engravings of St Peter that we consulted in the print collections of the Bibliothèque Nationale show him with his face covered with tears after he hears the cock crow for the third time. Indeed, it is rare to see him with keys and book as his sole attributes and not the cock. Peter's repentance finds its full meaning as a symbol of the sacrament of penance, a sacrament that the Protestants refused to recognize. Other scenes from the life of this disciple that were engraved in workshops on the rue Saint Jacques included his receiving his mission from Christ and his being martyred upside down on a cross. It is worth noting that St Paul is rarely associated with St Peter and does not seem to have enjoyed the same favour in private homes that he had on church altars. He is figured either holding a sword and a book or in ecstasy on the road to Damascus.

After St Peter, the most frequently portrayed saint is John. It is rarely specified in the inventories, however, whether this is John the Evangelist or John the Baptist. The latter is mentioned almost exclusively in connection with the baptism of Jesus, so that we have classified those occurrences with the Christological subjects. The traditional attributes of John the Evangelist are the book and the eagle, or a chalice from which a sort of serpent surges forth.

In third place among the male intercessors stands St Jerome: he is shown half-naked, kneeling before a crucifix and a skull in the desert. A hermit like Mary Magdalene, he, too, embodies penance and urges the sinner to take up solitary retreat. His attributes, the book, the quill and the lion's head, are also symbols of science. In an engraving by Dossier, inspired by a painting by Antoine Dieu, this doctor of the Church is seated in a grotto. He holds a quill in his hand poised above a book, and is surrounded by his symbols, the crucifix and the lion's head. He has paused from his writing to observe the mouthpiece of a heavenly trumpet,[43] in a literal depiction of the words that have been attributed to him: 'Whether I am waking or sleeping, whether eating or drinking, I always believe I hear the trumpet of Judgement Day of which St Paul spoke.' And indeed, the Hieronymites, a powerful eremitic order during the sixteenth and seventeenth centuries, chose St Jerome as their patron and tried to imitate his coenobitic (austere) life.

Mentions of other saints are more unusual. Among them, however, martyrs enjoyed great favour. Like penance, suffering was exalted by the Counter-Reformation as a theme on which Christians should meditate. The most popular martyr was St Catherine of Alexandria, the patron saint of students, and in particular of the faculty of theology at the University of Paris. In addition to the traditional crown and palm branch, her attributes include a sword and a wheel, the instrument of her martyrdom. The other martyrs appearing most often among the images kept by our Parisians were St Margaret of Antioch, the protector of women during childbirth, and the Roman St Susanna. St Barbara was dearly beloved of rural churches because of her ability to offer protection from lightning and therefore from sudden death; her image was rare, however, in these urban households. Among the male saints were St Andrew, the apostle of Jesus, who appears either carrying his X-shaped cross or still attached by soldiers to the instrument of his martyrdom; St Lawrence, burned on a grill in the presence of a large crowd; and St Sebastian, tied to a tree, his body pierced with arrows. One engraving published by Nicolas Bazin was entitled *S. Sebastien Capitaine Chrestien et Martyr de Jesus-Christ*. A sign of the sufferings sent by God, Sebastian was a healer whose name was invoked with special fervour against epidemics of the plague.

Other saints revered in the households of these Parisians were honoured either because they had been close to Jesus or because their patronage had made them popular. Both in engravings and in the niches of altarpieces, St Anne is usually presented teaching the Virgin Mary to read. Though the cult of St Joseph had been restored to honour as the patron of the Good Death during the Catholic Reformation, he makes few appearances outside the setting of the Holy Family. Two final figures among those close to Christ are St Elizabeth, Mary's cousin and the mother of John the Baptist, and St Veronica, associated with the Passion: one engraving from 1652 based on a canvas by Nicolas Loir shows the latter raising her tear-filled eyes to heaven and holding up the holy shroud.[44]

Of all the patron saints admired by Parisians, St Genevieve held a special place as the protector of Paris. Of the numerous processions that took place in the city, the most solemn and extraordinary was that of St Genevieve's reliquary, which was actually carried to Notre Dame cathedral eight times during the seventeenth century, but only twice in the century thereafter. In an engraving done by Audran from a painting by Le Brun which decorated the chapel of the Carmelites in the faubourg Saint-Jacques, she is shown kneeling with a candle in her hand, busily watching over her sheep on a hill overlooking a besieged city. At her feet lie her attributes, a pair of keys, a distaff and an open book. Angels appear in the heavens above her. Another engraving with very similar iconography is accompanied by an 'antiphon and prayer to Saint Genevieve' in Latin.[45]

The patron of the monarchy, St Louis, had his feast day celebrated on 25 August with another procession and public festivities, and his image appears in a few households. Wearing a crown and robed in a fleur-de-lis cape and ermine mantle, he holds a sceptre and a crown of thorns in his hand. Parisians had recourse to him and to three other saints in their prayers: St Francis of Assissi, often represented in ecstasy, bearing the stigmata as a sign of his divine election, St Antony – either the hermit or the Franciscan from Padua – and St Dominic. We should point out, with reference to this last saint, that the theme of the rosary said to have been entrusted by the Virgin and the infant Jesus to St Dominic and St Catherine of Siena was totally absent from our sample. This subject had, however, been incorporated into many altarpieces belonging to the Brotherhoods of the Rosary in churches of western France.

Traditional saints played a much larger part in the piety of these Parisians than recently canonized saints elevated by the post-Tridentine Church. Among these saints of the Counter-Reformation, such figures as St Charles Borromeo, St Francis Xavier, St Francis of Sales, and St Jeanne of Chantal were mentioned. In the life of St Francis Xavier, the apostle of the Indies, it was the episode of his death on a Chinese island that held the interest of painters and engravers, as a print by Nicolas Bazin drawn from a painting by Antoine Dieu reveals. The missionary of the Company of Jesus is stretched out on a rock by the sea, clutching a rosary and a crucifix, with his eyes turned toward the cherubim appearing in the sky.[46] St Francis of Sales, the bishop and prince of Geneva, is most often shown in glory, surrounded by angels bearing him up. His hands are clasped in an attitude of prayer, or else he holds his crosier in one hand and a radiant flaming heart in the other, bearing the inscription, 'Vive Jésus' ('Long live Jesus').

It is interesting to note that in certain families, a particular saint is especially revered because he or she is the patron of the deceased. The presence of this saint within the household is perfectly natural in such cases, though such correlations can hardly be made on a general scale.

Old Testament themes were uncommon: they were less familiar and, because of their intellectual nature, less inspirational for meditation, though they were not completely missing from these abodes. The story of Adam reminded Christians of the origins of sin, while Abraham's offering of his only son Isaac to his God prefigured the sacrifice of the incarnate Christ, a new Adam come to earn remission of sins for humanity. It was the biblical characters foreshadowing the Son of God who enjoyed the greatest favour with seventeenth- and eighteenth-century Christians: Moses plucked from the water, Jesus escaping from the Massacre of the Innocents, Job being tested by God or the unjustly stricken Tobit, all of whom foretell Christ's passion. Among other Old Testament figures, two Jewish heroines appear, Judith and Susannah. Judith, a symbol of Yahweh's triumph over his enemies, inspired the engraver Herman Weyen to produce a series of ten small pictures narrating the various episodes of the victory over Holophernes. The story of the chaste Susannah, most frequently illustrated by the bathing scene, illustrates the power of divine grace to deliver believers from the hands of evil. The biblical figure of Susannah was summoned in a prayer for the dying: 'Deliver, Lord, this soul as you delivered Daniel from the lions' den, the three Hebrews from the furnace, and Susannah from a false accusation.[47]

Last of all, in the 'miscellaneous' category, we placed all the sundry themes: the major subjects here were God the Father, generally represented in the symbolic form of a bearded elder holding the earthly globe and surrounded by a host of angels, as he appeared above numerous retables, the Holy Trinity, the Last Judgement, scenes from the Apocalypse, and the Seven Sacraments.

If we look more closely at this pious imagery, two things stand out: first, the figure of Christ, especially Christ crucified, alone or between his mother and St

John, and second, the Virgin and the saints. These figures predominate over all other scenes from the Old or New Testament. Unlike pictures displayed on altars, these images which our Parisians kept in their daily midst did not depict subjects rich in catechismal lessons; rather, they offered themes for meditation and edification.

Since the inhabitants of these households preferred the scenes of the life of Jesus telling of his Passion and Crucifixion, it seems appropriate that the saints in Paradise whom they admired most were the penitents and the martyrs who had shared Christ's condition. Other members of the Church – its teachers, evangelists, doctors and bishops – take second place in these homes. The purpose of these devotional images was in fact not so much to instruct as it was to provide a support for individual prayer. It was the chamber of the master of the house, which was reserved for individual or family prayer, that contained the majority of these images: the inventories indicated that 62 per cent of them were found in the chamber of the deceased.

The intercessors to whom these Parisians turned at the hour of their deaths were those whom they invoked in their testaments: the suffering Christ who would deliver them from their sins and save them from death through his sacrifice on the cross, bringing them to eternal life in the fullness of divine love; the Virgin Mary, the greatest of all intermediaries, whom they implored daily to pray for all sinners, 'now and in the hour of our death'; and finally, all the saints of the heavenly kingdom who had answered God's call and who, through their exemplary lives of penitence and sacrifice, would help and encourage them to bear the hardships and sufferings of this world and to face death trusting in their coming reunion with Christ.

Though the inventories provide a very incomplete picture of the range of these themes, this pious imagery places a major emphasis on sin, death and the necessity of suffering and propitiatory penance. These are simply an expression of the religious sensitivities of the age.[48] The piety of Parisians in the seventeenth and eighteenth centuries was imbued with a Christocentrism that emphasized the 'dolorist' tendencies fostered by the preaching of the times. It was also marked by a Jansenist discourse that insisted through numerous writings on the difficulty of attaining salvation and on the weakness of many of the chosen. And indeed, the devotional images that these Christians chose to guide their spiritual journey seemed to focus more on the painful mysteries of the life of Christ than on the joyful and glorious ones, on sin rather than on divine mercy, on penance rather than on love, and on the fear of judgement more than on hope.

Objects of Piety

Devotional books and images were not the only clues to domestic piety: they were supplemented in 45 per cent of the households in our sample set by various sorts of religious objects. This percentage seems to have remained constant for the entire period covered by our study. Though the frequency of these items is slightly lower than that of devotional images, it is higher than that of books. The fact that the value of these objects was often low made them accessible to even the most humble households, and they were to be found in all social categories. In the home of a day labourer, two skulls were found in 1665, and servants at the end of the seventeenth century commonly owned 'a small Christ in ivory on his cross in ebony wood', whose price ranged from 10 to 30 sols. The wife of a floor polisher in 1751 owned fourteen reliquaries kept under clear glass. A journeyman turner in 1761 possessed 'three ex-votos, two completely in glass and the other with a Holy Virgin in gilded wood', as well as 'a tiny grotto representing the Holy Virgin, another grotto painted white and gilded in which the infant Jesus lies'.

Objects of piety of some value, however, were to be found only in well-to-do households: a silver crucifix and five reliquaries, one of which was 'in enamelled gold valued at 180 L' were inventoried in the home of Jean Amelot, the *Premier Président* of the Grand Council, in 1644. In the assessment performed in 1640 of the estate of a Chevalier of the royal order and *maréchal de camp et d'armée,* 'a reliquary in gold with the image of Our Lady trimmed with diamonds ... and two rosaries, one in amber and the other in coral' with a total value of 120 L were listed. In the home of the wife of a draper in 1751, the notaries observed an ivory crucifix with a rosewood cross on a black velvet background with a frame in carved and gilded wood, worth 50 L, as well as a silver stoup adorned on top with a Christ surrounded by the attributes of his Passion and estimated at 60 L. Some of these objects of piety, such as the crosses, could be considered as jewellery of great value. One cross ornamented with five pink diamonds in silver settings belonged in 1746 to the wife of a master dyer and merchant and was valued at 200 L. Among the many jewels belonging to the Marquise de Traisnel there figured three crosses, one of which was composed of an emerald and five diamonds surrounded by fourteen tiny brilliants, valued at the considerable sum of 3000 L.

The sacred value attributed to some of these articles can be perceived through the notarial vocabulary. The widow of one of the squires of the Duchesse de Guise possessed twelve rosaries in 1651, one of which was made of ebony and trimmed with relics. The wife of a gardener and florist had kept as a precious possession a 'tiny cross set with relics' in 1748. As for the wood used to make the crucifix inventoried in 1772 in the home of a merchant beverage seller, the valuers specified that it had been brought from Judaea.

The number of religious objects per household was rarely very high, generally ranging from one to four. But were such articles simply neglected by the valuers in many cases, as were the small pious images, because of their negligible market value? The more modest the household, the more likely these poor objects were to be ignored. Nevertheless a few inventories do prove that there were deceased persons, often from the working classes, who had collected these tangible signs of their faith and fervour. In 1673, one master cobbler left behind a Christ in a wooden frame, a crystal cross on a chain, a reliquary, two little Virgins, a small cross in white silver and a gold cross. A simple but fortunate vinegar maker from the faubourg Saint-Antoine, whose estate was hardly worth more than 600 L, had amassed nineteen devotional objects in his chamber in 1761, including a 'Christ in ivory placed on his cross in blackened wood'. The wife of a master candle maker in 1772 owned eleven objects of piety, and we have already mentioned the fourteen reliquaries belonging to a floor polisher, as well as the twelve rosaries owned by the widow of a squire of the Duchesse de Guise.

There does not seem to be any correlation between the possession of devotional objects or images and specific social category. The sex ratio, on the other hand, appears to play a more determining role. Just as women seemed more eager to leave wills than men, their homes, especially those of widows and spinsters, were also more open to these humble objects used in their daily devotional practices. We should recall the significant number of single women in Paris at that time, and the important role they played in the spiritual life of the capital.

The absence of religious objects in ecclesiastical households, however, comes as a total surprise. Almost a third of the priests whose inventories were analysed here possessed neither a crucifix nor a prie-dieu nor any pious images. But these clerks without any devotional objects were practising priests and simple students – men without lodgings they could truly call their own, living in communities. Some were very much alone, having settled only recently in the city. In the homes of priests in which objects of piety were noted, the religious decor was most often restricted to a single room in their dwellings: a single crucifix hanging on the wall or placed on the mantelpiece, or on the desk of a chamber. In the other rooms, all that is mentioned are 'so-called devotional paintings', without any further description. It would seem that pious decoration remained essentially a function of the financial situation and social standing of each priest, more than of his place in the ecclesiastical hierarchy. In the homes of such figures as Jean Desmoulins and André Tullou, the curés of Saint-Jacques-du-Haut-Pas and Saint-Benoît, in that of Nicolas du Moustier, vicar of Saint-Séverin, and in the homes of the Abbé Paul de Curduchesne and Pierre Deblanges, vicar general of the bishop of Coutances, all doctors of the Sorbonne, the religious decor blends into the daily living area. These men of the Church, however, constituted the elite of Parisian clergy, in terms of their duties and their powers as well as their family and social connections.

It is also striking to observe the almost total absence of objects of piety inventoried in the homes of priests who died towards the middle of the eighteenth century. It is rare to find more than a single crucifix, except in the homes of high-ranking members of the clergy such as Claude-François Thomassin, doctor of the Sorbonne and curé of Saint-Pierre-des-Arcis, or Jean-Charles Tissu, *licencié* in theology from the faculty of Paris, prior of La Verdre and honorary canon at Saint-Nicolas-du-Louvre. In any case, the apparent indifference of priests toward religious objects cannot be considered to indicate a lack of piety on their part. These ecclesiastics officiated in a church or a chapel every day, where they were surrounded by religious decoration. Did they feel the same need as lay people to be surrounded by devotional objects in the setting of their domestic lives? Could they not be considered to compensate for this absence with the sometimes exceptional collections of religious books they possessed? As men of the Church in the service of God and the souls he had confided to them, they might understandably neglect material goods and even the decoration of their homes, be it secular or pious, in favour of the spiritual and intellectual nourishment which in many cases constituted a significant part of their fortunes.

What were the different types of pious objects mentioned by the valuers? Despite their gaps and their lack of detail, the inventories provide a wealth of information on the many sorts of devotional objects belonging to the deceased. Often detailed descriptions of the form, materials and colours used give us an idea of the physical appearance of these supports for piety. We shall look over these various objects in decreasing order of incidences recorded.

More than 50 per cent of them – 646 or 51 per cent of a sample of 1270 artefacts – were crucifixes. It was in the fifth century that sculptures of the body of Christ on the cross first appeared; in the twelfth century he began to be figured with his legs twisted and an expression of suffering on his face, whereas until then he had been shown alive, his eyes open, standing in an attitude of triumph. Though the crucifix was the object of piety most frequently cited by the valuers, it appeared in only 26 per cent of all households in the second half of the seventeenth century as well as at the beginning of the age of the Enlightenment. It may seem astonishing that three-quarters of these households did not possess this quintessential symbol of faith in a period when religious fervour was riding high. It is true, though, that a painted or engraved image of the Crucifixion, a scene from the Passion or an *Ecce Homo* might well replace the crucifix in the chamber of the deceased. Perhaps, too, in these modest interiors, a simple wooden cross, of absolutely no value and therefore neglected by the valuers, might take the place of a crucifix. Then too, this familiar object, laden with emotional and religious meaning, was held out so that the dying person might kiss it, and was traditionally buried with the deceased, either nailed on to the coffin or slipped into the hands of the corpse. This custom would explain the relatively small number of 'Christs on the cross' mentioned in the inventories. Like the images representing the Son of God in all his human suffering, the crucifix reminded Christians of the mystery of Redemption, in keeping with the Christocentric doctrine of the Council of Trent.

What form did these objects take? It is important first of all to distinguish the material used for the body of Christ from that of the cross supporting it, which was always different, as a few examples show: 'a Christ in ivory placed on his cross in blackened wood', 'a Christ in gilded wood on a background of black velvet, in a golden frame', or 'a Christ in copper on a varnished wood cross'. The most frequently used material for fashioning the body of Christ was ivory. Not only was its colour reminiscent of flesh, but it also had the advantage of being a noble material worthy of the greatness of the subject. White when new, it yellowed over the years, and its fine, tight grain could take a beautiful polish. The second most common material was either pure, bronzed or silver-plated copper. Red in its natural state, this metal could be yellowed using calamine in order to give it a golden appearance. Bronze or *airain*, as well as *potin*, a copper-based alloy, were also mentioned. These crucifixes, crafted out of metals known to be resistant, were made to last. They were familiar objects, to which their owners became attached, and were not replaced lightly, for they were charged with emotional and spiritual force. After metals, wood is the most commonly employed material. Easy to sculpt, it gave each object a unique character imparted by the craftsman's hand. Unlike metal, wood could not be used to produce numerous copies. Plaster, painted or protected by a layer of bronze, could be used to produce series of inexpensive crucifixes. Models in bone were more expensive and bore a resemblance to those in ivory. The most precious and most costly of all, and therefore the most rare, were the so-called crucifixes *d'eau* or *en eau*, literally 'crucifixes of water', made of aquamarine, a marvellously pure blue stone.

The overwhelming majority of the supports for the crucified body of Christ were designated as '(on) his cross in blackened wood' or 'in varnished wood'. The coloured wood used most frequently was pearwood, employed in an attempt to imitate ebony, the noblest of woods. When the wood type is specified, it is ebony, *palissandre*, purpleheart, mahogany, boxwood, oak, walnut or pearwood. In all, the most commonly encountered crucifix was the model 'in ivory on a cross in blackened wood', for which the dark colour of the support highlighted the paleness of Christ's body. A number of these crucifixes were set against a velvet background, usually black or occasionally green. Other backgrounds mentioned included painted wood, tapestry or violet moiré. The border around these crucifixes was usually in gilded wood. It might be described as sculpted and gilded, varnished or painted wood. When the shape was indicated, it was said to be arched. Present in all levels of the Parisian population, these crucifixes were habitually hung on the wall. Standing models placed on a piece of furniture or the mantelpiece over the fireplace were much more rare.

After the crucifix, the most widespread object of piety was the reliquary. Most unfortunately, the notaries' descriptions are hardly sufficient to satisfy our curiosity about their contents, or even the shape and colour of these reliquaries. It seems probable that these were usually objects brought back from a place of pilgrimage, intended to contain a bit of earth from a famous tomb, water from a miraculous fountain, or the remains of some charismatic figure. One notorious example of such an individual was the deacon François de Pâris, whose hair, garments and furniture were distributed in 1727 as relics to Jansenist fanatics. The valuers rarely describe the appearance of these reliquaries: they are content to define them as large, small or 'of different sizes', or to identify a 'reliquary picture' or 'picture as reliquary'.

Such an object might take the form of a vase or a box, and might be made of varnished wood, silver or a cross of gold. When it took the form of a picture, it was framed in gilded, carved and gilded or varnished wood, or in horn with copper plating, and was usually fitted with a glass pane to protect it. It might represent a paschal lamb, or contain wax figures. Some of these reliquaries belonging to wealthy individuals were in precious metals. We have already mentioned the reliquary in enamelled gold, worth 180 L, belonging to Jean Amelot. The wife of Jacques-Honoré Barentin, a *Maître des Requêtes*, possessed a very fine reliquary in gilded vermeil in 1665 which was an exceptional piece. The reliquary was a quintessential sacred object endowed with protective powers, and sometimes with a sentimental value as well. Yet it does not seem to have been a sign of popular devotion only, since it was to be found in the most diverse milieux.

The stoup implied making a gesture, and therefore a religious observance. It was almost always associated with a crucifix, though it was much less common-place (12 per cent of pious objects noted). It took the form of a more or less rounded hemisphere filled with holy water. It could be made of various materials, such as silver or, more modestly, copper, pewter, bronzed lead or even gilded and sometimes sculpted wood, crystal, glass, enamel, marble or tortoiseshell. The most beautiful of these stoups, especially those made of silver, were sometimes finely crafted. Among these models is one decorated with a cherub, found in 1654 in the home of Jacques Galland, the *Secrétaire Ordinaire* of the Council of State and Direction des Finances. On another model, inventoried in 1644 in the home of a surgeon, 'was set the representation of the Virgin with Francis'. As for the stoup belonging to Pierre Gargan, the *Intendant des Finances* who died in 1657, it showed 'Our Lady in miniature' and was worth 100 L. Some of these stoups were equipped with sprinklers.

In a small number of households, religious figurines were inventoried. These were sculptures of the infant Jesus, the Virgin or various saints, in different materials: 'a small Jesus in gilded wood in its niche fitted with a small clear glass pane', a little Virgin in white wax in its niche', a statue of St John in painted marble, or a Magdalene in bronze against a black velvet background in a frame. These statuettes were often enclosed in a niche, like the one found in the single room inhabited by a master painter in 1735: 'a St Anne on a pedestal in gilded wood, a niche with a little Jesus in white wax, a niche with a St Genevieve in plaster'. The materials most commonly used for producing these sculptures were copper, plaster, wax and wood, though marble, crystal, alabaster and bronze were also mentioned.

The frequency of religious jewellery in these interiors was approximately the same as that of figurines, or 6 per cent. Half of these jewellery pieces are crosses, almost always in a noble material such as gold, silver, crystal, coral, diamonds, brilliants or garnet. Their value varied greatly, depending on the material used and on the presence or absence of diamonds. The wife of an official at the Grand Bureau de la Monnaie owned a simple 'little cross of stones from the Temple' valued at just 40 sols in 1746, while the diamond-studded crosses of the wife of a master dyer and merchant and of the Marquise de Traisnel were estimated respectively at 200 L and 3000 L. These crosses, made to be worn around the neck, were sometimes accompanied by a chain or a velvet ribbon. Others were said to be *à la dévote* or hanging, reliquaries or trimmed with relics. Aside from crosses, sacred jewellery mainly took the form of medallions and rings with religious designs: one silver medallion of Pope Alexander VII with a small silver stamp showing the cross of Jerusalem was valued at 3 L; 'a gold ring in which is set a black stone where there is the face of Christ' was valued at 100 sols; a gold ring bearing the name of Jesus was also found.

Rosaries constituted only 3 per cent of all objects of piety and apparently figured in the inventories only when they had some value as jewellery. By definition, a rosary was portable and was kept in the bottom of a pocket, a drawer or a jewellery box, where it usually escaped the valuers' notice. As a personal object that had accompanied its owner along the path of the spirit throughout his or her life, it accompanied the deceased once more in the coffin, where it was slipped between his or her fingers. This custom of burying the dead with their rosaries could explain the rarity of this object in the inventories. We should note that it is almost completely absent throughout the eighteenth century. It seems to capture the attention of the valuers only when it is made from a precious material, like gold, coral, amber, agate, *cornaline* (a type of red agate) or ebony. Rosaries were sometimes ornamented with a cross in gold, silver or crystal, which could take the place of a reliquary. Among the twelve rosaries belonging to the widow of a squire of the Duchesse de Guise, the one in ebony was trimmed with relics, another in cornaline was equipped with an enamel reliquary and a little cross in crystal, and a third, worth 100 sols, had a silver cross.

The prie-dieu, a more space-consuming and relatively expensive object of piety, was very rare and was to be seen only in the dwellings of priests and particularly fervent individuals. It implied the practice of prayer in a place propitious to reflection. Owners of prie-dieux generally had space available and owned other devotional objects as well. Though it fitted into the familiar setting of the chamber, the prie-dieu stood at the centre of a space set apart for prayer in the home of Nicolas du Moustier, the vicar of Saint-Séverin: like an altar, 'a prie-dieu in oak wood and a retable closing with a key, with a copper medallion on which were the commandments of God' stood between 'two prints, the first representing Our Lord on the cross, the second St Nicolas (his patron saint) and two small Christs in copper on their crosses with stands in blackened wood'. The prie-dieu belonging to Jean Desmoulins, curé at Saint-Jacques-du-Haut-Pas, was also reminiscent of a decorated retable: 'a prie-dieu closed by two shutters, around which is a wooden frame on which Our Lord on the cross is represented; the Virgin and St John are on the two sides and two angels above, with a Holy Spirit in bronze; with ornaments in gilded wood above and to the sides.' Among the lay people possessing a prie-dieu were Denis-Jérôme Notte, a master pastry maker, and Marie-Anne Blanquet, a spinster. The former owned, at the time of his death in 1744, a prie-dieu in oak and pine 'fitted with a shutter with a bronze-wire grill' and the latter, who died two years later, had placed 'a prie-dieu with a kneeler, fitted with two shutters and a walnut lectern', estimated at 8 L, in her chamber.

Finally, under the heading of 'various', we have grouped objects as disparate as a confessional and a skull, making up a real miscellany. An *agnus* or *Agnus Dei*, for example, was generally valued with the reliquaries, prints and holy shrouds. This term designated either a type of medallion in clay or wax blessed by the pope, on which the figure of the paschal lamb had been printed, or else a tiny pious image decorated with embroidery and intended for children. Unless the valuers offer some further description, e.g. 'painted both on canvas and on enamel', or mention an '*agnus* picture' or a 'picture with *agnus*', we can hardly visualize these little aids to piety.

While a skull, a grotto with a Virgin, or a nativity scene all stimulated reflection and prayer, other objects, which we have classified as various, were used in a service celebrated in the church: the *tavayolle* or *tanviolle*, generally listed with the household linen, was a lining for the basket used for distributing consecrated bread; a set of sacerdotal ornaments including a chasuble, a stole and a maniple in red damask with gold and silver trim, all enveloped in a protective cloth, was valued at 60 L. Sacred vessels and linen, such as altar dressings for a chapel, a small chalice cover in black velvet with two crosses in satin, cruets, a box for the wafers, a bell, a chalice, a paten and so forth, were inventoried almost exclusively in the households of priests. Finally, we identified objects used by those participating in the offices: 'a crimson red velvet bag for kneeling at church' or 'a church bag' (*sac d'église*) in crimson velvet, trimmed with a fine gold ribbon, in which the owner could store a missal, valued at 40 L. These two articles both belonged to ladies of high society.

Whether they were intended to elevate the soul towards the Lord or to manifest the glory of God, these various objects generally revealed an aesthetic preoccupation and a richness conferred upon them by their form or the precious or semi-precious material in which they were made. Especially in seventeenth-century homes, in which the decor was little more than tapestries and a few pictures on the walls, an ivory crucifix or a silver stoup stood out as luxury items. But in an age when the religious tide was running high, it was natural that sacred objects in the service of faith should be the most beautiful of all.

Though the inventories help us, through the valuers' indications, to identify different types of objects that were most likely produced in quantity, they tell us nothing about the origins of these goods or how they were distributed. Were these articles sold by pedlars or by merchants established in Paris? From the inventories of a few haberdashers, it emerges that objects of piety were part of their habitual stock of merchandise. In 1639, the inventory of one painter and merchant haberdasher who had possessed a shop in the galleries of the Louvre as well as a stall at the Saint-Germain fair, reveals that his stock of goods was a surprisingly sundry mixture of objects: medals and medallions, Persian dishware, scientific instruments, exotic souvenirs, shells and 216 drawings, prints and paintings. In particular, among the paintings and engravings of religious subjects, the valuers noted a 'crucifix with a Virgin and St John, in painted wood, worth 40 sols'.

Several inventories of shopkeepers in Saint-Denis are equally enlightening as to the sources of these devotional objects. Marguerite Régnier, a haberdasher who died in 1757, sold not only laces, buttons and toiletry mirrors, but also catechism books, alphabets and little books. These various articles, as well as toys and jewellery, were lumped together with devotional objects of little value: 'six crosses in red-stained wood for children, at 1 sol ... three dozen Holy Spirit crosses and medals in lead, valued together at 6 sols ... two dozen necklaces and rosaries in wood, glass, and wax, valued together at 36 sols'. Another series of religious objects was inventoried in 1770 in the home of Pierre Bottet, a gold-smith from Saint-Denis: 'several Christ-Holy-Spirits, flat crosses ... a reliquary, a cross with framing ... a package of turquoise wedding rings and gold crosses set with pearls, valued together at 34 L'.

It would appear, then, that it was very easy for Parisians and the inhabitants of outlying villages to acquire these inexpensive objects of piety in the shops of haberdashers and goldsmiths. A tiny number of these articles may have come from the sites of pilgrimages on which the deceased had gone with members of his or her family as a devotional act. It is interesting to remember Montaigne's account in his *Journal de voyage en Italie* of having bought devotional objects in the village of Loreto for 50 écus.

Where were these religious objects located within the living space of the home? Like pious images, the majority of them were found in the chamber, and above all the chamber of the deceased, the father of the family and master of the household. While secular art works were encountered in greater number in other rooms of the home, and especially in the common room, more than half the crucifixes were listed in the death chamber. This was also the primary location for holy water stoups, reliquaries, figurines and prie-dieux. It is more difficult to affirm that crosses and medals were arranged in a similar manner, since they were usually inventoried separately, with the silver and jewellery.

What do we know about the way these objects of piety were arranged in the chamber of the deceased? The inventory done after death gives hardly any information about their positions within the room. But the grouping together of some of these items suggests that the most devout households had set up a special area for prayer, in accordance with the precepts of Jesus: 'When thou prayest, enter into thy closet, and when thou hast shut thy door, pray to thy Father which is in secret' (Mt. 6:6). Different examples offer us a glimpse of this prayer corner installed by a few Parisians in their bedchambers: a priest and sacristan at Saint-Martin had placed 'two stoups and a crucifix set on a background of black panne' in his chamber, and these no doubt created an environment for his prayers. A professor at the Collège d'Autun and *bachelier* (student) priest of the Sorbonne, could withdraw into his chamber and kneel on 'a prie-dieu in white-painted wood' before 'a Christ in ivory on the cross, with its frame in blackened wood, posed on a background of black velvet'. In both the chamber of Jean Desmoulins and that of Nicolas du Moustier, the prie-dieu and the objects surrounding it constituted a pious decor reminiscent of a church altar.

Priests were not the only people to set aside a space in their chambers for prayer. In other households, arrangements like the following were found in the chamber of the deceased: a crucifix surrounded by two or four candlesticks, recalling the way an altar is laid out. In the chamber of a haberdasher in 1665 the valuers inventoried a 'cross with its Christ and two candlesticks in ebony' valued at 3 L. This presentation was frequently seen on prints of the period, showing the saints praying before a crucifix surrounded by candelabra.

In the town houses inhabited by rich office holders like Aignan de Beauharnais, *Commissaire aux Requêtes du Palais*, Jacques Galland, *Secrétaire Ordinaire* of the Council of State and Direction of Finances, or Roland Gruyn, *Secrétaire des Finances*, a chapel or oratory was installed in one room, near the common room, or perhaps in a study, However, the inventories of these individuals make no allusions to the furnishings of these spaces.

These objects, signs of how piety was lived out in the privacy of the home, were the practical tools for daily religion. Concentrating these objects in the main chamber and setting up a holy space used as an oratory facilitated the gestures that accompanied prayer and set the rhythm of the Christian's day. In front of the crucifix, these men and women crossed themselves before and after their morning and evening prayers and at mealtimes during the blessing. If the household had a stoup, its members could cross themselves with holy water and sprinkle their home and the things they used in order to sanctify them. The prie-dieu was more conducive to a kneeling position and encouraged a physical stance propitious to meditation and prayer, with hands folded or crossed on the chest, eyes raised toward the crucifix or a pious image or turned towards a book placed on the lectern of the prie-dieu, such as *L'Imitation de Jésus-Christ* or a collection of psalms. And of course, telling the beads of a rosary in honour of the Virgin was a spiritual exercise accessible to everyone. These are the gestures called to mind by the presence of these pious objects. Iconography helps us restore them visually to their context: a print engraved by Daumont, at the Aigle d'Or in the rue de la Ferronnerie, presented a comparison between 'the life of a good man and a debauched man'. One of the images shows the pious man, kneeling in the morning, his hands folded, before a crucifix set on a low table. At his side is another, smaller prostrate figure, perhaps his son. The caption comments,

> Qui prie Dieu soir et matin
> Ne manquera jamais de rien.
>
> (He who prays to God morning and evening
> Will never want for anything.)

Another vignette illustrates the ritual of the blessing or *Benedicite*: before the family eats its meal together, the father, surrounded by his wife and child, recites the blessing. The caption reads:

> Dieu bénit la nourriture
> A ceux qui vont en droiture.
>
> (God blesses the food
> Of those who follow the path of righteousness.)

Was this the impact of post-Tridentine teaching through imagery, making itself felt on these Parisian households that faithfully perform their daily devotions? As they express their faith in God by their piety within the family, they certainly appear to be true domestic units of the church.

Though devotional objects were encountered in only 45 per cent of these dwellings, their absence may be compensated by the presence of painted or engraved pious images or religious books. If we take into account the possession of these three sorts of objects, 70 per cent of our Parisians demonstrated their religious feelings within their familiar home environment. For these faithful, the Christian life was not restricted to going to mass on Sunday and on obligatory feast days, to vespers and other offices, and to participating in the sacraments and the various processions. It was equally inseparable from all the moments spent under God's watching eye, whether in Church or at home. This level of 70 per cent would seem to represent a minimum.

Actually, in many inventories, it is possible that the books, images, and other objects which were not described were of a religious nature. And of course the crucifixes and rosaries buried with the deceased left no trace. For all these reasons, it seems reasonable to estimate that only 10–20 per cent of all households contained no religious objects whatsoever, at least before the middle of the eighteenth century. The Parisians who were without any devotional objects were often either people at the bottom of the social scale, or impoverished individuals, such as widows who had only minimal resources. During the first

half of the eighteenth century, more than three-quarters of those who died without pious objects left behind less than 1000 L after their deaths. The proportion
of households owning objects of piety was greatest in the wealthy levels of society.

We should emphasize that those who possessed religious books and those who
owned devotional images and objects were not always one and the same. We have
already highlighted the case of priests who displayed a strong predilection for
written materials as opposed to other objects. The will left by André Tullou, the
curé of Saint-Benoît and doctor of theology at the Faculty of Paris, is very
revealing on this point: he requests that his body be buried, not with his crucifix,
but with the Gospel: 'I want the Gospel of Jesus Christ to be placed on my
stomach, in my bier, as certain witness to my faith in the divine word, in accordance with the example of the first Christians.'

In the working classes, however, where the literacy rate was often low, painted
and sculpted images were preferred over books. The most fervent Parisians, and
especially single women, collected both written works and images and objects of a
religious nature. This was the case of Marie-Anne Blanquet, a spinster, who in
1746 had accumulated three portraits of bishops and cardinals, six paintings
figuring Christ or the Virgin, four crucifixes, a prie-dieu, 'a veil of silk tapestry
bearing the Holy Name of Jesus in the middle' which decorated her antechamber, and almost 400 pious books in her abode.

This issue of pious images, books and objects within Parisian households
would be worth developing and pursuing further. Already, our study, complemented by specific research on the subject, demonstrates how important the
religious element was in all social categories, and not just during the 'century of
the saints' but even up to a late date during the Enlightenment. It is true that
objects such as rosaries and stoups, related to religious gestures, were gradually
disappearing from inventories during Voltaire's time. However, pious images and
books were still present in great numbers in the interiors of the middle classes of
the population in the 1770s. It is also true that in some well-to-do homes belonging to the city's intellectual or artistic elite the complete absence of any religious
books or objects could be observed during the same period. The break that
became visible in the tone of testamentary language by the middle of the century
was hardly perceptible in the study of objects of piety before the 1780s, and thus
lies beyond the limits of our study. The sharp decline of these devotional objects,
with the simultaneous collapse of traditional acts and beliefs, is the subject of a
new study directed by Pierre Chaunu and based on inventories done between
1775 and 1830.

Conclusion

Now that we have reached the end of our wanderings in the company of the notaries, what final impressions remain from this investigation of 2783 Parisians households? During this long stroll through space and time, we have gone through so many doors, climbed and descended so many staircases, from the cellar to the attic or from one room to another in these lodgings spread over several stories. We have inquisitively opened so many cupboards and closets, and sorted through so many belongings of all kinds.

Perhaps it is this accumulation of such a diversity of objects owned by these Parisians two or three centuries ago that strikes us most. What a fascinating and rich imaginary museum they create! If they could be presented in chronological order, they would reveal the substantial multiplying effect of the eighteenth century. Large numbers of tiny technical advances, the fruits of the inventive minds and ingenuity of the men and women of the Enlightenment, combined with an increasing desire for greater well-being and a profound aspiration for happiness, to embellish and improve the setting of daily life. Housing became a little more spacious and was designed in a more rational manner, with a horizontal layout. Rooms were somewhat better heated and lit and with the beginnings of specialization, greater privacy was achieved. These were the primary improvements enjoyed by Parisians born during the reign of Louis XV, in comparison with earlier generations. But what conferred an appealing personal character on these dwellings was above all the abundance and infinite variety of objects of all sorts that had been accumulated by the deceased during the eighteenth century. Marquetry commodes, mirrors, pier glasses, pendulums and other articles were not exclusively the privilege of princely and noble residences, but could also find their places in the interiors of the middle classes of the population. And the elegance and refinement of the creations of Parisian craftsmen blended with the richness of furnishing fabrics and wall coverings glowing with harmonious colours.

Just as Voltaire's use of language can be considered to represent a high point of French literature, so the decorative arts of this period also reached a state of perfection that we are able to glimpse through the inventories after death. After all, in the present day, furniture and curios in Louis XV and Louis XVI style are the subjects of financial transactions of incomparable magnitude. Parisians of the age of the Enlightenment – and not only the very rich – had the privilege of adorning their living environment with a profusion of fine objects that have become much sought after by antique dealers and art lovers today. Travellers from the provinces and from abroad acclaimed the pre-eminence of Paris in terms of the luxury, taste and intelligence they discovered there. The chronological analysis of the notarial valuations helps us to understand how the households of the capital were enriched and embellished during the eighteenth century, in comparison with the previous century and with the rest of France. What a contrast there is between the sombre and austere Parisian interiors of the dark seventeenth century, stripped of any superfluous element, and those of the age of the Enlightenment, filled with so many lovely pieces of furniture and decorative objects of all kinds!

And what a contrast between Parisian lodgings and provincial ones. Even 'the most considerable city of the kingdom after Paris', as d'Expilly described Lyon, did not undergo changes in its habitat during the age of the Enlightenment comparable to those that took place within the Parisian urban fabric. With the exception of a few residences belonging to a tiny minority of rich bourgeois, 'most of Lyon's buildings', writes Maurice Garden, 'were old, narrow, high, dark and complicated by all sorts of adventitious constructions and successive additions, which often gave a miserable and sad aspect to these houses.'[1] While many one-room dwellings were often used simultaneously as workshops and contained only summary furnishings, the majority of the multi-room quarters occupied by merchants were starkly furnished, without much concern for their decoration. Even the *salons* of the city's wealthiest inhabitants seems relatively modest when compared to their Parisian counterparts. How much more rustic, then, did the village houses in the Cotentin, upper Berry, or lower Limousin regions appear in contrast with the average Parisian habitation, even though they were generally equipped with the articles indispensable to daily life.

But Paris owed its status as model and driving force of the kingdom in all domains to the fact that it was the capital. The extraordinary influence exercised by Paris was magnificently expressed by a contemporary of Louis XIV, the jurist Julien Brodeau, in his 1669 edition of *La Coutume de la Prévôté et Vicomté de Paris*:

The City of Paris is the royal capital of the kingdom, the centre of the state, the ordinary staying place of kings and their courts, the seat of the first and oldest Parlement and of the Cour des Pairs, the city source of laws, the common homeland of all the French, the pole of all the nations of the world, the France of France.[2]

The other functions of Paris, be they religious, intellectual or economic, all stemmed from the city's function as the political and administrative capital of the kingdom. The city, whose population grew from some 450,000 inhabitants in the 1680s to almost 600,000 on the eve of the Revolution, never stopped expanding throughout the eighteenth century, or affirming its influence and its power of attraction. Our study of the very heart of these households points out this eminent role of Paris in all the activities relating to housing: it was in the capital that fields as diverse as urban planning, construction, fine arts, decoration and luxury crafts all achieved their highest perfection, to the greater benefit of the city's inhabitants.

Improved living and housing conditions for Parisians by the end of the seventeenth century, and above all during the eighteenth century in the newly developed neighbourhoods to the west, were one of the factors behind this growth. It is true that in terms of material comfort, the small advances achieved in terms of heating, lighting and hygiene beginning in the 1750s seem slender indeed, if we compare them with the progress brought about by the industrial revolution a century later. The changes that were to alter completely the way Parisians lived did not come into effect until the second half of the nineteenth century and the dawn of the twentieth century, and they came in phases: indoor supplies of drinking water in 1860, under Haussmann's administration, the installation of gas and electricity beginning in 1878, and extension of mains drainage undertaken in 1883.

Though the many objects discovered in these interiors stricken by death appear still and mute at first glance, we have attempted not to visit these homes as if they were museums. Throughout these pages, we have sought to give a human face to the inhabitants of these places, to reconstruct the gestures of their daily life, and even, in certain cases, to lift the veil on the family's privacy. The valuations of their books, their works of art and their devotional objects have revealed their cultural tastes, their interests, and their religious sensibility to us. Some of these Parisians, belonging to the full range of social categories, have become almost familiar acquaintances: Nicolas du Moustier, the vicar of Saint-Séverin, filled with great piety and ardour for catechizing his parishoners; the rich and sumptuous Marquise de Traisnel, a woman of excellent taste who collected jewellery, silver and porcelain, as well as precious bibelots, and who was also a fervent admirer of Louis XV. She respectfully kept the portrait that had been given by the *Bien-Aimé* (the 'well-loved' king) to her father, the Secretary of State. We have also met the wealthy bookseller Frédéric Léonard and his wife Marie-Anne des Essarts, owners of several keyboard instruments, various types of games and a superb furniture collection; the servant Jeanne Dameron, wet-nurse to the Duc de Bourbon and first chambermaid to the Duchesse de Bourbon, who was so attached to her masters that she possessed their portraits; the spinster Marie-Anne Blanquet, as knowledgeable and open to the progress of the Enlightenment as she was pious; and many others.

Though these inventories, unlike analytical texts or private diaries, give us only a fairly superficial look at the personalities of these men and women, they are in contrast rich with information on the gestures and behaviour involved in everyday life. To the eyes of a twentieth-century observer, the rituals of sociability which existed not only within the peasantry, but in the city as well, are what is most striking. The bonds created by blood, neighbourliness and work were a means of struggling against the difficulties and uncertainties of existence, and especially against solitude. The malaise that reigns in today's urban agglomerations was already familiar to the inhabitants of eighteenth-century Paris, and especially to widowed and unmarried women.

For the many Parisians who practised their piety within their households, human relationships were not all that mattered; their relationship with God remained essential. These Christians who had become children of God through the sacrament of baptism knew that they were loved by their Father in Heaven, and that in their solitude, in sickness and in the hour of their deaths, they could plead for his infinite mercy.

At the end of this imaginary journey into the Paris of two or three centuries ago, why not admit that we have enjoyed lifting the roofs off these houses and entering into the very heart of the lives of their inhabitants? Why not recognize the affection we feel for these elegant and refined interiors from the age of the Enlightenment? After all, like the paintings of Watteau and Boucher, they evoke a bygone way of life that inspired Talleyrand to make his famous remark, long after the fall of the *ancien régime*: 'Those who did not live before 1789 cannot know what it means to live the gentle life.'

Appendices

Appendix 1   Main Bed Types Listed in the Inventories

High-post
Low-post
Bâtard
Twin
On castors
With columns
With turned posts
A l'antique
En tombeau (tomb-shaped)
A l'impériale
A la Duchesse

Polish style
Turkish style
Italian style
Roman style
Baldaquin
Children's
Cradle
Wicker basket
Trestle
Baudet (Trestles)
Collapsible

On trestles
Camp bed
On the ground
Straw mattress
Day
Room
Sleeping bench
With two backboards
English style

Appendix 2   Various Types of Lighting Elements and Frequency of Appearance

Mobile elements		*Fixed elements*	
Candleholder	63%	Branch	9%
Torch	15%	Chandelier	0.5%
Martinet	5%		
Lamp	3%		
Lantern	2%		
Bougeoir (candle stick)	1.5%		
Nightlight }	1%		
Candelabrum }			

Appendix 3   Vocabulary for Furnishing Fabrics (definitions based on *Dictionnaire de Trévoux*)

Bouracan or *barracan*: Coarse *camelot* or fabric woven from goat hair, used to make raincoats.

Brocatelle: Light fabric made of cotton or raw silk, to imitate brocade.

Cadis: A type of inexpensive light wool fabric.

Calico (*indienne*): Fabric made partly of silk and partly of wool.

Calmande, calamande, calamandre, or *callemandre*: A type of woollen fabric, highly lustred, in black or various other colours.

Camelot: Fabric usually made from goat hair, with wool or silk.

Damask (*damas*): Fabric made of silk, with pattern in relief featuring flowers or other figures.

Lace (*dentelle*): Small braid or work in threads of silk, gold or silver, made on a spindle and used to trim clothing or linens.

Drap: Very warm fabric used to make winter clothing. Made of wool for wearing, and with gold and silver for furnishings and church hangings.

Droguet: Inexpensive wool fabric, a type of *drap*, but very thin and narrow.

Estame: Work with threads of wool, woven and interlaced with each other in stitches.

Etamine: Light, very thin fabric, worked like *toile*.

Futaine: Fabric made of yarn and cotton.

Gauze (*Gaz*): *Toile* and fabric very loosely woven, through which daylight can be seen.

Gros de Tours: Silk fabric whose weave is diagonally ribbed and which looks coarse and thick.

Linon: Very loosely woven cloth, made of fine linen.

Moiré: Entirely silk fabric, both warp and woof, with a tight weave.

Molleton: Type of light wool fabric, very soft and spongy.

Moquette: Woollen fabric worked like velvet.

Muslin (*mousseline*): Very light-coloured cotton cloth, fine and loosely woven, which is not smooth, but makes little billows like foam.

Panne: Entirely silk fabric whose warp is composed of, and forms, a sort of pile that is longer than velvet and shorter than plush.

Plush (*peluche*): Fabric made entirely of silk, whose warp pile is cut like that of panne and of velvet, but whose pile is left longer.

Pinchina: A type of woollen fabric without diagonal rib, which is a sort of coarse and solid *drap*.

Ras de Saint-Maur: A type of fabric with diagonal rib, like serge.

Satin: Silk fabric, polished and shiny, whose warp is very fine and stands out, and whose weft is coarse and hidden, which gives it its lustre. Bruges satin: Fabric with weft in thread and whose warp is in silk.

Satinade: Common satin fabric, or one which imitates satin.

Serge: Common, light fabric of diagonally ribbed wool.

Siamoise: Fabric blended from silk and cotton, which was seen for the first time in France when the ambassadors of the king of Siam came there during the reign of Louis XIV. This is also a fabric of thread and cotton. It is striped. The warp is in thread and linen, and the weft in cotton.

Silk: Extremely soft and loose thread, which is used to make beautiful, costly fabrics.

Taffeta: Thin, plain-coloured silk fabric.

Toile: Cloth with interwoven threads, of which some run lengthwise, and the others widthwise.

Tripe or *Tripe de velours*: Wool fabric which is manufactured and cut like velvet.

Velvet (*velours*): Fabric made entirely of silk, whose pile is wound around a little copper shaft, on which it is then cut, which produces a cloth with nap shorter than panne.

Appendix 4   Vocabulary for Furnishing Fabric Colours

Agate	Flaxen grey	Pewter grey
Apricot	Frog green	Pink
Ash	Garnet	Plum
Ashen chestnut	Gingerbread	Plum green
Aurore (dawn)	Gold	Prairie green
Autumn leaves	Golden	Purple
Bis (grey-brown)	Golden yellow	Red
Black	Grey	Ruby
Blond	Grey (*petit*)	Sand
Blue	Grey-blue	Scarlet
Brown	Grey-brown	Sea green
Celadon (grey-green)	Grey-white	Silver
Chamois	*Grisaille* (grizzle)	Slate
Changing green	Hazel grey	Slate grey
Cherry	Hazelnut	Thorn grey
Chestnut	Isabelle (light tan)	Tobacco
Cinnamon	Jasper	Tree bark
Clove	Lemon	Turkish blue
Coffee	Light grey	Vermeil
Crimson	Lilac	Vermilion
Daffodil	Mauve	Violet
Dapple grey	Mouse grey	Water green
Dark cinnamon	Olive	White
Ecru (natural)	Orange	Wine-coloured
Fawn	Pale blue	Yellow
Fire	Pale hazelnut	Yellowish
Fire grey	Pale pink	
Flambé	Pearl grey	

Notes

Notes to Introduction

1. Martin Lister, *A Journey to Paris in the Year 1698*, London, 1699, p. 5.
2. Louis-Sébastien Mercier, *Le Tableau de Paris*, 12 vols, Amsterdam, 1781–8, vol. XI, p. 3.
3. Louis-Sébastien Mercier, *Parallèle de Paris et de Londres*, Introduction and notes by Claude Bruneteau and Bernard Cottret, Paris, 1982, p. 140.
4. Mercier, *Tableau*, vol. I, ch. 88: 'On bâtit de tous côtés'.
5. Ibid., vol. XI, 'Il fait bon crier un peu.'
6. The theses by these students may be consulted at the Centre de Recherches sur la Civilisation de l'Europe Moderne at the Université Paris-Sorbonne, 1 rue Victor Cousin, 75005 Paris, France.
7. The Minutier Central des Notaires, 87 rue Vieille du Temple, 75003 Paris, France, is part of France's National Archives.
8. Roland Mousnier, *Recherche sur la stratification sociale à Paris aux XVIIe–XVIIIe siècles*, Paris, 1976.
9. On the subject of Paris, three interesting works based mainly on the use of inventories compiled after death are: Françoise Lehoux, *Le Cadre de vie des médecins parisiens, aux XVIe et XVIIe siècles*, Paris, 1976; Michel Marion, *Les Bibliothèques privées à Paris au milieu du XVIIIe siècle*, Paris, 1978; and Daniel Roche, *Le Peuple de Paris*, Paris, 1981.
10. We refer in particular to the following books and articles: *Les Actes notariés source de l'histoire sociale, XVIe–XIXe siècles*, Actes du Colloque de Strasbourg (March 1978), Strasbourg, 1979, articles by Micheline Baulant, 'L'Analyse par ordinateur des inventaires après décès de la région de Meaux', p. 197; Jean Jacquart, 'L'Utilisation des inventaires en histoire socioculturelle', p. 241; Daniel Roche, R. Arnette and F. Ardellier, 'Inventaires après décès parisiens et culture matérielle au XVIIIe siècle', p. 231; *Probate Inventories* (papers presented at the Leeuwenborch Conference, Wageningen, 5–7 May 1980), Utrecht, 1980, articles by Micheline Baulant, 'Typologie des inventaires après décès', p. 33 and 'Enquêtes sur les inventaires après décès autour de Meaux aux XVIIe et XVIIIe siècles', p. 141; Madeleine Connat, 'Etude sur les inventaires après décès de Paris, 1500–1560' in *Position de Thèses de l'Ecole Nationale des Chartes*, Nogent-le-Rotrou, 1942.

11. Roche, *Le Peuple de Paris*, p. 60.

12. Jean-Paul Poisson, 'Introduction à l'étude du rôle socio-économique du notariat à la fin du XVIIe siècle' in *Notaires et société*, Paris, 1985, p. 247.

13 Poisson, 'Introduction à l'étude du rôle socio-économique du notariat au XVIIIe siècle: Quatre offices parisiens en 1749' in *Notaires*, p. 367.

14. Roche, *Le Peuple de Paris*, p. 60.

15. Mercier, *Tableau*, vol. II, ch. 115, p. 21, 'Notaires'. See also vol. 4, ch. 37, p. 31, 'Les Affiches': 'Un inventaire grossoyé rapporte beaucoup plus qu'un bon livre.'

16. J. Kaplow, *Les Noms des rois, les pauvres de Paris à la veille de la Révolution*, Paris, 1974; A. Farge, *Le Vol d'aliments*, Paris, 1974; M. Botlan, *Domesticité et domestiques à Paris, dans la crise (1770–1790)*, doctoral thesis at the Ecole des Chartes, Paris, 1976; S. Lartigue, *Les Populations flottantes à Paris au XVIIIe siècle*, master's thesis, Paris I, 1980.

17. Translator's note: the notary in France traditionally had greater powers than his British or American counterpart, resembling those of an attorney or solicitor.

18. On the subject of these psychological and social conditions, see Jean Queniart, 'L'Utilisation des inventaires en histoire socioculturelle', p. 241 in *Les Actes notariés source d'histoire sociale, XVIe–XIXe siècles*, Actes du colloque de Strasbourg (March 1978), Strasbourg, 1979; Jean-Paul Poisson, 'L'Inventaire notarié (atmosphère psychologique et matérielle)', communication at Pierre Chaunu's seminar, 31 January 1978.

Notes to Chapter 1

1. Bibliothèque Nationale (BN), Ms. fr. 21695, fo. 268.

2. Joseph Saugrain, *Dictionnaire universel de la France ancienne et moderne et de la Nouvelle France*, 3 vols (in-folio), Paris, 1726.

3. Abbé Expilly, *Dictionnaire géographique, historique et politique des Gaules et de la France*, 5 vols, Paris, 1762, vol. V, p. 401.

4. The estimates made by Hurtaut and Magny in *Dictionnaire historique de la Ville de Paris et de ses environs*, 4 vols, Paris, 1779, which claim that there were 50,000 residential buildings in Paris, seem inflated. A. Beraud and P. Dufey write in *Dictionnaire historique de Paris*, 2 vols, Paris, 1832, vol. I, p. 428, that there were approximately 29,400 such buildings in Paris in 1830.

5. Abbé Expilly, *Dictionnaire géographique*, vol. V, p. 480.

6. Adrien Friedmann, *Paris, ses rues, ses paroisses du Moyen Age à la Révolution*, Paris, 1959.

7. Ibid., pp. 345ff.

8. Robert Descimon, Jean Nagle, 'Les Quartiers de Paris du Moyen Age au XVIIIe siècle: évolution d'un espace plurifonctionnel', *Annales* (1979), p. 956.

9. Jaillot, *Recherches critiques, historiques et topographiques sur la ville de Paris*, 5 vols, Paris, 1782, vol. V.

10. A. Du Pradel, *Livre commode des adresses pour 1692*, 2 vols, Paris, 1878.

11. Jèze, *Etat ou tableau de la ville de Paris*, Paris, 1765.

12. Henri Sauval, *Histoire et recherches des antiquités de la ville de Paris*, 3 vols, Paris, 1724, vol. I, p. 26.

13. BN, Ms. fr. 21692, fo. 302.

14. Jeanne Pronteau, *Les Numérotages des maisons de Paris du XVe siècle à nos jours*, Paris, 1966.
15. BN, Ms. fr. 21695, fo. 270.
16. Marcel Marion, *Dictionnaire des institutions de la France aux XVIIe et XVIIIe siècles*, Paris, 1923, p. 205.
17. G.-A. Guyot, *Répertoire universel et raisonné de jurisprudence*, 17 vols, Paris, 1784–5, vol. VII, p. 5.
18. Jaillot, *Recherches critiques*, vol. I, 'Quartier du Palais-Royal', p. 23.
19. Sauval, *Histoire et recherches*, vol. I, p. 26.
20. Hurtaut and Magny, *Dictionnaire historique*, vol. II, p. 153.
21. Louis-Sébastien Mercier, *Le Tableau de Paris*, vol. IV, p. 95.
22. Ibid., vol. I, ch. 85, 'Le Fauxbourg Saint-Marcel', p. 271.
23. Daniel Roche, *Le Peuple de Paris*, pp. 256f.

Notes of Chapter 2

1. Roland Mousnier, *Les Institutions de la France*, 2 vols, Paris, 1980, vol. I, p. 251.
2. Roland Mousnier, *Paris au XVIIe siècle*, Les Cours de Sorbonne, 4 vols, Paris, 1961, p. 337.
3. Alfred Franklin, *Dictionnaire historique des arts, métiers et professions exercés dans Paris depuis le treizième siècle*, Paris, 1906, p. 170.
4. Abbé Expilly, *Dictionnaire géographique*, vol. V, p. 402. In *Figaro et son maître: les domestiques au XVIIIe siècle*, Paris, 1984, Jacqueline Sabattier estimates the number of servants in Paris at 50,000 for 550,000 to 650,000 inhabitants. They would therefore have represented almost 10 per cent of the population.
5. Louis-Sébastien Mercier, *Le Tableau de Paris*, vol. IV, ch. 304, 'Filles nubiles', p. 23–4.
6. Marcel Reinhard, *Paris pendant la Révolution*, Les Cours de Sorbonne, 2 vols, Paris, 1963–5, vol. I, p. 50.
7. Gianpaolo Marana, *Lettre d'un Sicilien à un de ses amis*, introduction and notes by Abbé Valentin Dufour, Paris, 1883.
8. Joachim-Christopher Nemeitz, *Séjour à Paris, c'est-à-dire instructions fidèles pour les voyageurs de condition ... durant leur séjour à Paris*, Leiden, 1727, p. 588 (translated from German).
9. Mrs Cradock, *La Vie française à la veille de la Révolution (1783–1786). Journal inédit*, Paris, 1911.
10. Baroness d'Oberkirch, *Mémoires*, Paris, 1970.
11. Reinhard, *Paris pendant la Révolution*, vol. I, p. 81.
12. Jacques Savary des Bruslons, *Dictionnaire universel de commerce*, 4 vols in-folio, Copenhagen, 1760. The first edition was published in 1725.
13. Mousnier, *Les Institutions*, vol. I, p. 201.
14. Madeleine Foisil, 'L'Ecriture du for privé', in *Histoire de la vie privée: de la Renaissance aux Lumières*, vol. III, edited by Philippe Ariès and Georges Duby, Paris, 1986, p. 331.
15. Jean-Paul Poisson, *Notaires et société*, 'L'Apport des inventaires à la connaissance de la démographie parisienne ancienne: le règne de François Ier', p. 515.
16. Philippe Ariès, *L'Enfant et la vie familiale sous l'ancien régime*, Paris, 1973.

17. Peter Laslett, *Household and Family in Past Time*, Cambridge, 1972. See also Pierre Chaunu, *Histoire, science sociale*, Paris, 1974.
18. Mercier, *Tableau*, vol. VIII, ch. 626, 'Grisettes', p. 77.
19. Mercier, *Le Tableau de Paris*, introduced and edited by Jeffry Kaplow, Paris, 1979, p. 54.
20. *La Mort à Paris*, Paris, 1978, p. 393.
21. Daniel Roche, *Le Peuple*, p. 59.
22. Sabattier, *Figaro*, p. 28.

Notes to Chapter 3

1. Louis-Sébastien Mercier, *Le Tableau de Paris*, vol. X, ch. 847, 'Payer son terme', p. 211.
2. Among other works, see Jean-Pierre Babelon, *Demeures parisiennes sous Henri IV et Louis XIII*, Paris, 1965.
3. Jean-Pierre Labatut, *Les Ducs et pairs de France au XVIIe siècle*, Paris, 1972, p. 302.
4. Yves Durand, *Les Fermiers généraux au XVIIIe siècle*, Paris, 1971, p. 473.
5. Martin Lister, *A Journey to Paris in the Year 1698*.
6. Letter from a descendant of the Huguenots. This woman, a Protestant refugee living in Kassel, was visiting Paris for the first time in 1773. In *La Cité* (Bulletin de la Société Historique et Archéologique du 4ème Arrondissement), 1904, p. 47–51.
7. J. Nicot, *Thrésor de la langue française*, Paris, 1606.
8. Madeleine Foisil, *Le Sire de Gouberville*, Paris, 1981.
9. C. S. Walther, *Manuel de la toilette et de la mode (Essai d'un petit dictionnaire des modes)*, Paris, 1776, vol. I, part 1, p. 43.

Notes to Chapter 4

1. Gaston Bachelard, *La Poétique de l'espace*, Paris, 1938.
2. In addition to the major seventeenth- and eighteenth-century dictionaries mentioned above, the following works contain information on beds: Henri Havard, *Dictionnaire de l'ameublement et de la décoration depuis le XVIIe siècle jusqu'à nos jours*, 4 vols, Paris, 1887–90; Guillaume Janneau, *Lits de repos et lits*, Paris, 1977; Charles Oulmont, *La Maison, la vie au XVIIIe siècle*, Paris, 1929.
3. Martin Lister, *A Journey to Paris in the Year 1698*, p. 23.
4. Quoted by Michèle Sacquin, *Voyageurs anglais en France et voyageurs français en Angleterre*, thesis for the Ecole des Chartes, 3 vols, Paris, 1978.
5. Henry Coxe, *The Gentleman's Guide in his Tour through France*, London, 1817, p. li.
6. Fernand Braudel, *Civilisation matérielle, économie et capitalisme*, vol. I: *Les Structures du quotidien*, Paris, 1979, p. 106.
7. Lister, *Journey to Paris*, p. 144.
8. François Bluche, *La Vie quotidienne au temps de Louis XIV*, Paris, 1984, p. 169.
9. Ibid.
10. Braudel, *Civilisation matérielle*, p. 165.
11. Louis-Sébastien Mercier, *Parallèle de Paris et Londres*, p. 74.
12. *La Cuisinière bourgeoise, suivie de l'office …*, Bruxelles, 1753, p. 305.
13. Braudel, *Civilisation Matérielle*, p. 192.

14. Jean Jacquart, 'Les Paysanneries à l'épreuve' in Pierre Léon, *Les Hésitations de la croissance 1580–1740: histoire économique et sociale du monde*, vol. II, Paris, 1978.

15. Louis-Sébastien Mercier, *Le Tableau de Paris*, vol. VII, p. 225.

16. Lister, *Journey to Paris*, p. 128.

17. A. Furetière, *Roman bourgeois*, Paris, 1666, p. 918.

18. In addition to Henri Havard's book, mentioned earlier, on the subject of furniture in general, cf. Pierre Verlet, *L'Art du meuble à Paris au XVIIIe siècle*, 'Que sais-je?', Paris, 1968, and *La Maison au XVIIIe siècle en France*, Paris, 1966; Geneviève Souchal, *Le Mobilier français du XVIIIe siècle*, Paris, 1962.

Notes to Chapter 5

1. Louis-Sébastien Mercier, *Le Tableau de Paris*, vol. I, ch. 23, 'Des Cheminées', p. 39.

2. J.-J. Volkmann, *Neueste Reisen durch Frankreich …*, 3 vols, Leipzig, 1787–8, vol. 1, p. 153.

3. Mercier, *Tableau*, vol. X, ch. 836; vol. I, ch. 23, 'Cheminées', p. 182.

4. J.-J. Volkmann, op. cit., vol. I.

5. Mercier, *Tableau*, vol. X, p. 183.

6. *Le Voyageur fidèle, ou le guide des étrangers dans la Ville de Paris*, Paris, 1716, p. 351.

7. Andrée Corvol, *L'Homme et l'arbre sous l'ancien régime*, Paris, 1984, p. 553.

8. Mercier, *Tableau*, vol. VII, ch. 567, 'Bois à brûler', p. 85.

9. Ibid., vol. I, ch. 23, 'Cheminées', p. 39.

10. Round table on heating wood, chaired by Andrée Corvol, session of Pierre Chaunu's seminar, 10 March 1981.

11. Mercier, *Tableau*, vol. VII, p. 85.

12. E. Meininger, *Voyage en France fait en l'an 1663 par Jean-Gaspard Dolfuss* (translated from German), Mulhouse, 1881, p. 29.

13. *Le Voyageur fidèle*, p. 350.

14. Martin Lister, *A Journey to Paris in the Year 1698*, p. 154.

15. On this issue, the following period documents may be consulted: Jacques Hippolyte Ronesse, *Vues sur la propreté des rues de Paris*, n.p., 1782, and J.-A. Dulaure, *Nouvelle Description des curiosités de Paris*, Paris, 1785. Other (modern) references include Jean Bouchary, *L'Eau à Paris à la fin du XVIIIe siècle*, Paris, 1946, and Jean-Pierre Goubert, *La Conquête de l'eau*, Paris, 1986.

16. Mercier, *Tableau*, vol. I, ch. 49, 'Porteurs d'eau', p. 90.

17. William Cole, *A Journal of my Journey to Paris in the Year 1765*, London, 1931, p. 42.

18. Goubert, *Conquête de l'Eau*, p. 50.

19. Lister, *Journey to Paris*, p. 154.

20. Cole, *Journal*, p. 41.

21. On this point, see Madeleine Foisil, 'Les Attitudes devant la mort au XVIIIe siècle: sépultures et suppressions de sépultures dans le cimetière parisien des Saints-Innocents', *Revue Historique* (1974), p. 303.

22. Dulaure, *Nouvelle Description*, p. 200.

23. Quoted in Goubert, *Conquête de l'Eau*, p. 173.

24. Ronesse, *Vues sur la propreté*, pp. 34–5.

25. These lines are quoted in Georges Vigarello, *Le Propre et le sale, l'hygiène du corps*

depuis le Moyen Age, Paris, 1985. p. 22. They are taken from T. Renaudot, *Recueil général des questions traitées et conférences du bureau d'adresse*, Paris, 1655.

26. Quoted in Roland Mousnier, *Paris capitale au temps de Richelieu et de Mazarin*, Paris, 1978, p. 130.

27. Bibliothèque Nationale Prints, Qb 1685, Hennin Collection, vol. 62, and Oa 52, p. 151.

28. Mercier, *Tableau*, vol. XI, 'Latrines', p. 34.

Notes to Chapter 6

1. Martin Lister, *A Journey to Paris in the Year 1698*, p. 24.

2. Louis-Sébastien Mercier, *Le Tableau de Paris*, vol. I, ch. 89, 'Ameublement', p. 166.

3. *Horace Walpole's Correspondence*, edited by W. S. Lewis, 34 vols, New Haven, 1955–74, vol. XXXI, p. 87.

4. Quoted in Pierre Chaunu, *La Civilisation de l'Europe des Lumières*, Paris, 1971, p. 432.

5. J.-J. Guiffrey, *Table générale des artistes ayant exposé aux salons du XVIIIe siècle*, Paris, 1873, and Hélène Zmijewska, 'La Critique des salons en France avant Diderot', *Gazette des Beaux-Arts* (July–August 1970).

6. Krzysztof Pomian, 'Marchands, connaisseurs, curieux à Paris au XVIIIe siècle', *Revue de l'Art* (1979), p. 23.

7. Pons-Augustin Alletz, *Manuel de l'homme du monde*, Paris, 1761, p. xiv.

8. Abbé Laugier, *Manière de bien juger des ouvrages de peinture*, Paris, 1771, pp. 32–3.

9. 'Lettre sur le choix et l'arrangement d'un cabinet curieux, écrite par M. Des Allier d'Argenville ...', *Revue universelle des arts*, 18 (1863), p. 163.

10. Jean Adhemar, *La Gravure originale au XVIIe siècle*, Paris, 1963.

11. Henri Sauval, *Histoire et recherches des antiquités de la ville de Paris*, vol. V, bk. 6, p. 665.

12. François Bluche, *Les Magistrats du Parlement de Paris au XVIIIe siècle*, Besançon, 1960, p. 326.

13. Georges Wildenstein, 'Le Goût pour la peinture dans la bourgeoisie parisienne au début du règne de Louis XIII', *Gazette des Beaux-Arts* (1959), and 'Le Goût pour la peinture dans le cercle de la bourgeoisie parisienne autour de 1700', *Gazette des Beaux-Arts* (1958).

14. La Font de Saint-Yenne, *Réflexions sur quelques causes de l'état de la peinture en France*, The Hague, 1747.

15. Ibid., p. 8.

16. Ibid., p. 13.

17. Mercier, *Tableau*, vol. IX, 'Manufactures royales de glaces', p. 186.

18. Ibid., vol. XII, 'Pendules', p. 170.

19. Pierre Verlet, *Le Grand livre de la tapisserie*, Paris, 1965, p. 99.

20. M. Mauclerc, *Traité des couleurs et vernis*, Paris, 1773, p. 108.

21. Daniel Roche, *Le Peuple de Paris*, p. 193.

Notes to Chapter 7

1. Henri-Jean Martin, *Livre, pouvoirs et société à Paris au XVIIe siècle*, 2 vols, Paris, 1969, and Michel Marion, *Les Bibliothèques privées à Paris au milieu du XVIIIe siècle*,

Paris, 1977. We are grateful to M. Marion and to Denis Crouzet for the help they kindly provided in identifying certain works.

2. We have not identified this book.

3. Not identified

4. This may be a work by John Locke, translated into French as *De l'Education des enfans*, Amsterdam, 1695.

5. Not identified.

6. This may be a work by Gommar Huygens entitled *La Méthode que l'on doit garder dans l'usage du sacrement de pénitence*, Paris, 1676.

7. Not identified.

8. By Antonio de Molina, translated from Spanish, Paris, 1624.

9. By Luis of Granada, translated from Spanish, Paris, 1583. Numerous other translations and reprints appeared during the seventeenth century.

10. Antoine Arnauld and Pierre Nicole, *La Logique, ou l'art de penser*, Paris, 1662.

11. *Cas de conscience proposé par un confesseur de province touchant la constitution d'Alexandre VII*, Liège, 1701.

12. This is probably a work by the Protestant author Jacques Abbadie entitled *Traité de la vérité de la religion chrétienne*, Rotterdam, 1684.

13. Dom Nicolas Alexandre, *Médecine et chirurgie des pauvres ...*, Paris, 1714.

14. This may be *Histoire de l'hérésie des iconoclastes* by Mainbourg, Paris, 1674, or *Histoire de l'hérésie de Viclef, Jean Hus et Jérôme de Prague*, by Antoine Varillas, Lyon, 1682.

15. Adrien Baillet, *Histoire des démeslez du pape Boniface VIII avec Philippe Le Bel, roy de France*, Paris, 1718.

16. This may be the *Mémoires* of Cardinal Richelieu, begun in 1600.

17. This could be either of the following works: Pierre Coste, *Histoire de Louis de Bourbon II du nom, prince de Condé*, Cologne, 1693, or Jean de La Brune, *Histoire de la vie de Louis de Bourbon, prince de Condé*, 1693.

18. Sandras de Courtilz, *La Vie de Jean-Baptiste Colbert*, Cologne, 1695.

19. Pierre du Val, *La Description et l'alphabet d'Espagne et de Portugal*, Paris, 1659.

20. By Blomberg, translated from English, Utrecht, 1705.

21. By Baron Charles-Louis de Poellnitz, Amsterdam, 1734.

22. By Temple Stanyan, translated from English, Amsterdam, 1714.

23. Aubery du Maurier, *Mémoires pour servir à l'histoire de Hollande et des autres Provinces-Unies*, Paris, 1680.

24. Grégoire Leti, *La Vie d'Elizabeth, reine d'Angleterre*, translated from Italian, Amsterdam, 1694.

25. By Andrew M. Ramsay, Paris, 1727.

26. François Bluche, *La Vie quotidienne au temps de Louis XIV*, p. 295.

27. By Pierre Pithou, Paris, 1594.

28. Nicolas Coëffeteau, *Response au livre intitulé*: Le Mystère d'iniquité, *du Sieur du Plessis*, Paris, 1614.

29. Not identified.

30. By Comte Roger de Bussy-Rabutin, Liège, n.d.

31. By Claude-Joseph Dorat, Amsterdam and Paris, 1772.

32. By Baron de Poellnitz, Amsterdam, 1734.

33. Françoise Lehoux, *Le Cadre de vie des médecins parisiens aux XVIe et XVIIe siècles*, Paris, 1976.

34. Louis-Sébastien Mercier, *Le Tableau de Paris*, vol. XII, 'Revendeurs de livres', p. 151.
35. Not identified.
36. On this subject, see Pierre Chaunu, *La Civilisation de l'Europe des Lumières*, p. 410, and the work of Norbert Dufourcq and Josiane Bran-Ricci, *Les Instruments de musique au XVIIIe siècle: France et Grande-Bretagne*, London, 1973.
37. Diderot, *Salons*, Oxford, 1960, vol. II, p. 112.
38. Victor-Lucien Tapié, *Baroque et classicisme*, Paris, 1957, 1972, and Victor-Lucien Tapié, Jean-Paul Le Flem and Annik Pardailhé-Galabrun, *Retables baroques de Bretagne*, Paris, 1972.
39. Michèle Ménard, *Mille retables de l'ancien diocèse du Mans*, Paris, 1980.
40. Pierre Chaunu, *La Mort à Paris*, pp. 375f.
41. Prints, Bibliothèque Nationale, Da 35, fol., p. 128, item 144.
42. Ibid., Db 10, in-fol., p. 25.
43. Ibid., Db 10, in-fol., p. 23.
44. Ibid., Ed 33, fol., p. 25.
45. Ibid., Da 35, in-fol., p. 140.
46. Ibid., Db 10, in-fol., p. 25.
47. Quoted in Louis Réau, *Iconographie de l'art chrétien*, Paris, 1956, vol. II, 'Iconographie de la Bible', p. 393.
48. Jean Delumeau, *Le Péché et la peur*, Paris, 1983.

Notes to Conclusion

1. Maurice Garden, *Lyon et les Lyonnais au XVIIIe siècle*, Paris, 1970, p. 405.
2. R. Lick, 'Les Intérieurs domestiques dans la seconde moitié du XVIIIe siècle, d'après les inventaires après décès de Coutances', *Annales de Normandie* (1970).

Suggested Reading

The following list is not a bibliography of Paris. A selection of this size would be insufficient. For the written work that we have directed, the documentation that we use is drawn directly from the national archives, especially from the Minutier Central. The following are simply a few of the books that particularly enriched our thinking.

Ariès, Philippe, *L'enfant et la vie familiale sous l'Ancien Régime*, Paris, Seuil, 1973.

Ariès, Philippe, Duby, Georges (eds), *Histoire de la vie privée*, vol. III: *De la Renaissance aux Lumières*, Paris, Seuil, 1986.

Babelon, Jean-Pierre, *Demeures parisiennes sous Henri IV et Louis XIII*, Paris, Le Temps, 1965.

Bluche, François, *Les Magistrats au Parlement de Paris au XVIIIe siècle*, Besançon, 1960.

—— *La Vie quotidienne au temps de Louis XVI*, Paris, Hachette, 1980.

—— *La Vie quotidienne au temps de Louis XIV*, Paris, Hachette, 1984.

Boudon, Françoise, André Chastel, Hélène Couzy, Françoise Hamon, *Système de l'architecture urbaine. Le Quartier des Halles à Paris*, CNRS, 1977.

Boudriot, Pierre-Denis, *La Construction locative parisienne sous Louis XV*, doctoral dissertation, Paris IV, 1981.

Braudel, Fernand, *Civilisation matérielle, économie et capitalisme*, Paris, A. Colin, 1979.

Brette, Armand, *Atlas de la censive de l'archevêché dans Paris*, Paris, Histoire Générale de Paris, 1906.

Chatelus, Jean, *Peinture et groupes sociaux: les goûts artistiques des marchands parisiens (1729–1759)*, doctoral dissertation, Paris X, 1973.

Chaunu, Pierre, *La Civilisation de l'Europe des Lumierès*, Paris, Arthaud, 1971.

—— *La Mort à Paris*, Paris, Fayard, 1978.

Delumeau, Jean, *Le Péché et la peur*, Paris, Fayard, 1983.

Durand, Yves, *Les Fermiers généraux au XVIIIe siècle*, Paris, PUF, 1971.

Farge, Arlette, *Vivre dans la rue au XVIIIe siècle*, Paris, Gallimard, 1979.

Foisil, Madeleine, *Le Sire de Gouberville*, Paris, Aubier, 1981.

Friedmann, Adrien, *Paris, ses rues, ses paroisses du Moyen Age à la Révolution*, Paris, Plon, 1959.

Gallet, Michel, *Demeures parisiennes. L'époque de Louis XVI*, Paris, Le Temps, 1964.

Goubert, Jean-Pierre, *La Conquête de l'eau*, Paris, Laffont, 1986.

Labatut, Jean-Pierre, *Les ducs et pairs de France au XVIIe siècle*, Paris, PUF, 1972.

La Monneraye, Jean de, *Terrier de la censive de l'archevêché dans Paris, 1772*, Histoire Générale de Paris, Paris, 1981.

Laslett, Peter, *The World We Have Lost*, London, Methuen, 1965.

Lehoux, Françoise, *Le Cadre de vie des médecins parisiens aux XVIe et XVIIe siècles*, Paris, A. and J. Picard, 1976.

Marion, Michel, *Les Bibliothèques privées à Paris au milieu du XVIIIe siècle*, Paris, Bibliothèque Nationale, 1978.

Martin, Henri-Jean, *Livre, pouvoirs et société à Paris au XVIIe siècle*, Genève, Droz, 1969.

Meyer, Jean, *La Vie quotidienne en France au temps de la Régence*, Paris, Hachette, 1979.

Mousnier, Roland, *Recherche sur la stratification sociale à Paris, aux XVIIe et XVIIIe siècles*, Paris, A. Pedone, 1976.

—— *Paris, capitale au temps de Richelieu et de Mazarin*, Paris, A. Pedone, 1978.

—— *Les Institutions de la France*, Paris, PUF, 1980.

Poisson, Jean-Paul, *Notaires et société*, Paris, Economica, 1985.

Pronteau, Jeanne, *Les Numérotages des maisons de Paris du XVe siècle à nos jours*, Paris, Commission des Travaux Historiques, 1966.

Reinhard, Marcel, *Paris pendant la Révolution*, Paris, CDU, 1963–5.

—— *Jacques Louis Menetra compagnon vitrier au XVIIIe siècle*, Paris, Montalba, 1982.

Roman, Christian, 'Mendiants et policiers à Paris au XVIIIe siècle', *Histoire, Economie et Société* (1982).

Sabattier, Jacqueline, *Figaro et son maître. Les domestiques au XVIIIe siècle*, Paris, Perrin, 1984.

Souchal, Geneviève, *Le Mobilier français du XVIIIe siècle en France*, Paris, Hachette, 1966.

Verlet, Pierre, *L'Art du meuble à Paris au XVIIIe siècle*, Paris, PUF, 1958.

Vigarello, Georges, *Le Propre et le sale. L'hygiène du corps depuis le Moyen Age*, Paris, Seuil, 1985.

Index